GEGE AKUTAMI

Two kilobytes.

GEGE AKUTAMI published a few short
works before starting *Jujutsu Kaisen*, which began
serialization in *Weekly Shonen Jump* in 2018.

JUJUTSU KAISEN

VOLUME 4
SHONEN JUMP MANGA EDITION

BY GEGE AKUTAMI

TRANSLATION Stefan Koza
TOUCH-UP ART & LETTERING Snir Aharon
DESIGN Shawn Carrico
EDITOR John Bae
CONSULTING EDITOR Erika Onabe

JUJUTSU KAISEN © 2018 by Gege Akutami
All rights reserved.
First published in Japan in 2018 by SHUEISHA Inc., Tokyo.
English translation rights arranged by SHUEISHA Inc.

The stories, characters and incidents mentioned
in this publication are entirely fictional.

No portion of this book may be reproduced
or transmitted in any form or by any means without
written permission from the copyright holders.

Printed in the U.S.A.

Published by VIZ Media, LLC
P.O. Box 77010
San Francisco, CA 94107

10 9 8 7 6 5
First printing, June 2020
Fifth printing, July 2021

PARENTAL ADVISORY
JUJUTSU KAISEN is rated T+ for Older Teen
and is recommended for ages 16 and up. This
volume contains fantasy violence.

viz.com

JUJUTSU KAISEN

4

I'M GONNA KILL YOU!

STORY AND ART BY GEGE AKUTAMI

JUJUTSU KAISEN
CAST OF CHARACTERS

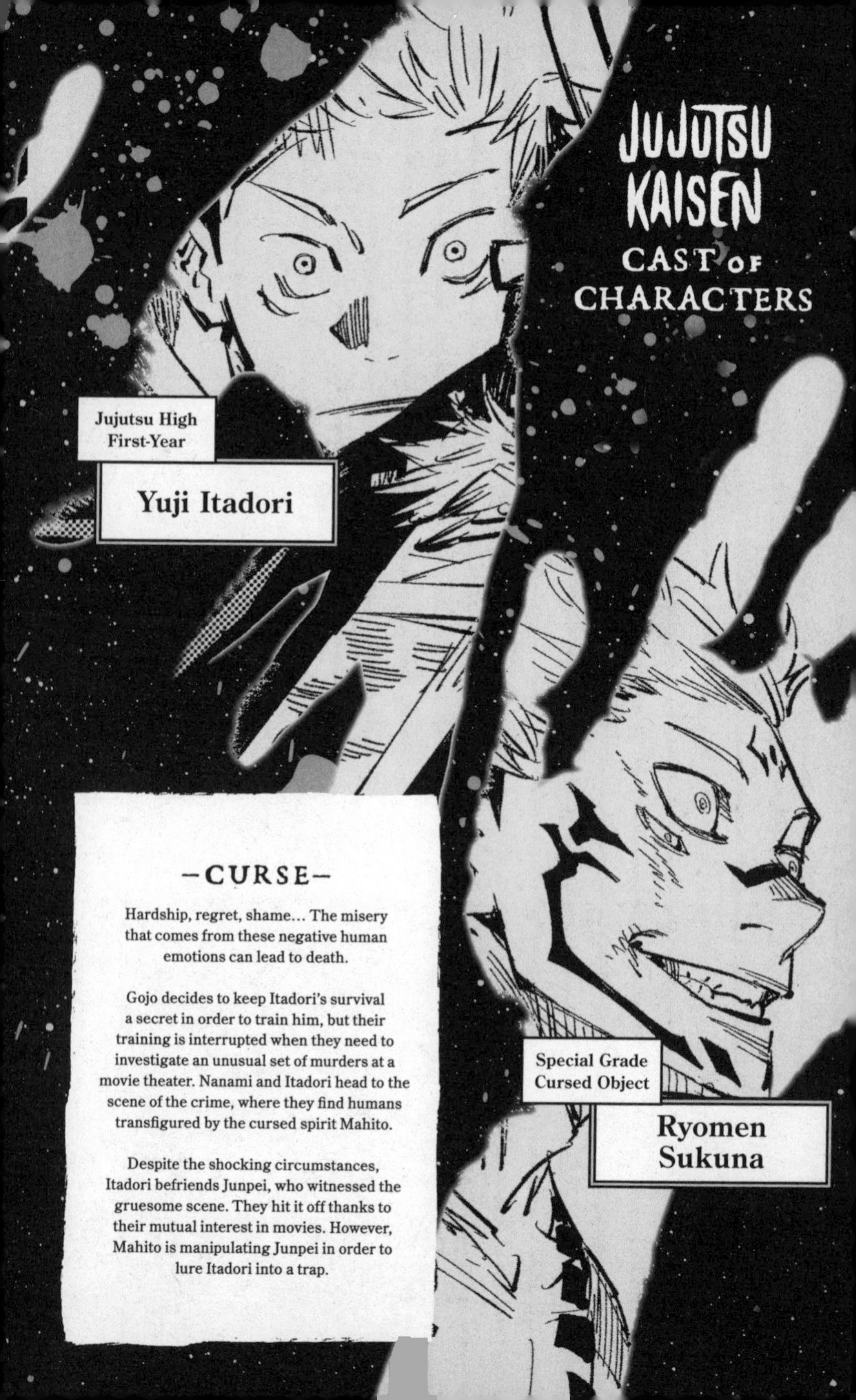
Jujutsu High
First-Year
Yuji Itadori
Special Grade
Cursed Object
Ryomen
Sukuna

—CURSE—

Hardship, regret, shame… The misery that comes from these negative human emotions can lead to death.

Gojo decides to keep Itadori's survival a secret in order to train him, but their training is interrupted when they need to investigate an unusual set of murders at a movie theater. Nanami and Itadori head to the scene of the crime, where they find humans transfigured by the cursed spirit Mahito.

Despite the shocking circumstances, Itadori befriends Junpei, who witnessed the gruesome scene. They hit it off thanks to their mutual interest in movies. However, Mahito is manipulating Junpei in order to lure Itadori into a trap.

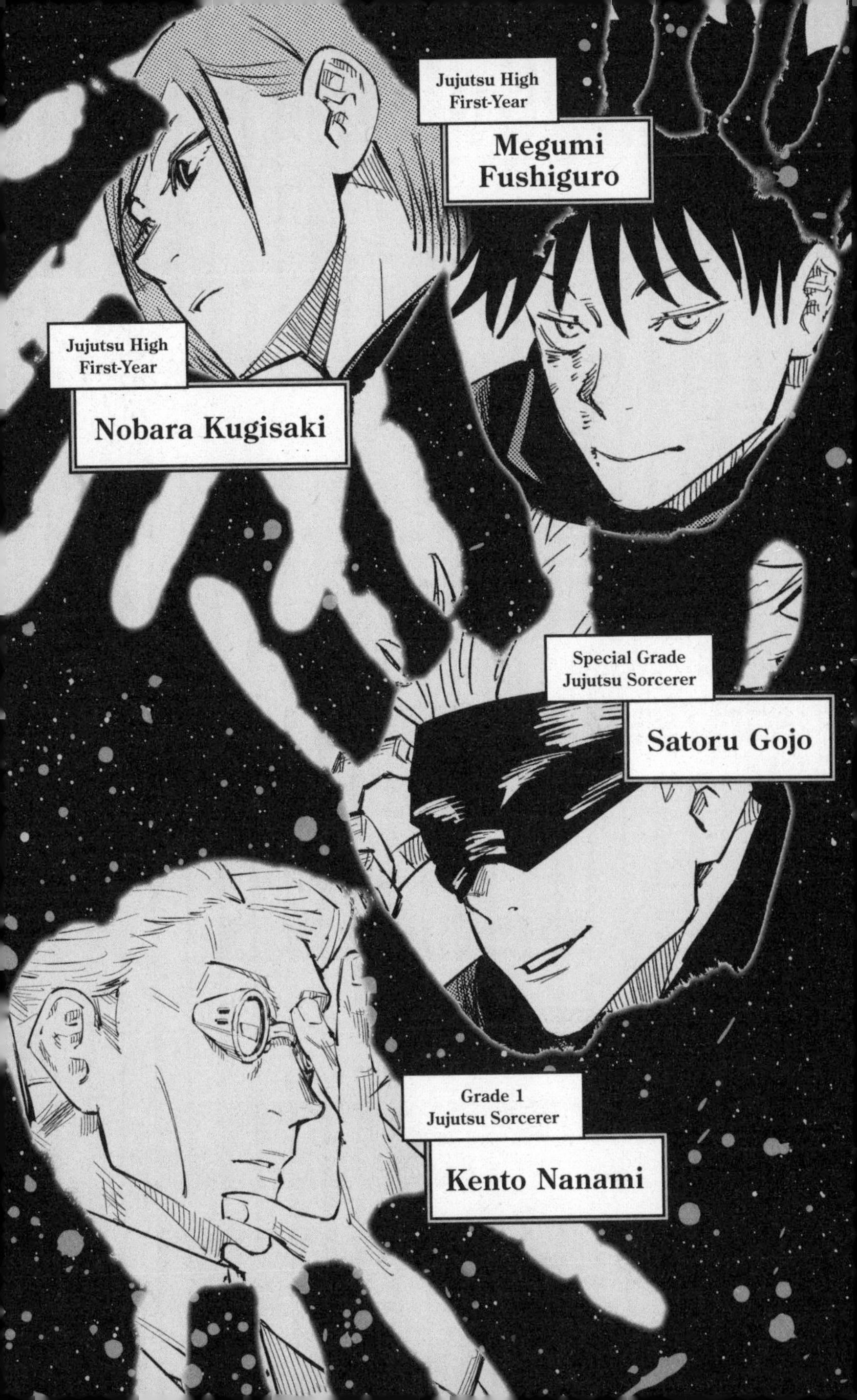
Jujutsu High
First-Year
Megumi
Fushiguro
Jujutsu High
First-Year
Nobara Kugisaki
Special Grade
Jujutsu Sorcerer
Satoru Gojo
Grade 1
Jujutsu Sorcerer
Kento Nanami

JUJUTSU KAISEN

4

I'M GONNA KILL YOU!

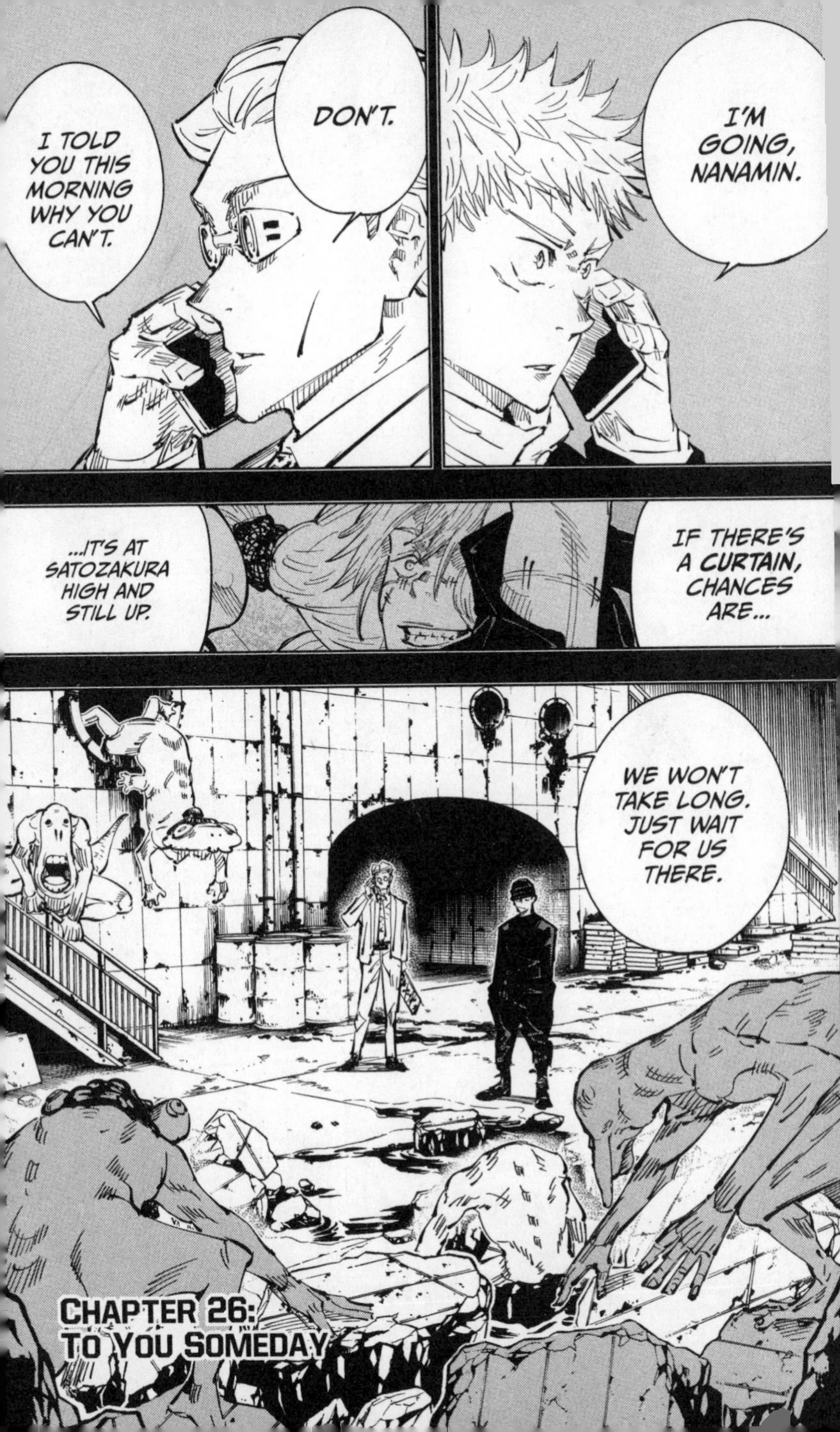
I'M GOING, NANAMIN.
DON'T.
I TOLD YOU THIS MORNING WHY YOU CAN'T.
IF THERE'S A CURTAIN, CHANCES ARE...
...IT'S AT SATOZAKURA HIGH AND STILL UP.
WE WON'T TAKE LONG. JUST WAIT FOR US THERE.

CHAPTER 26: TO YOU SOMEDAY

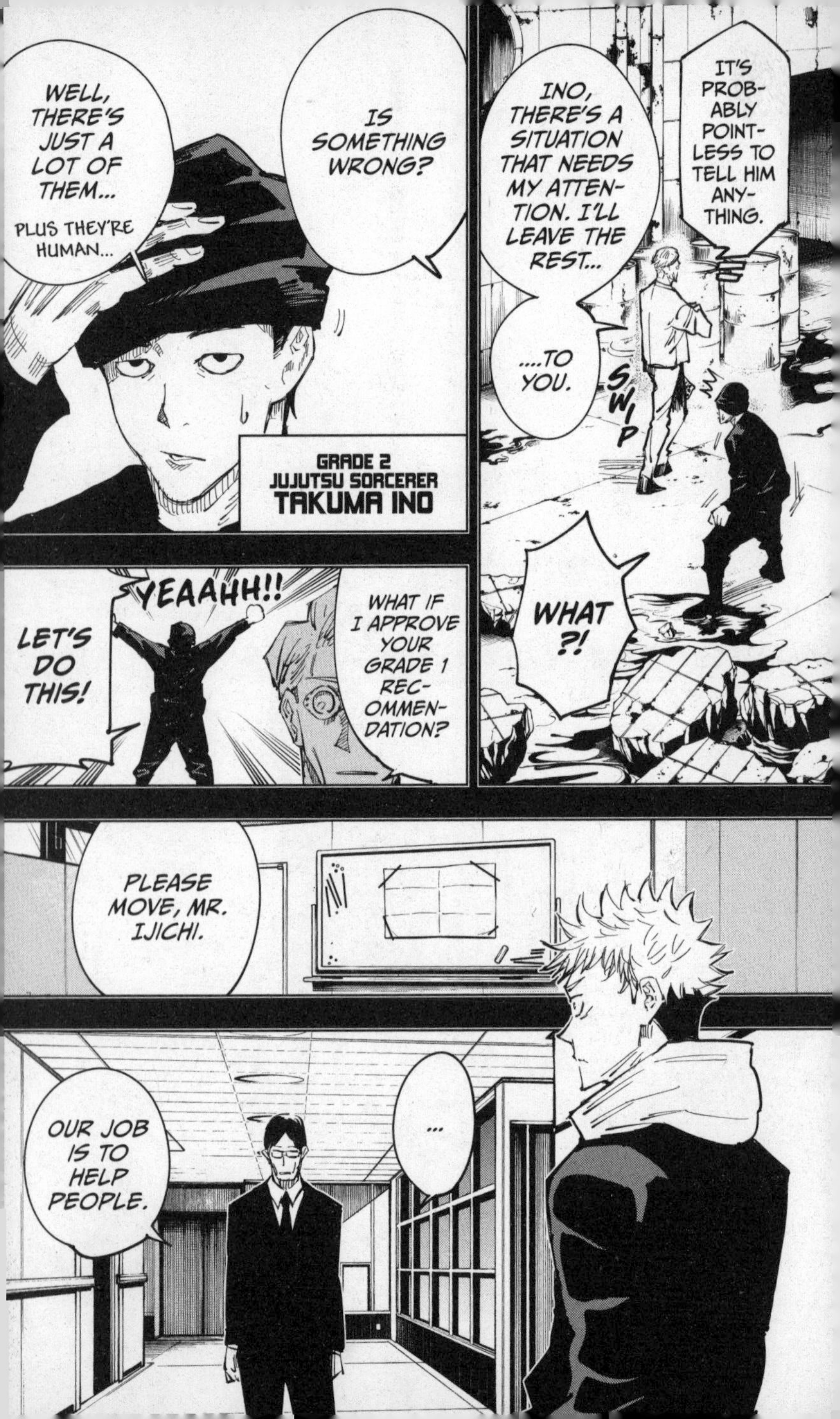
IT'S PROBABLY POINTLESS TO TELL HIM ANYTHING.
INO, THERE'S A SITUATION THAT NEEDS MY ATTENTION. I'LL LEAVE THE REST...
....TO YOU.
SWIP
WHAT?!
IS SOMETHING WRONG?
WELL, THERE'S JUST A LOT OF THEM... PLUS THEY'RE HUMAN...
GRADE 2 JUJUTSU SORCERER TAKUMA INO
WHAT IF I APPROVE YOUR GRADE 1 RECOMMENDATION?
YEAAHH!!
LET'S DO THIS!
PLEASE MOVE, MR. IJICHI.
...
OUR JOB IS TO HELP PEOPLE.

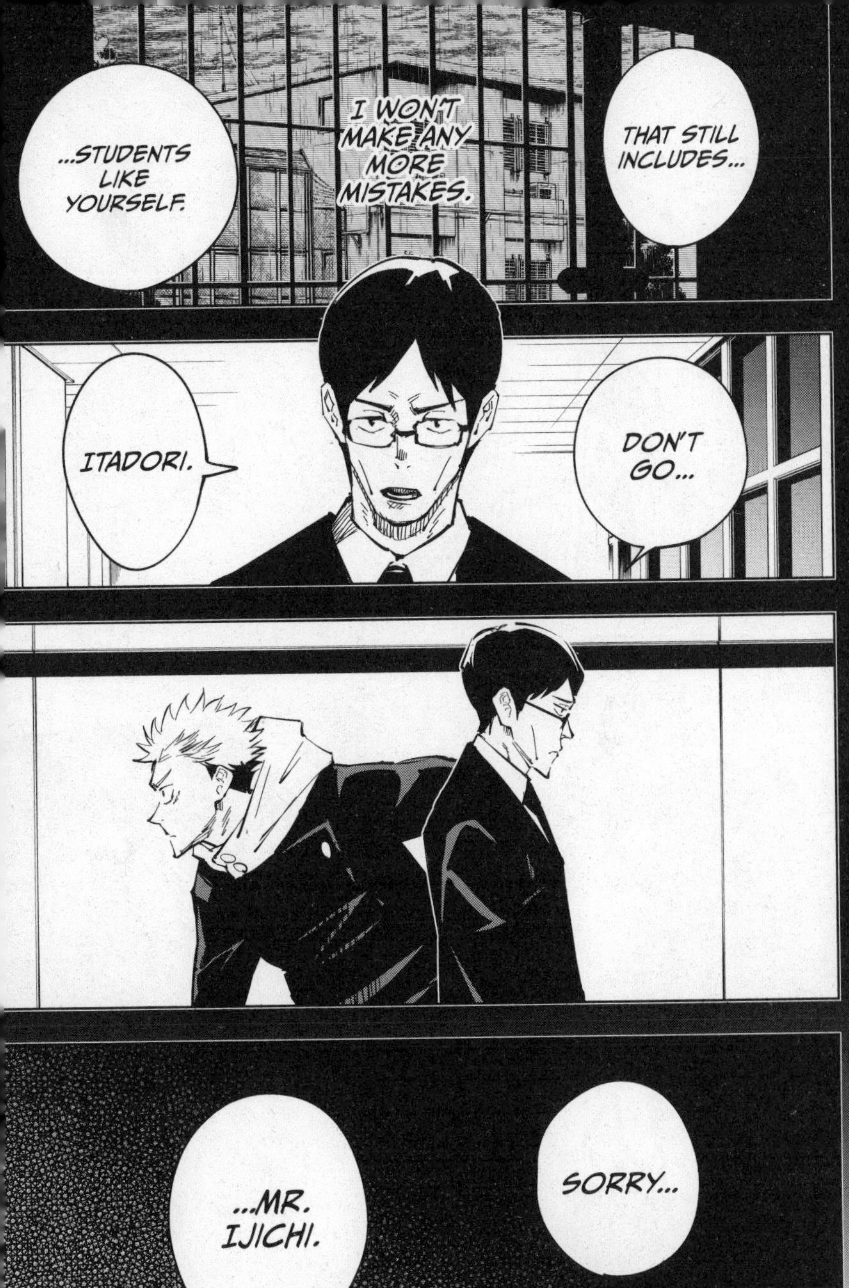
I WON'T MAKE ANY MORE MISTAKES.
THAT STILL INCLUDES...
...STUDENTS LIKE YOURSELF.
DON'T GO...
ITADORI.
SORRY...
...MR. IJICHI.

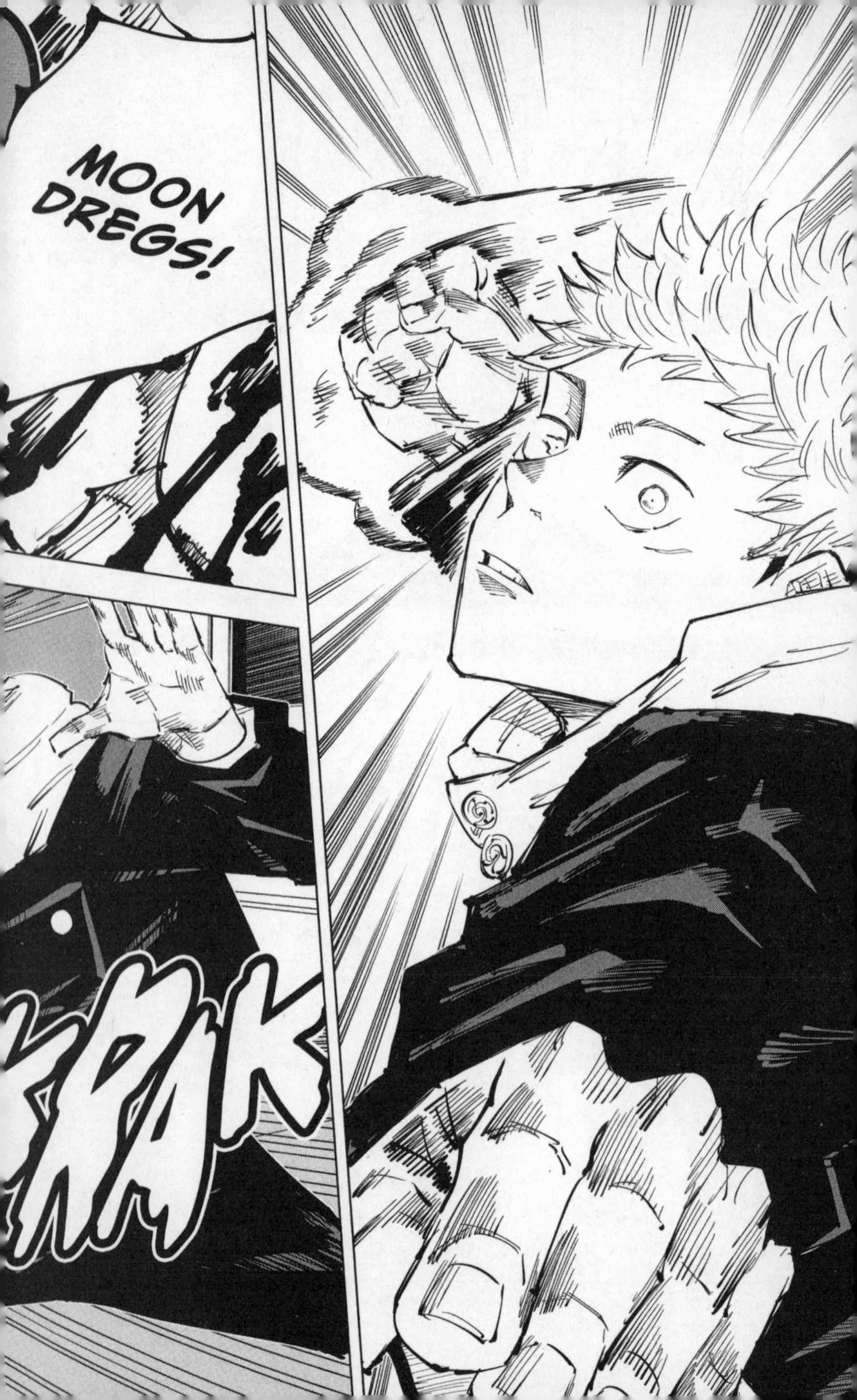
MOON DREGS!

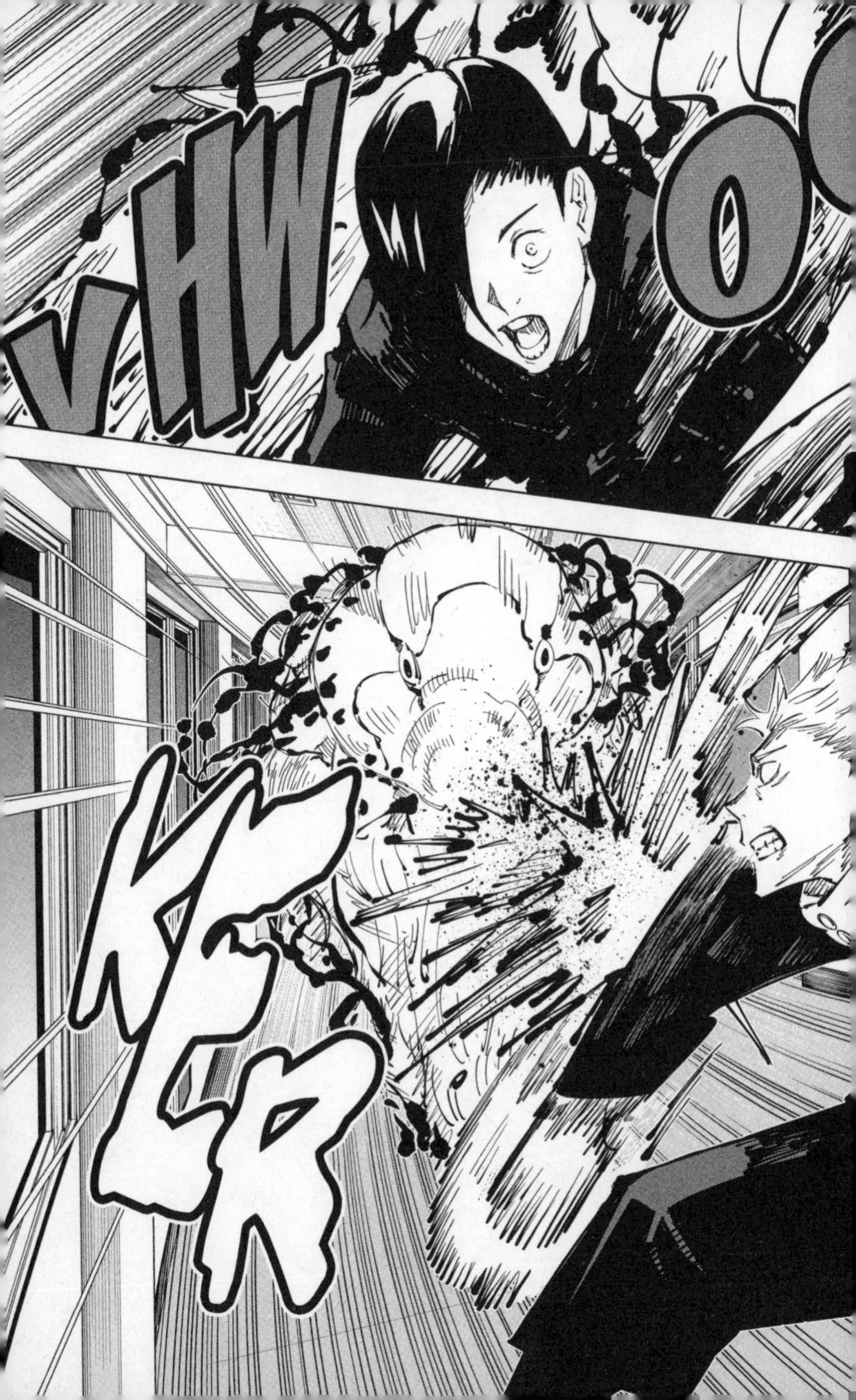
VHWO

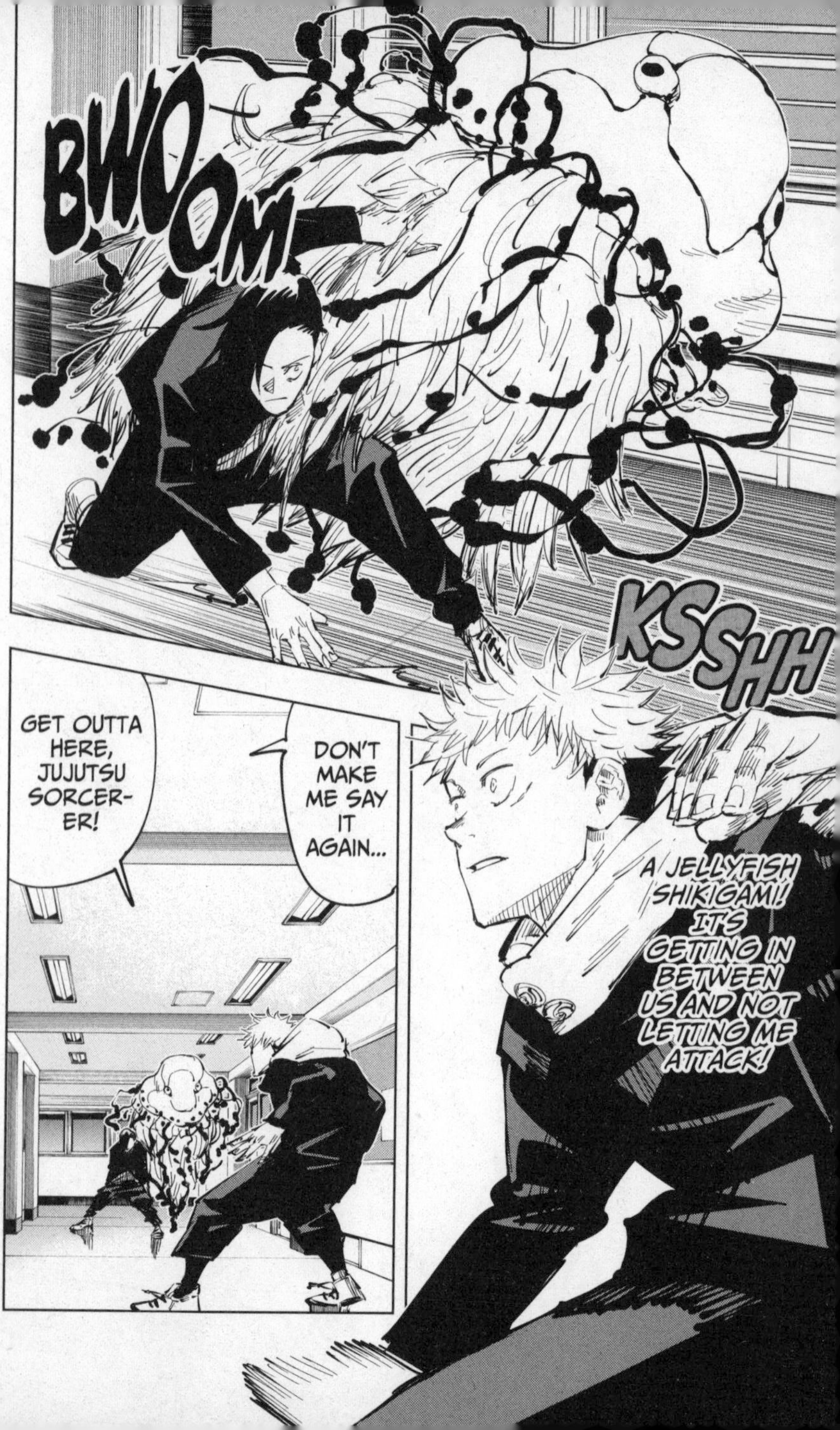
BWOOM
KSSHH
A JELLYFISH SHIKIGAMI! IT'S GETTING IN BETWEEN US AND NOT LETTING ME ATTACK!
DON'T MAKE ME SAY IT AGAIN...
GET OUTTA HERE, JUJUTSU SORCERER!

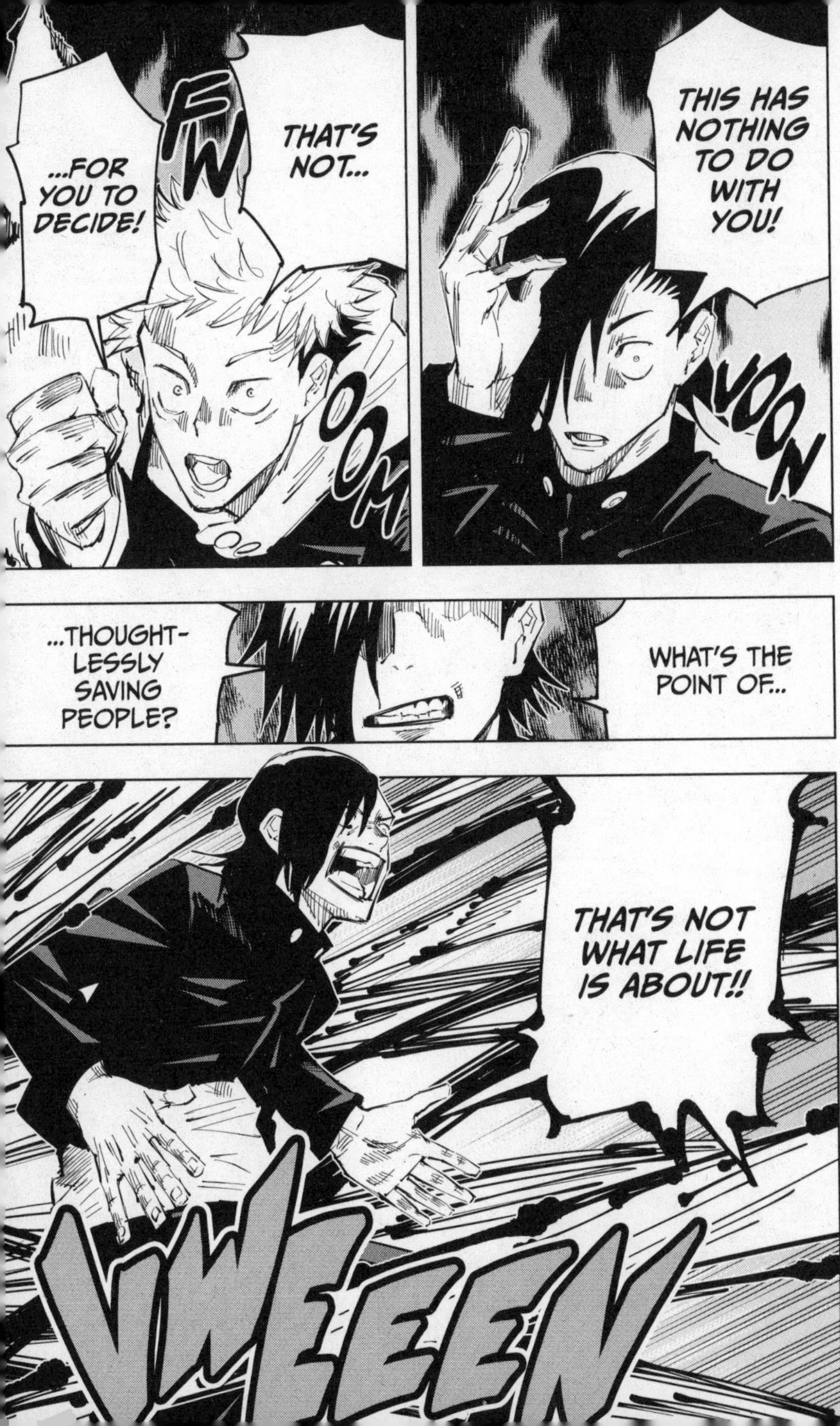
THIS HAS NOTHING TO DO WITH YOU!
VOON
THAT'S NOT...
FW
...FOR YOU TO DECIDE!
OOM
WHAT'S THE POINT OF...
...THOUGHTLESSLY SAVING PEOPLE?
THAT'S NOT WHAT LIFE IS ABOUT!!
VWEEEN

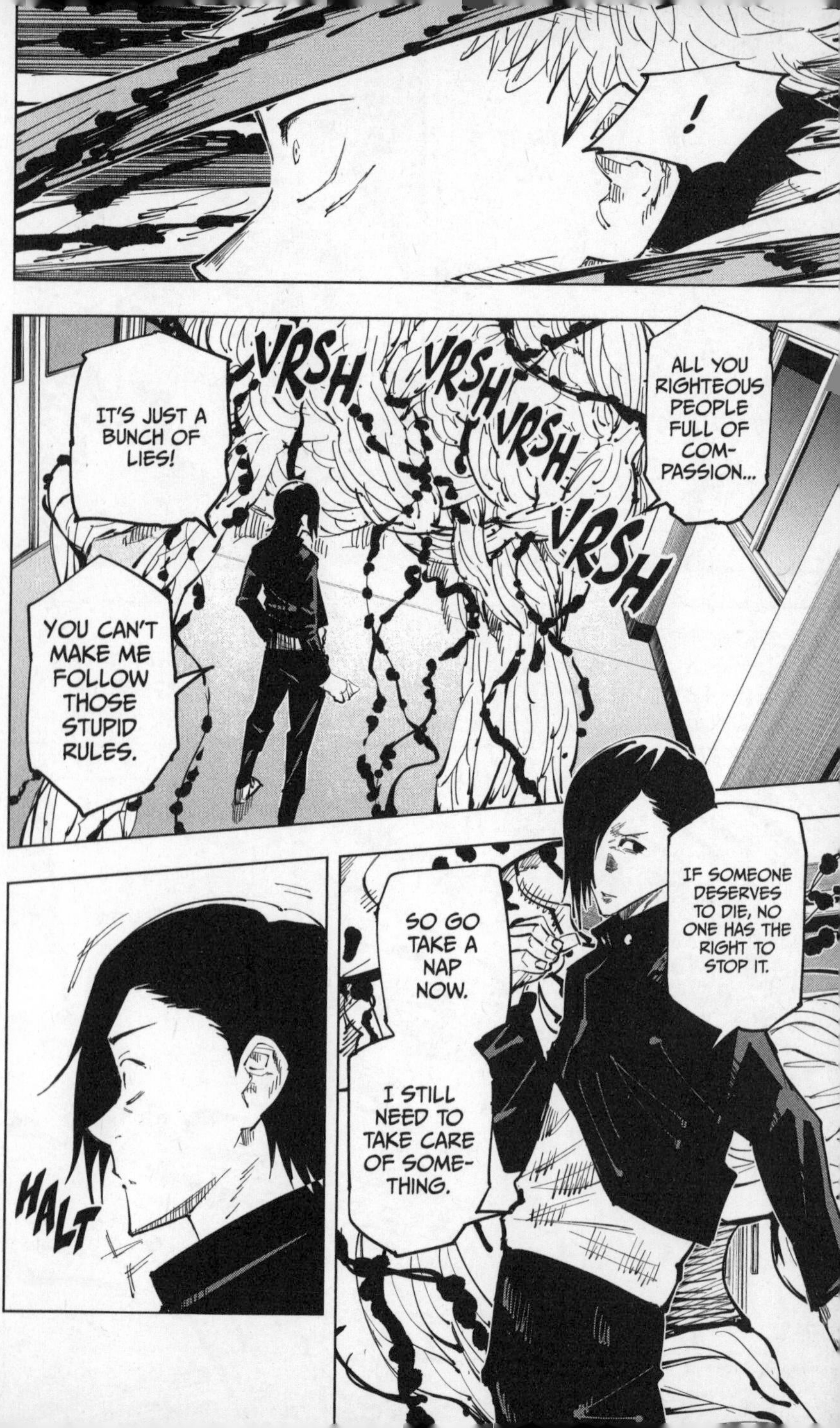
!
ALL YOU RIGHTEOUS PEOPLE FULL OF COM-PASSION...
VRSH VRSH VRSH VRSH VRSH
IT'S JUST A BUNCH OF LIES!
YOU CAN'T MAKE ME FOLLOW THOSE STUPID RULES.
IF SOMEONE DESERVES TO DIE, NO ONE HAS THE RIGHT TO STOP IT.
SO GO TAKE A NAP NOW.
I STILL NEED TO TAKE CARE OF SOME-THING.
HALT

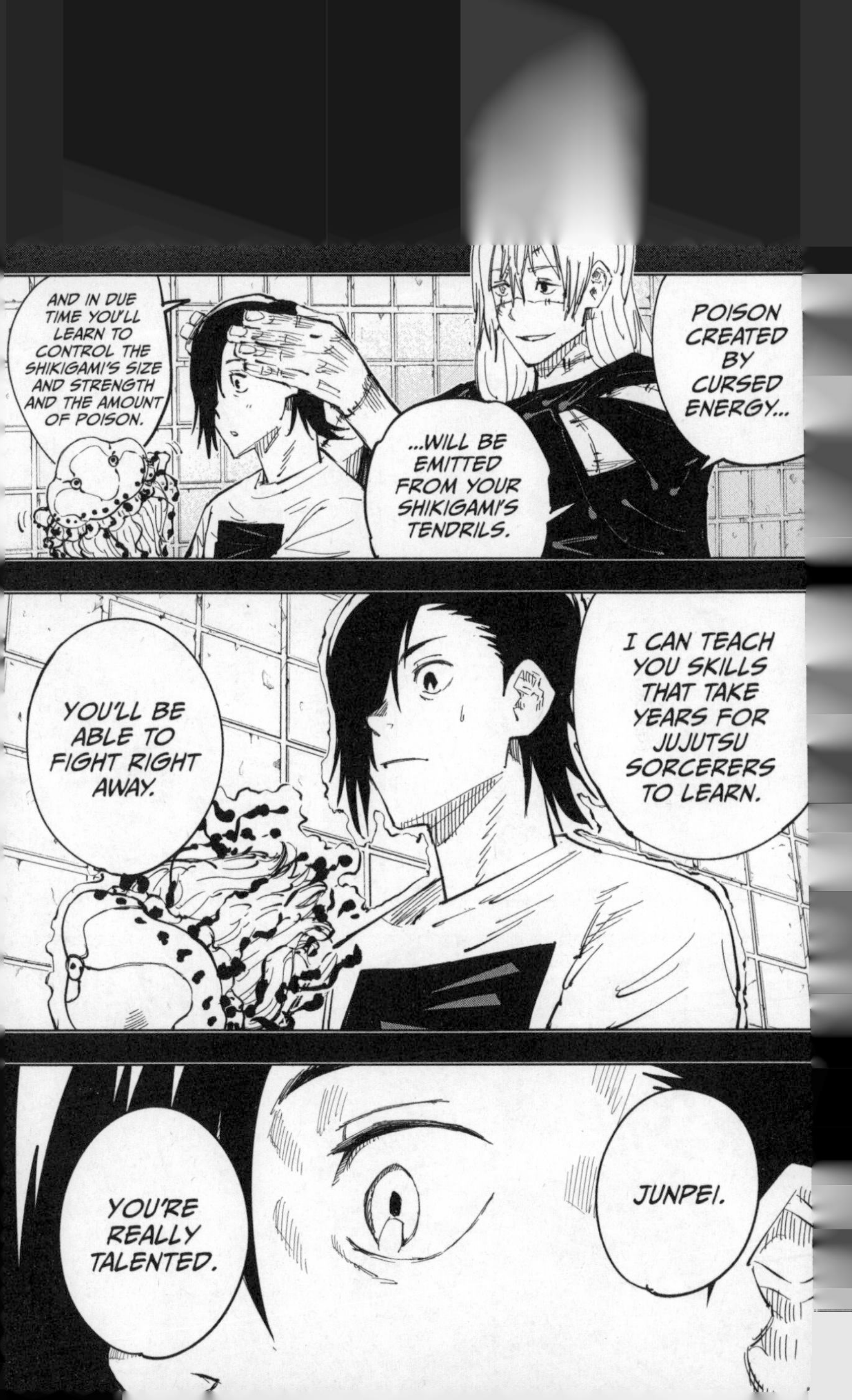
POISON CREATED BY CURSED ENERGY...
...WILL BE EMITTED FROM YOUR SHIKIGAMI'S TENDRILS.
AND IN DUE TIME YOU'LL LEARN TO CONTROL THE SHIKIGAMI'S SIZE AND STRENGTH AND THE AMOUNT OF POISON.
I CAN TEACH YOU SKILLS THAT TAKE YEARS FOR JUJUTSU SORCERERS TO LEARN.
YOU'LL BE ABLE TO FIGHT RIGHT AWAY.
JUNPEI.
YOU'RE REALLY TALENTED.

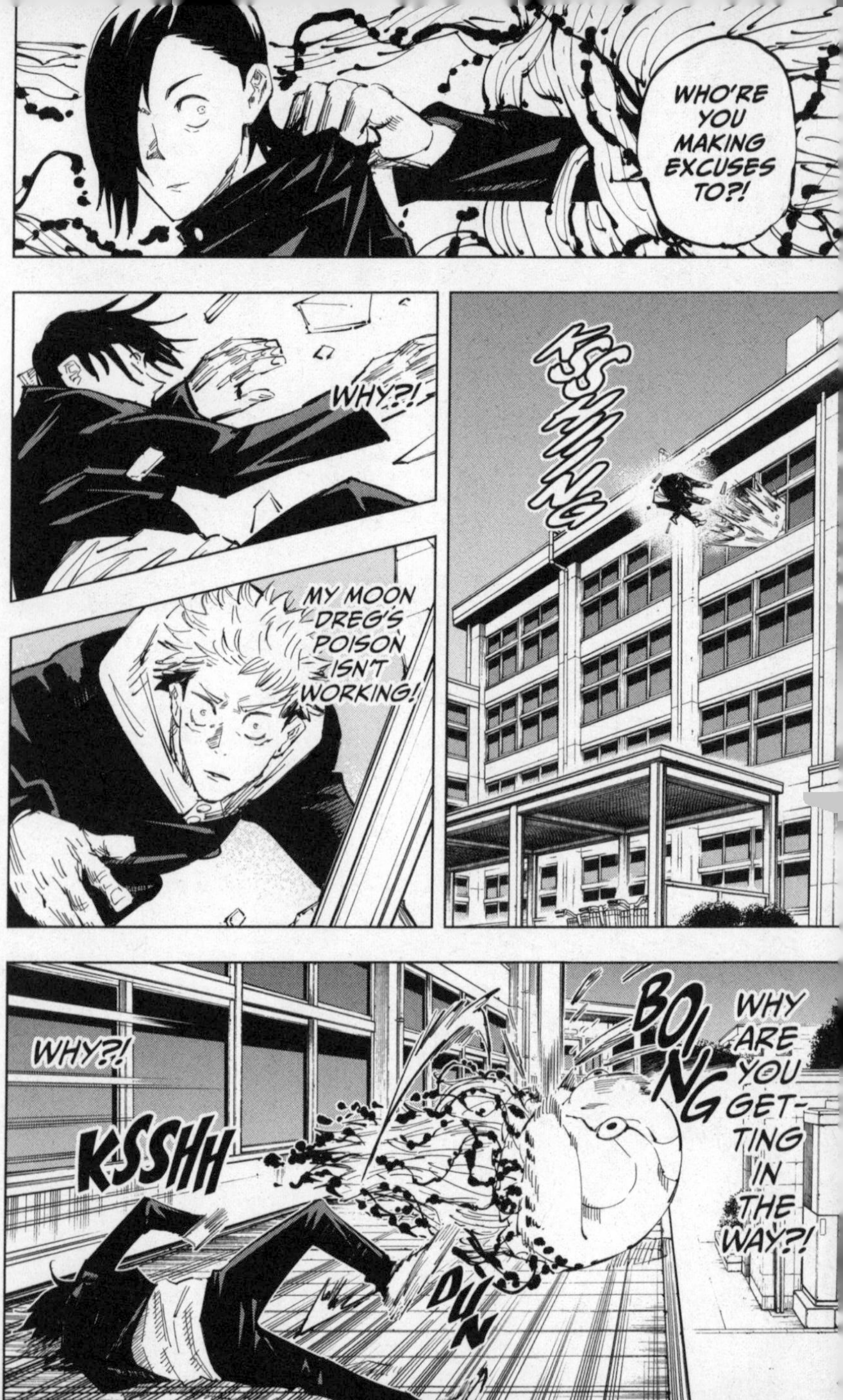
WHO'RE YOU MAKING EXCUSES TO?!
KSHIING
WHY?!
MY MOON DREG'S POISON ISN'T WORKING!
BOING
WHY ARE YOU GETTING IN THE WAY?!
WHY?!
KSSHH
DUN

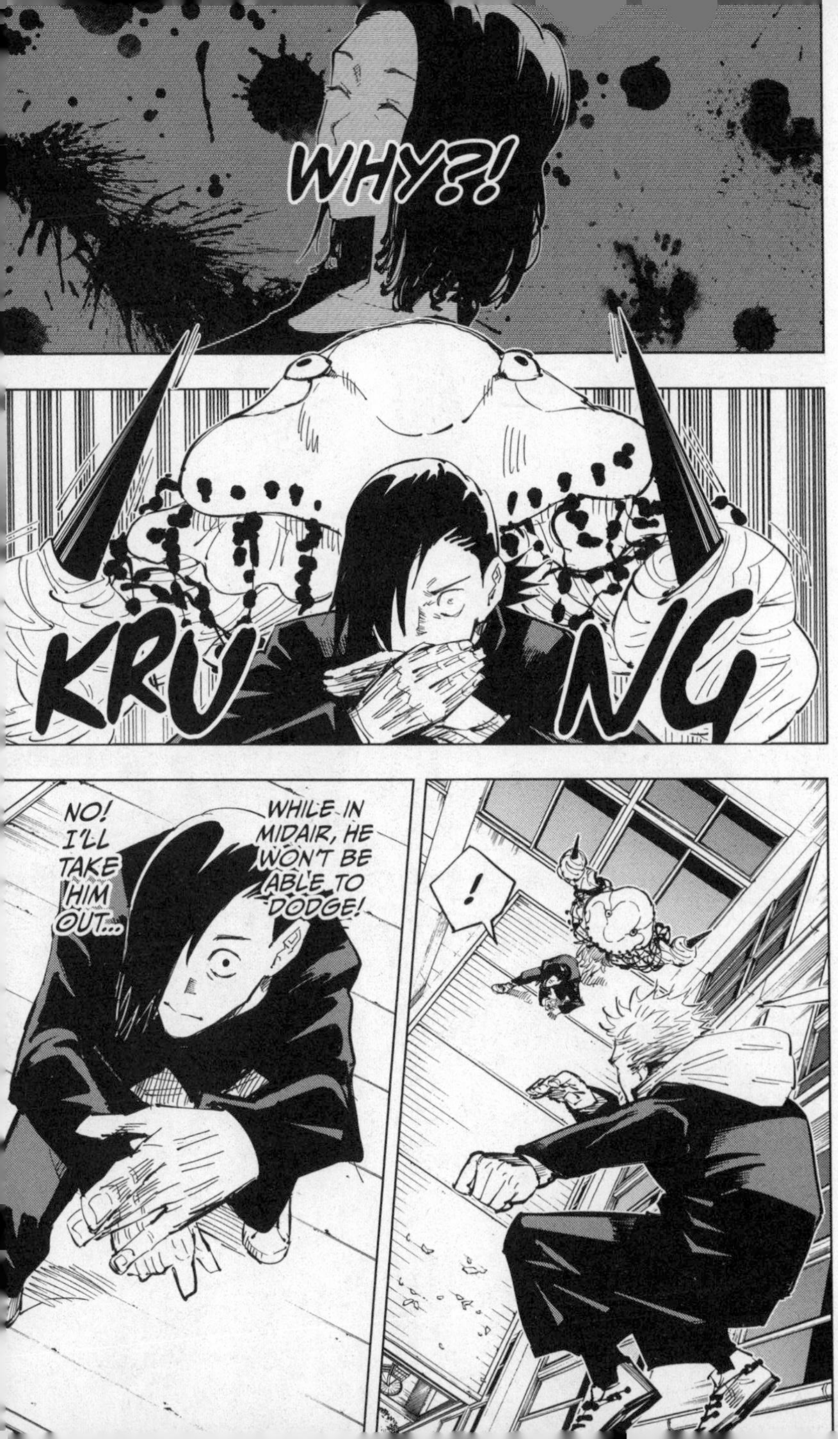
WHY?!
KRUNG
!
WHILE IN MIDAIR, HE WON'T BE ABLE TO DODGE!
NO! I'LL TAKE HIM OUT...

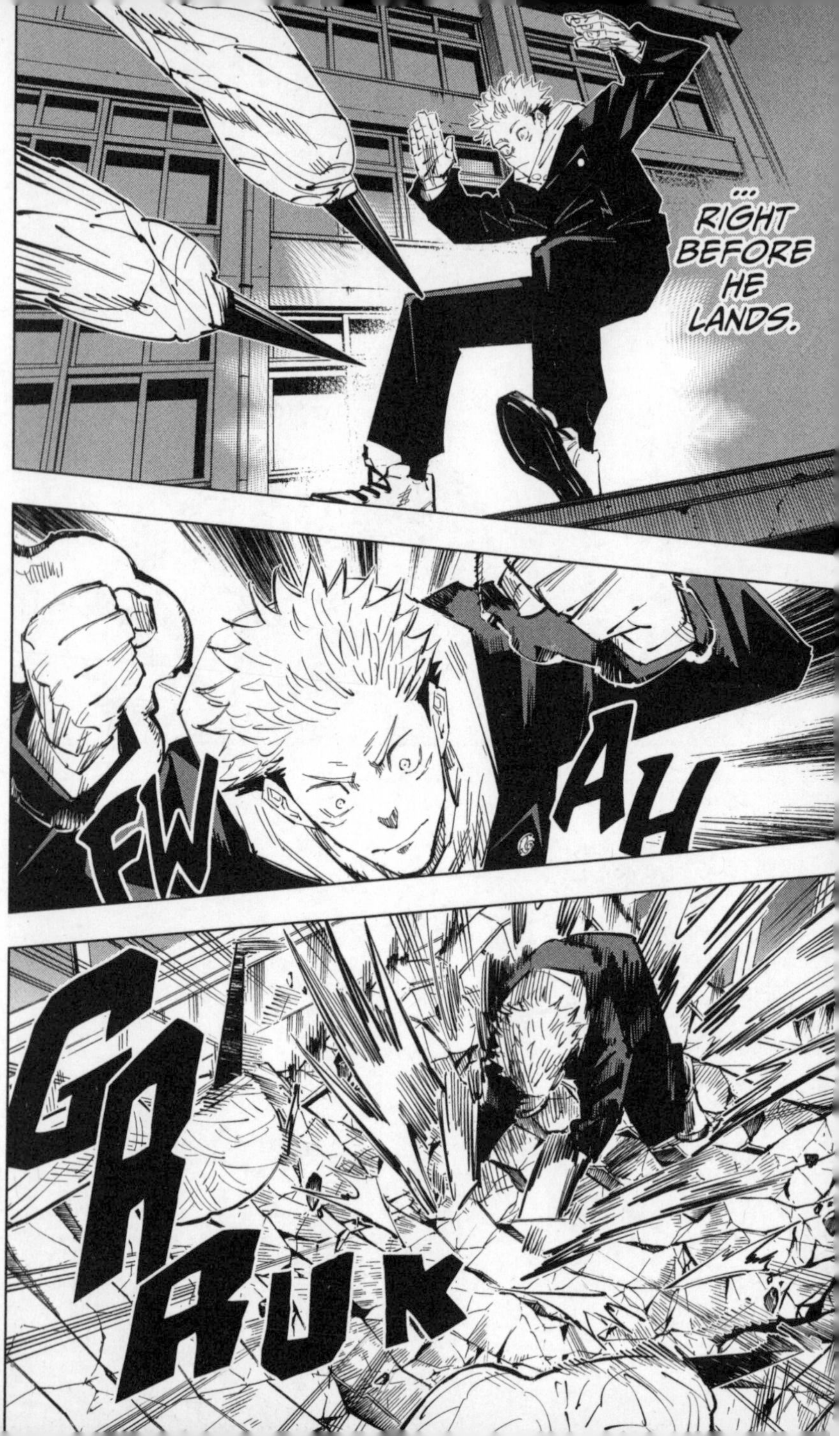
...RIGHT BEFORE HE LANDS.
FWAH
GABAUK

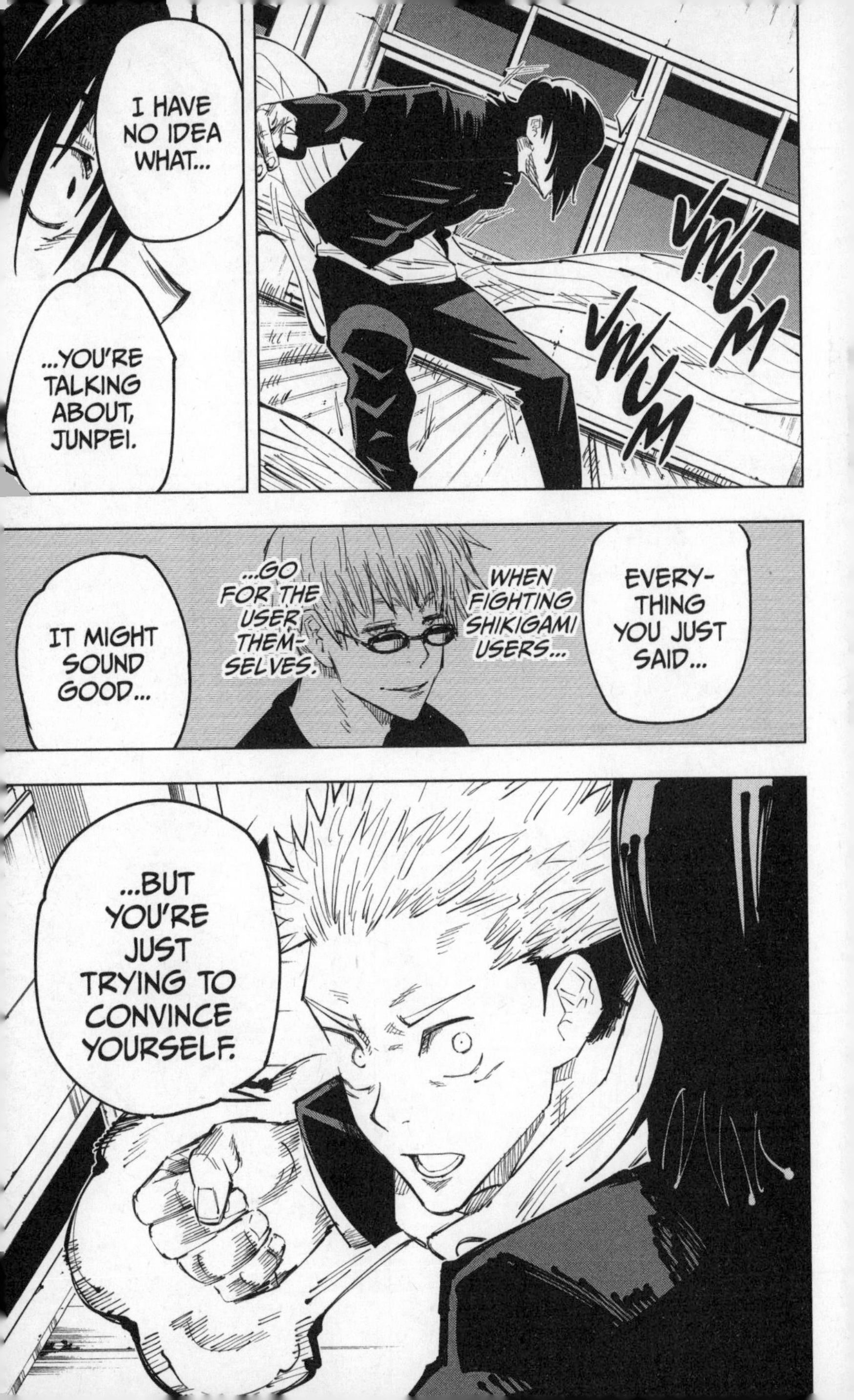
VWUM
VWUM
I HAVE NO IDEA WHAT...
...YOU'RE TALKING ABOUT, JUNPEI.
EVERY-THING YOU JUST SAID...
WHEN FIGHTING SHIKIGAMI USERS...
...GO FOR THE USER THEM-SELVES.
IT MIGHT SOUND GOOD...
...BUT YOU'RE JUST TRYING TO CONVINCE YOURSELF.

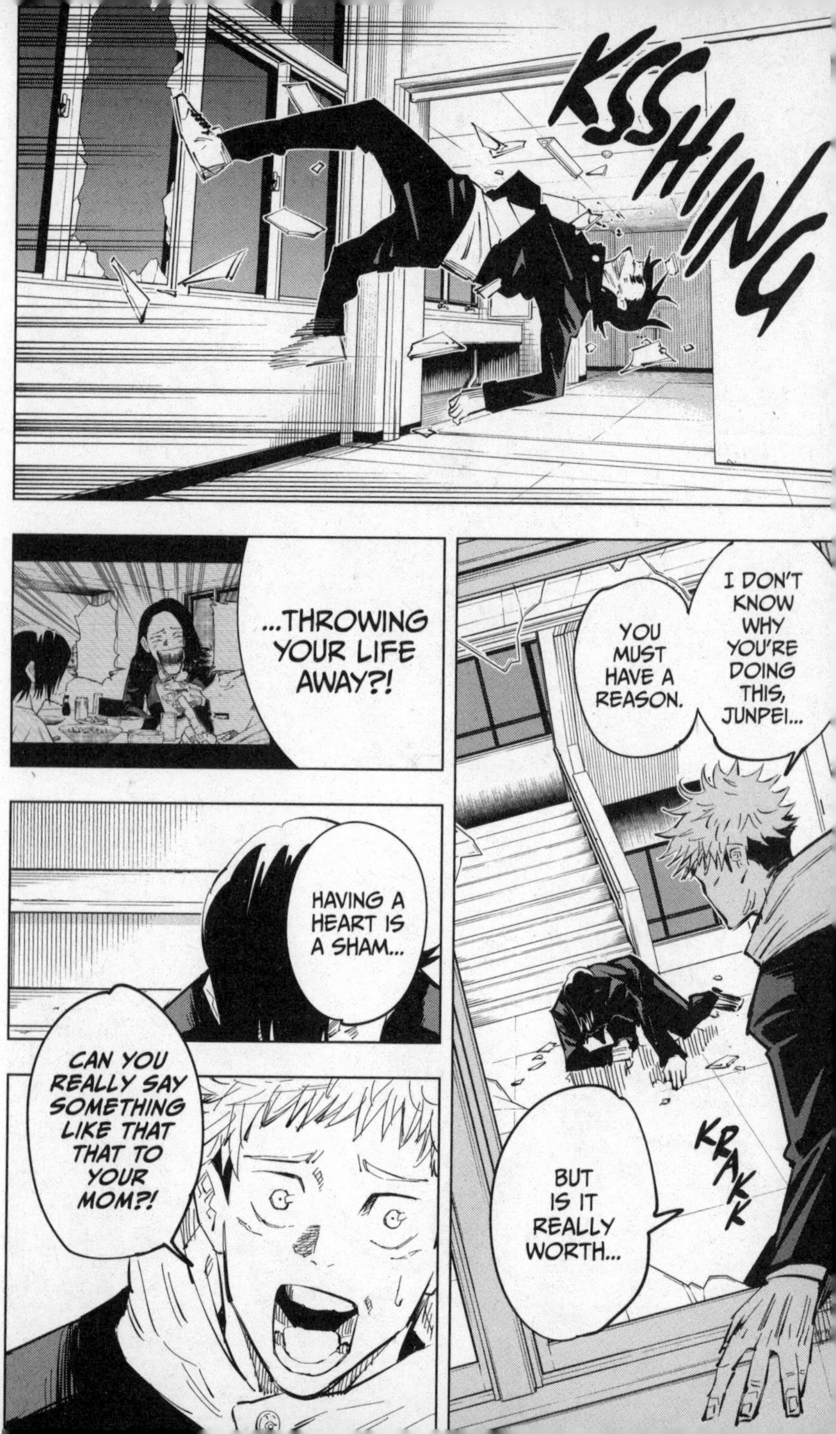
KSSHING
I DON'T KNOW WHY YOU'RE DOING THIS, JUNPEI...
YOU MUST HAVE A REASON.
KRAKK
BUT IS IT REALLY WORTH...
...THROWING YOUR LIFE AWAY?!
HAVING A HEART IS A SHAM...
CAN YOU REALLY SAY SOMETHING LIKE THAT THAT TO YOUR MOM?!

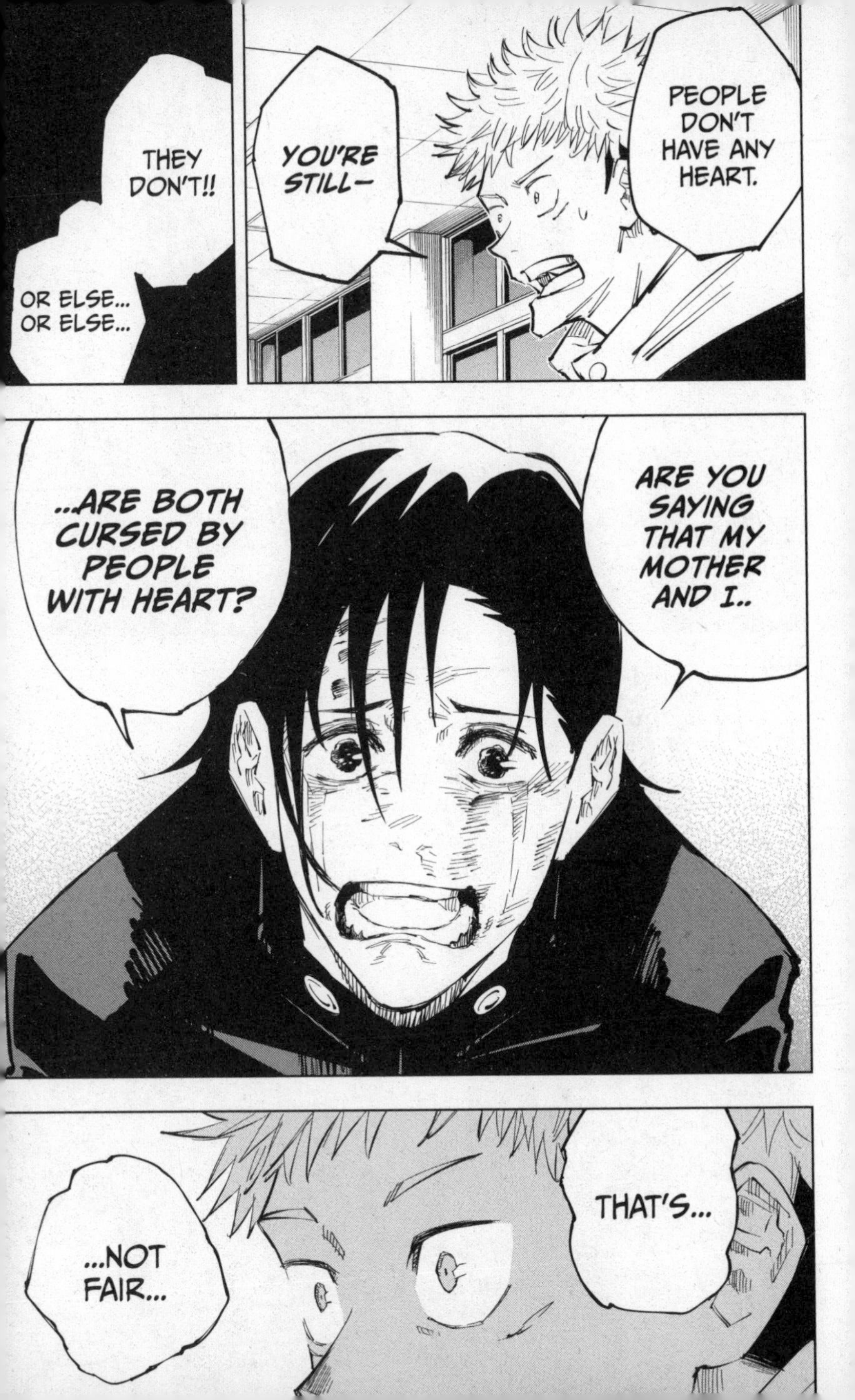
PEOPLE DON'T HAVE ANY HEART.
YOU'RE STILL—
THEY DON'T!!
OR ELSE... OR ELSE...
ARE YOU SAYING THAT MY MOTHER AND I..
...ARE BOTH CURSED BY PEOPLE WITH HEART?
THAT'S...
...NOT FAIR...

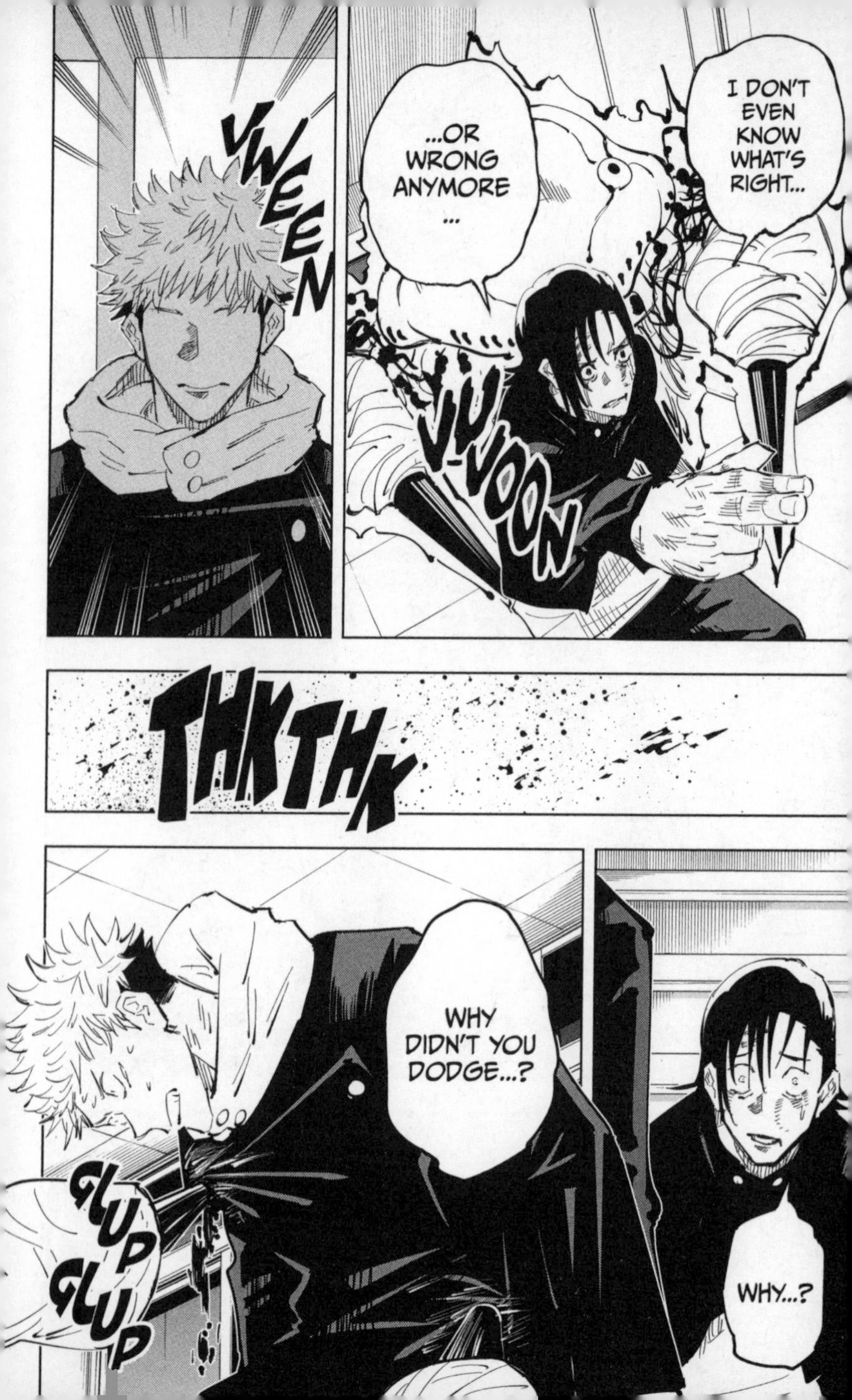
I DON'T EVEN KNOW WHAT'S RIGHT...
...OR WRONG ANYMORE ...
V-VOON
VWEEN
THKTHK
WHY...?
WHY DIDN'T YOU DODGE...?
GLUP GLUP

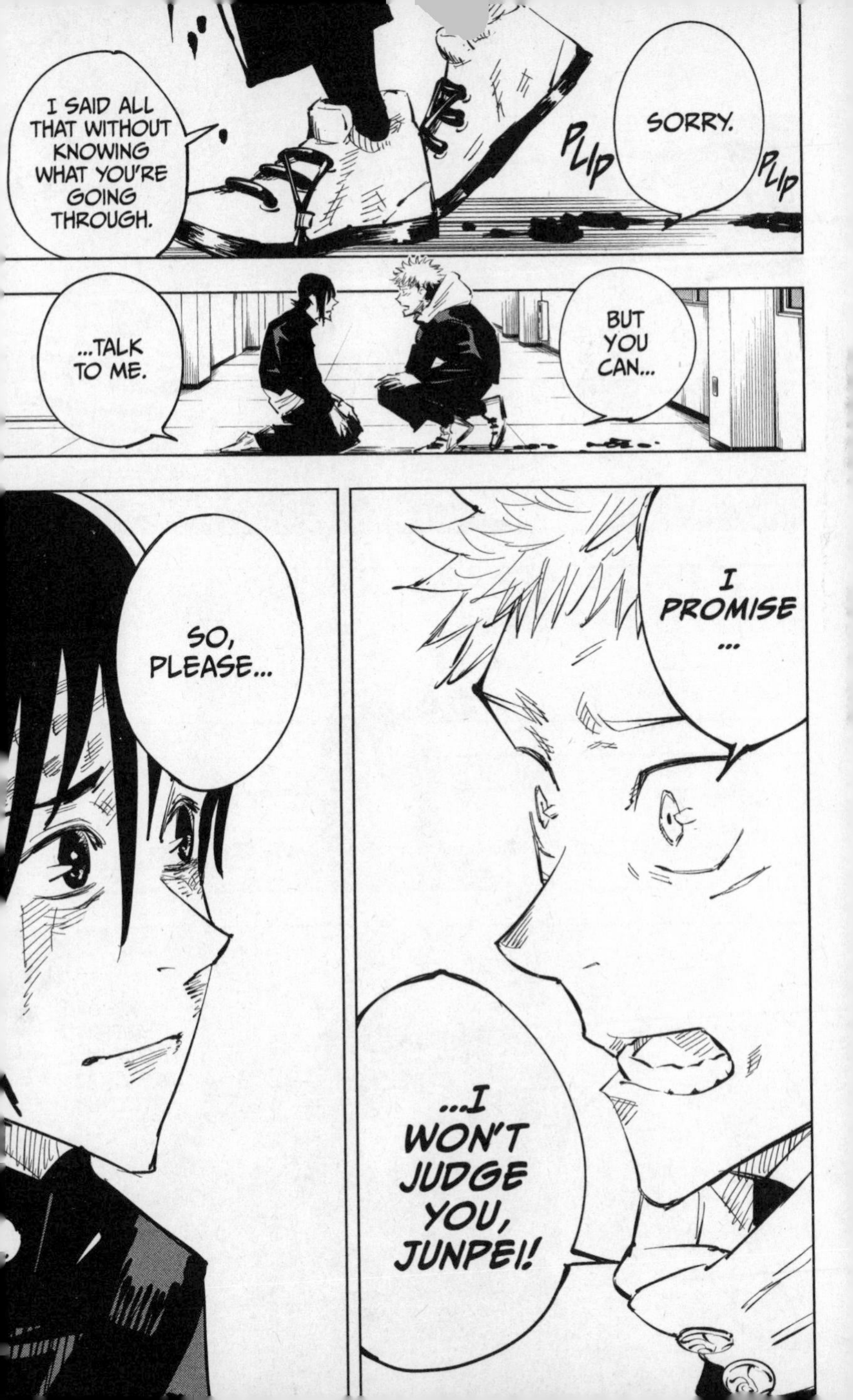
SORRY.
PLIP
PLIP
I SAID ALL THAT WITHOUT KNOWING WHAT YOU'RE GOING THROUGH.
BUT YOU CAN...
...TALK TO ME.
I PROMISE...
...I WON'T JUDGE YOU, JUNPEI!
SO, PLEASE...

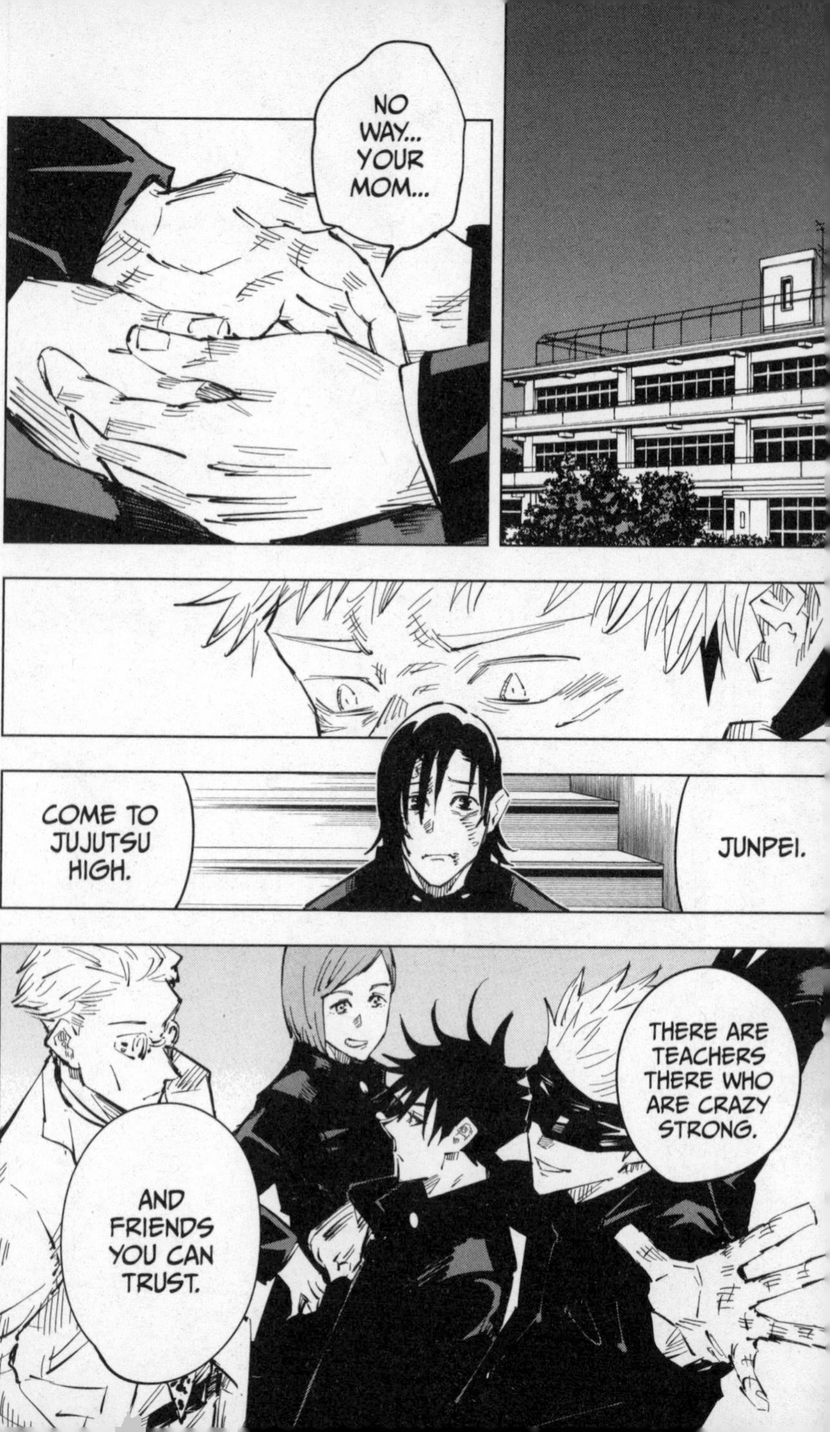
NO WAY... YOUR MOM...
JUNPEI.
COME TO JUJUTSU HIGH.
THERE ARE TEACHERS THERE WHO ARE CRAZY STRONG.
AND FRIENDS YOU CAN TRUST.

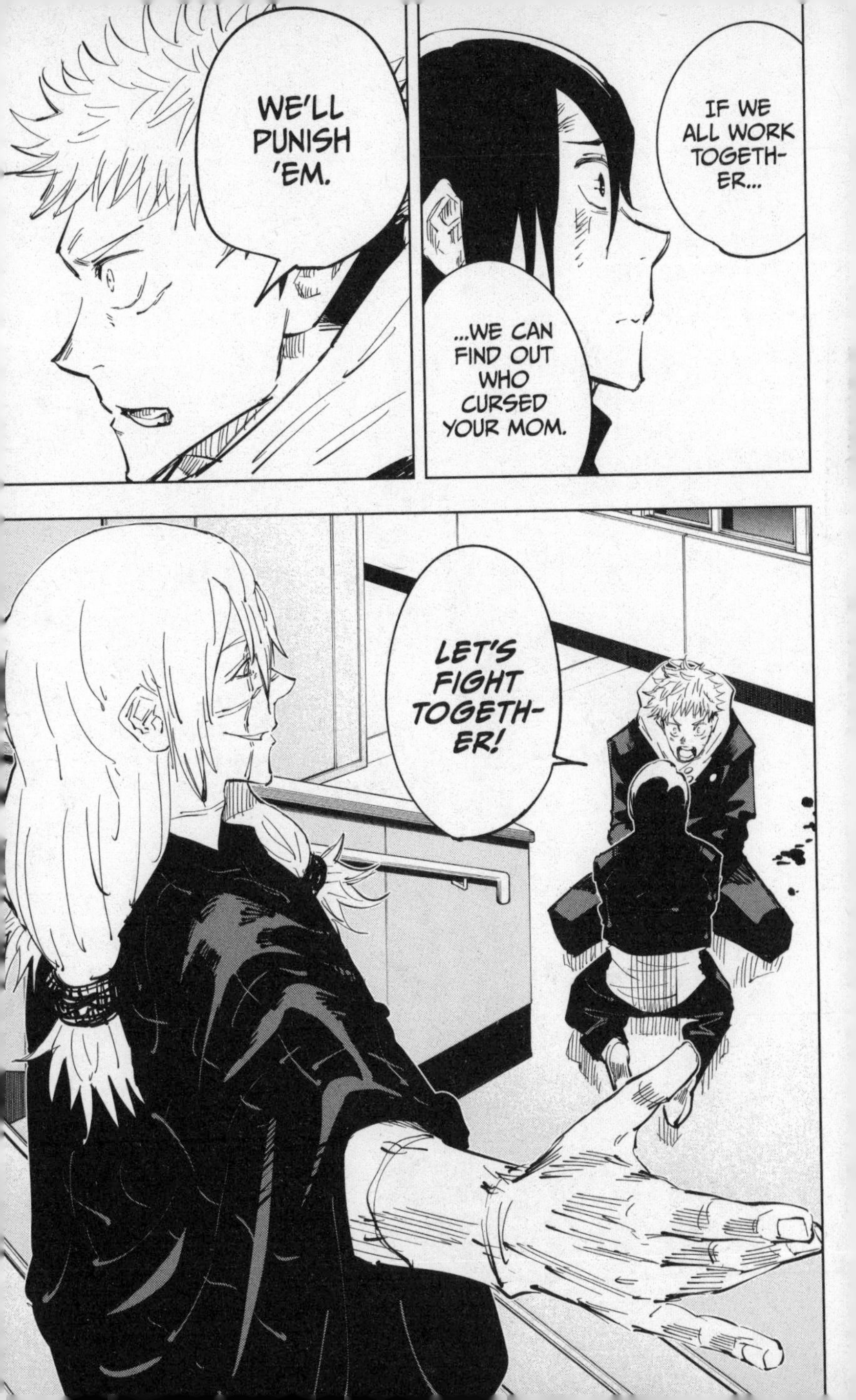
IF WE ALL WORK TOGETH-ER...
...WE CAN FIND OUT WHO CURSED YOUR MOM.
WE'LL PUNISH 'EM.
LET'S FIGHT TOGETH-ER!

TAKUMA INO
(21 YEARS OLD)

- Takuma is always getting help from others because of his little-brother vibe.
- With Gojo around, you start to lose perspective, but most great sorcerers are Grade 1 or 2. Takuma is not weak.
- He really respects Nanami after accompanying him on a mission.
- He hopes that he'll get Nanami's watch as a hand-me-down one day.
- He's only been in about four panels but already has a profile page. Good luck on making Grade 1!

Chapter 27: What If

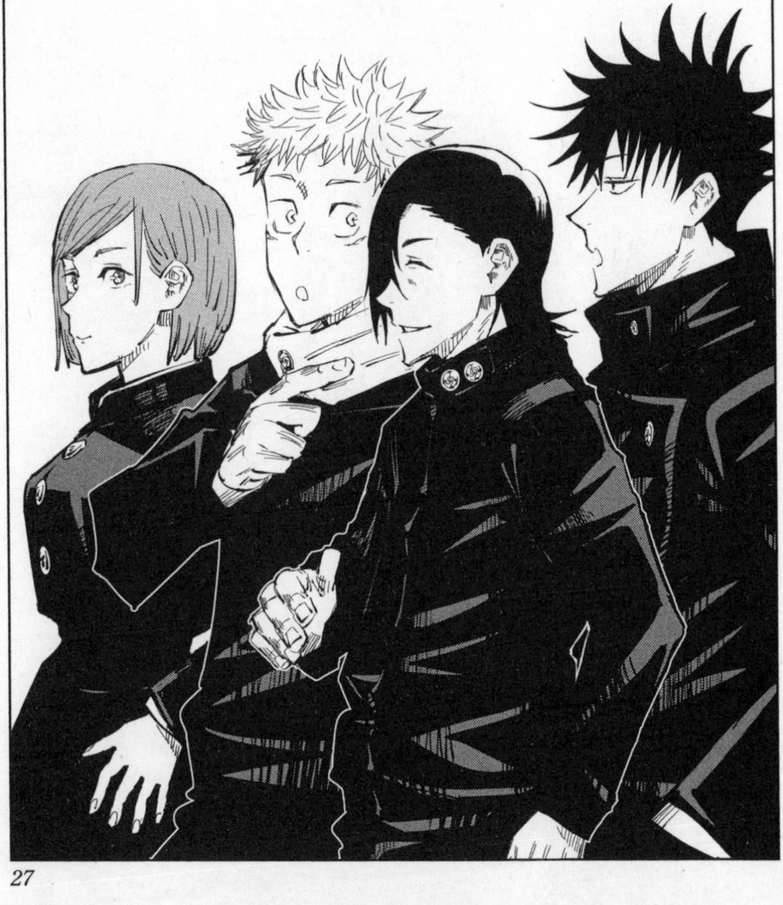

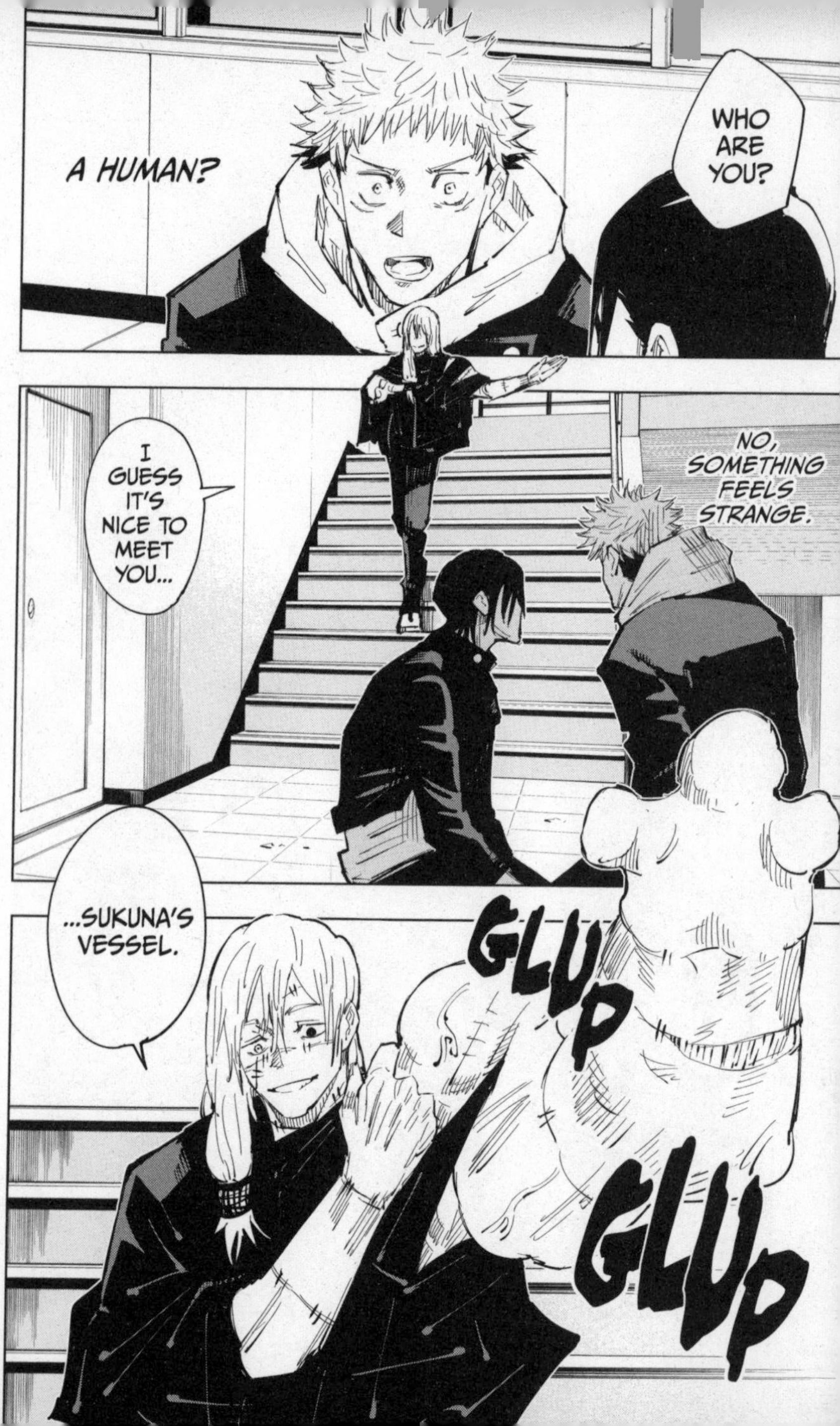
WHO ARE YOU?
A HUMAN?
NO, SOMETHING FEELS STRANGE.
I GUESS IT'S NICE TO MEET YOU...
...SUKUNA'S VESSEL.
GLUP
GLUP

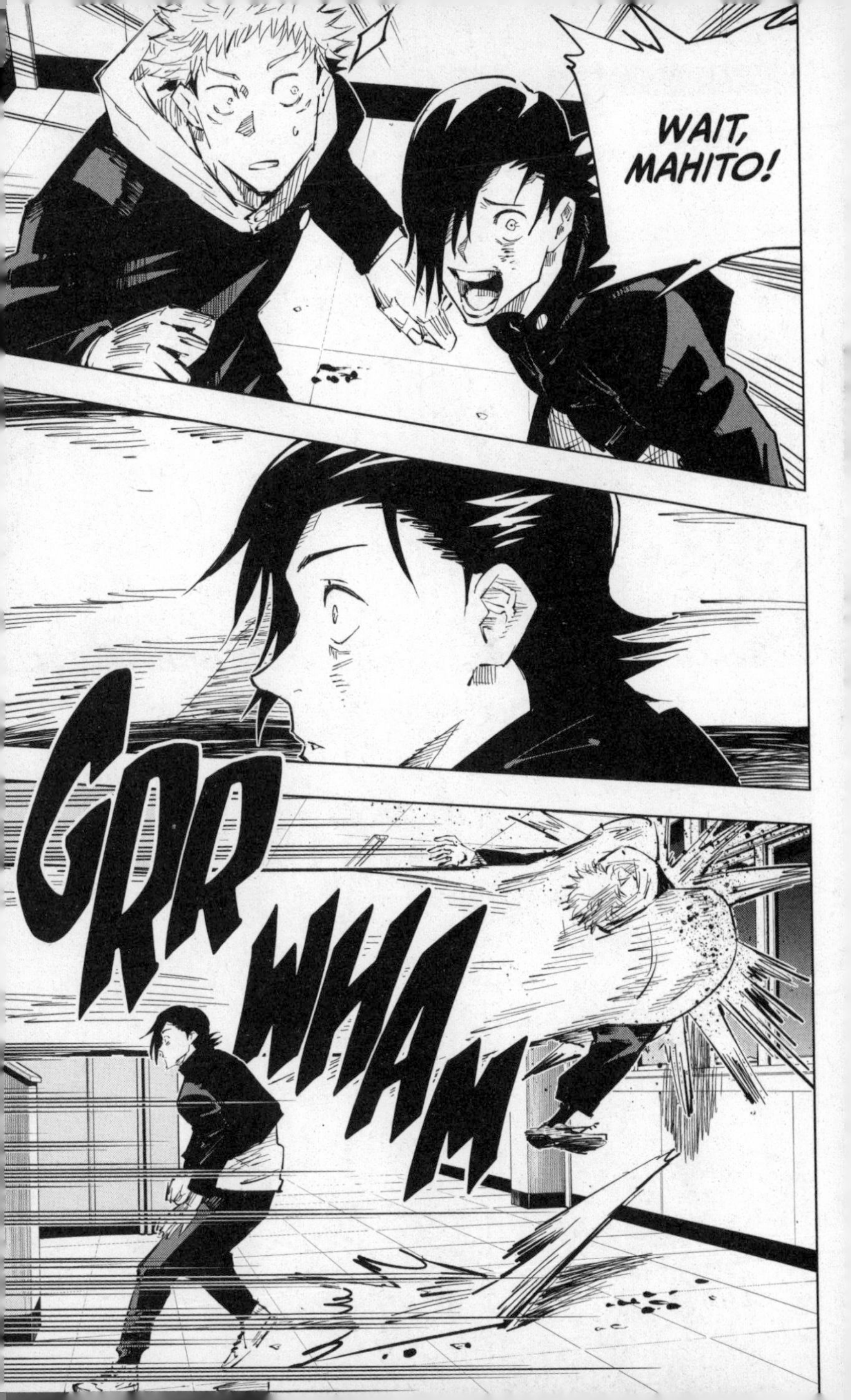
WAIT, MAHITO!
GDR
WHAM

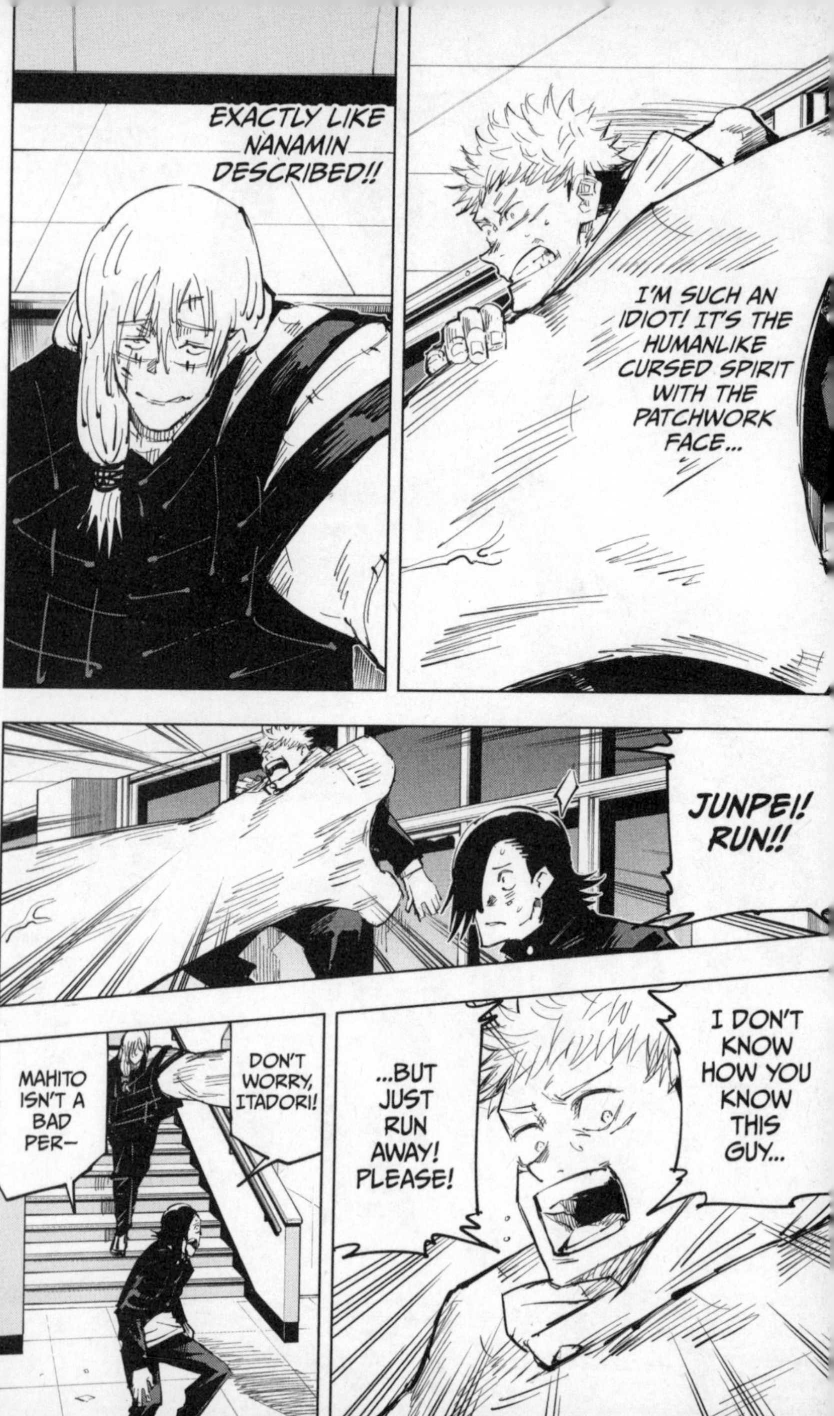
I'M SUCH AN IDIOT! IT'S THE HUMANLIKE CURSED SPIRIT WITH THE PATCHWORK FACE...
EXACTLY LIKE NANAMIN DESCRIBED!!
JUNPEI! RUN!!
I DON'T KNOW HOW YOU KNOW THIS GUY...
...BUT JUST RUN AWAY! PLEASE!
DON'T WORRY, ITADORI!
MAHITO ISN'T A BAD PER—

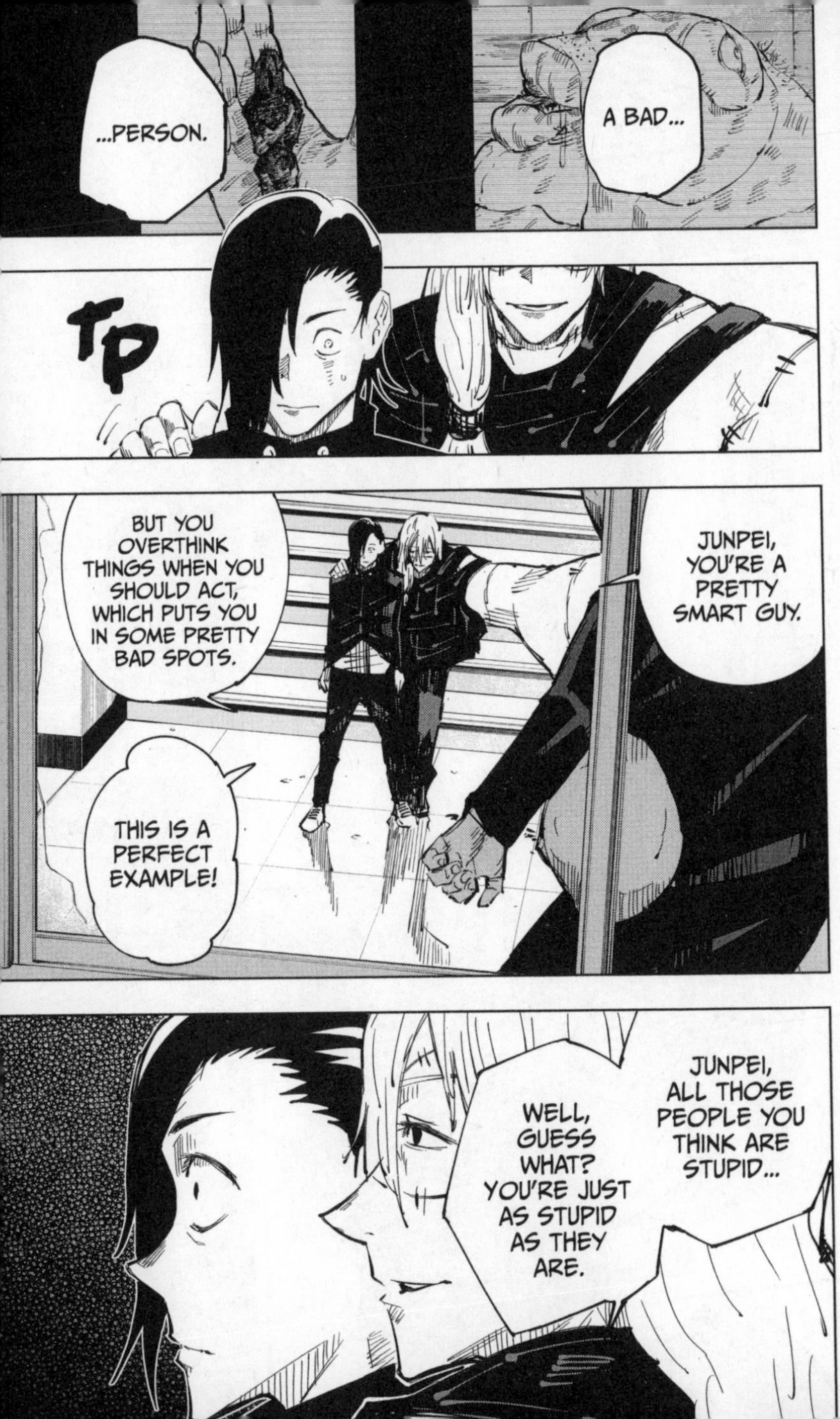
A BAD...
...PERSON.
TP
JUNPEI, YOU'RE A PRETTY SMART GUY.
BUT YOU OVERTHINK THINGS WHEN YOU SHOULD ACT, WHICH PUTS YOU IN SOME PRETTY BAD SPOTS.
THIS IS A PERFECT EXAMPLE!
JUNPEI, ALL THOSE PEOPLE YOU THINK ARE STUPID...
WELL, GUESS WHAT? YOU'RE JUST AS STUPID AS THEY ARE.

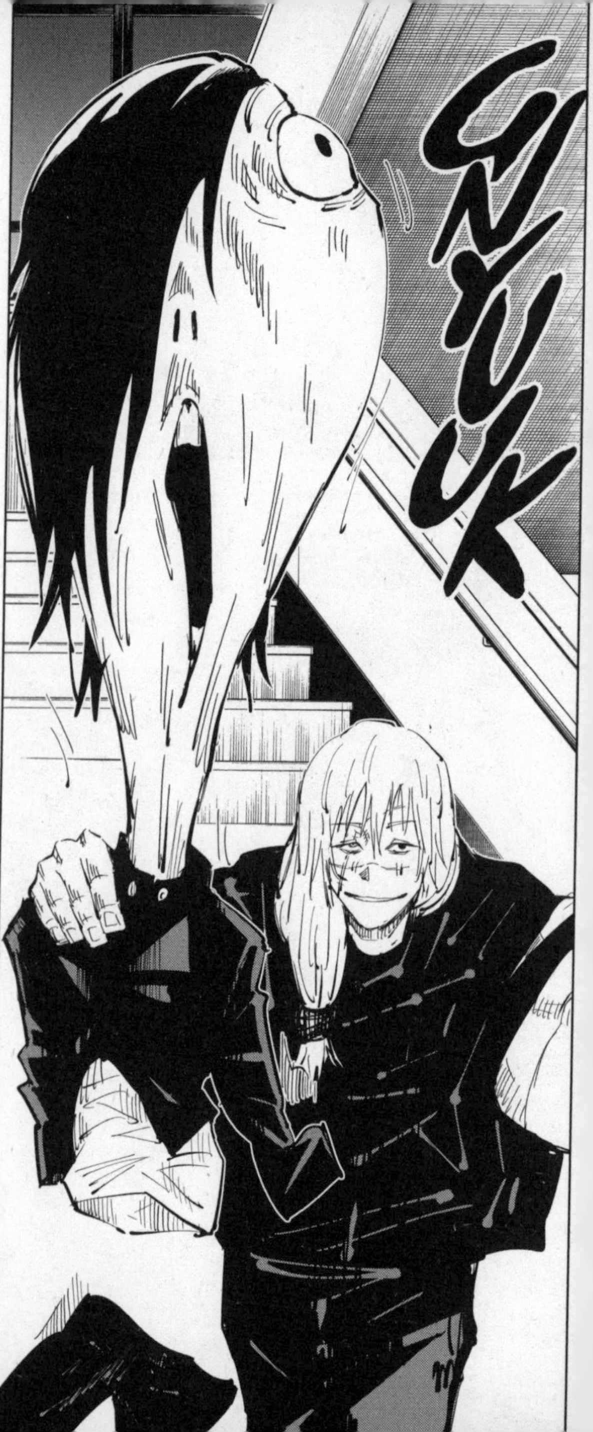

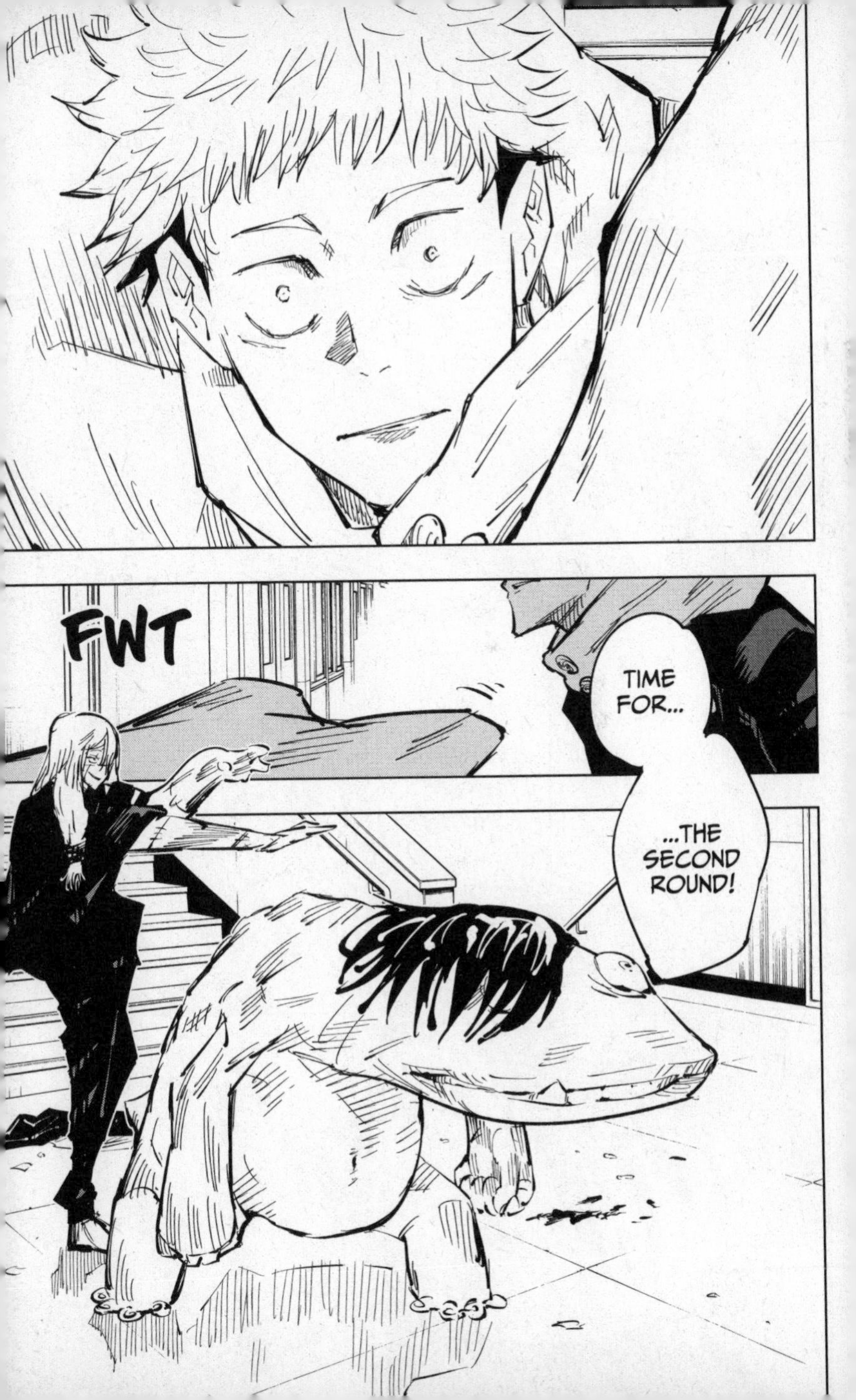
TIME FOR...
FWT
...THE SECOND ROUND!

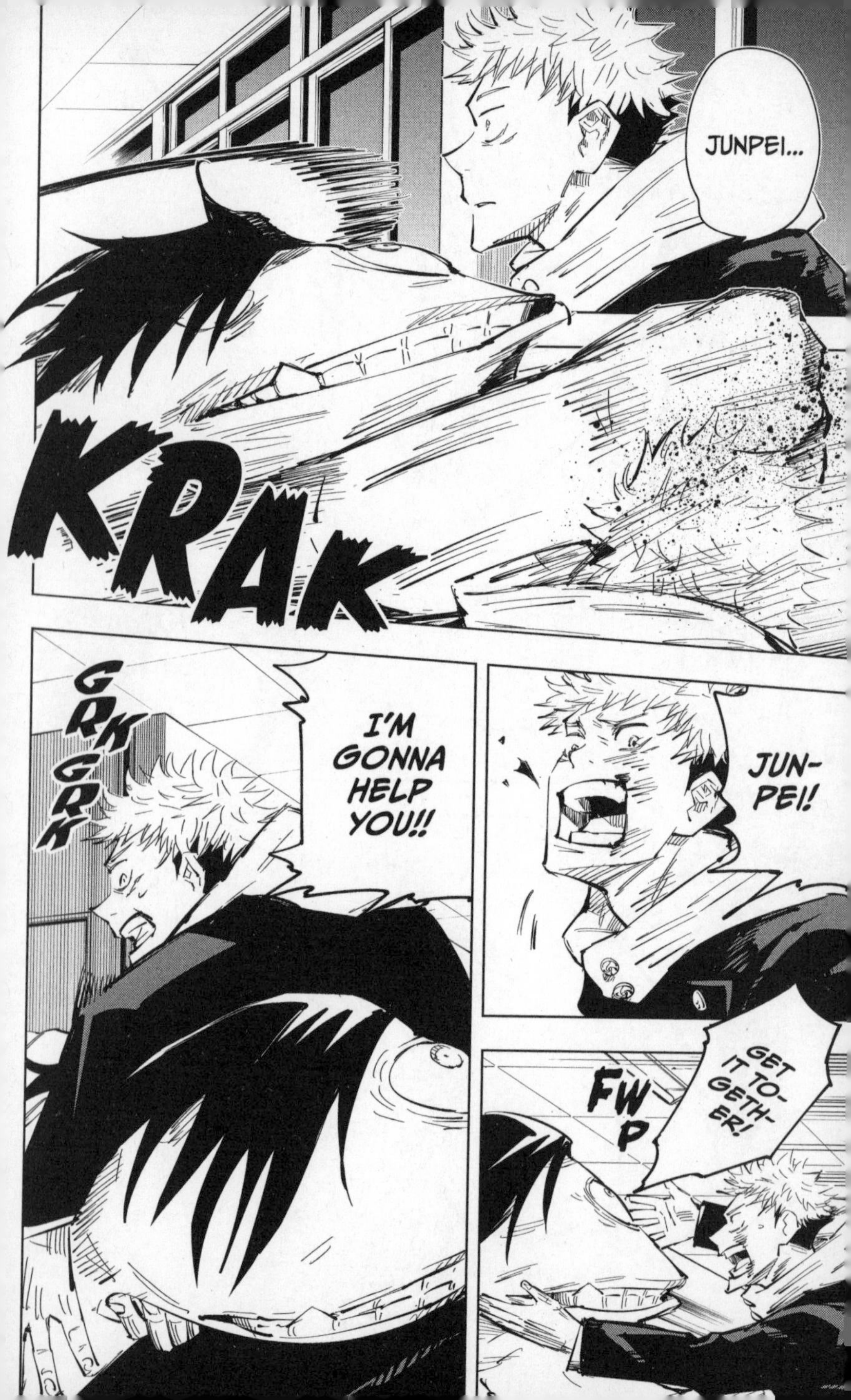

JUNPEI...
KRAK
JUN-PEI!
GET IT TO-GETH-ER!
FWP
I'M GONNA HELP YOU!!
GRK GRK

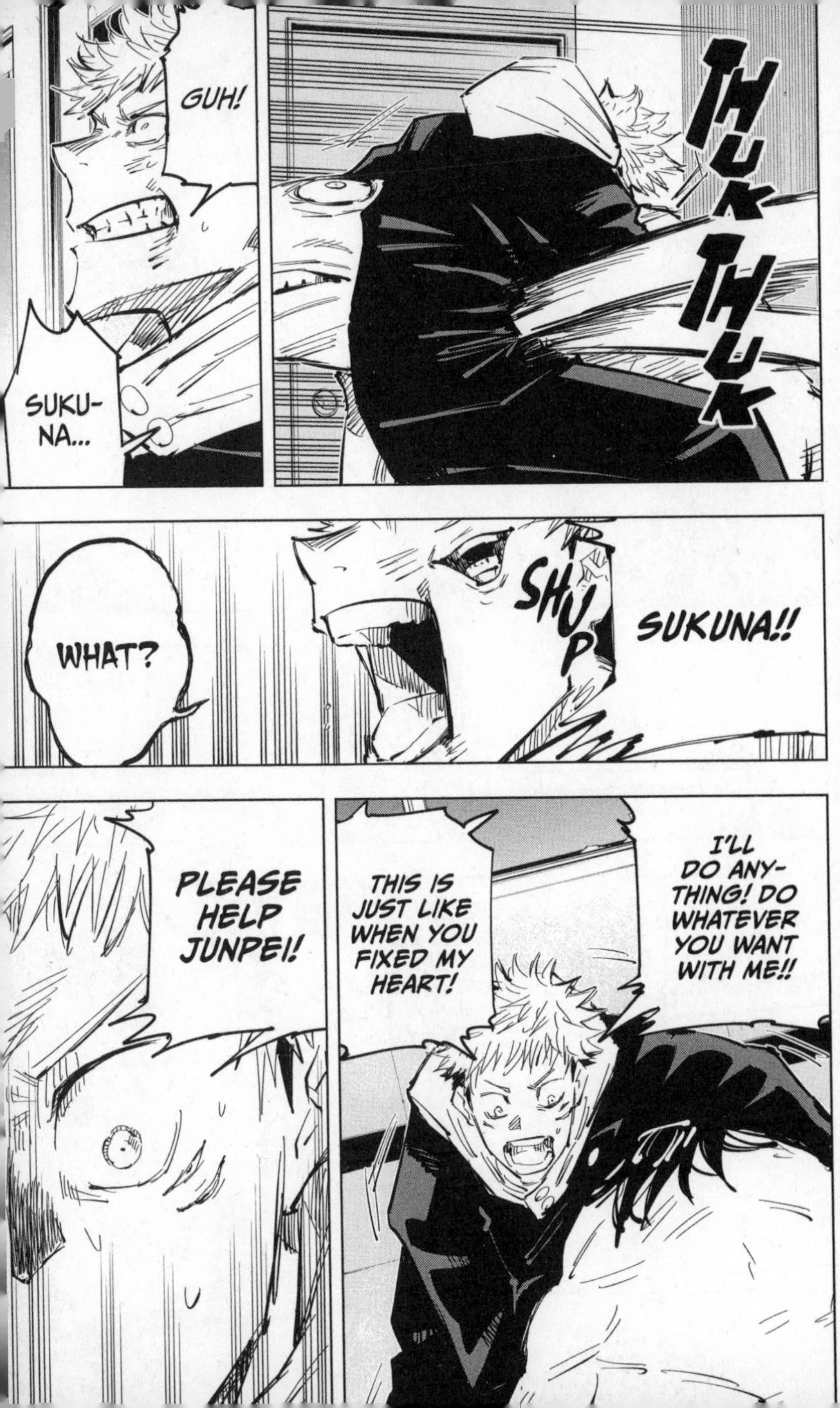
THUK THUK
GUH!
SUKU-NA...
SUKUNA!!
SHUP
WHAT?
I'LL DO ANYTHING! DO WHATEVER YOU WANT WITH ME!!
THIS IS JUST LIKE WHEN YOU FIXED MY HEART!
PLEASE HELP JUNPEI!

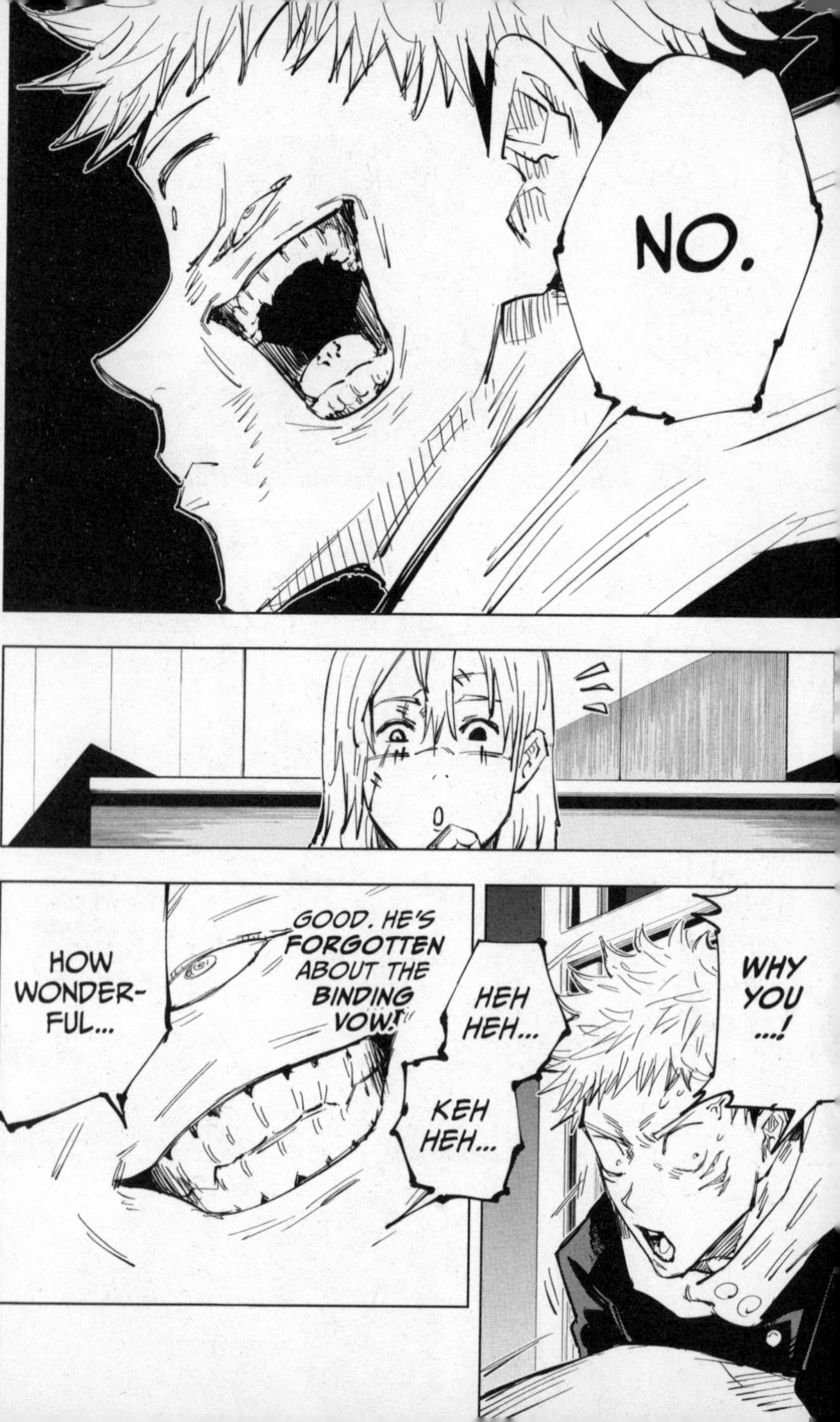
NO.
WHY YOU ...!
GOOD. HE'S FORGOTTEN ABOUT THE BINDING VOW!
HEH HEH...
HOW WONDER-FUL...
KEH HEH...

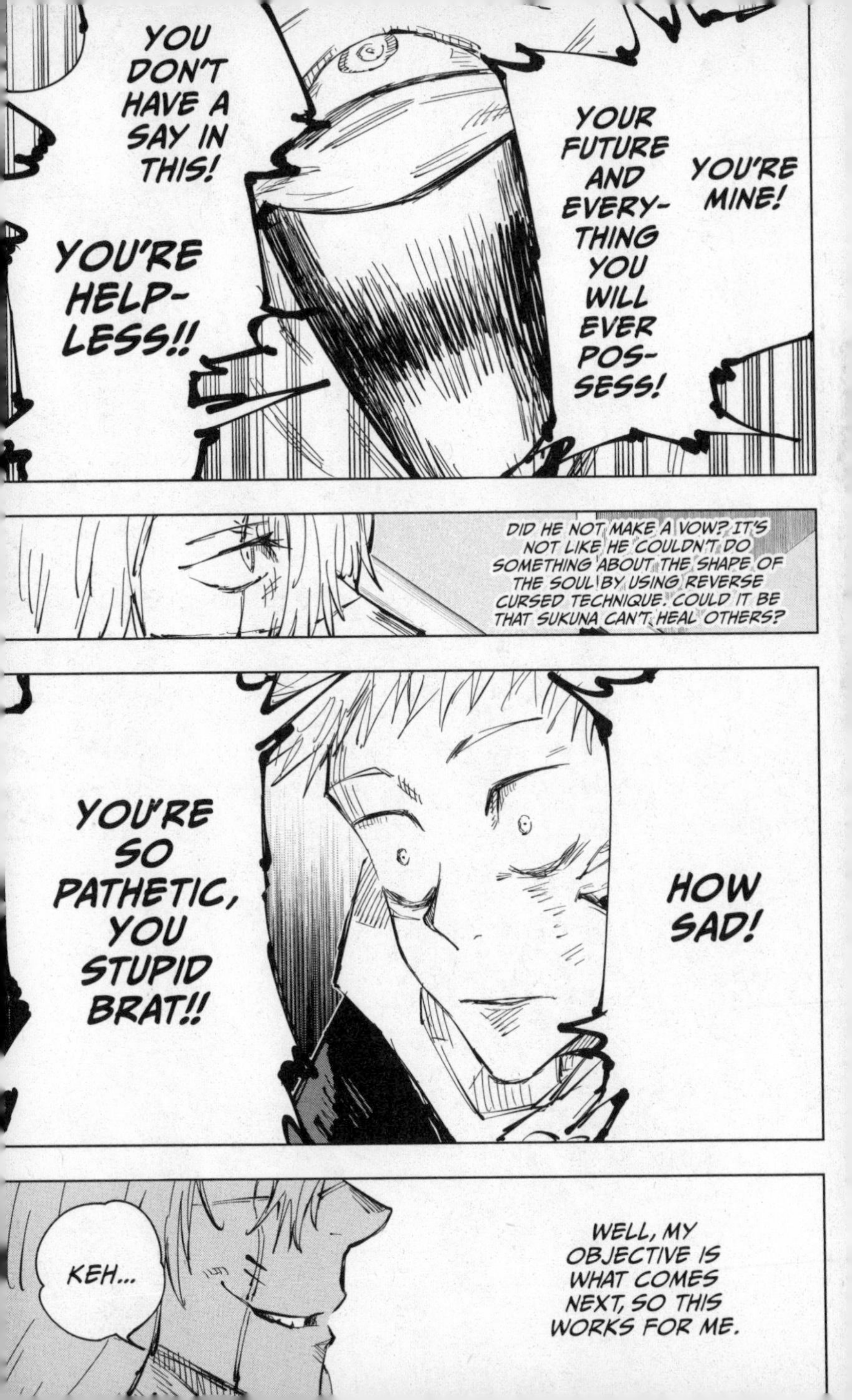
YOU'RE MINE!
YOUR FUTURE AND EVERYTHING YOU WILL EVER POSSESS!
YOU DON'T HAVE A SAY IN THIS!
YOU'RE HELPLESS!!
DID HE NOT MAKE A VOW? IT'S NOT LIKE HE COULDN'T DO SOMETHING ABOUT THE SHAPE OF THE SOUL BY USING REVERSE CURSED TECHNIQUE. COULD IT BE THAT SUKUNA CAN'T HEAL OTHERS?
HOW SAD!
YOU'RE SO PATHETIC, YOU STUPID BRAT!!
WELL, MY OBJECTIVE IS WHAT COMES NEXT, SO THIS WORKS FOR ME.
KEH...

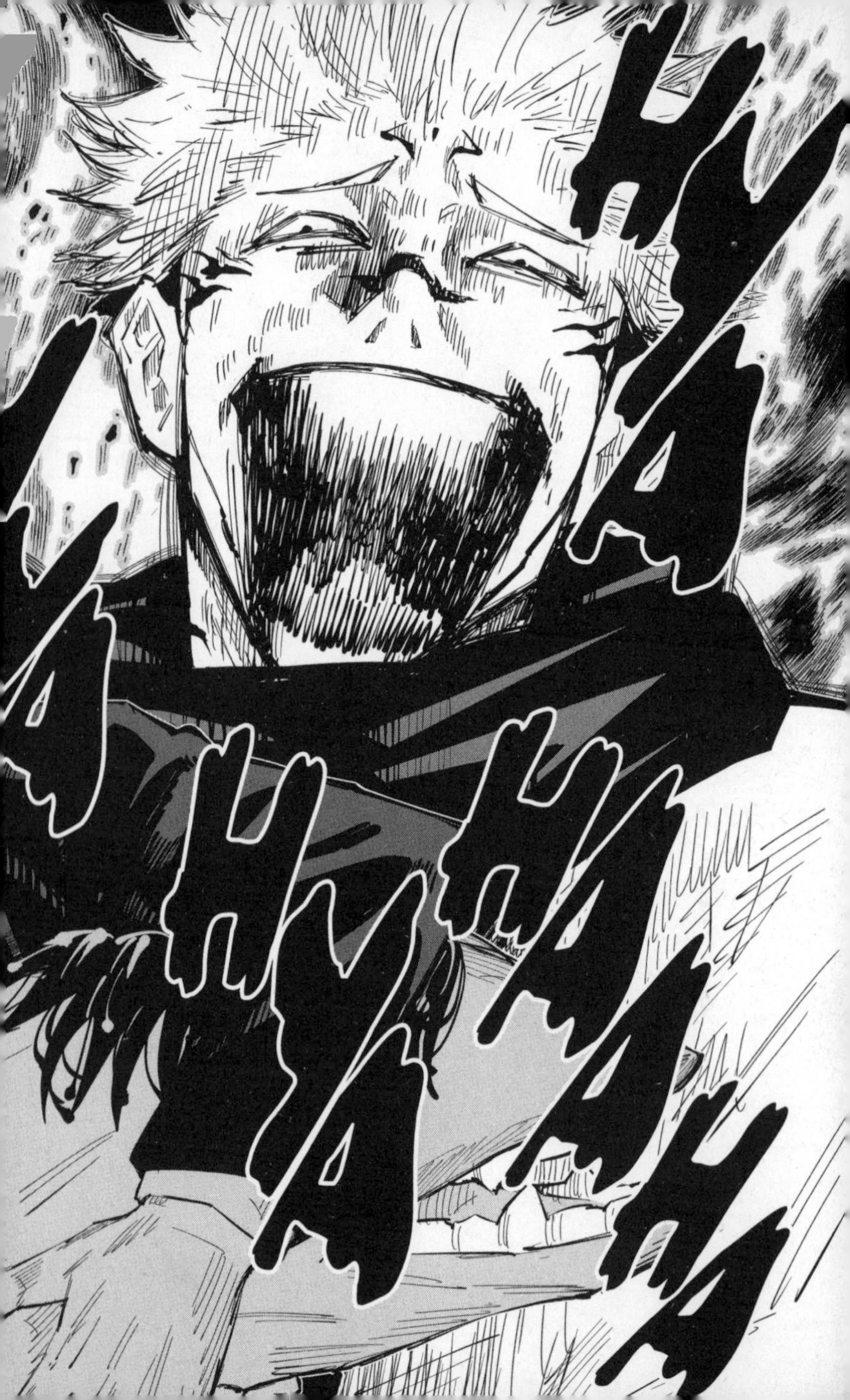
HA HAHAHAHA

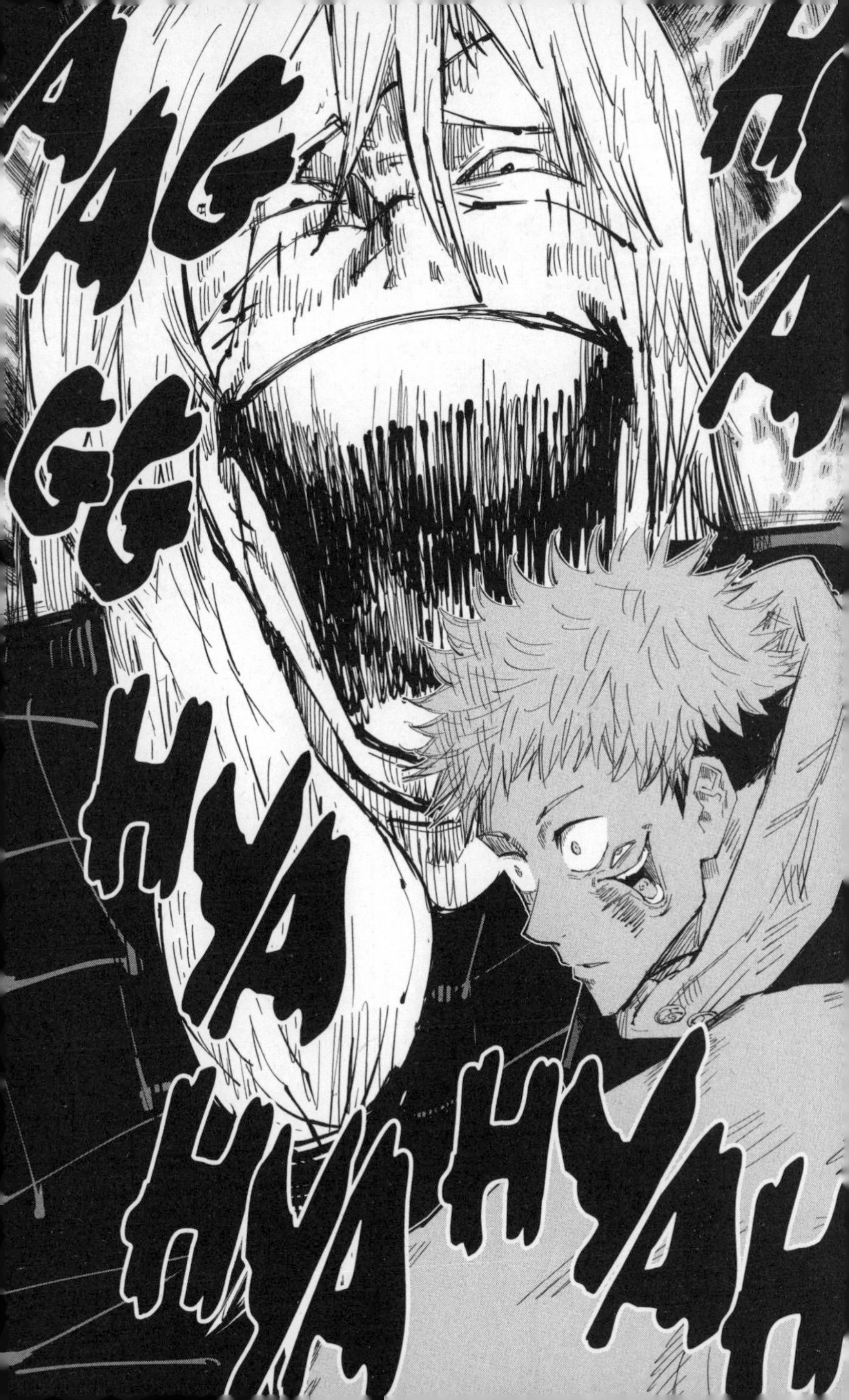
AA
AAGGGHYA
HYAHYAH

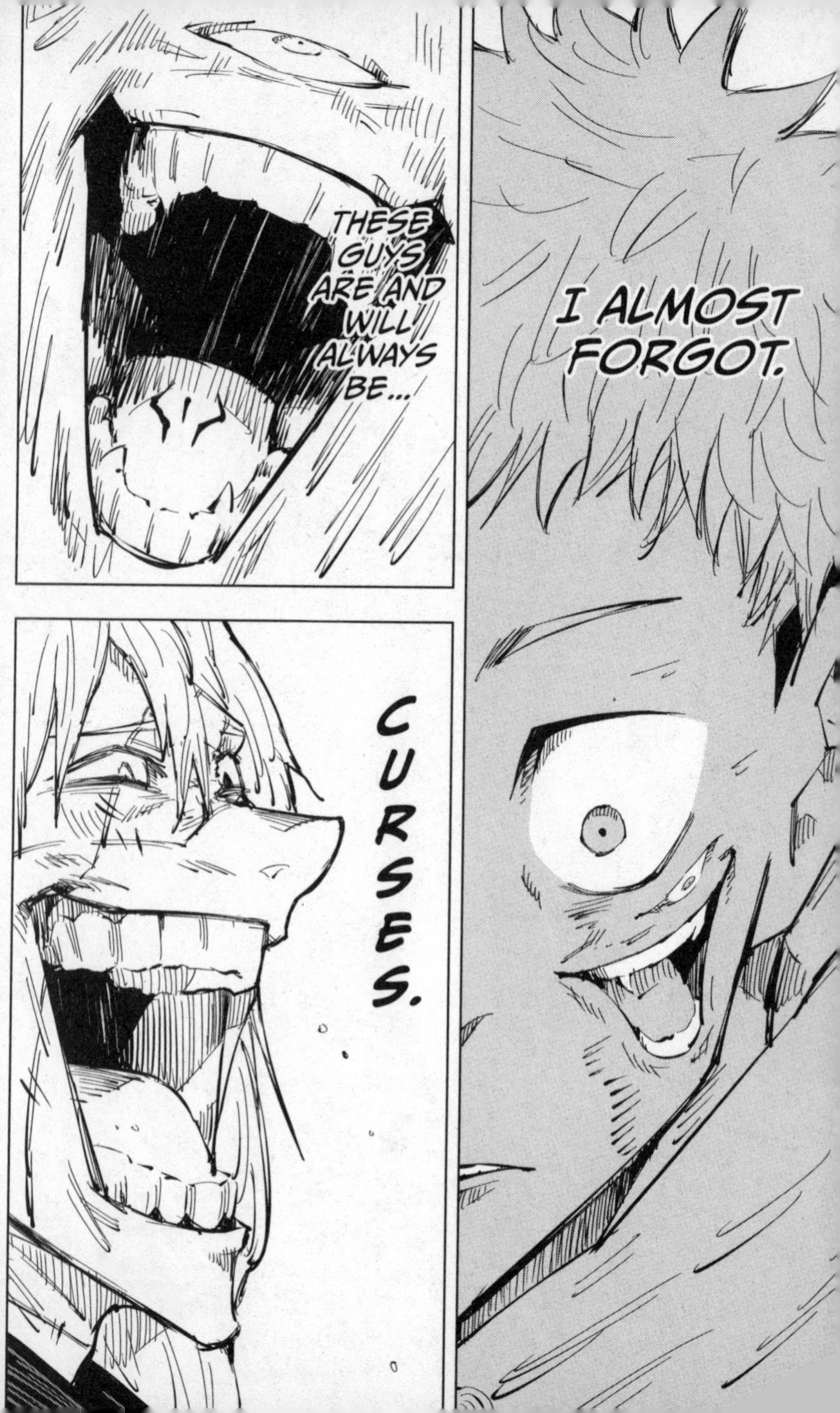
I ALMOST FORGOT.
THESE GUYS ARE AND WILL ALWAYS BE...
CURSES.

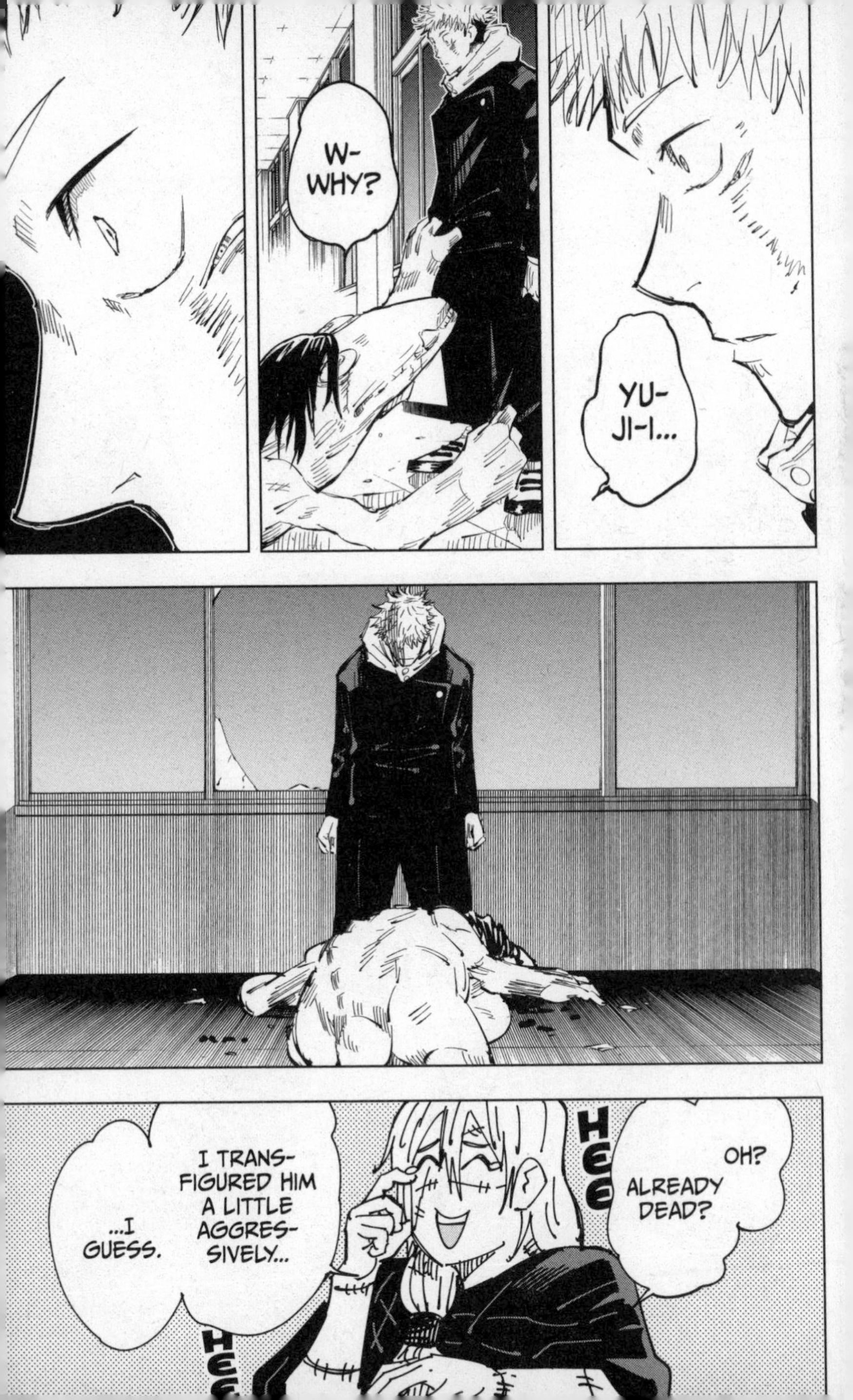
YU-JI-I...
W-WHY?
OH? ALREADY DEAD?
HEE
I TRANS-FIGURED HIM A LITTLE AGGRES-SIVELY...
...I GUESS.
HEE

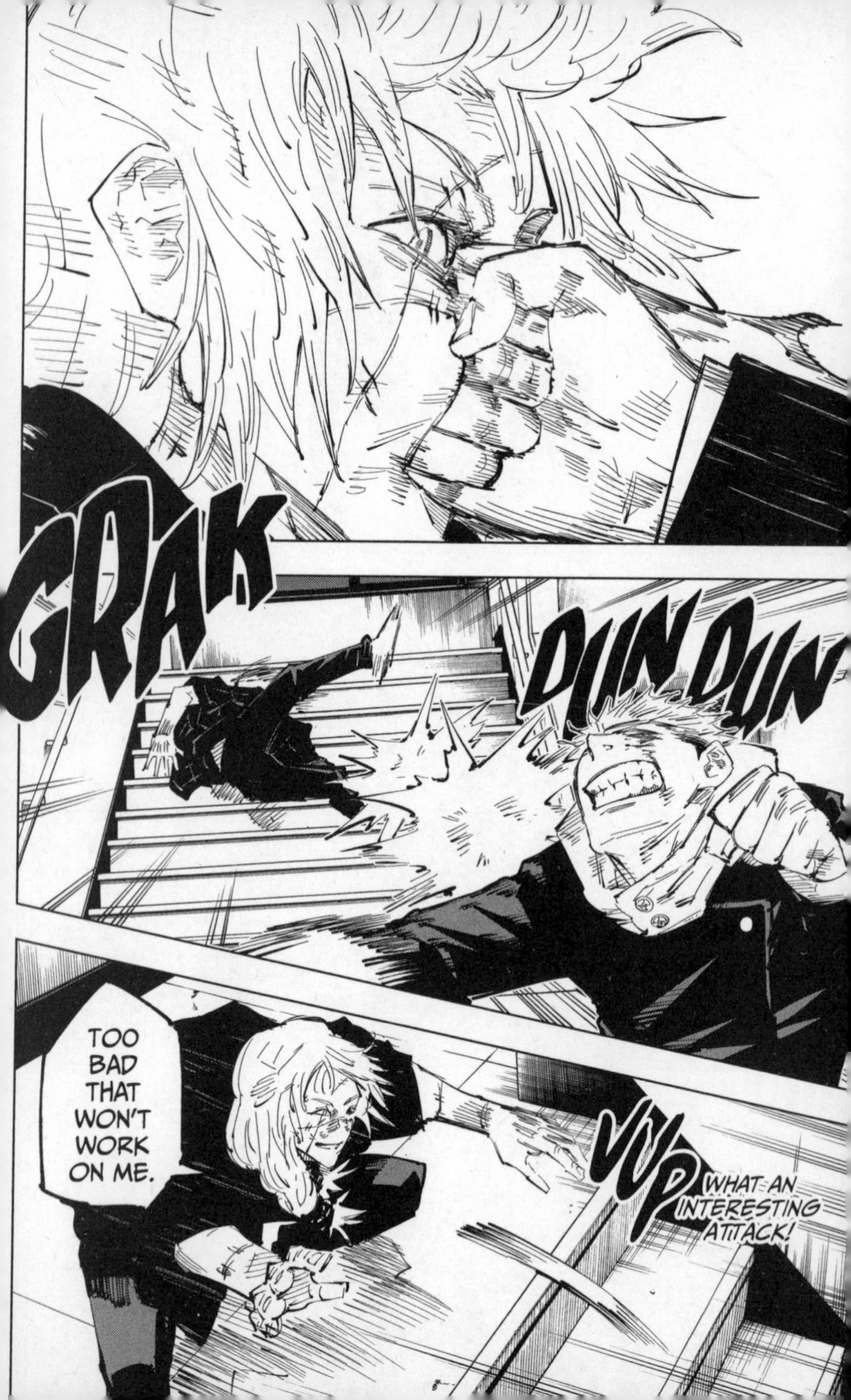
GRAK
DUN DUN
WHAT AN INTERESTING ATTACK!
VVP
TOO BAD THAT WON'T WORK ON ME.

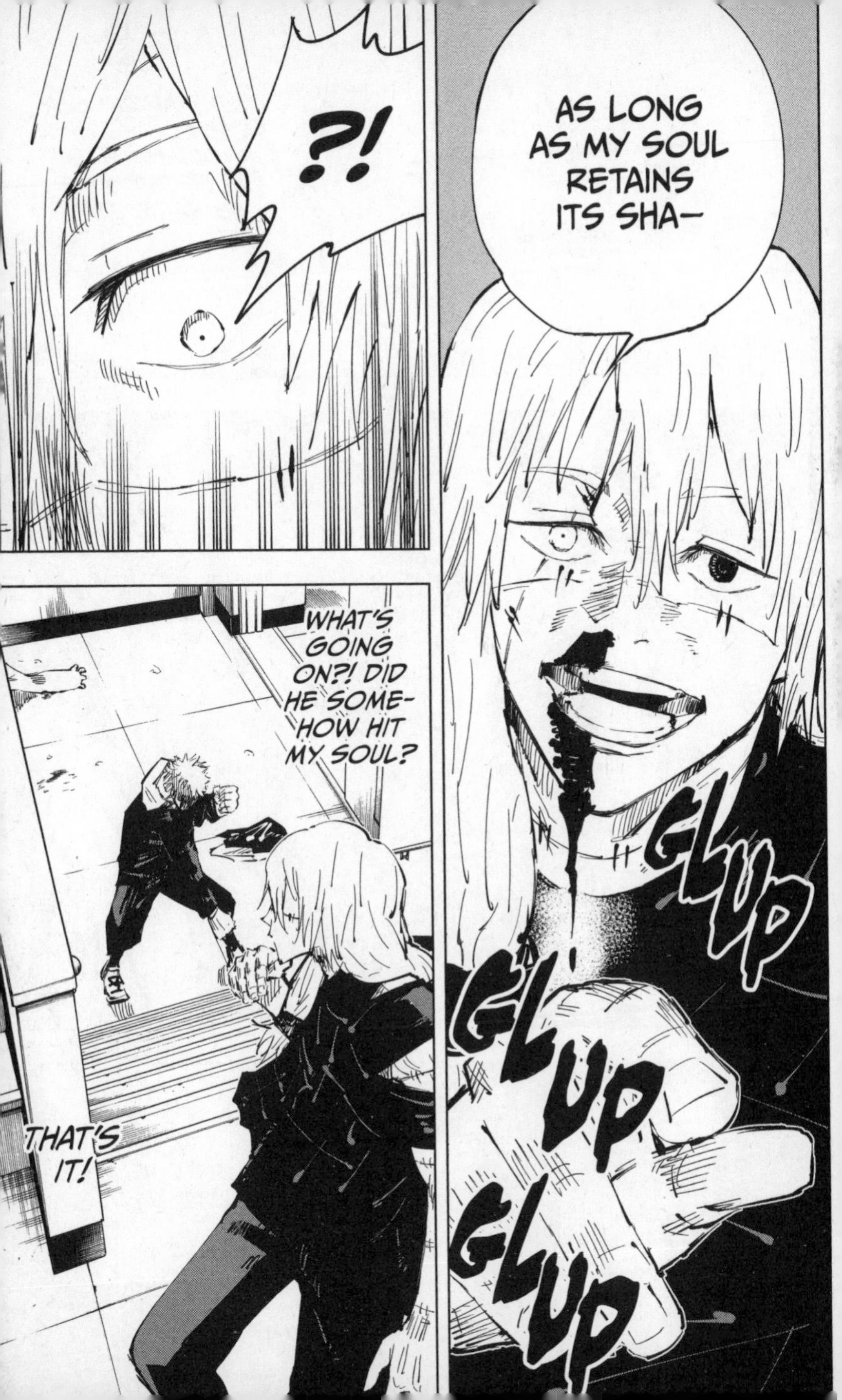
AS LONG AS MY SOUL RETAINS ITS SHA—
GLUP
GLUP
GLUP
?!
WHAT'S GOING ON?! DID HE SOME-HOW HIT MY SOUL?
THAT'S IT!

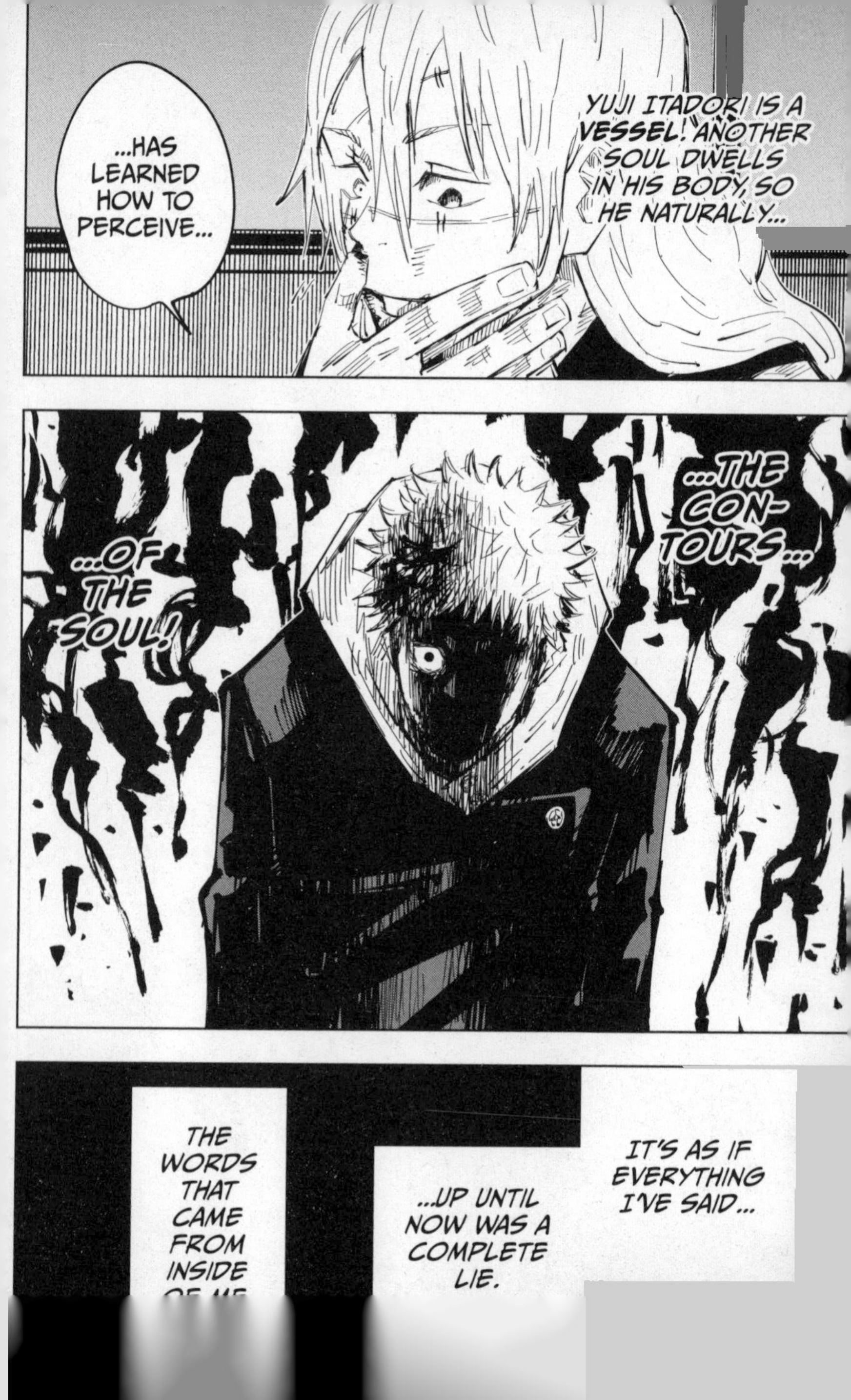
YUJI ITADORI IS A VESSEL! ANOTHER SOUL DWELLS IN HIS BODY, SO HE NATURALLY...
...HAS LEARNED HOW TO PERCEIVE...
...THE CON-TOURS...
...OF THE SOUL!
IT'S AS IF EVERYTHING I'VE SAID...
...UP UNTIL NOW WAS A COMPLETE LIE.
THE WORDS THAT CAME FROM INSIDE

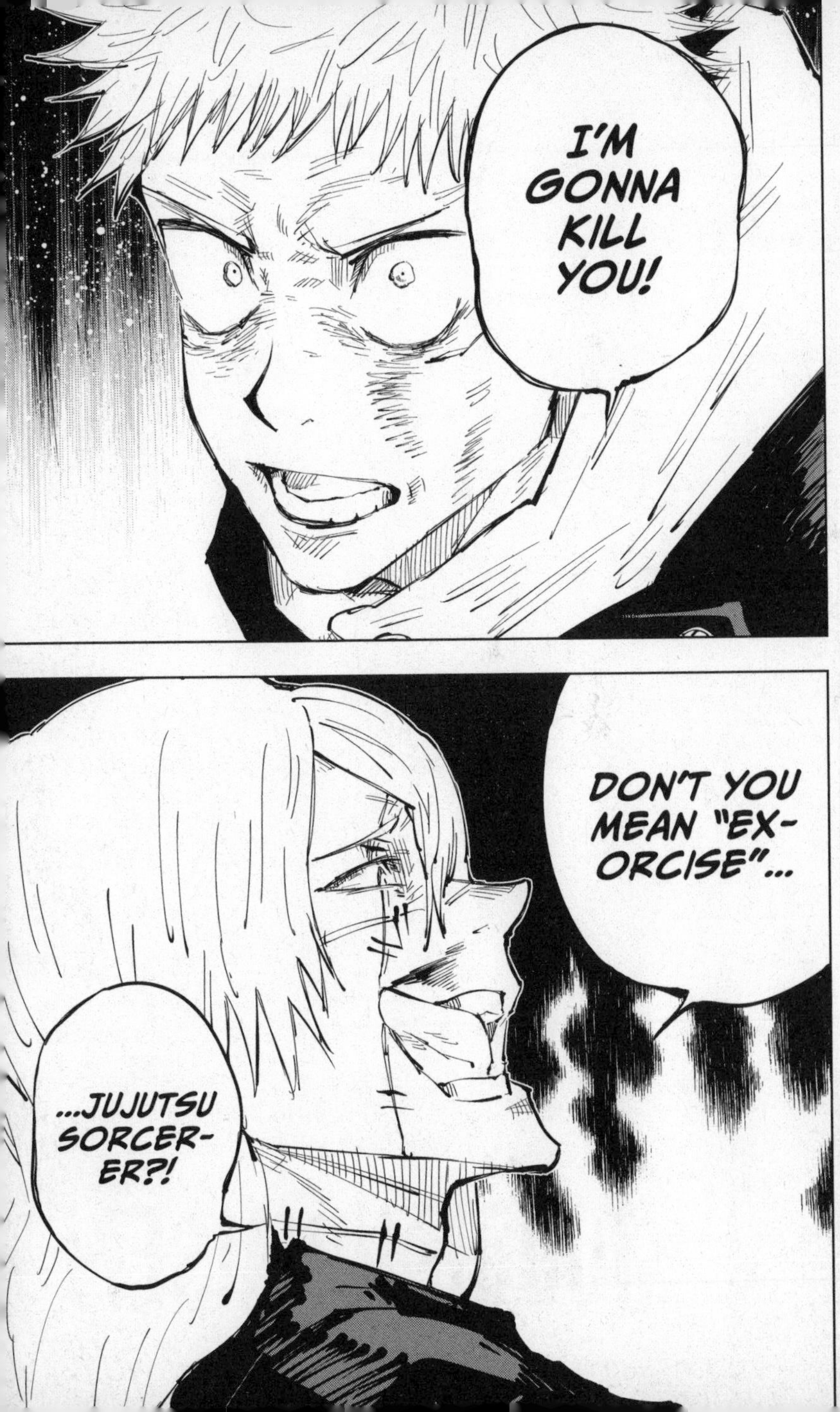
I'M GONNA KILL YOU!
DON'T YOU MEAN "EX-ORCISE"...
...JUJUTSU SORCERER?!

JUJUTSU KAISEN

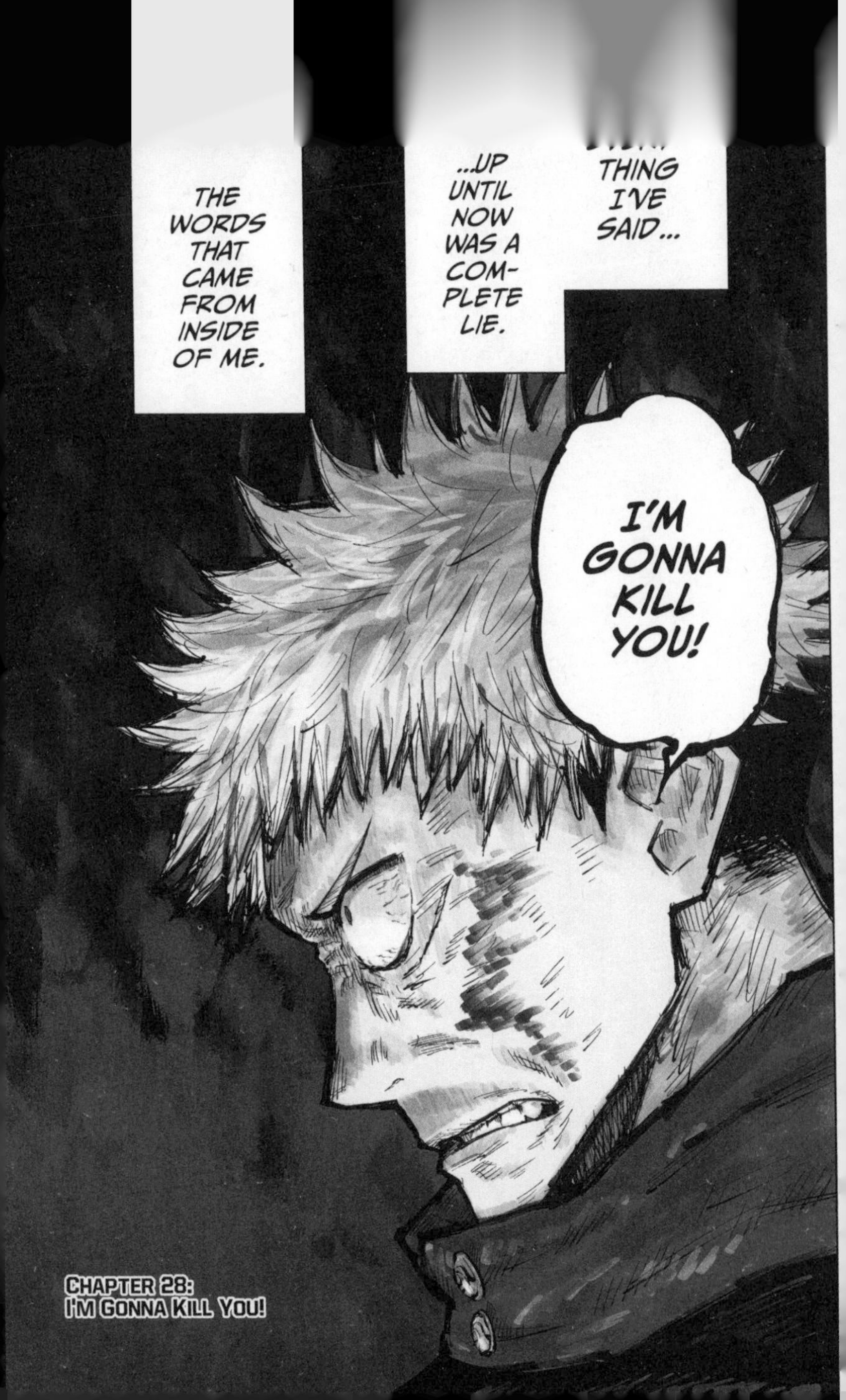
THING I'VE SAID...
...UP UNTIL NOW WAS A COMPLETE LIE.
THE WORDS THAT CAME FROM INSIDE OF ME.
I'M GONNA KILL YOU!
CHAPTER 28: I'M GONNA KILL YOU!

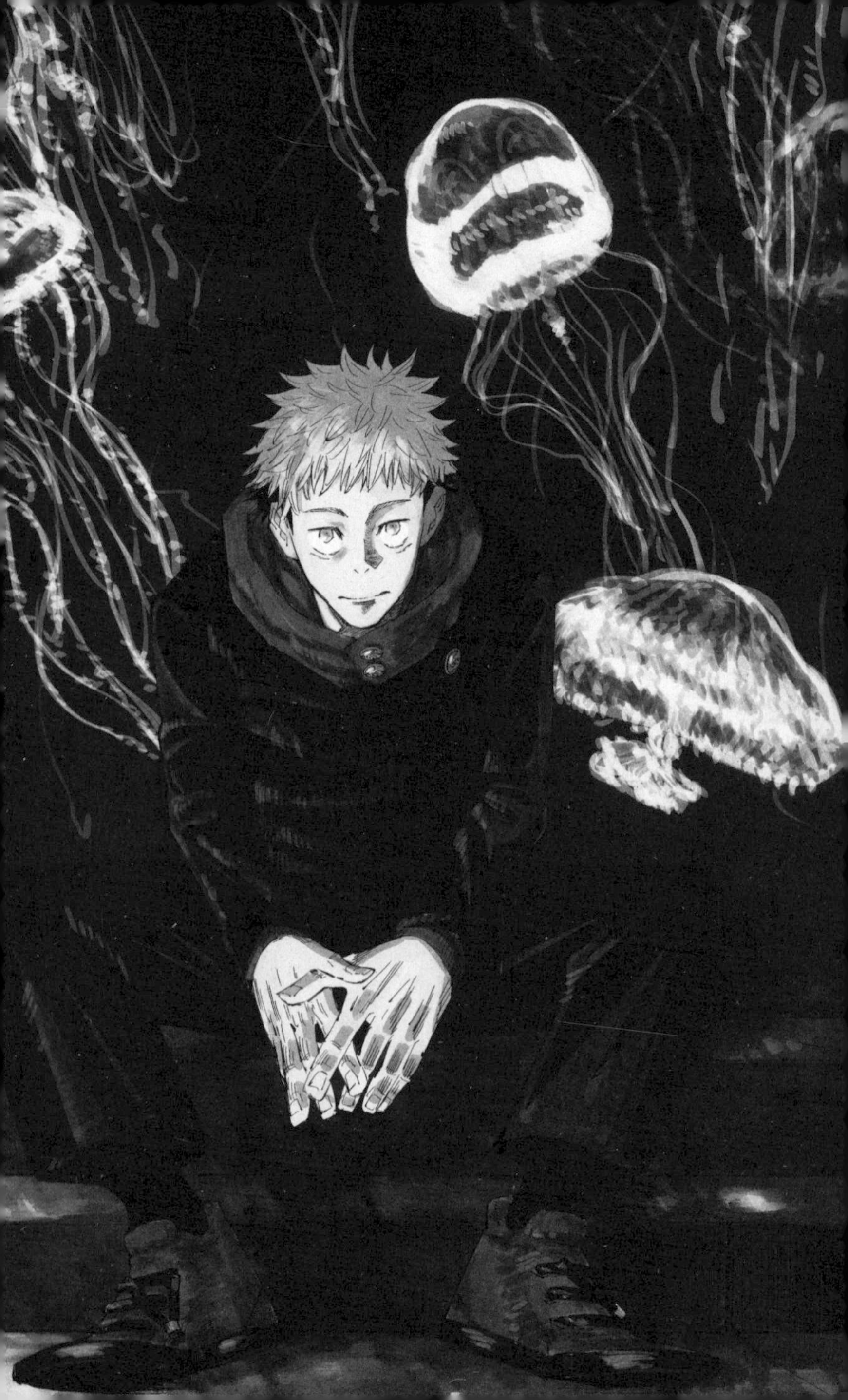

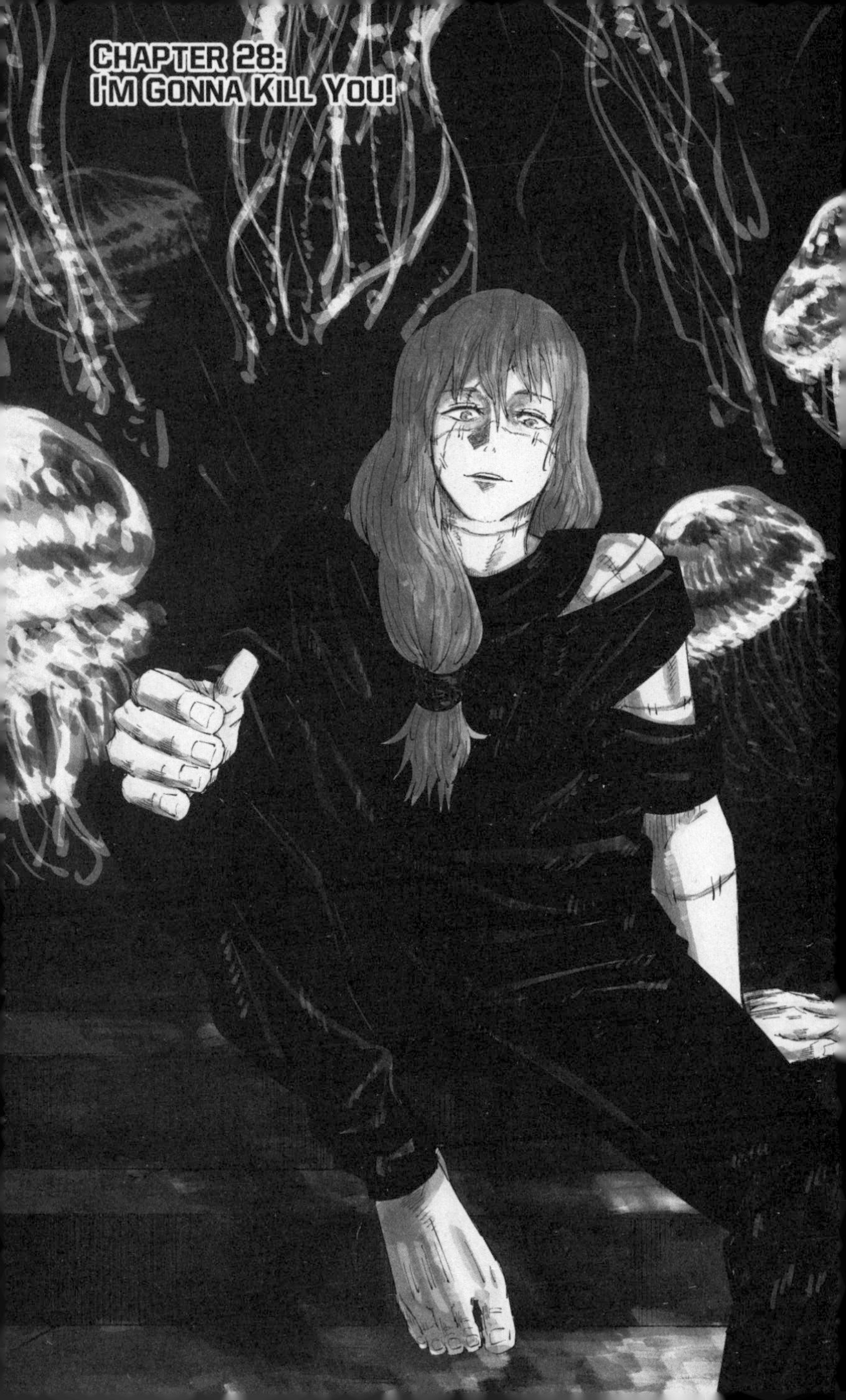
CHAPTER 28:
I'M GONNA KILL YOU!

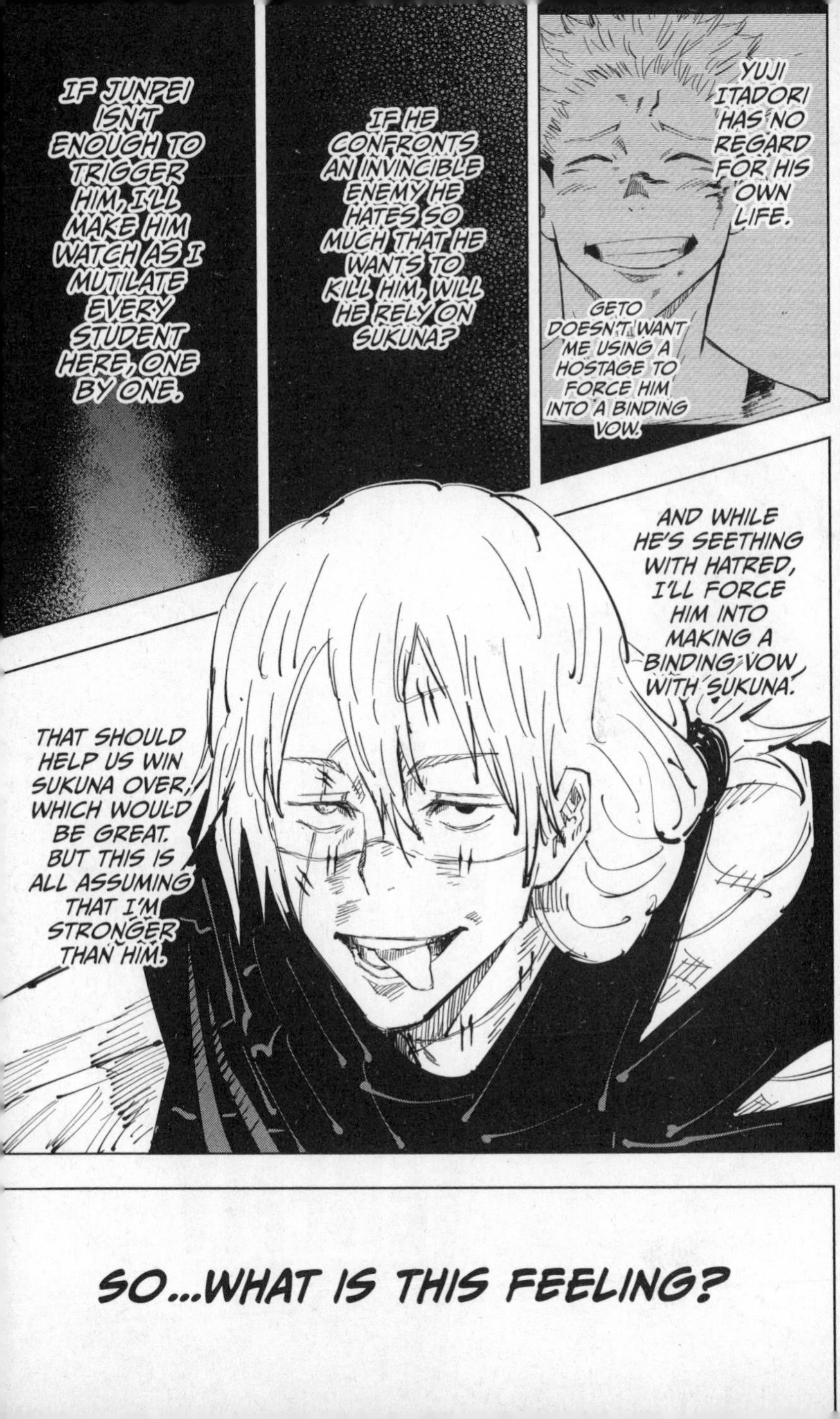
YUJI ITADORI HAS NO REGARD FOR HIS OWN LIFE.
GETO DOESN'T WANT ME USING A HOSTAGE TO FORCE HIM INTO A BINDING VOW.
IF HE CONFRONTS AN INVINCIBLE ENEMY HE HATES SO MUCH THAT HE WANTS TO KILL HIM, WILL HE RELY ON SUKUNA?
IF JUNPEI ISN'T ENOUGH TO TRIGGER HIM, I'LL MAKE HIM WATCH AS I MUTILATE EVERY STUDENT HERE, ONE BY ONE.
AND WHILE HE'S SEETHING WITH HATRED, I'LL FORCE HIM INTO MAKING A BINDING VOW WITH SUKUNA.
THAT SHOULD HELP US WIN SUKUNA OVER, WHICH WOULD BE GREAT. BUT THIS IS ALL ASSUMING THAT I'M STRONGER THAN HIM.
SO...WHAT IS THIS FEELING?

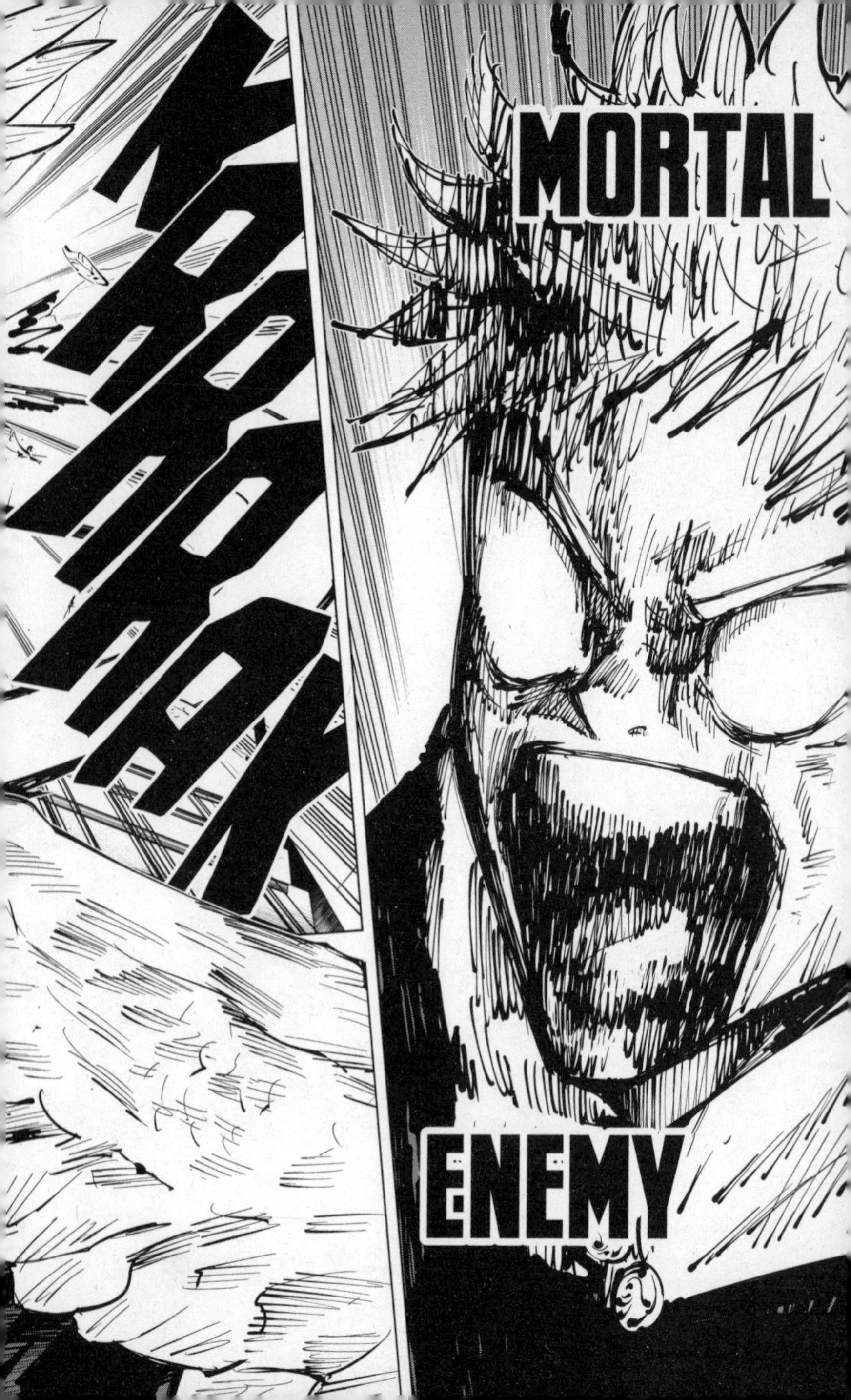
MORTAL
ENEMY

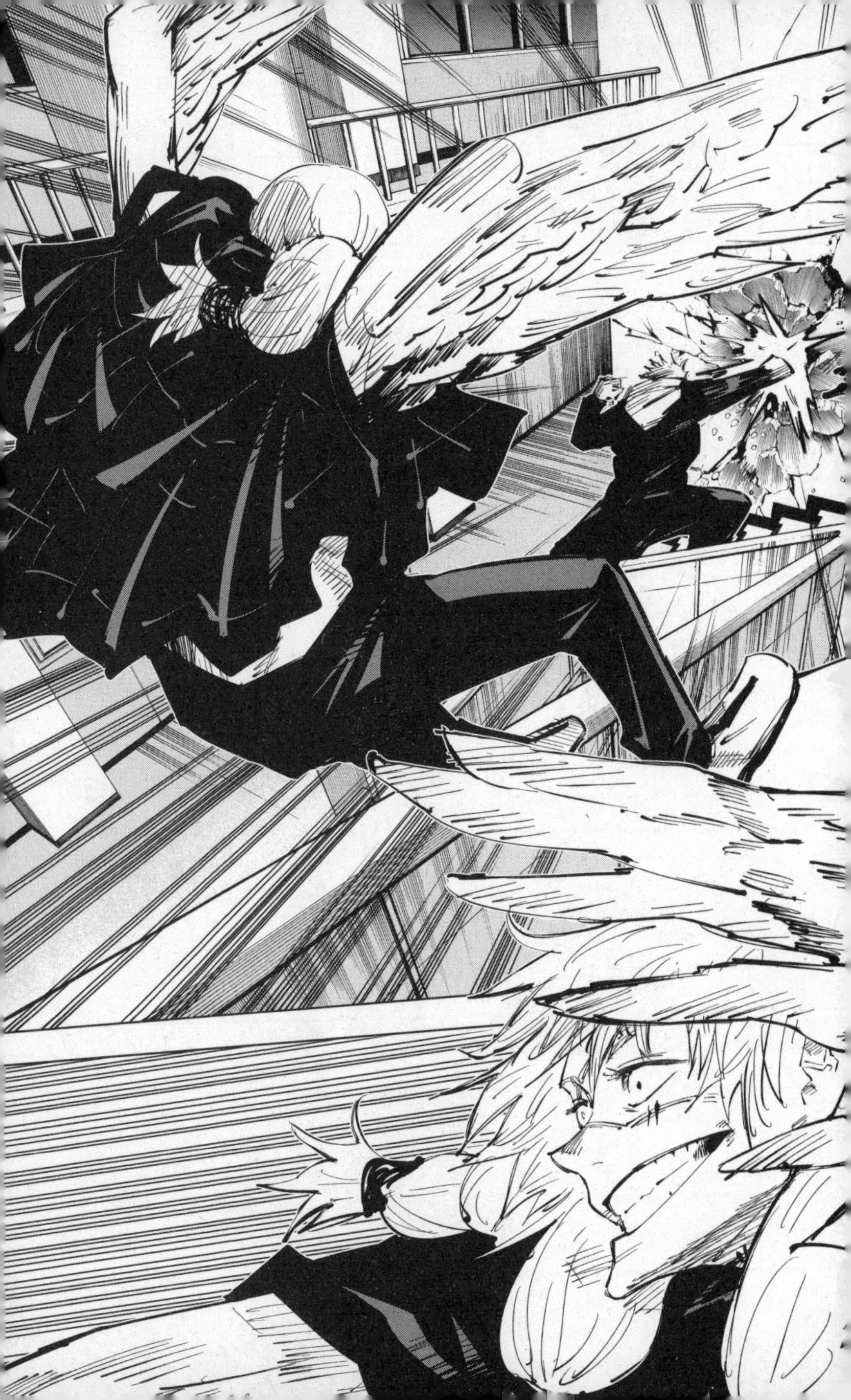

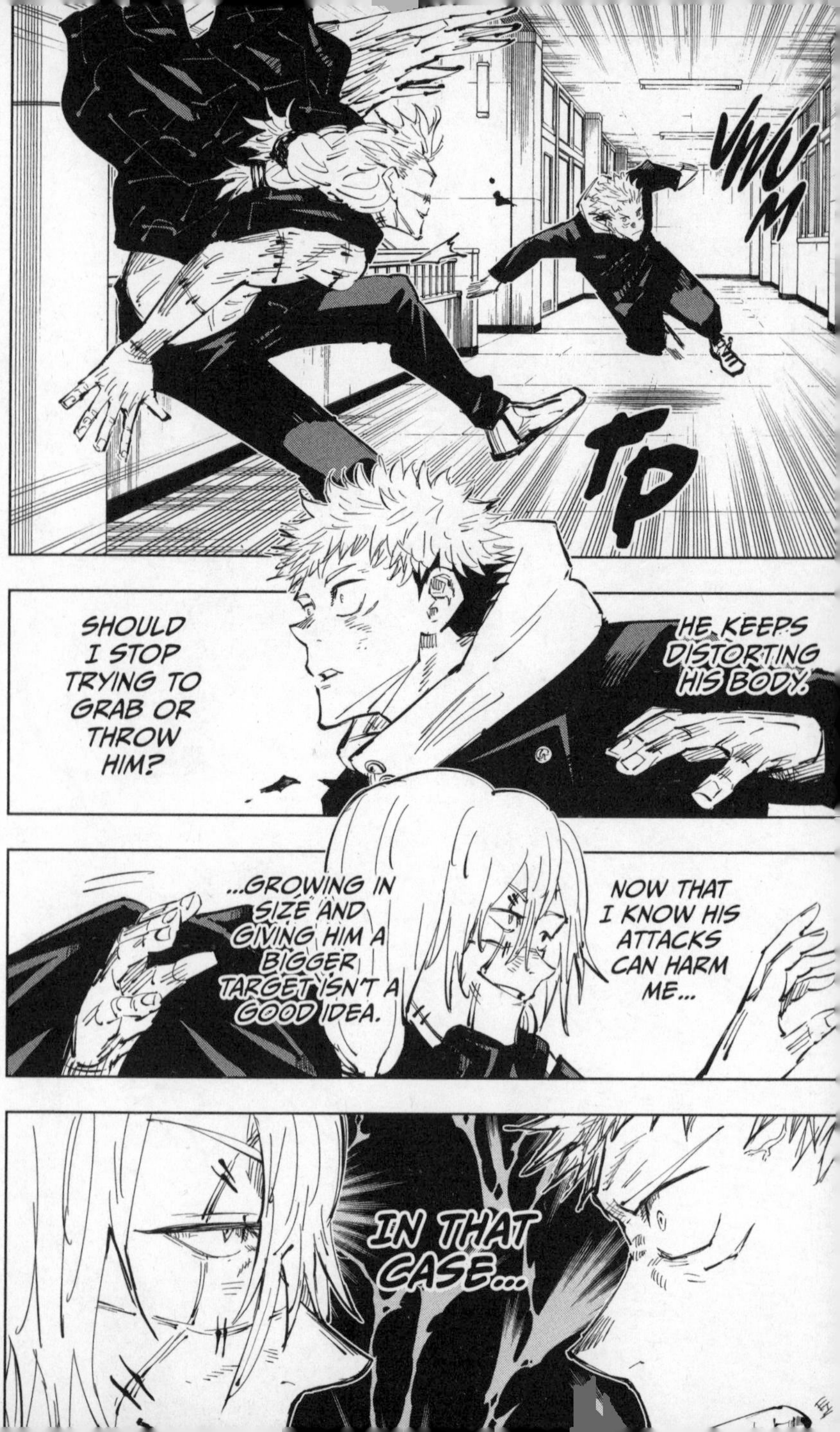
VMMM
TP
HE KEEPS DISTORTING HIS BODY.
SHOULD I STOP TRYING TO GRAB OR THROW HIM?
NOW THAT I KNOW HIS ATTACKS CAN HARM ME...
...GROWING IN SIZE AND GIVING HIM A BIGGER TARGET ISN'T A GOOD IDEA.
IN THAT CASE...

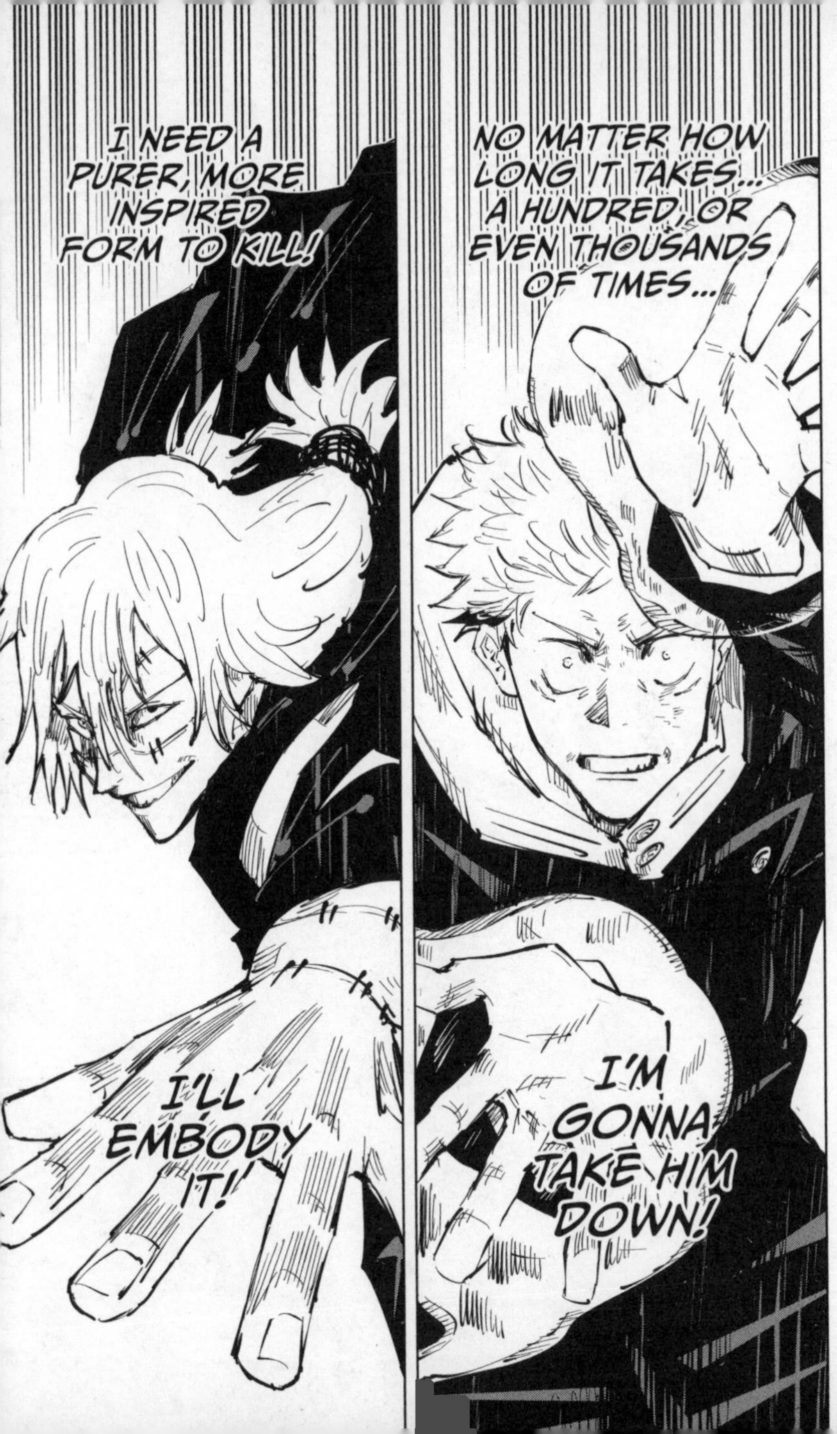
NO MATTER HOW LONG IT TAKES... A HUNDRED, OR EVEN THOUSANDS OF TIMES...
I'M GONNA TAKE HIM DOWN!
I NEED A PURER, MORE INSPIRED FORM TO KILL!
I'LL EMBODY IT!

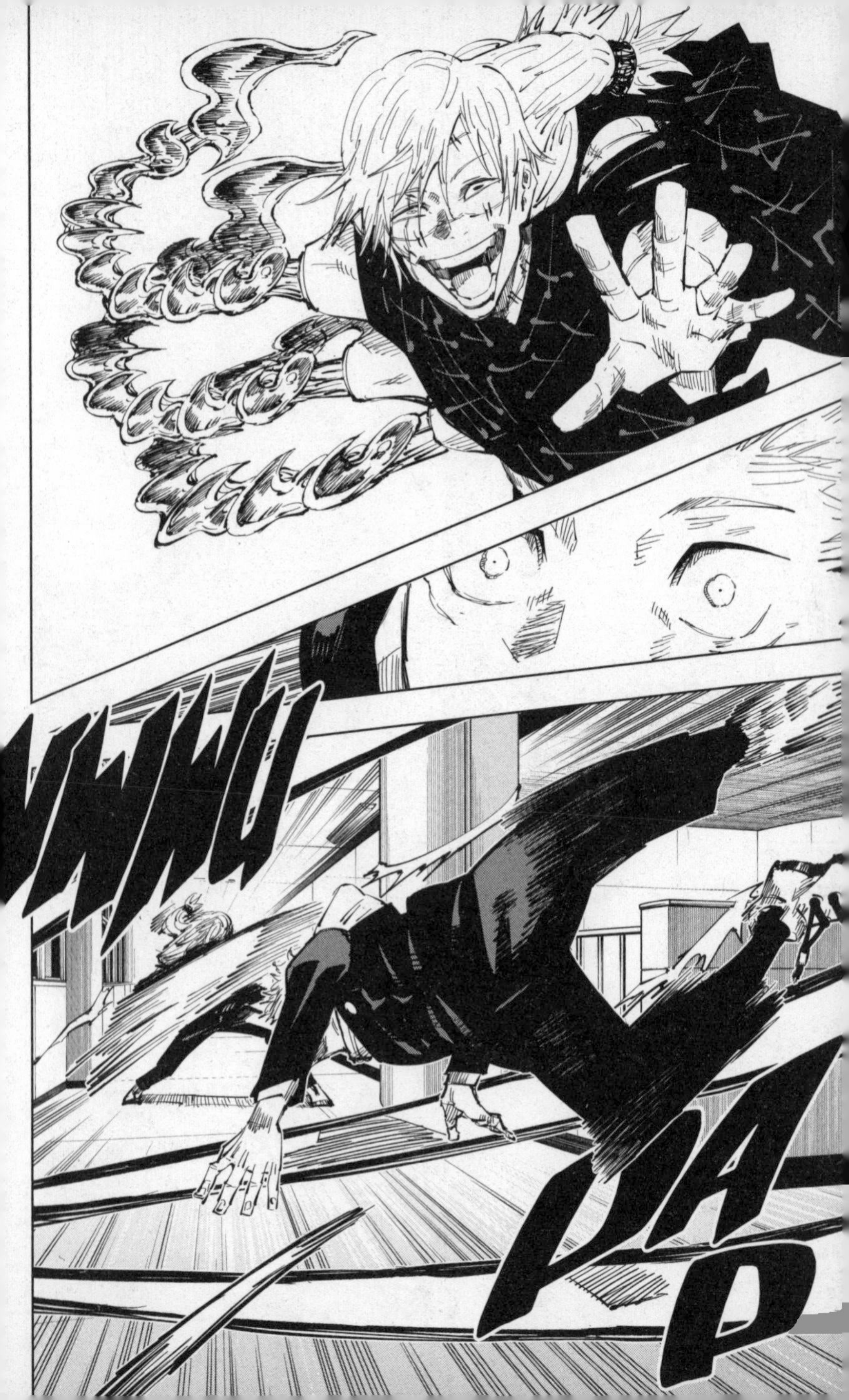

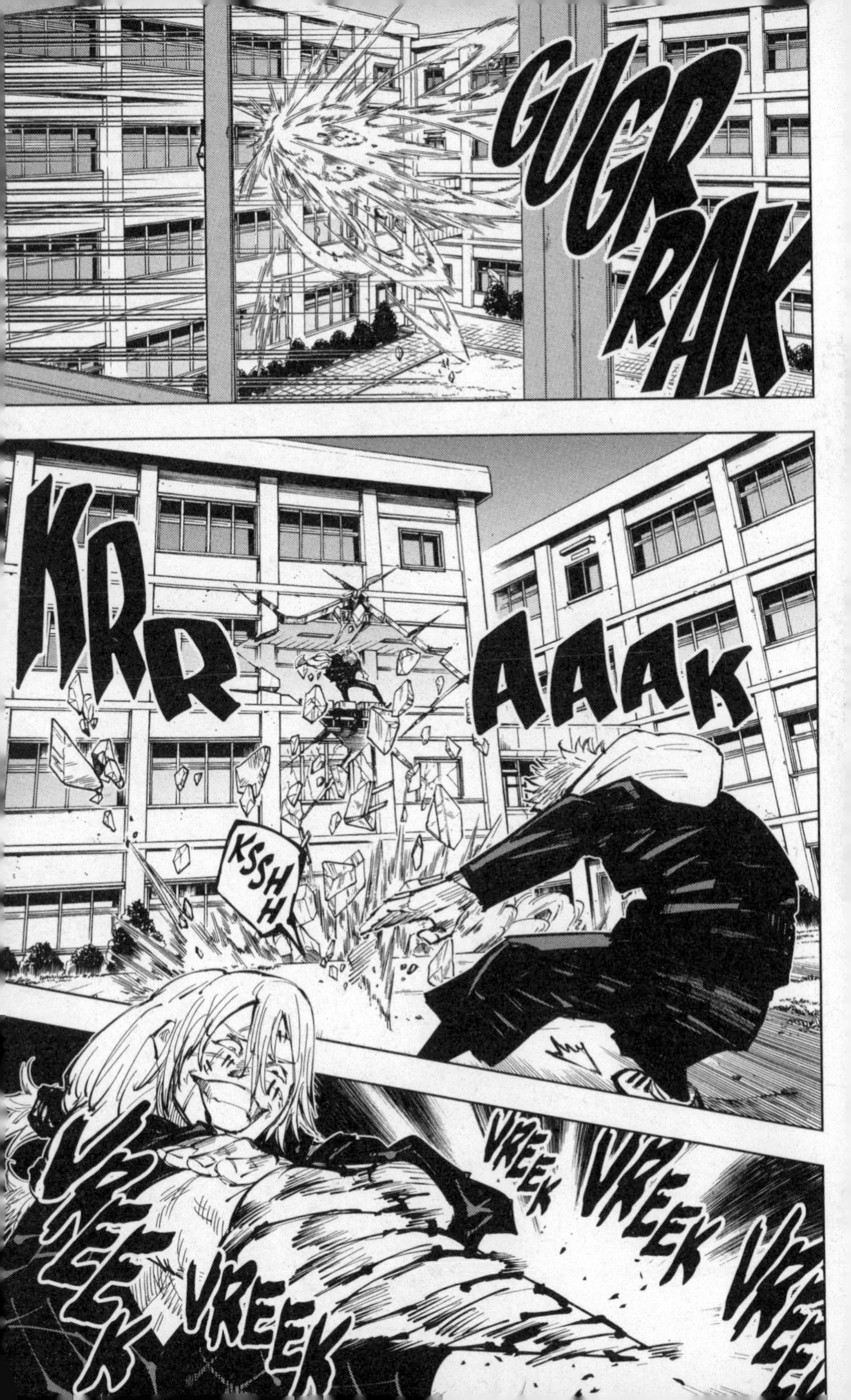
GUGRRAK
KRRAAAK
KSSHH
VREEK
VREEK
VREEK
VREEK

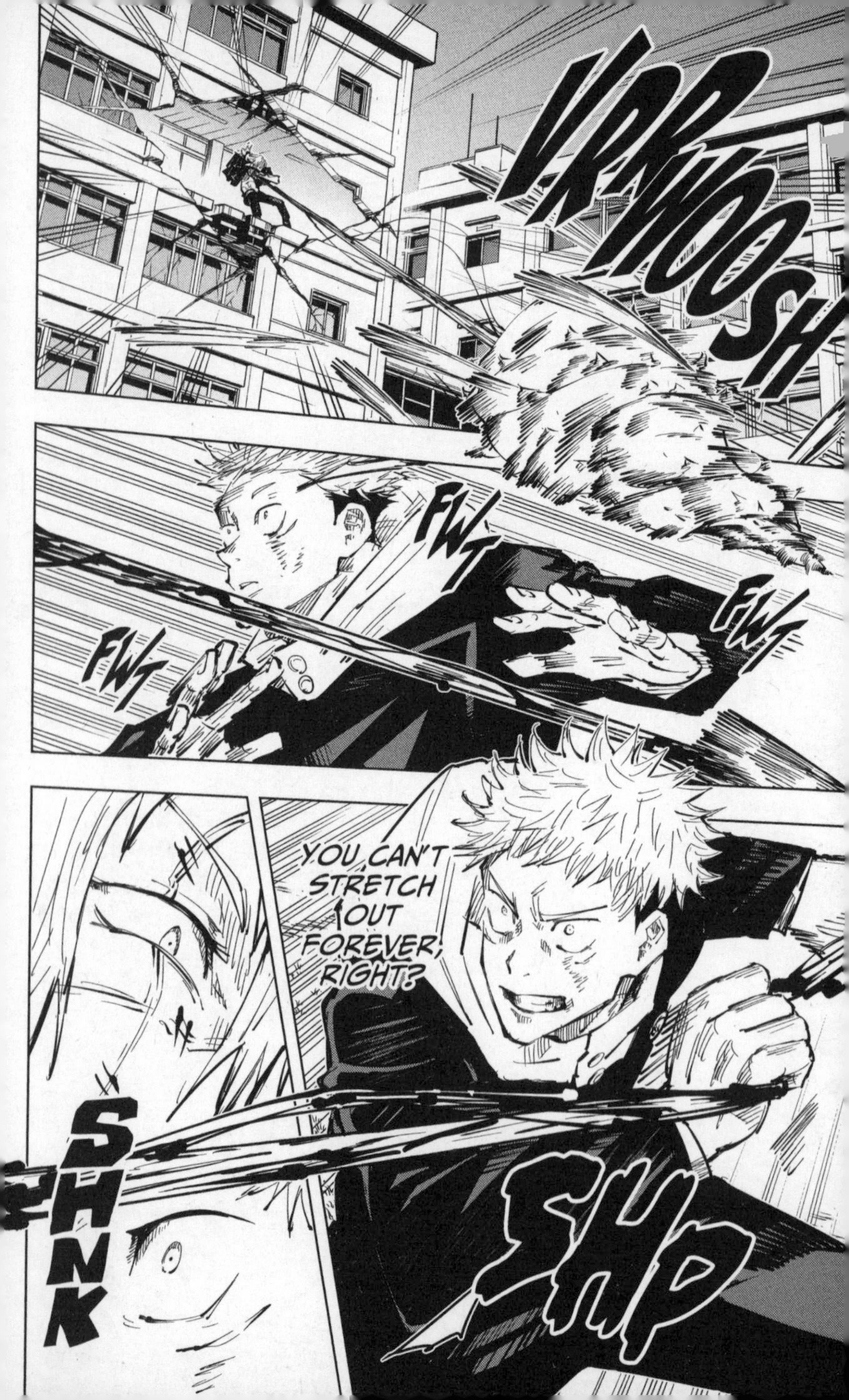
VROOSH
FWT
FWT
FWT
YOU CAN'T STRETCH OUT FOREVER, RIGHT?
SHP
SHNK

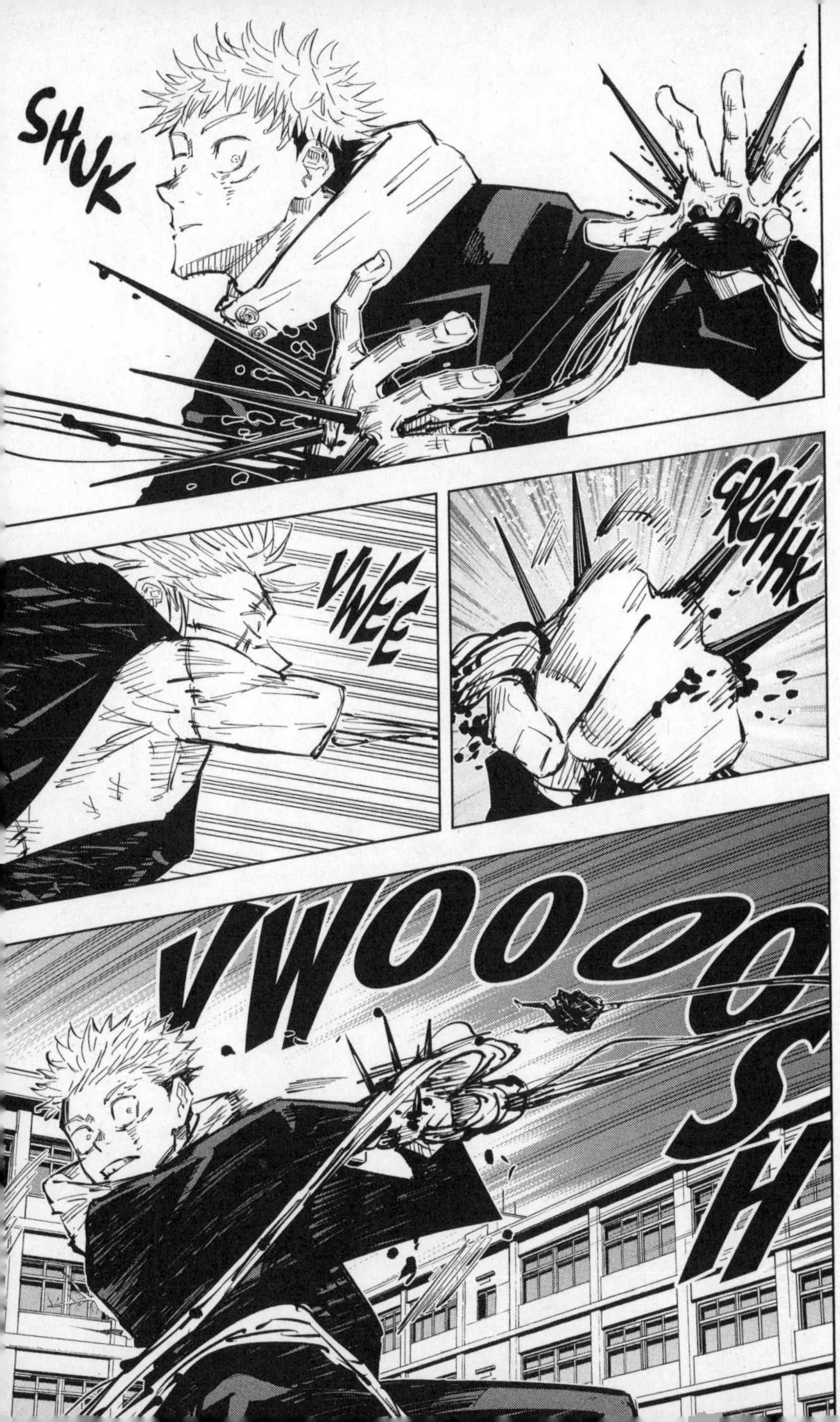
SHUK
GRCHHK
VWEE
VWOOOSH

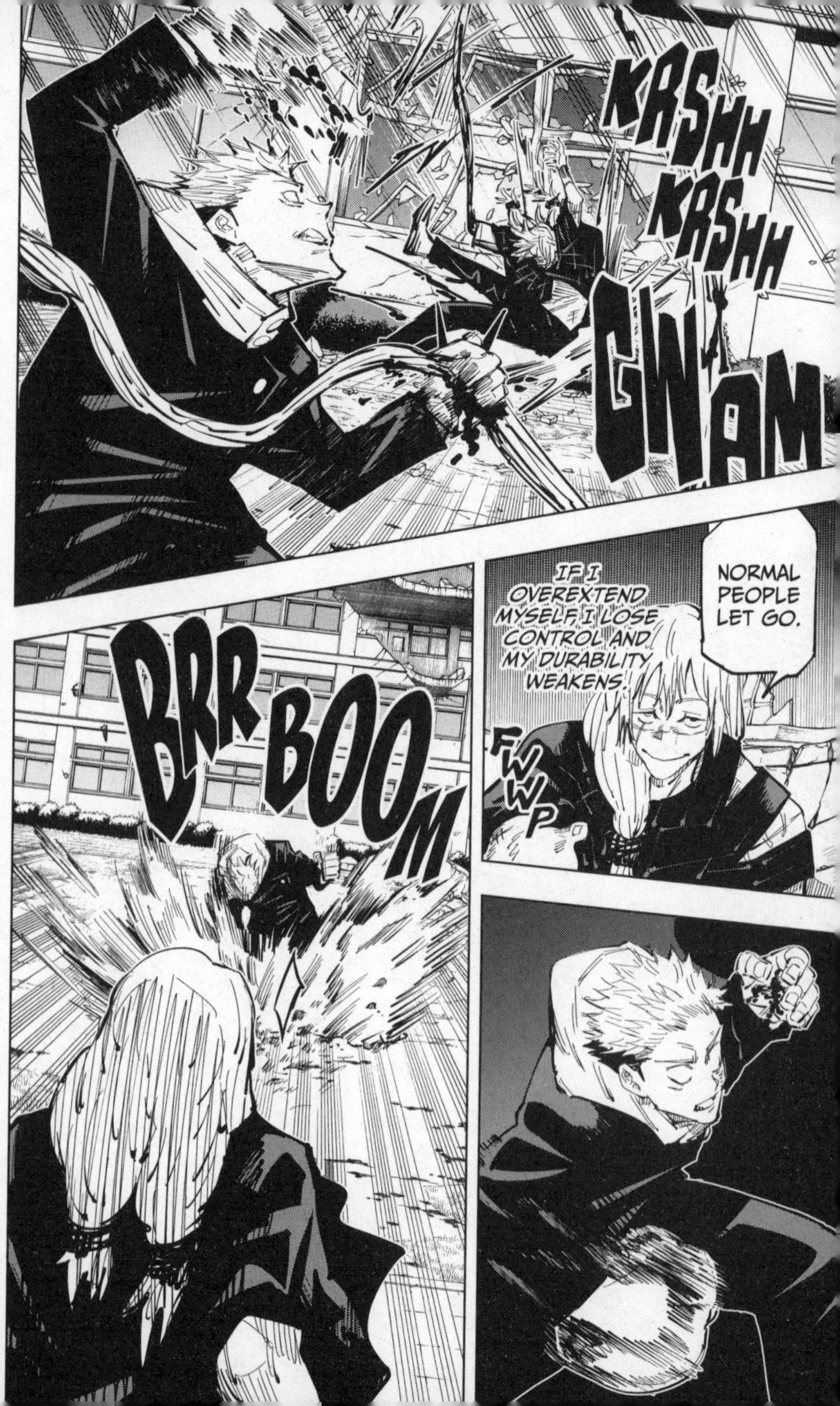
KRSHH
KRSHH
GWAM
NORMAL PEOPLE LET GO.
IF I OVEREXTEND MYSELF, I LOSE CONTROL AND MY DURABILITY WEAKENS.
FWWP
BRR BOOM

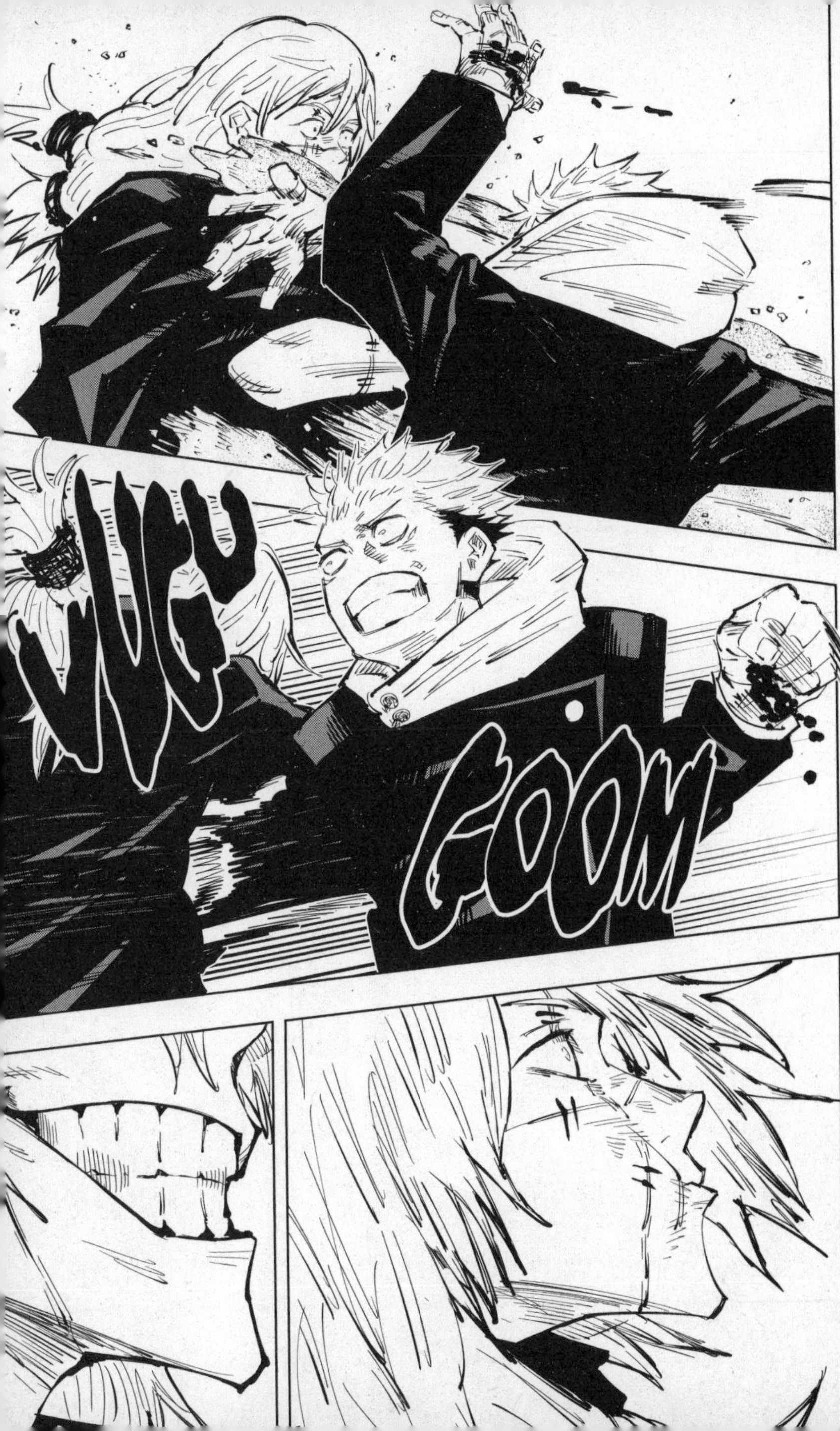
GOOM

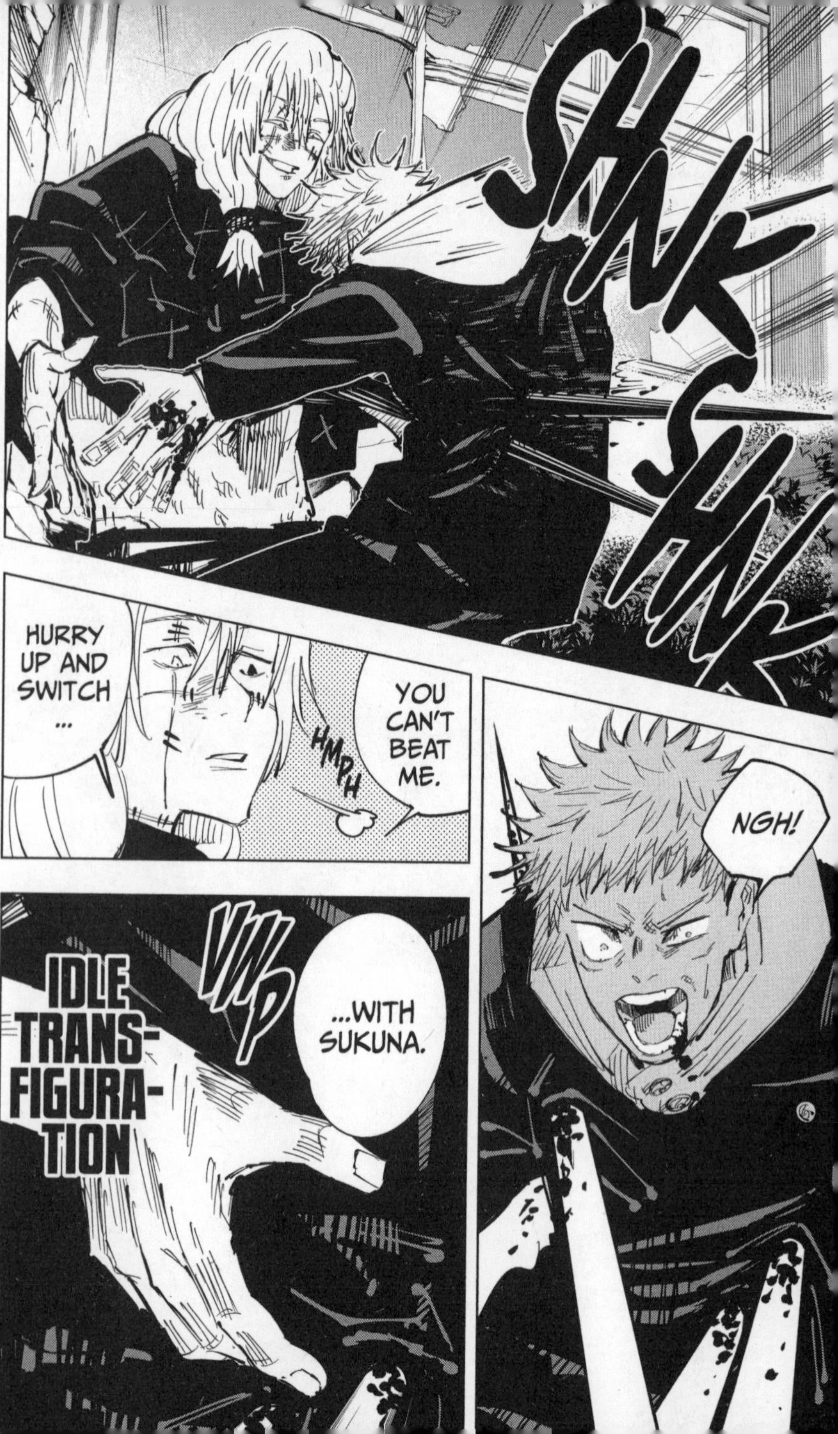
SHINK
SHINK
NGH!
YOU CAN'T BEAT ME.
HMPH
HURRY UP AND SWITCH ...
VWP
...WITH SUKUNA.
IDLE TRANS-FIGURA-TION

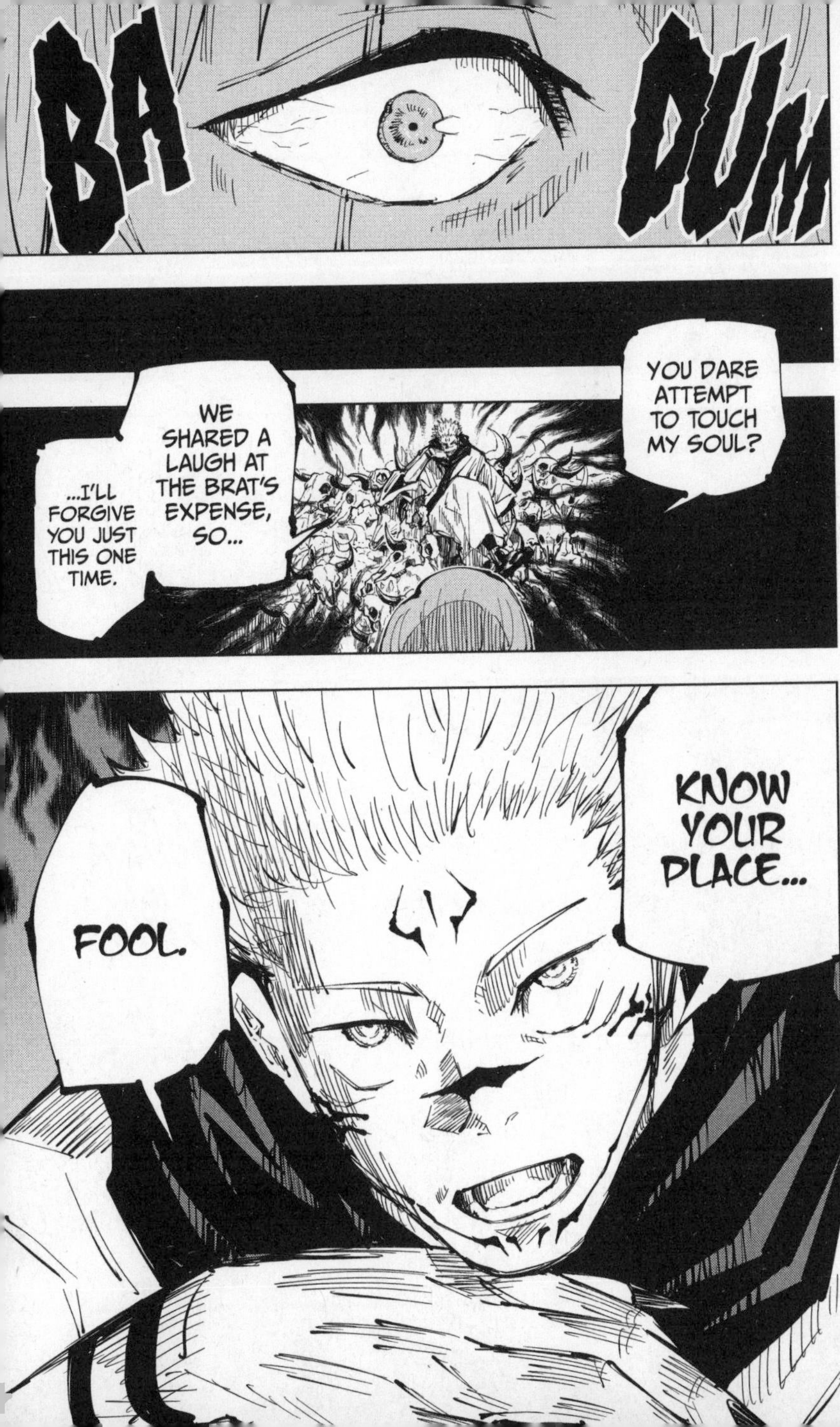
BA DUM
YOU DARE ATTEMPT TO TOUCH MY SOUL?
WE SHARED A LAUGH AT THE BRAT'S EXPENSE, SO...
...I'LL FORGIVE YOU JUST THIS ONE TIME.
KNOW YOUR PLACE...
FOOL.

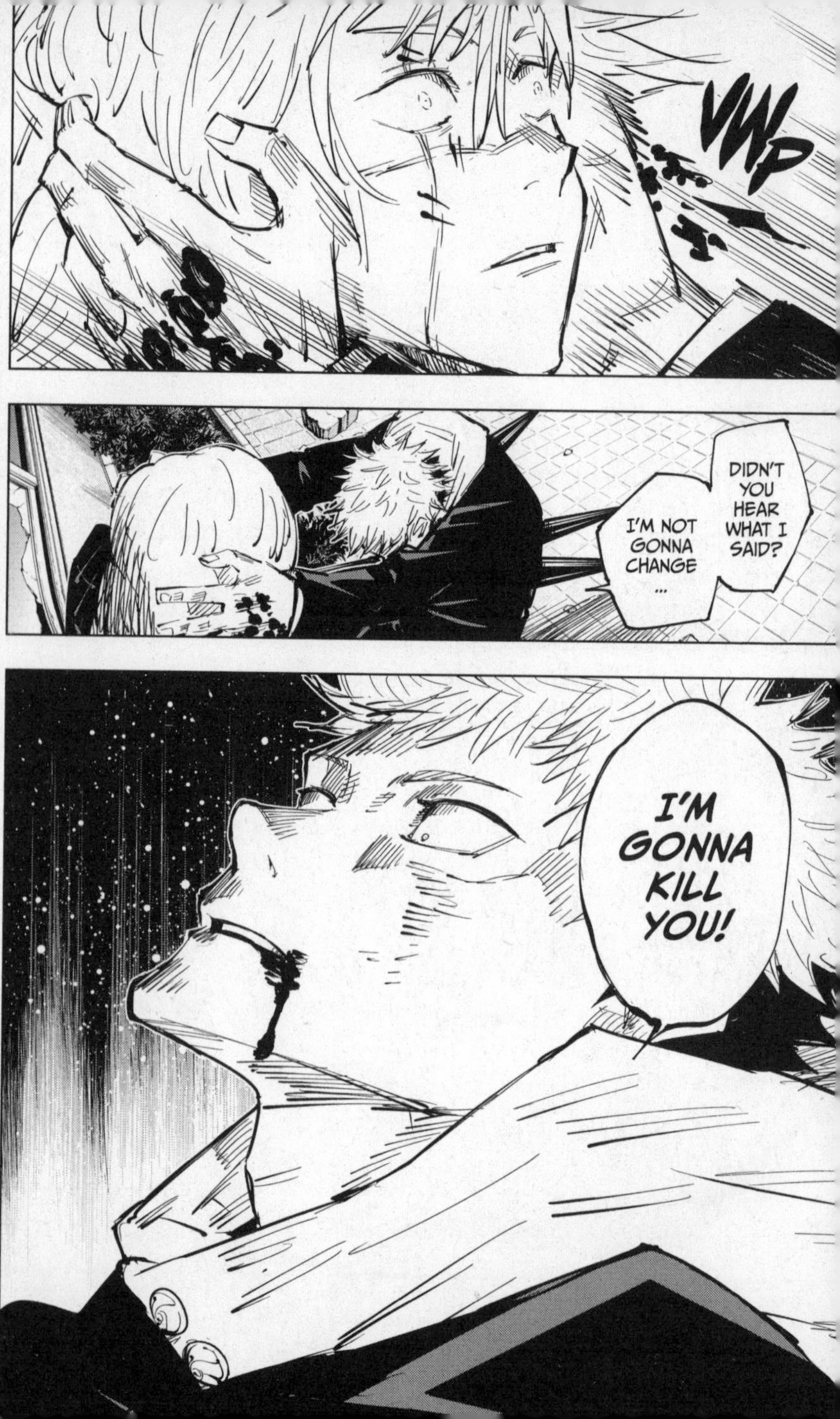
VWP
DIDN'T YOU HEAR WHAT I SAID?
I'M NOT GONNA CHANGE ...
I'M GONNA KILL YOU!

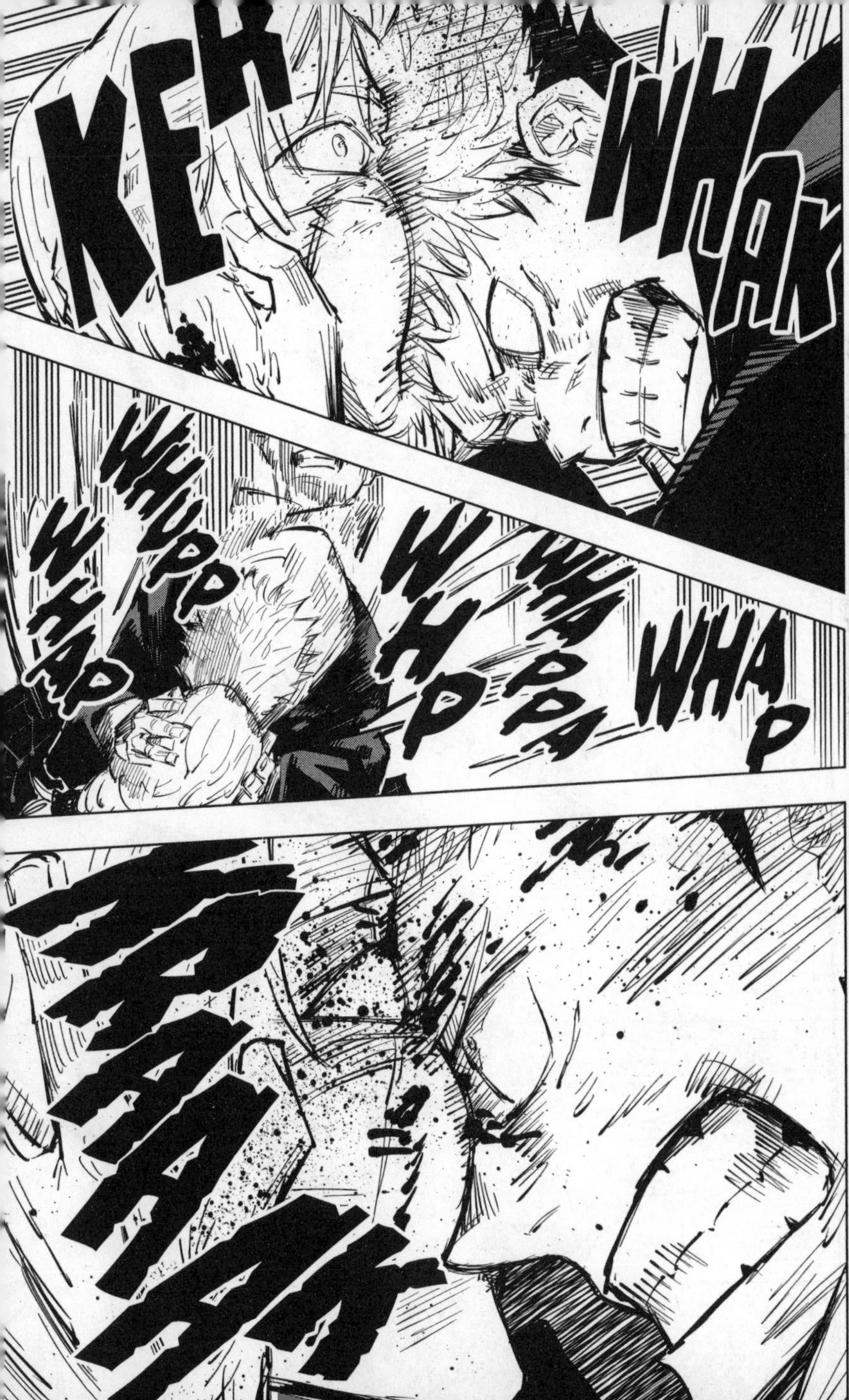
WHAK
KEH
WHAP
WHAPPA
WHAP
WHUPP
WHAP

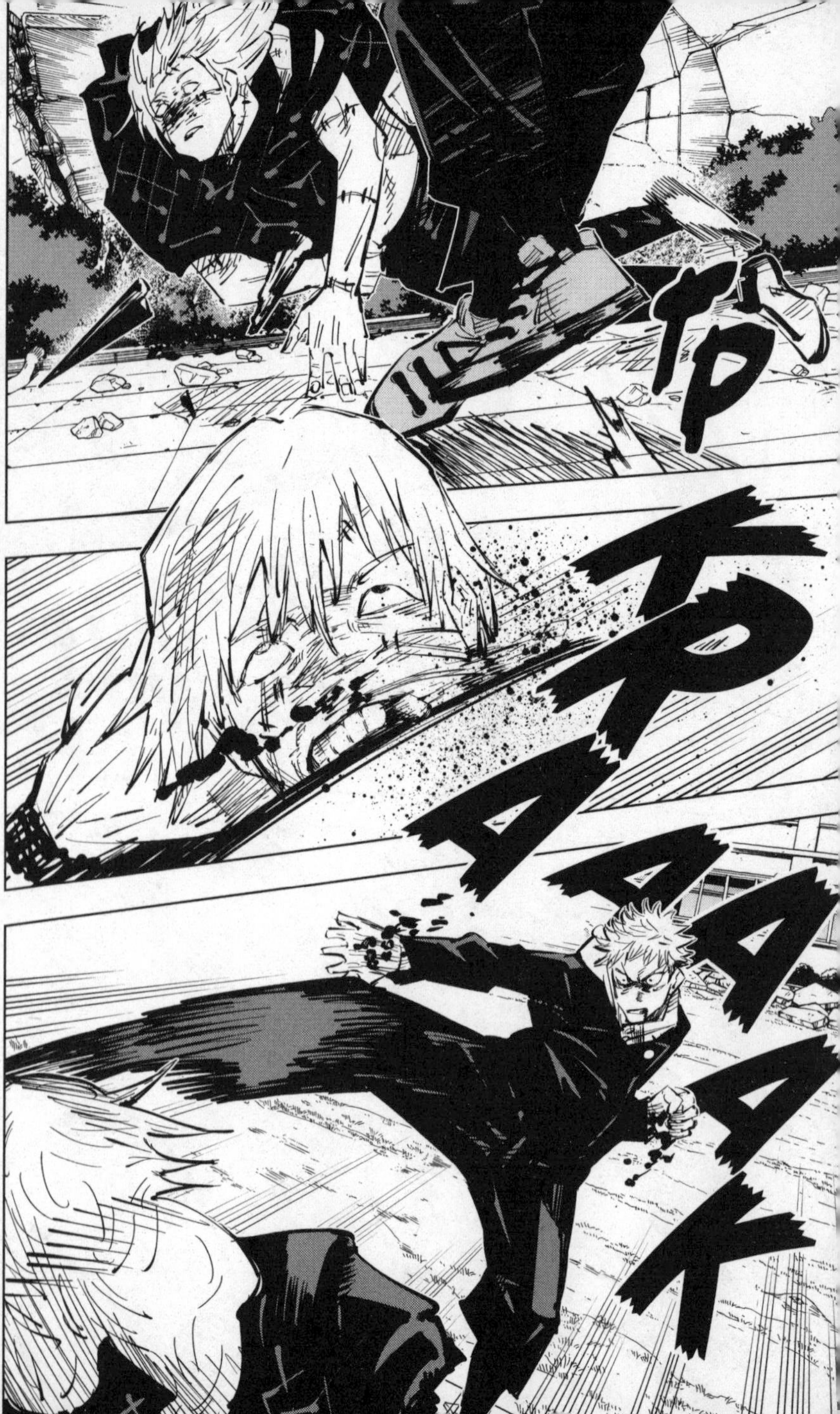
TP
TRAAAAK

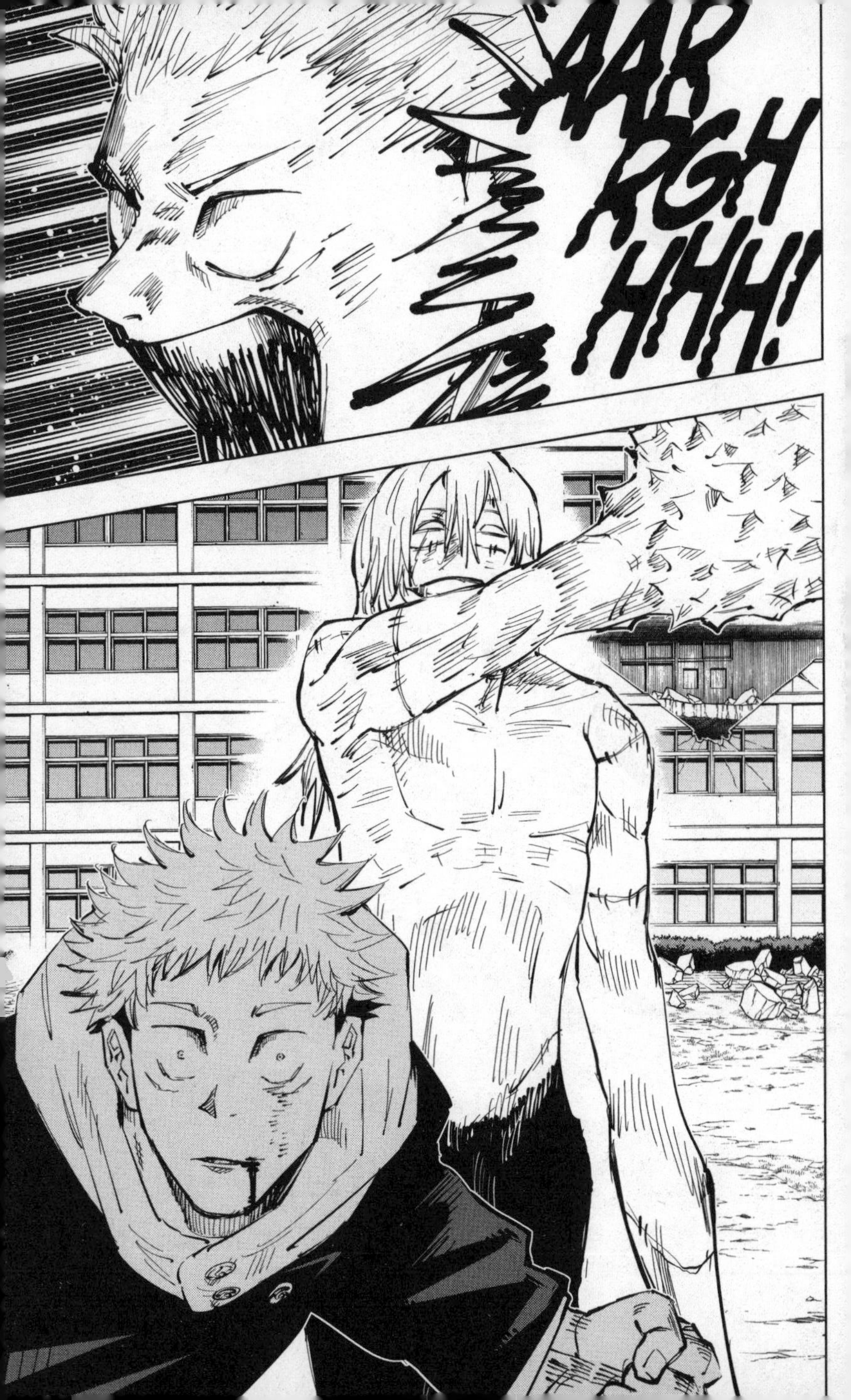
AARRGHHHH!

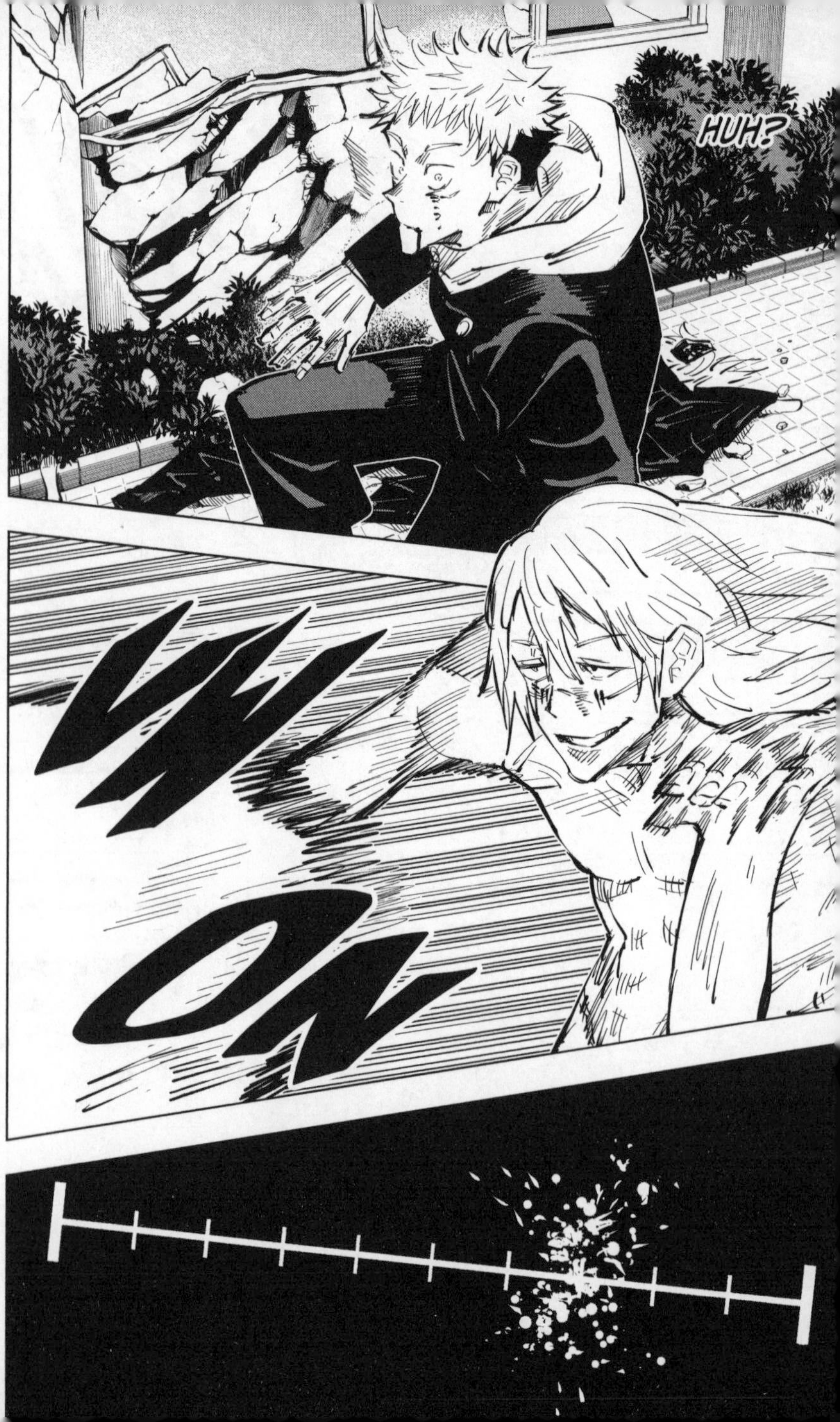
HUH?

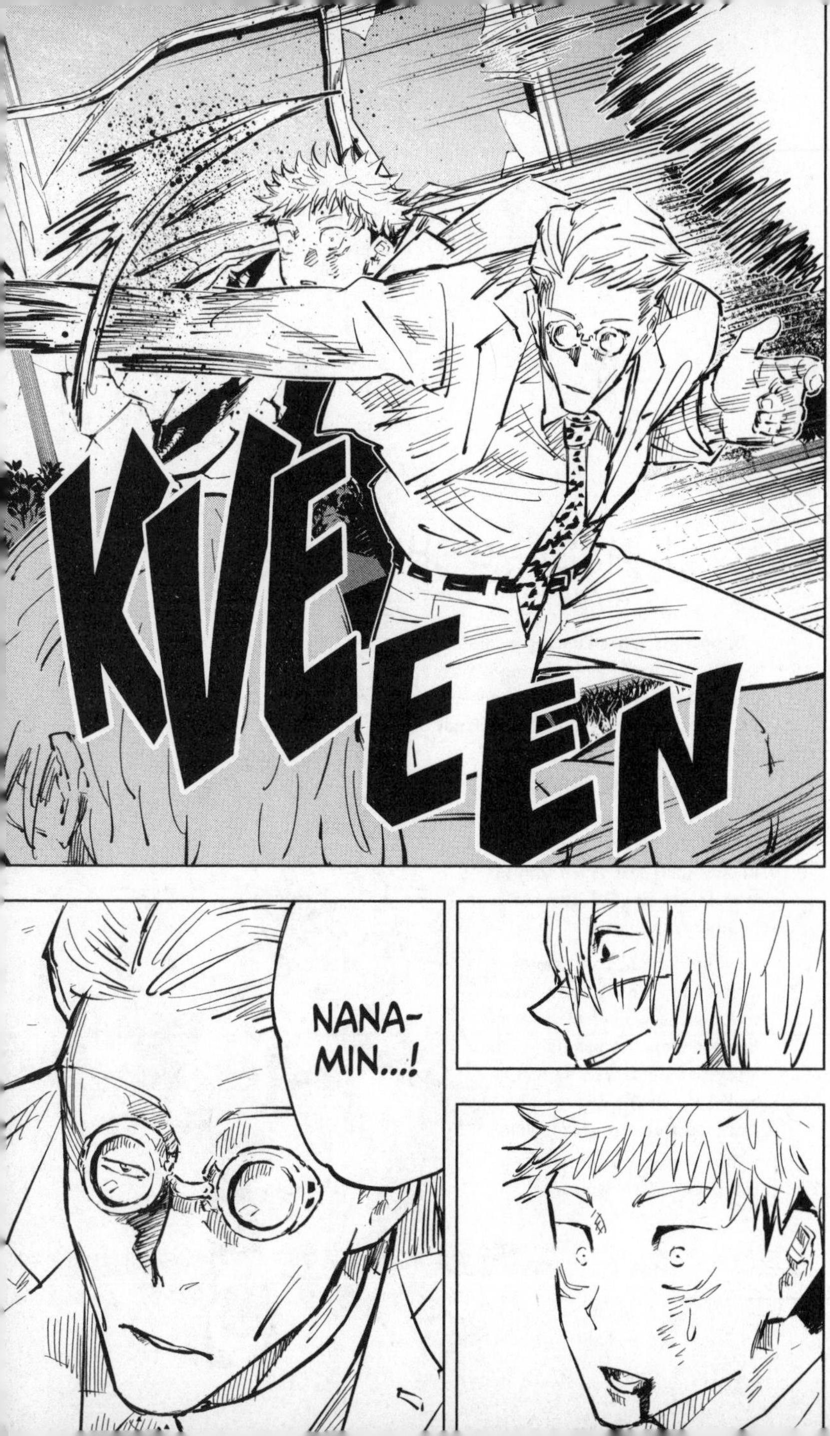
KVEEEN
NANA-
MIN...!

JUNPEI YOSHINO
(17 YEARS OLD)

• Junpei started a film appreciation club with two of his friends during his first year of high school. The club room became a spot for Ito and his friends to hang out.

• Since he was the only one to defend the club, he became a target for bullies. The club disbanded, and he gradually lost touch with his friends. He stopped going to school by his second year.

• I think I could have shown more of his good side if I had drawn these scenes. Since his fate was decided from the beginning, the story was influenced by that, and I ended up mostly depicting his troubled side. Sorry, Yoshino.

• He's probably a fan of the *Scary Movie* franchise.

CHAPTER 29: GROWTH

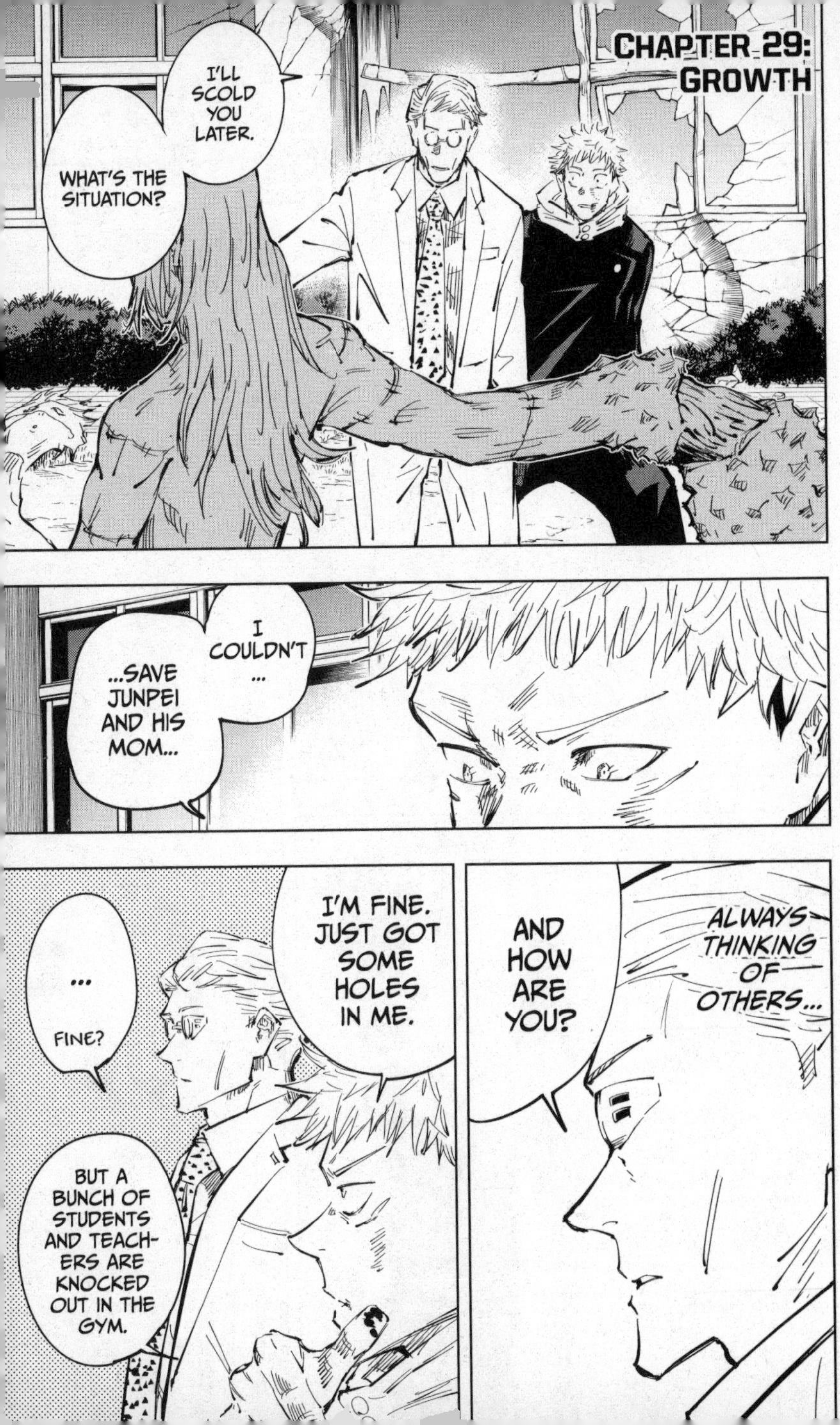
I'LL SCOLD YOU LATER.
WHAT'S THE SITUATION?
I COULDN'T ...
...SAVE JUNPEI AND HIS MOM...
ALWAYS THINKING OF OTHERS...
AND HOW ARE YOU?
I'M FINE. JUST GOT SOME HOLES IN ME.
...
FINE?
BUT A BUNCH OF STUDENTS AND TEACHERS ARE KNOCKED OUT IN THE GYM.

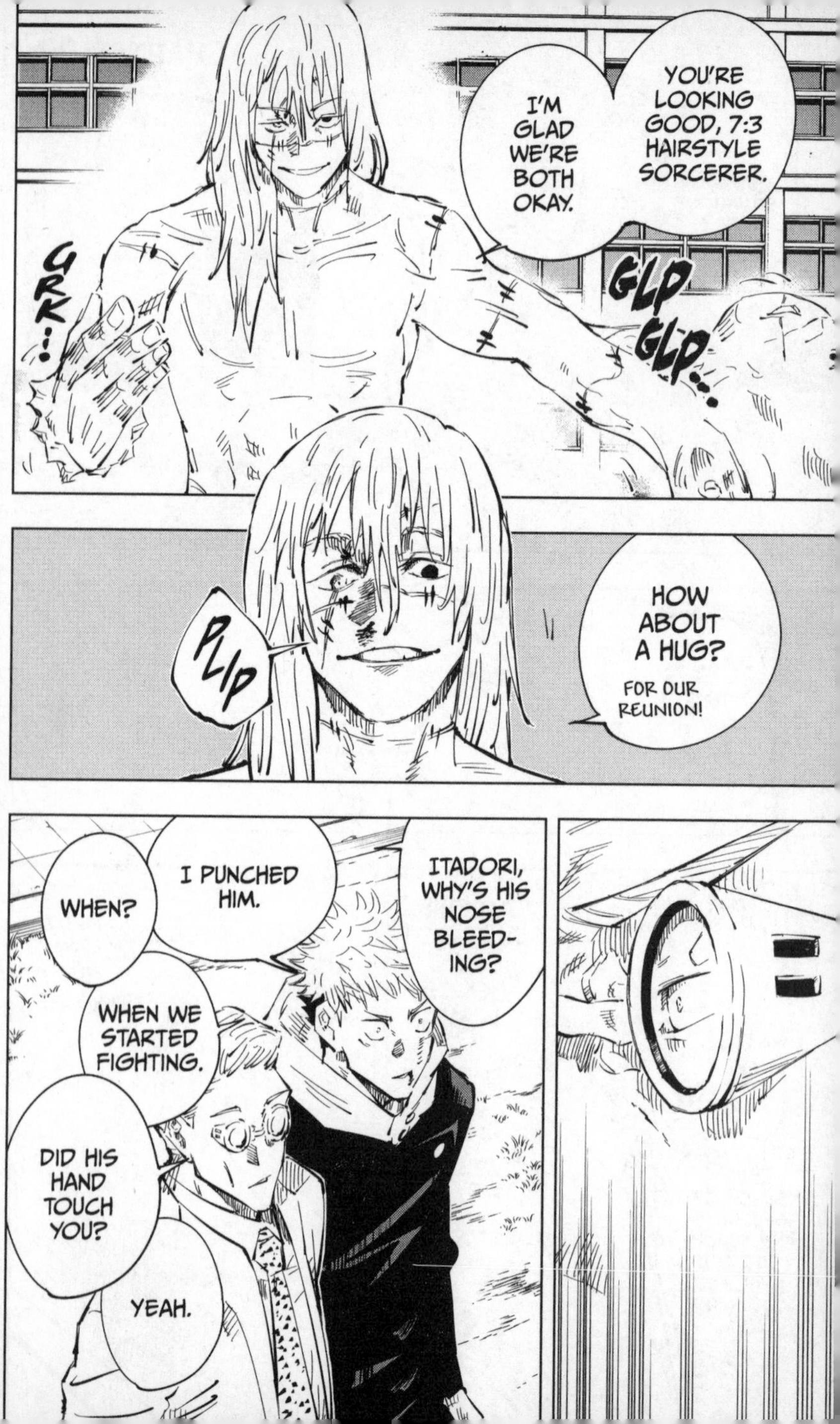
YOU'RE LOOKING GOOD, 7:3 HAIRSTYLE SORCERER.
I'M GLAD WE'RE BOTH OKAY.
GLP GLP...
GRK!!
HOW ABOUT A HUG?
FOR OUR REUNION!
PLIP
ITADORI, WHY'S HIS NOSE BLEEDING?
I PUNCHED HIM.
WHEN?
WHEN WE STARTED FIGHTING.
DID HIS HAND TOUCH YOU?
YEAH.

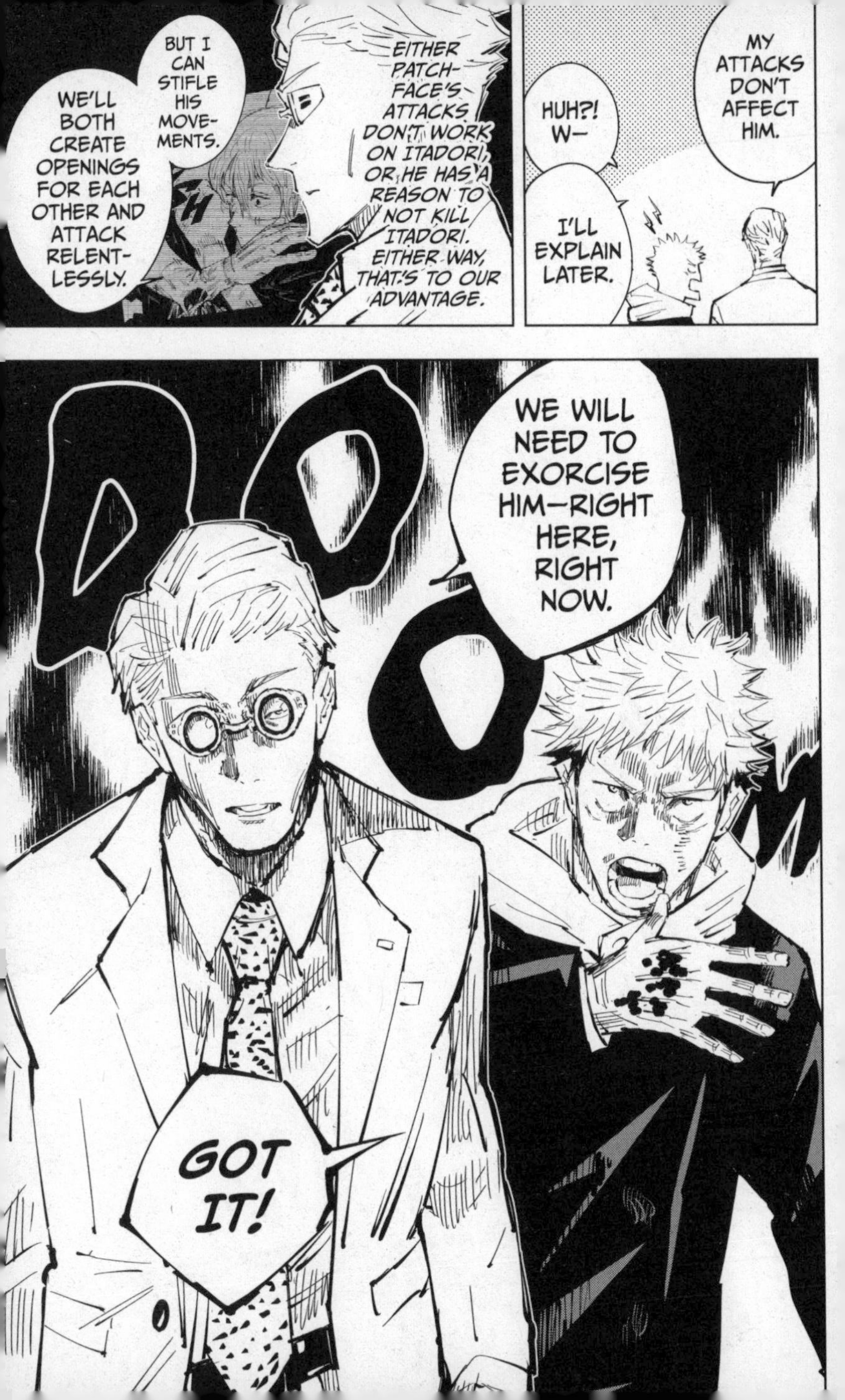
MY ATTACKS DON'T AFFECT HIM.
HUH?! W—
I'LL EXPLAIN LATER.
EITHER PATCH-FACE'S ATTACKS DON'T WORK ON ITADORI, OR HE HAS A REASON TO NOT KILL ITADORI. EITHER WAY, THAT'S TO OUR ADVANTAGE.
BUT I CAN STIFLE HIS MOVEMENTS.
WE'LL BOTH CREATE OPENINGS FOR EACH OTHER AND ATTACK RELENTLESSLY.
WE WILL NEED TO EXORCISE HIM—RIGHT HERE, RIGHT NOW.
GOT IT!

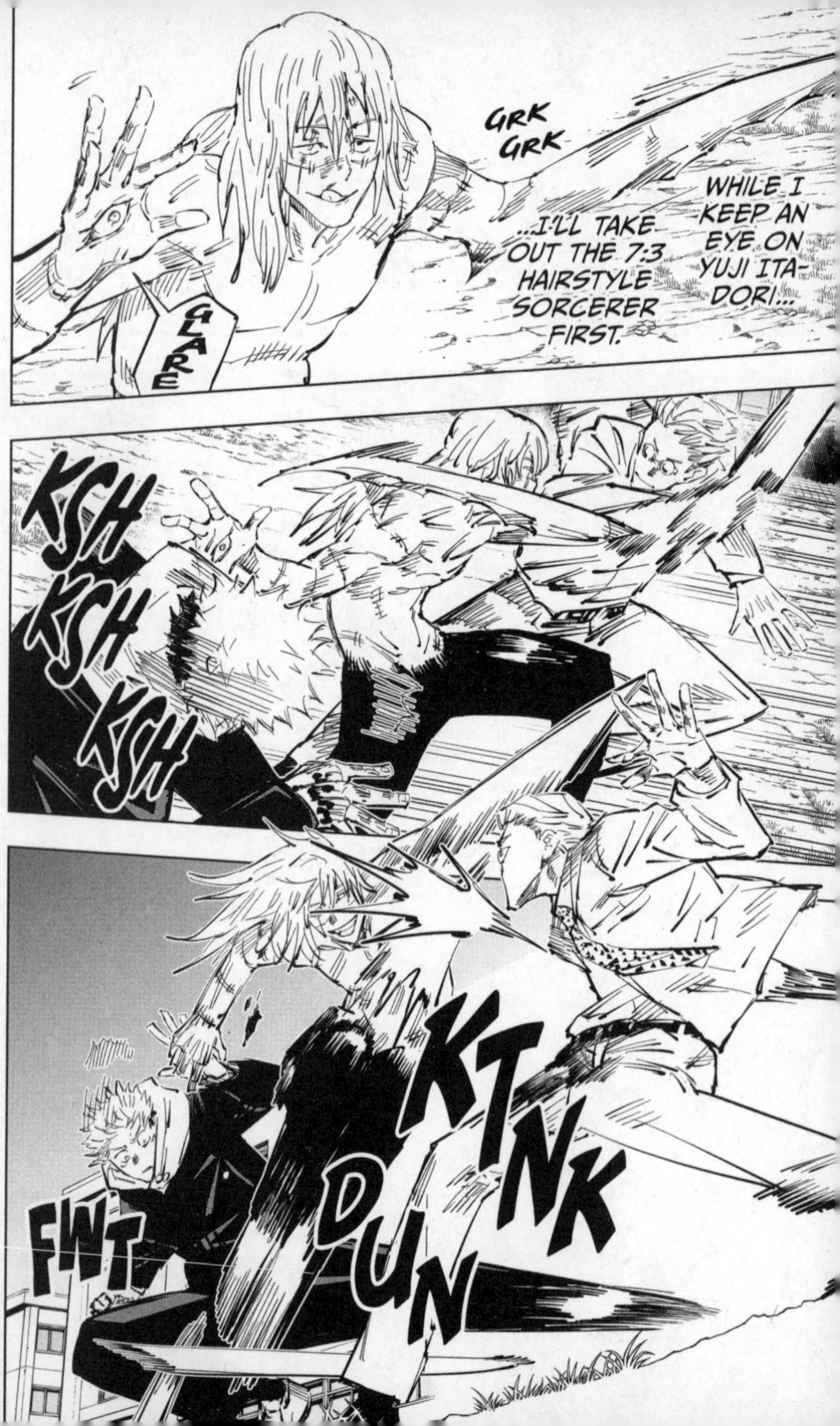
GRK GRK
WHILE I KEEP AN EYE ON YUJI ITA-DORI...
...I'LL TAKE OUT THE 7:3 HAIRSTYLE SORCERER FIRST.
GLARE
KSH KSH KSH
KTINK
DUN
FWT

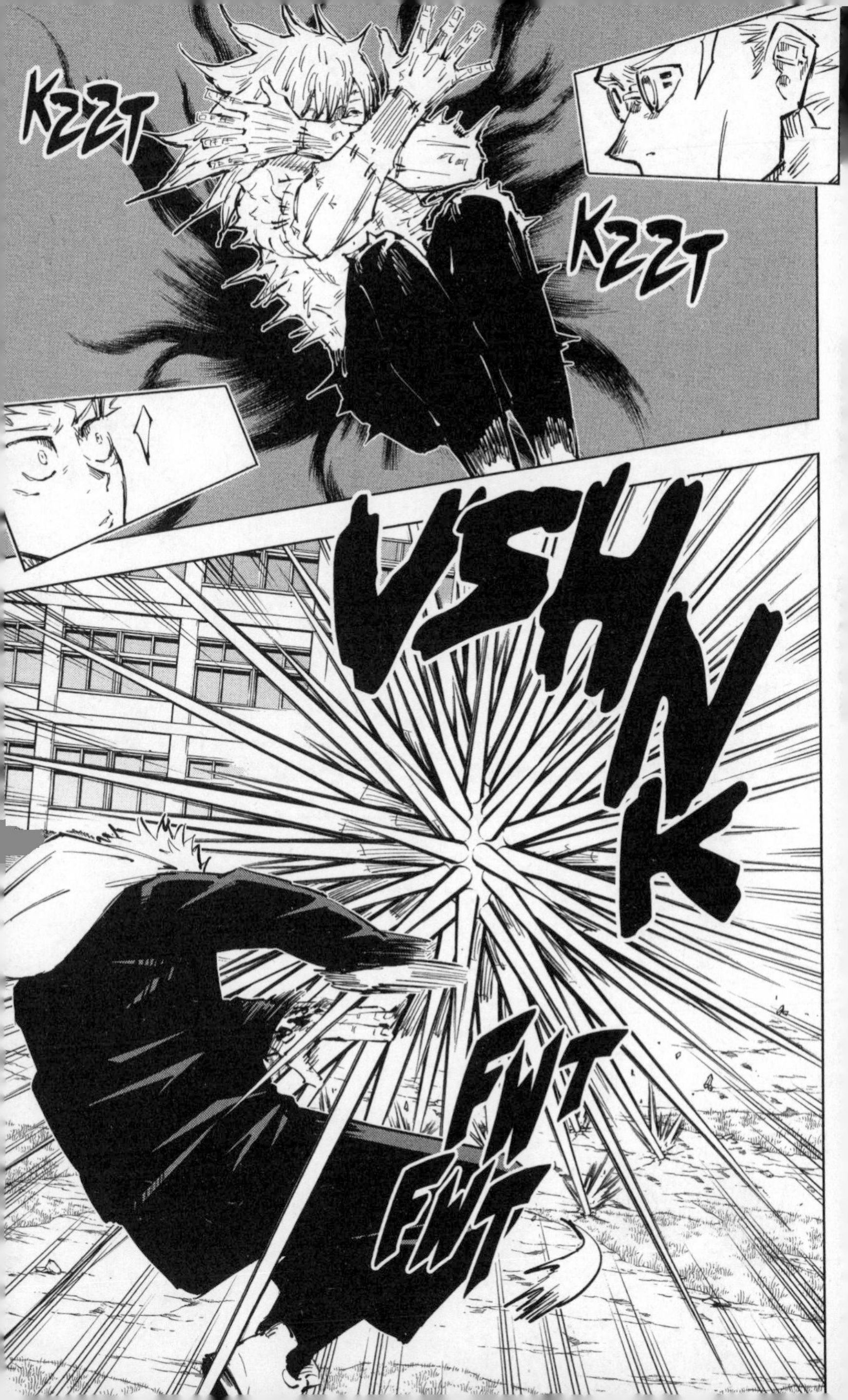
KZZT
KZZT
VSHNK
FWT
FWT

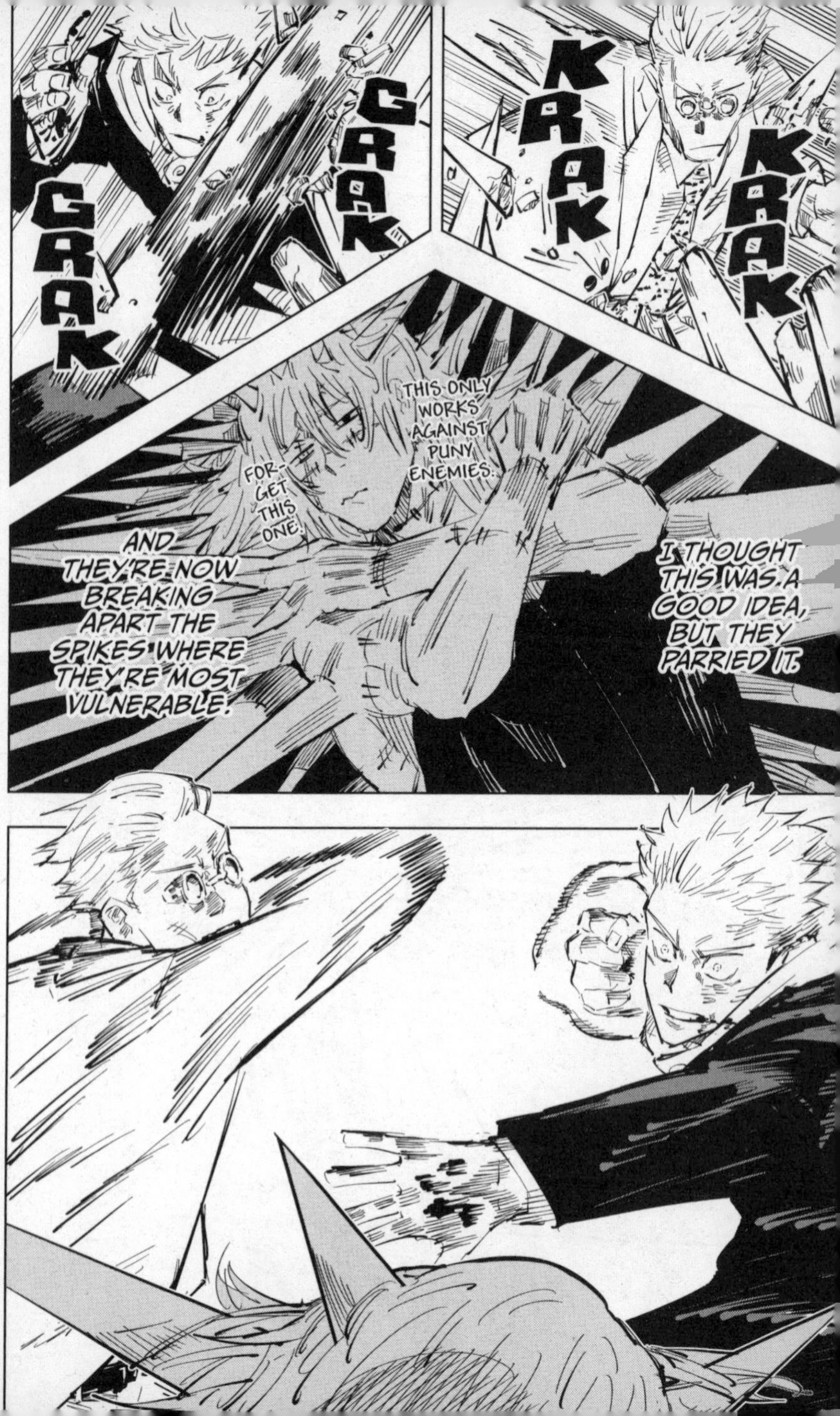
KRAK KRAK
GRAK GRAK
I THOUGHT THIS WAS A GOOD IDEA, BUT THEY PARRIED IT.
THIS ONLY WORKS AGAINST PUNY ENEMIES.
FOR-GET THIS ONE.
AND THEY'RE NOW BREAKING APART THE SPIKES WHERE THEY'RE MOST VULNERABLE.

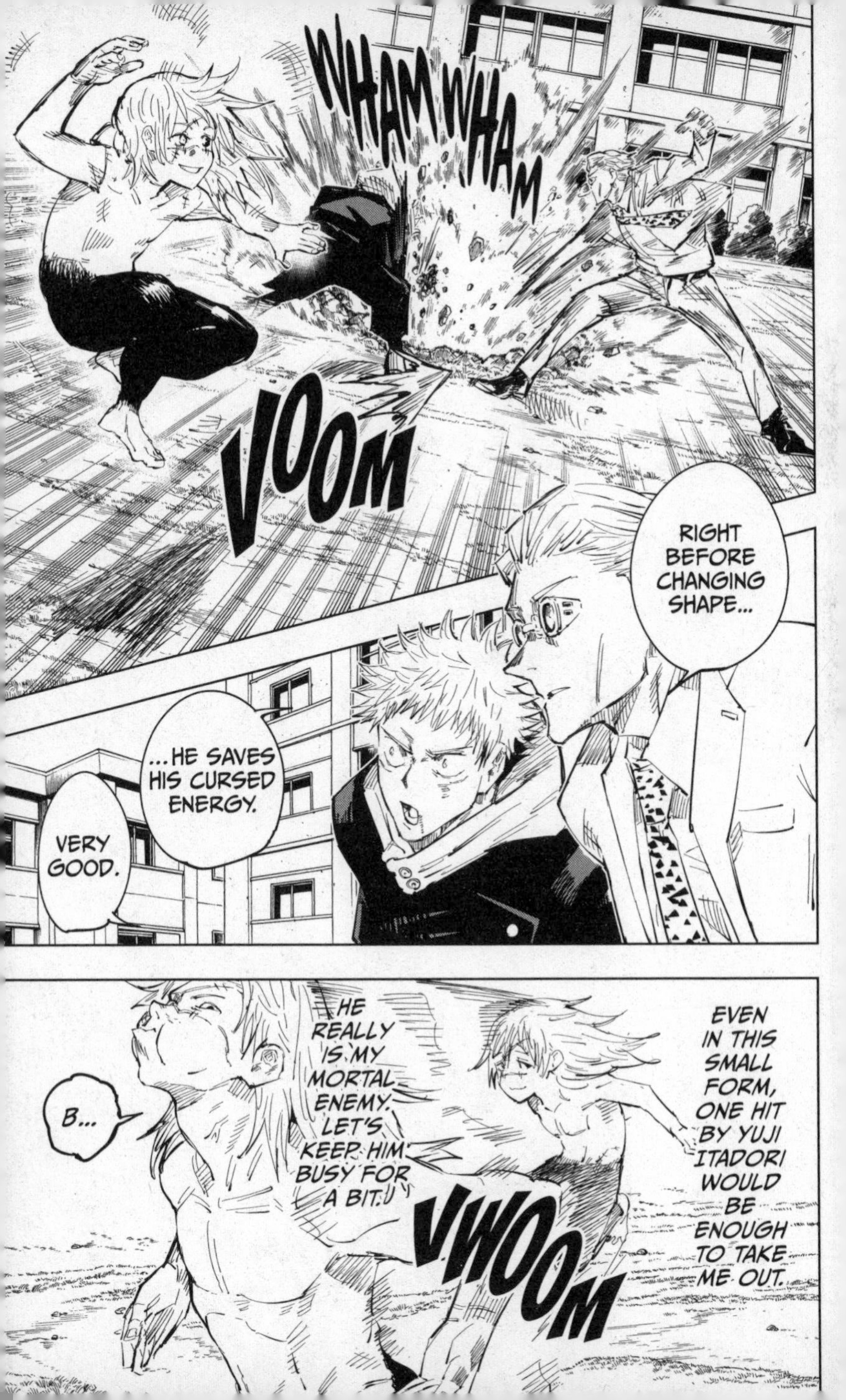
WHAM WHAM
VOOM
RIGHT BEFORE CHANGING SHAPE...
...HE SAVES HIS CURSED ENERGY.
VERY GOOD.
EVEN IN THIS SMALL FORM, ONE HIT BY YUJI ITADORI WOULD BE ENOUGH TO TAKE ME OUT.
VWOOM
HE REALLY IS MY MORTAL ENEMY. LET'S KEEP HIM BUSY FOR A BIT.
B...

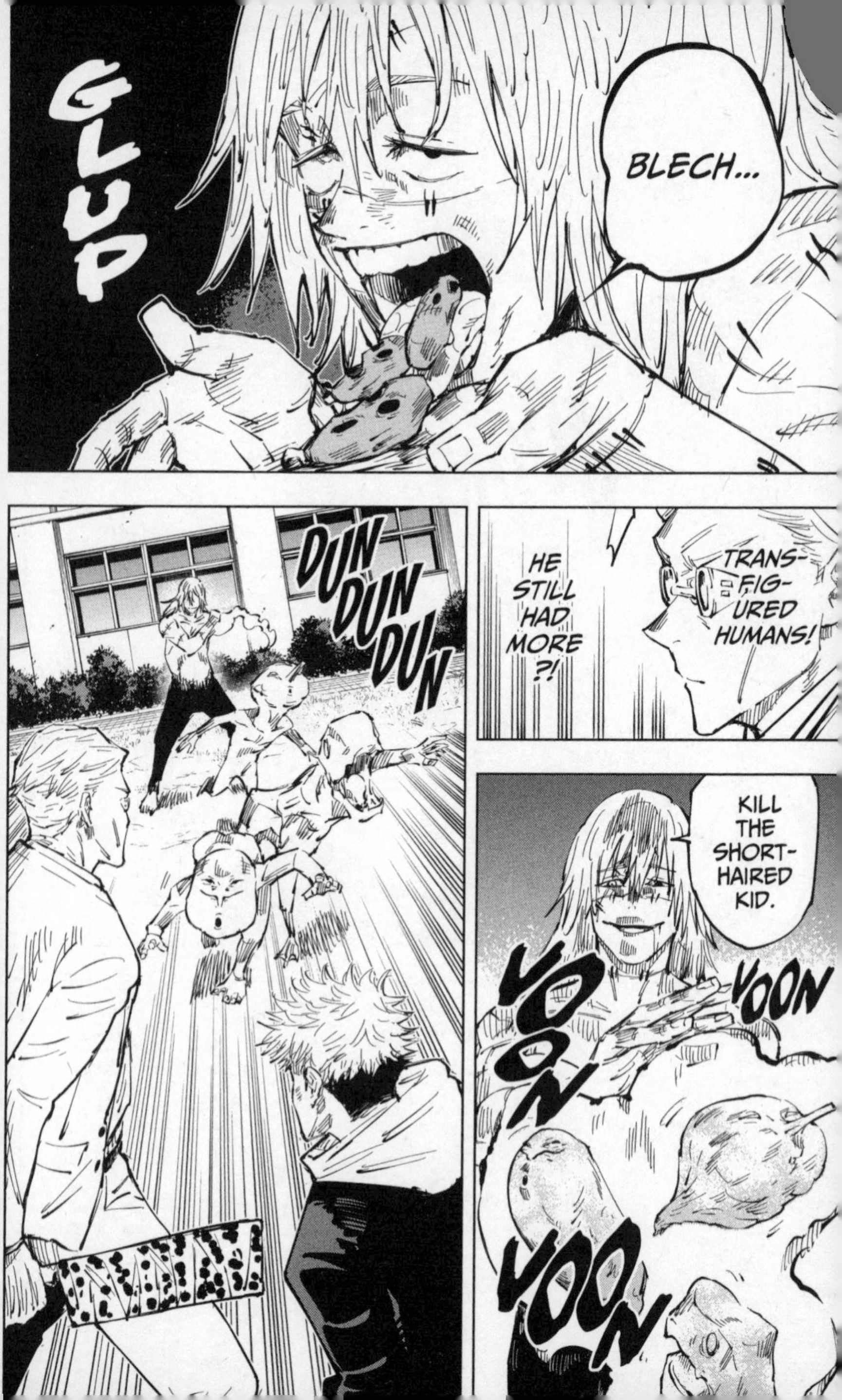
BLECH...
GLUP
TRANS-FIGURED HUMANS!
HE STILL HAD MORE ?!
KILL THE SHORT-HAIRED KID.
VOON
VOON
VOON
DUN DUN DUN

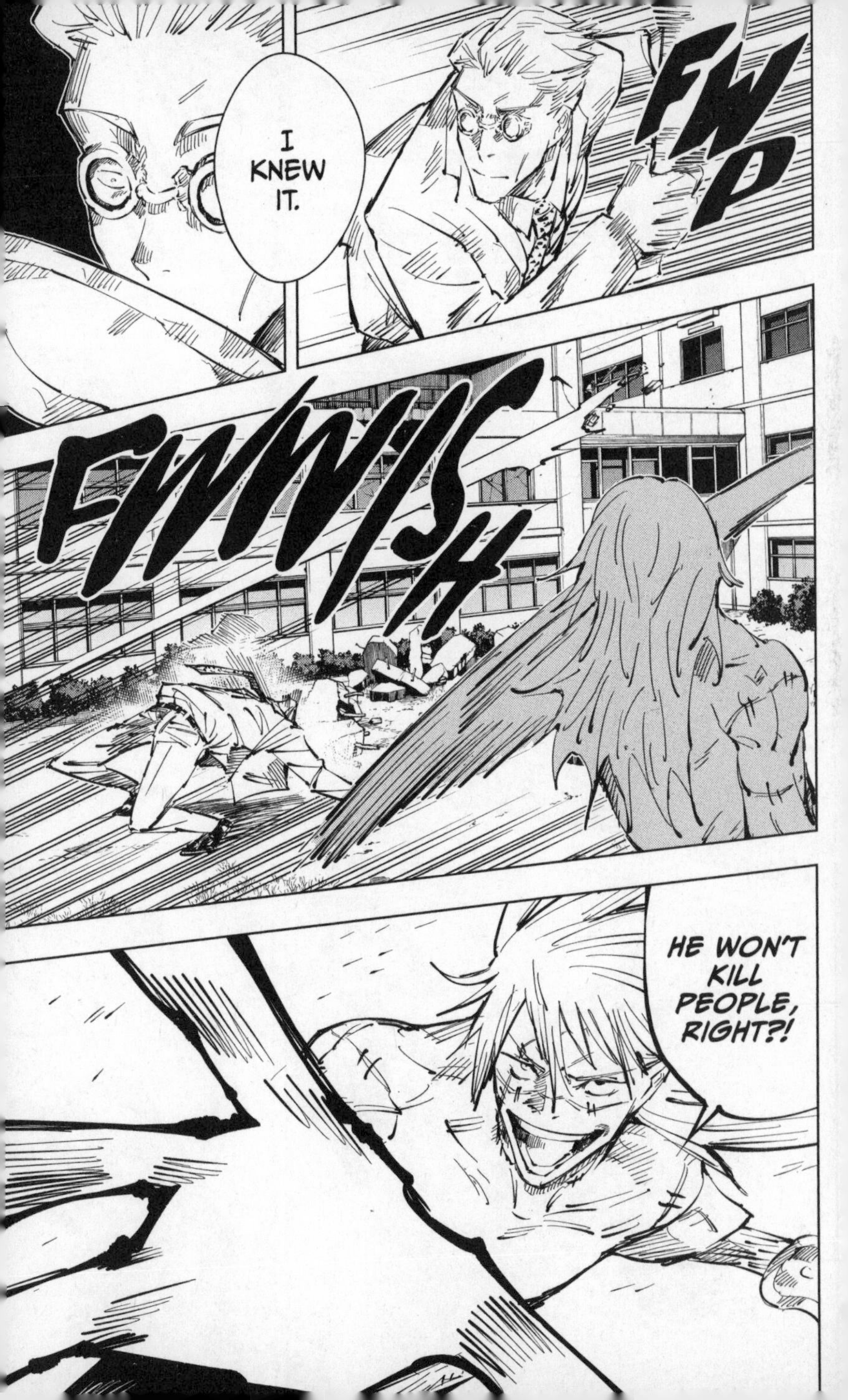
FWD
I KNEW IT.
FWISH
HE WON'T KILL PEOPLE, RIGHT?!

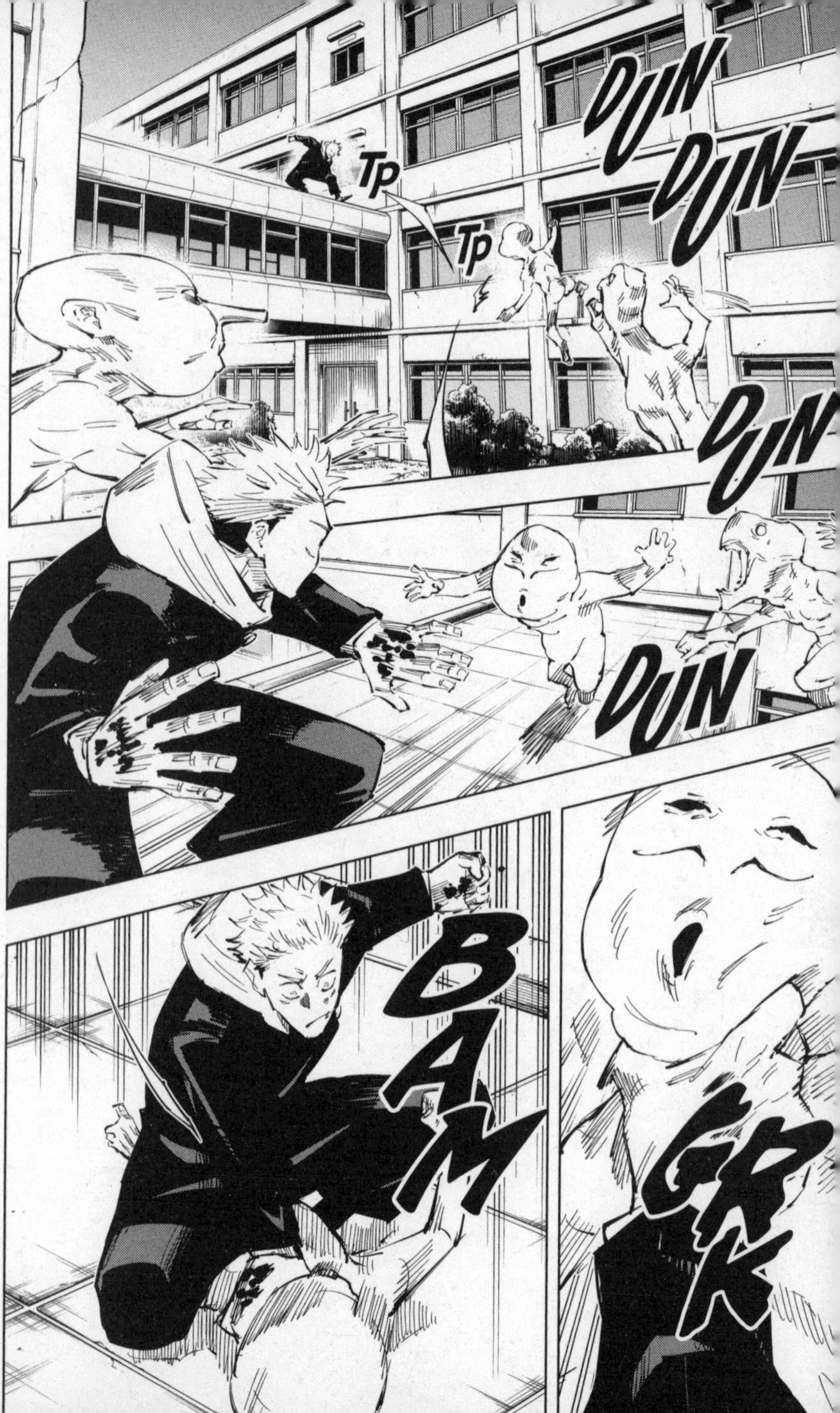
DUN DUN
TP
TP
DUN
DUN
GRK
BAM

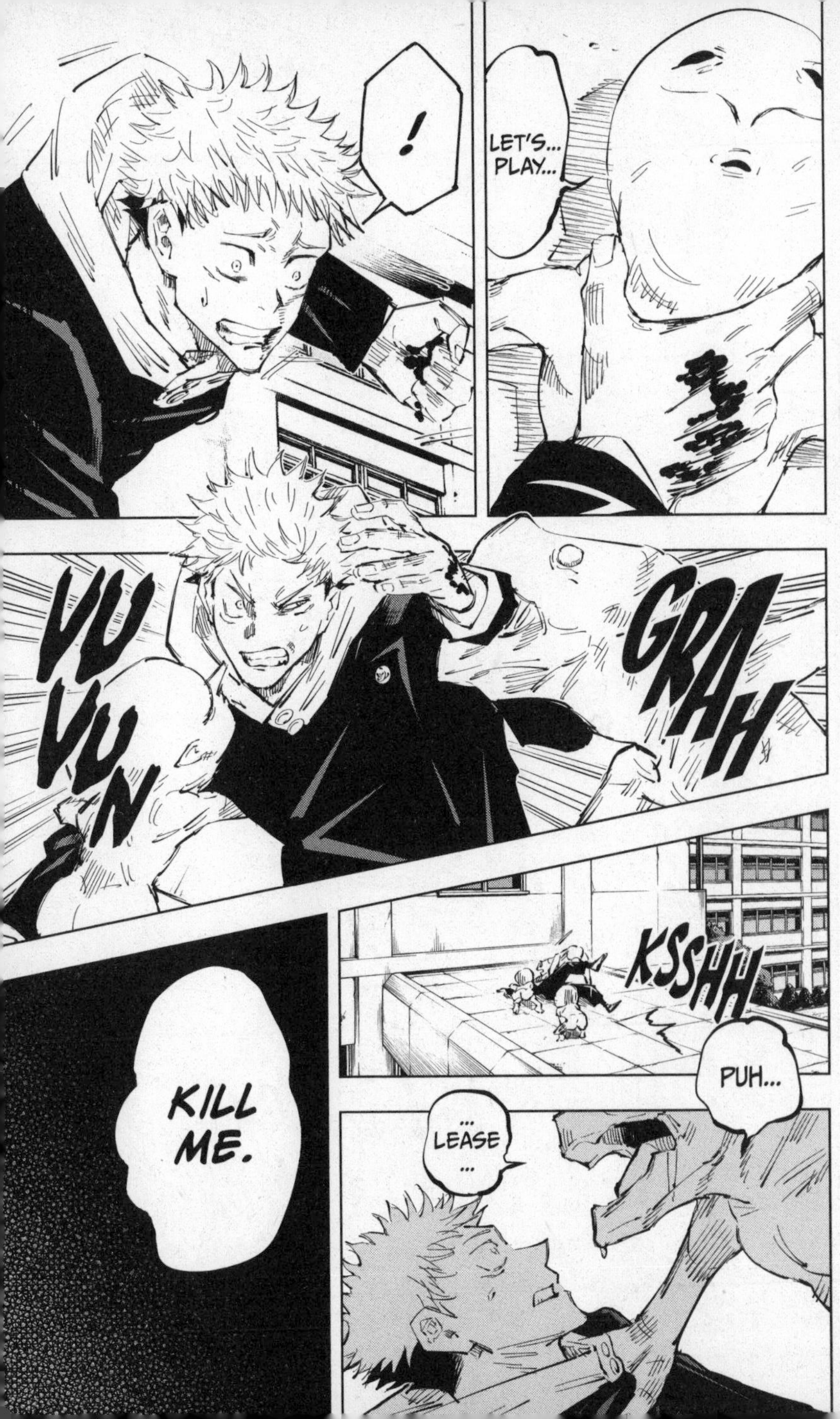
LET'S... PLAY...
!
GRAH
VUUN VUUN
KSSHH
PUH...
...LEASE...
KILL ME.

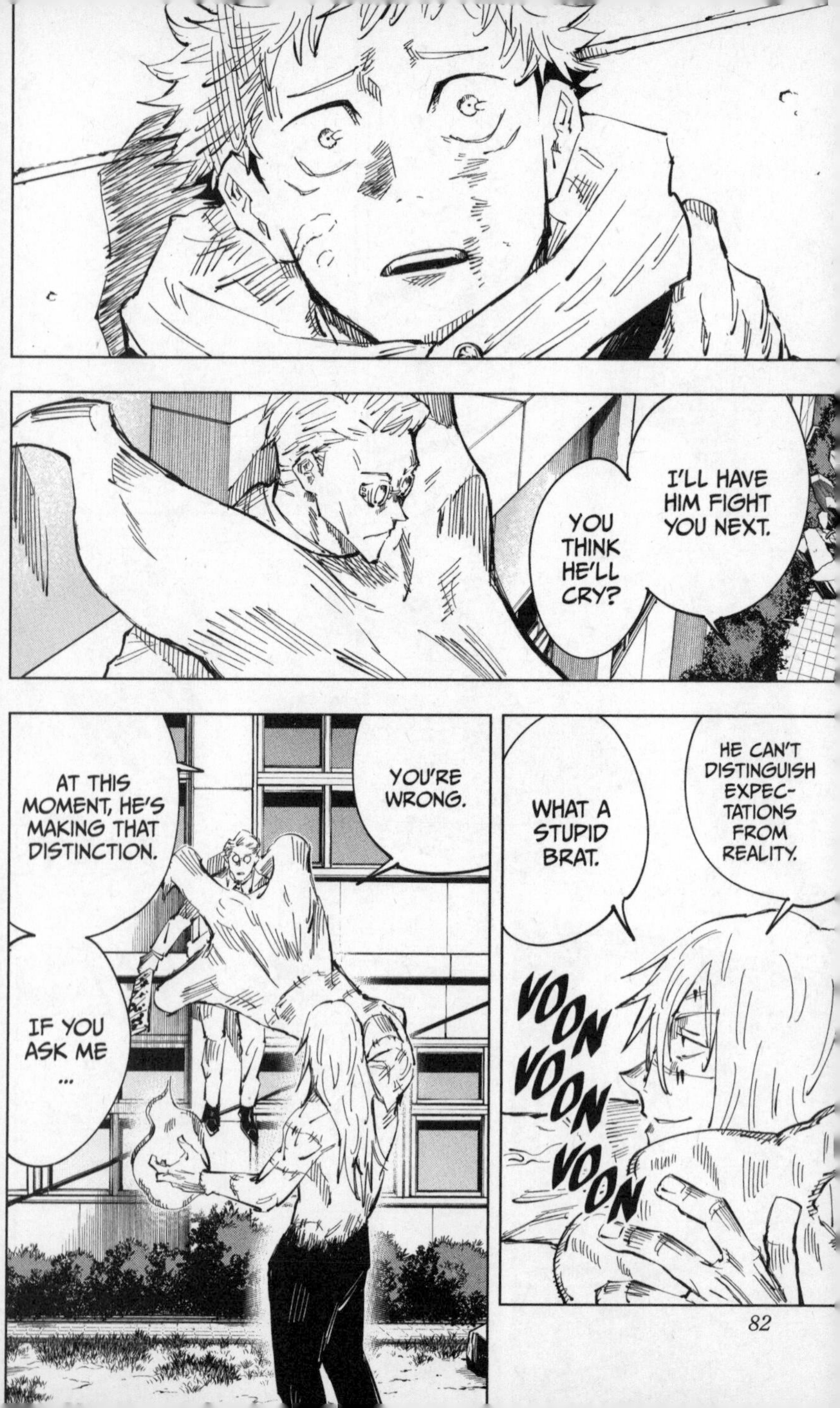
I'LL HAVE HIM FIGHT YOU NEXT.
YOU THINK HE'LL CRY?
HE CAN'T DISTINGUISH EXPECTATIONS FROM REALITY.
WHAT A STUPID BRAT.
VOON VOON VOON VOON
YOU'RE WRONG.
AT THIS MOMENT, HE'S MAKING THAT DISTINCTION.
IF YOU ASK ME ...

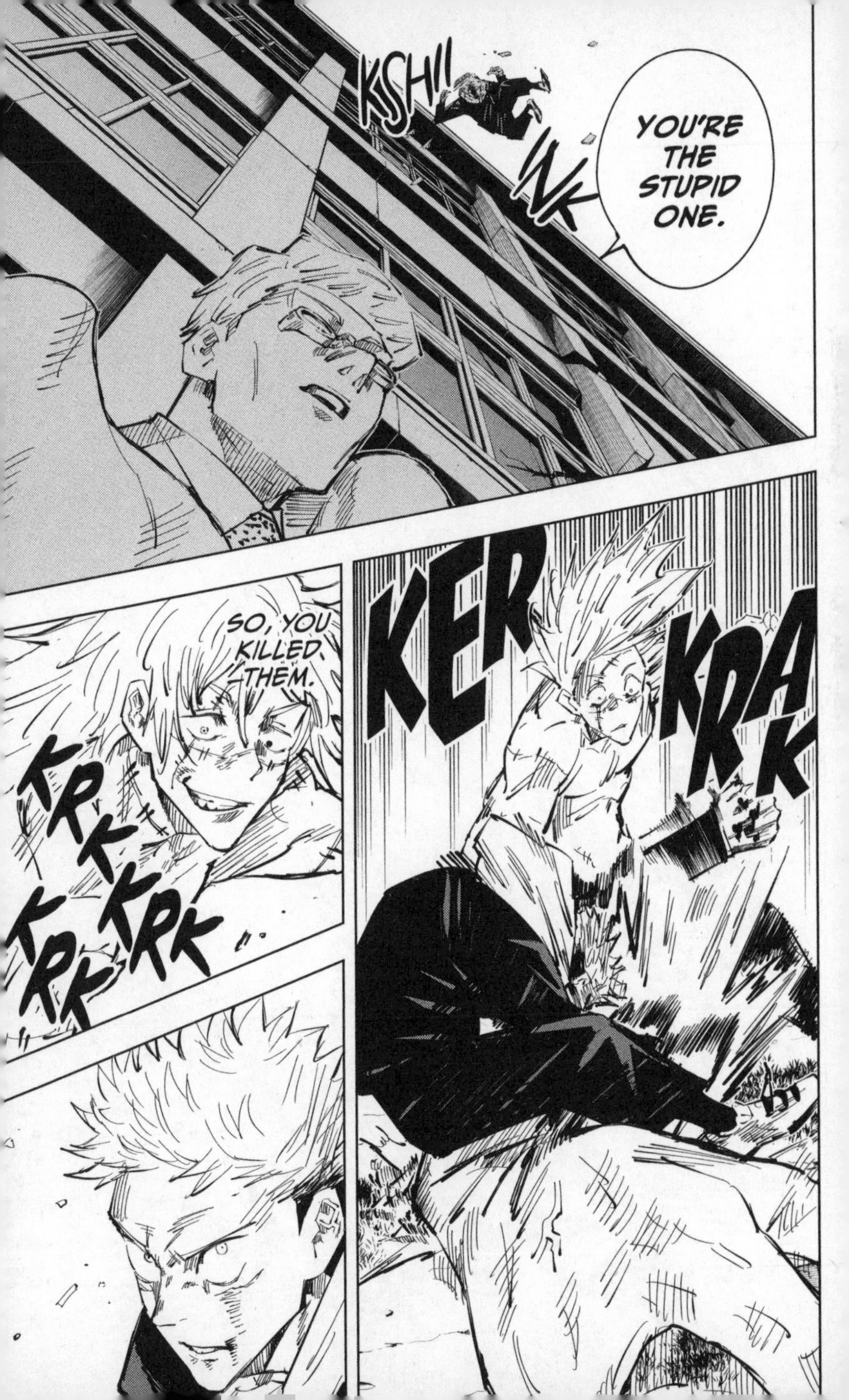
KSHIINK
YOU'RE THE STUPID ONE.
KERKRAK
SO, YOU KILLED THEM.
KRKRK KRKRK

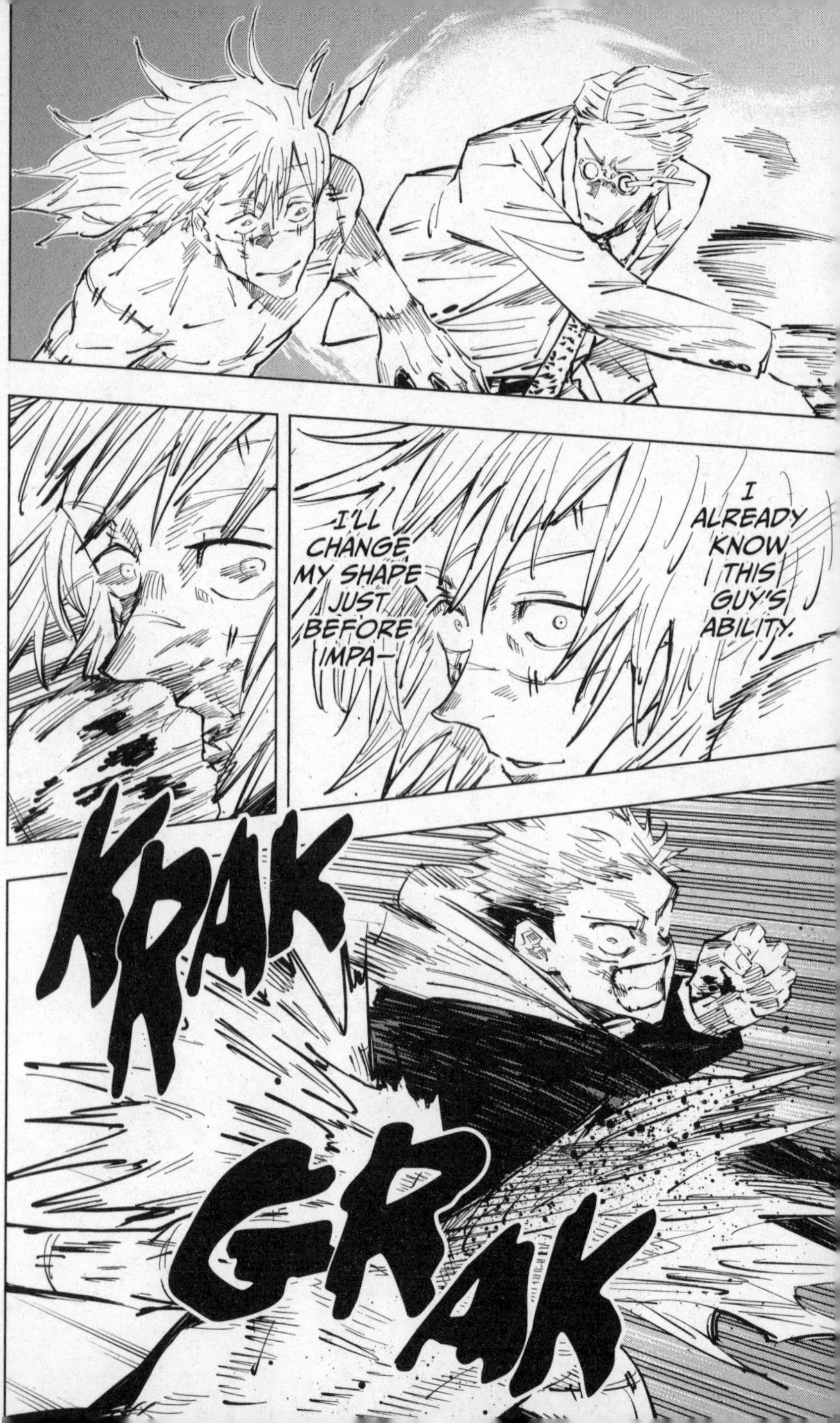
I ALREADY KNOW THIS GUY'S ABILITY.
I'LL CHANGE MY SHAPE JUST BEFORE IMPA—
KRAK
GRAK

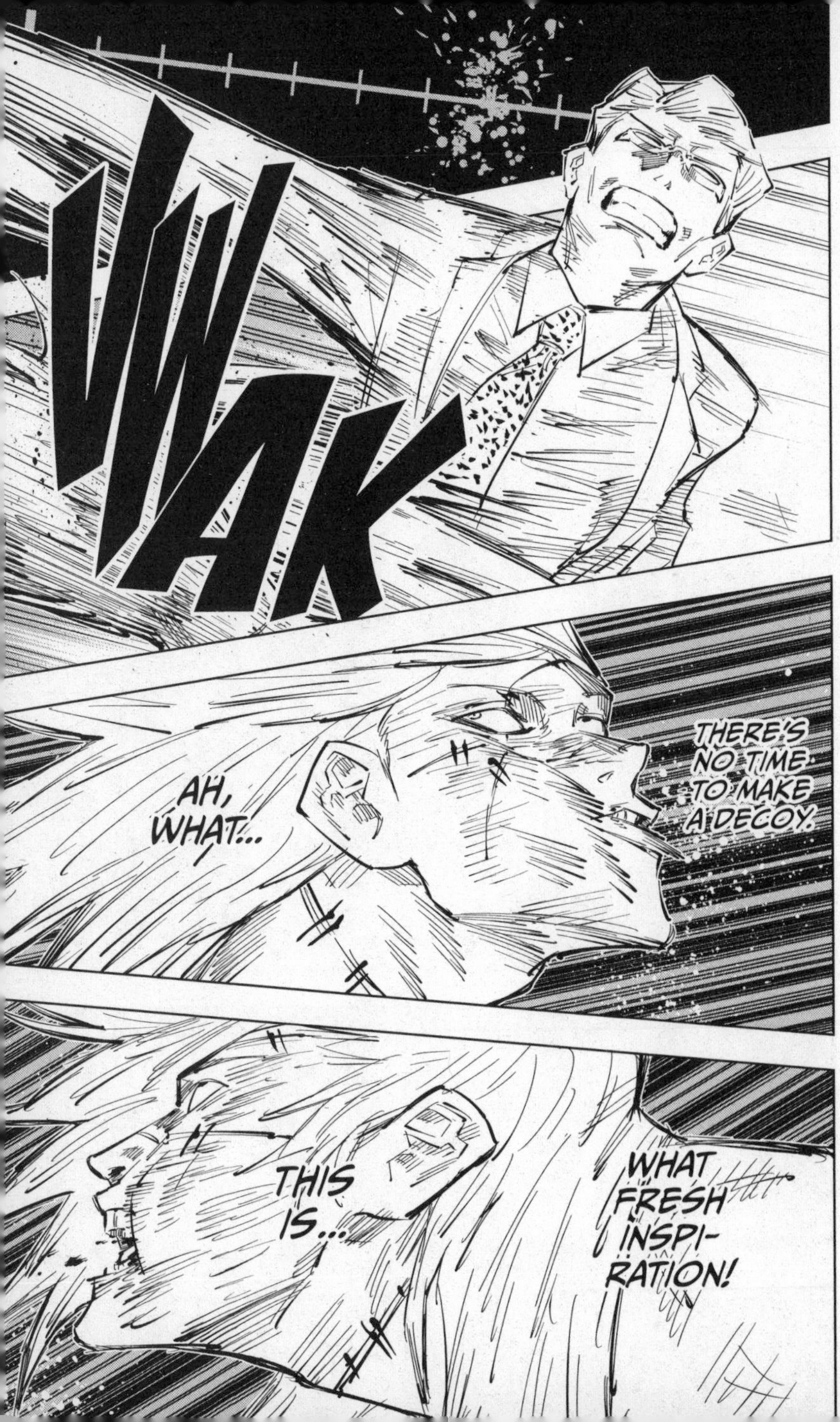
VVAK
THERE'S NO TIME TO MAKE A DECOY.
AH, WHAT...
WHAT FRESH INSPI-RATION!
THIS IS...

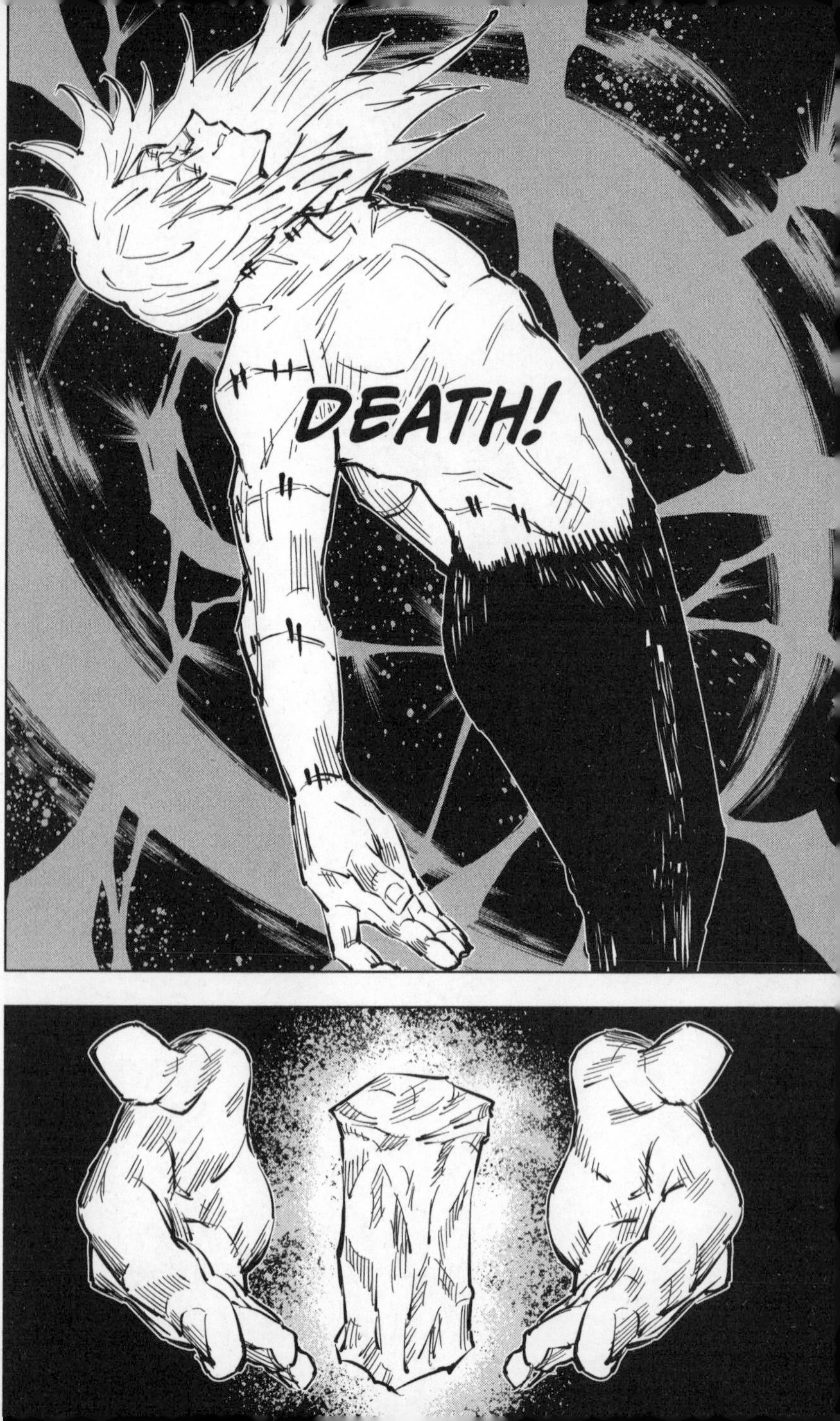
DEATH!

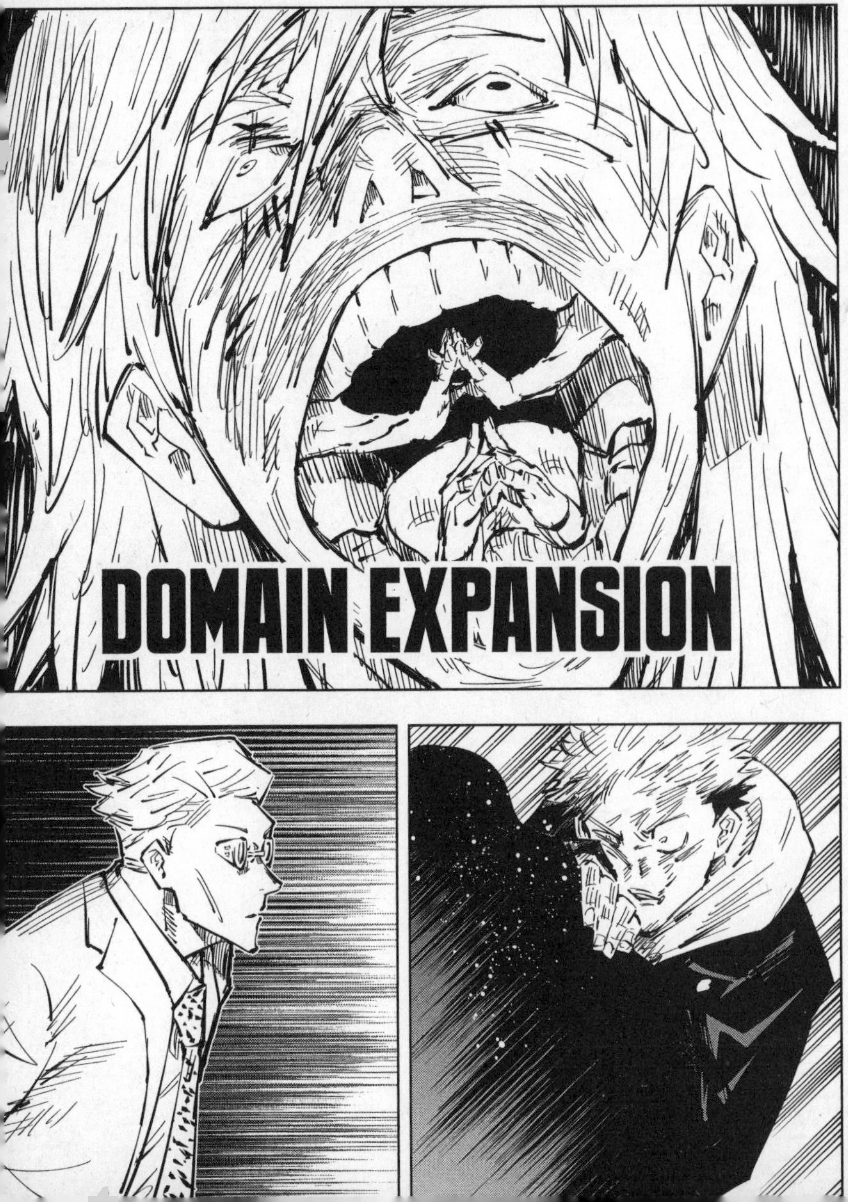
DOMAIN EXPANSION

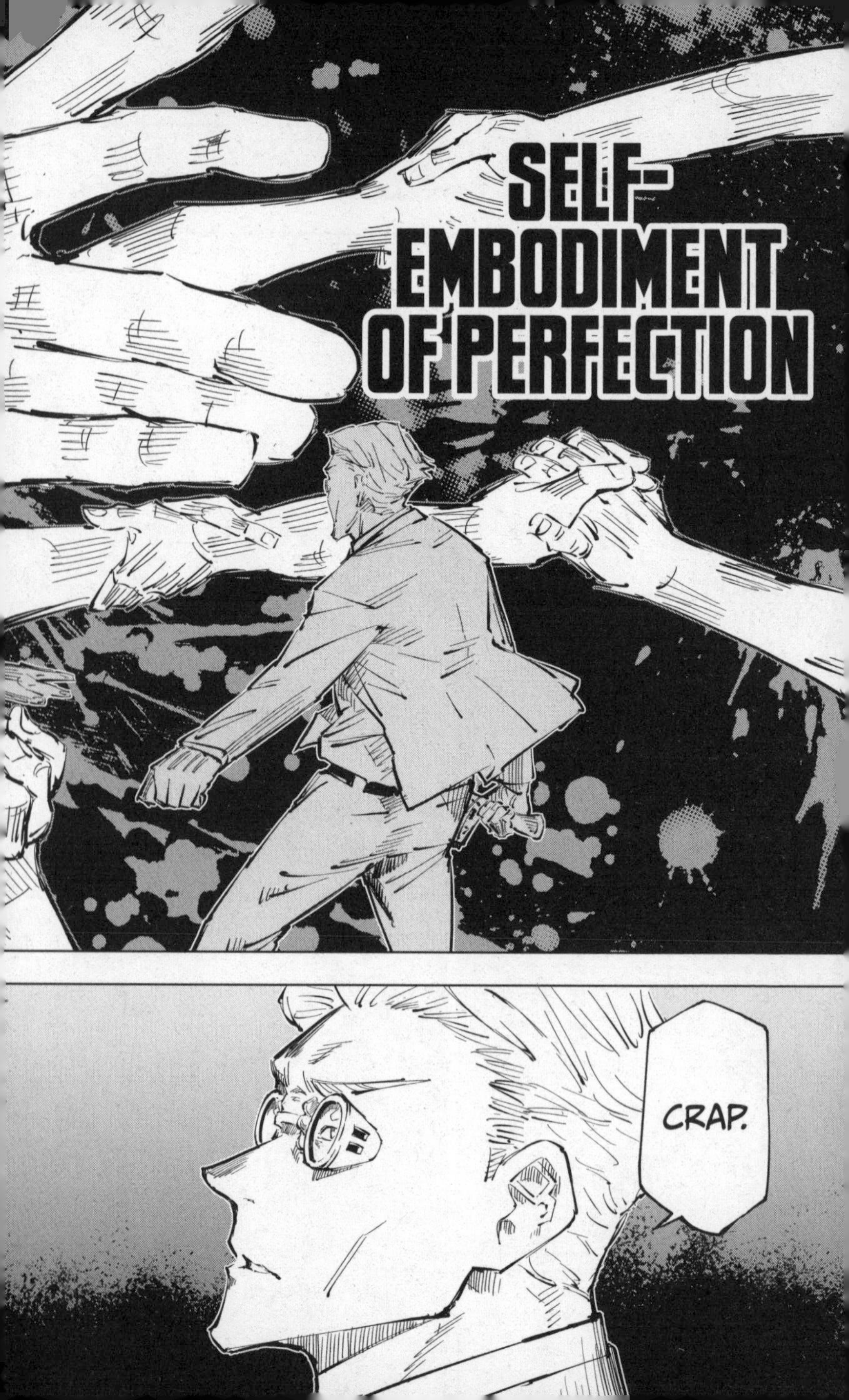
SELF-EMBODIMENT OF PERFECTION
CRAP.

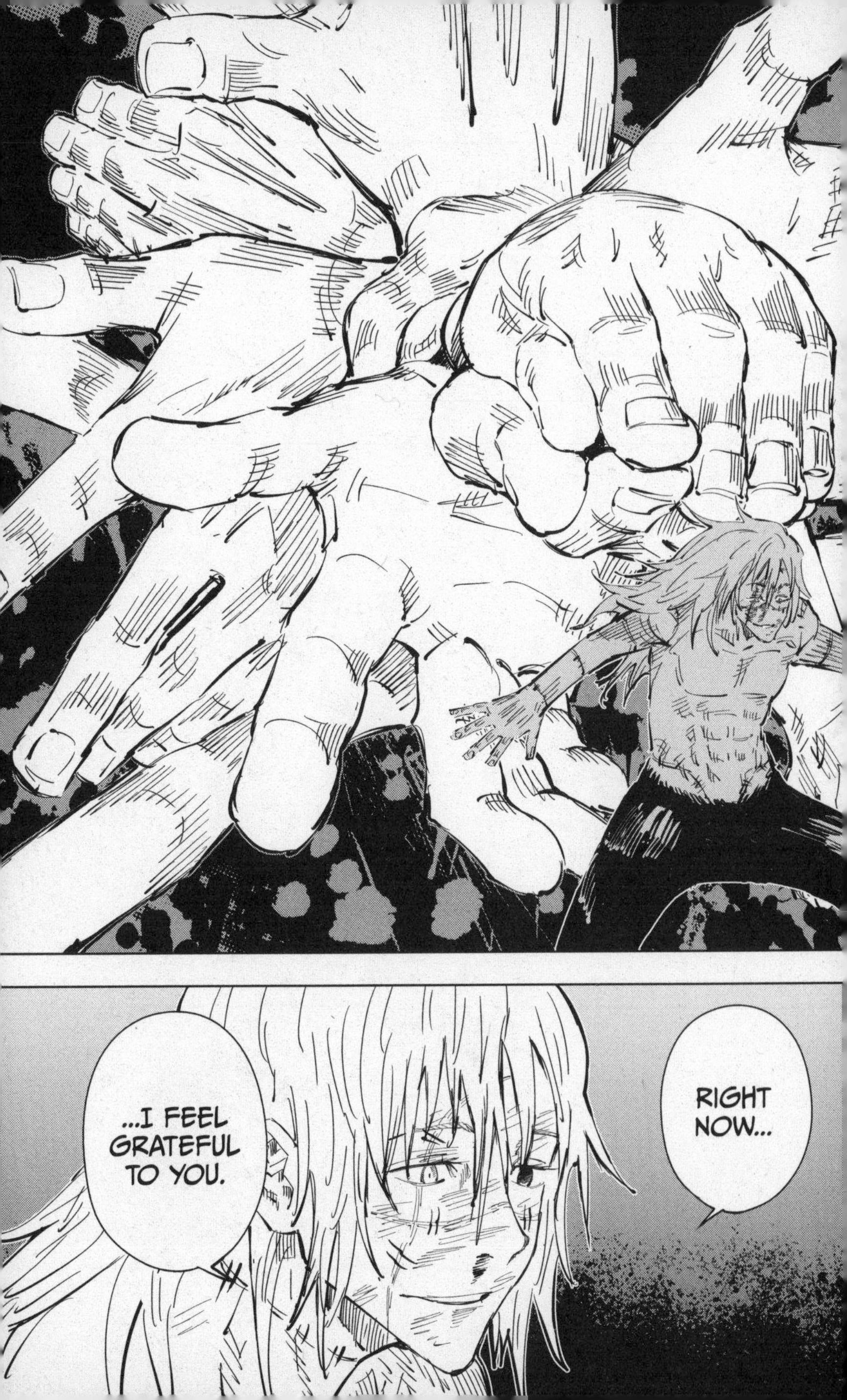
RIGHT NOW...
...I FEEL GRATEFUL TO YOU.

MAHITO'S FIGHT EXPLANATION, PART 1

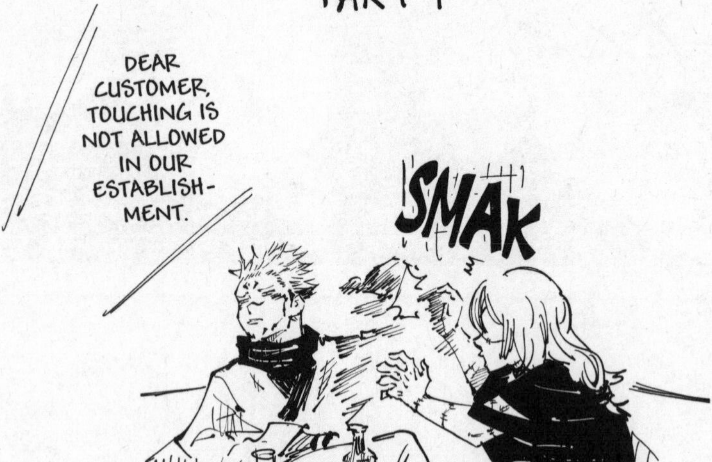
DEAR CUSTOMER, TOUCHING IS NOT ALLOWED IN OUR ESTABLISHMENT.
SMAK

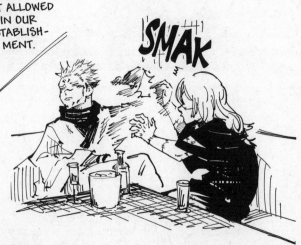

Chapter 30: Selfishness

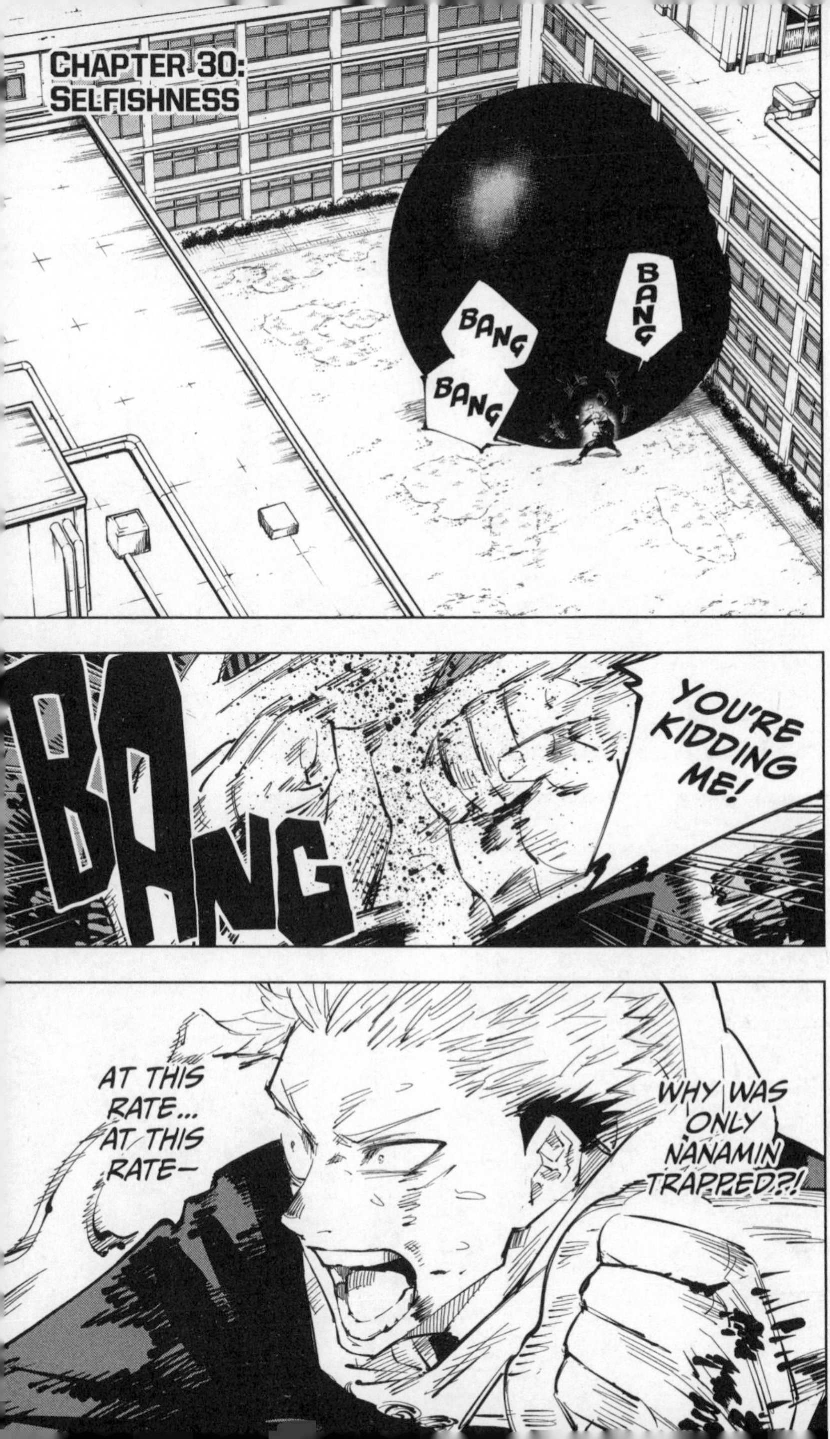
BANG
BANG
BANG
YOU'RE KIDDING ME!
BA BANG
WHY WAS ONLY NANAMIN TRAPPED?!
AT THIS RATE... AT THIS RATE—

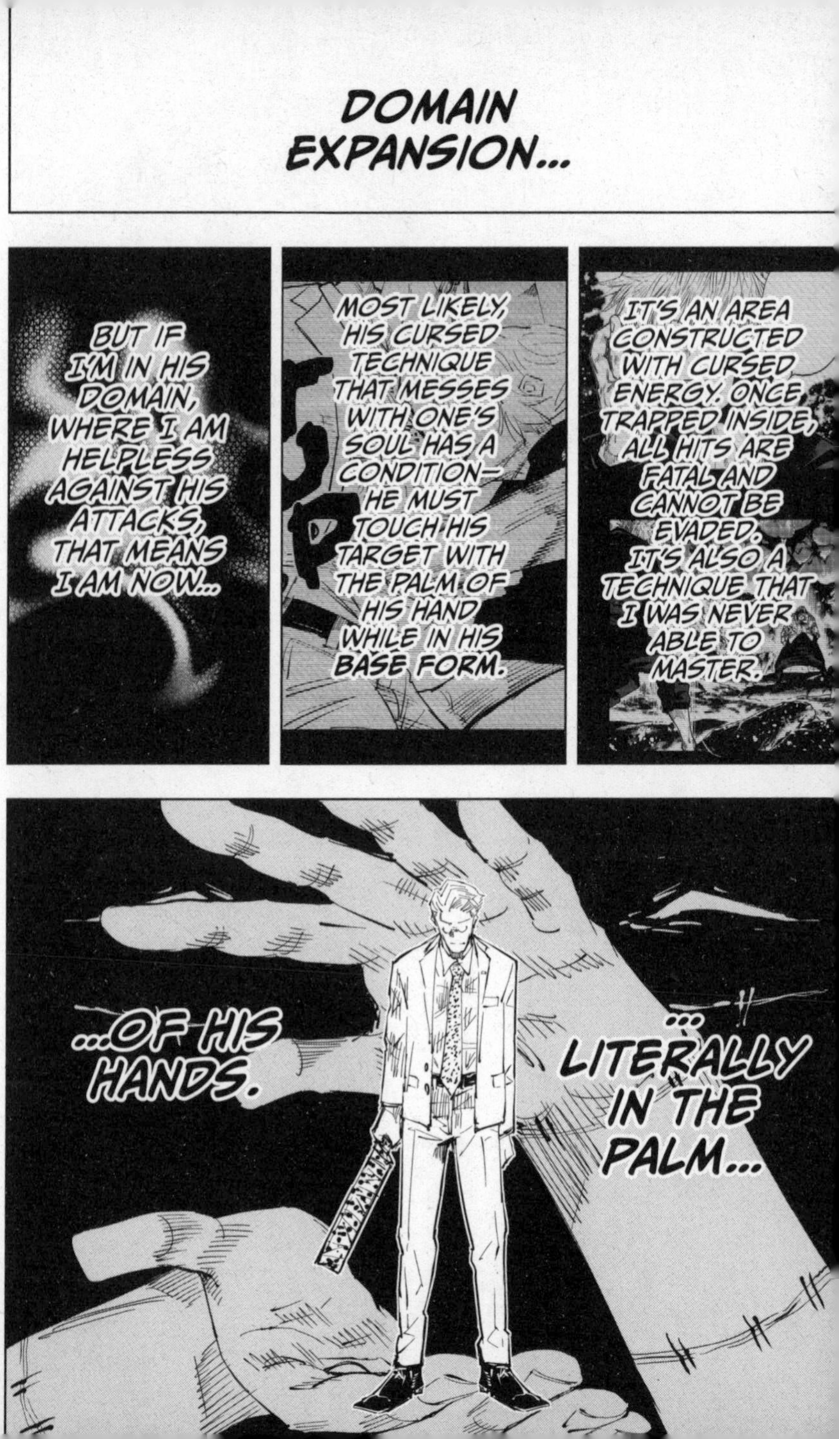
DOMAIN EXPANSION...
IT'S AN AREA CONSTRUCTED WITH CURSED ENERGY. ONCE TRAPPED INSIDE, ALL HITS ARE FATAL AND CANNOT BE EVADED. IT'S ALSO A TECHNIQUE THAT I WAS NEVER ABLE TO MASTER.
MOST LIKELY, HIS CURSED TECHNIQUE THAT MESSES WITH ONE'S SOUL HAS A CONDITION— HE MUST TOUCH HIS TARGET WITH THE PALM OF HIS HAND WHILE IN HIS BASE FORM.
BUT IF I'M IN HIS DOMAIN, WHERE I AM HELPLESS AGAINST HIS ATTACKS, THAT MEANS I AM NOW...
... LITERALLY IN THE PALM...
...OF HIS HANDS.

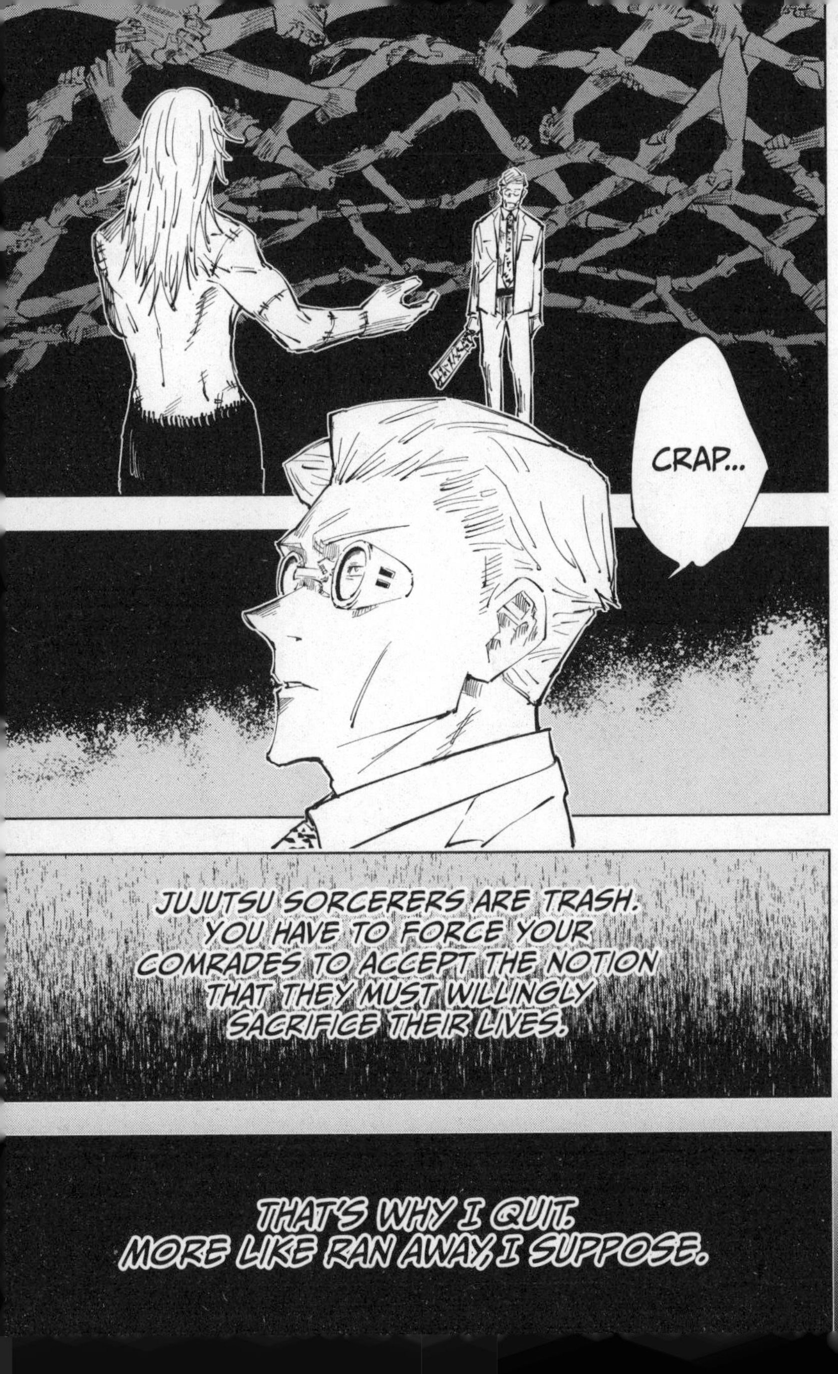
CRAP...
JUJUTSU SORCERERS ARE TRASH. YOU HAVE TO FORCE YOUR COMRADES TO ACCEPT THE NOTION THAT THEY MUST WILLINGLY SACRIFICE THEIR LIVES.
THAT'S WHY I QUIT. MORE LIKE RAN AWAY, I SUPPOSE.

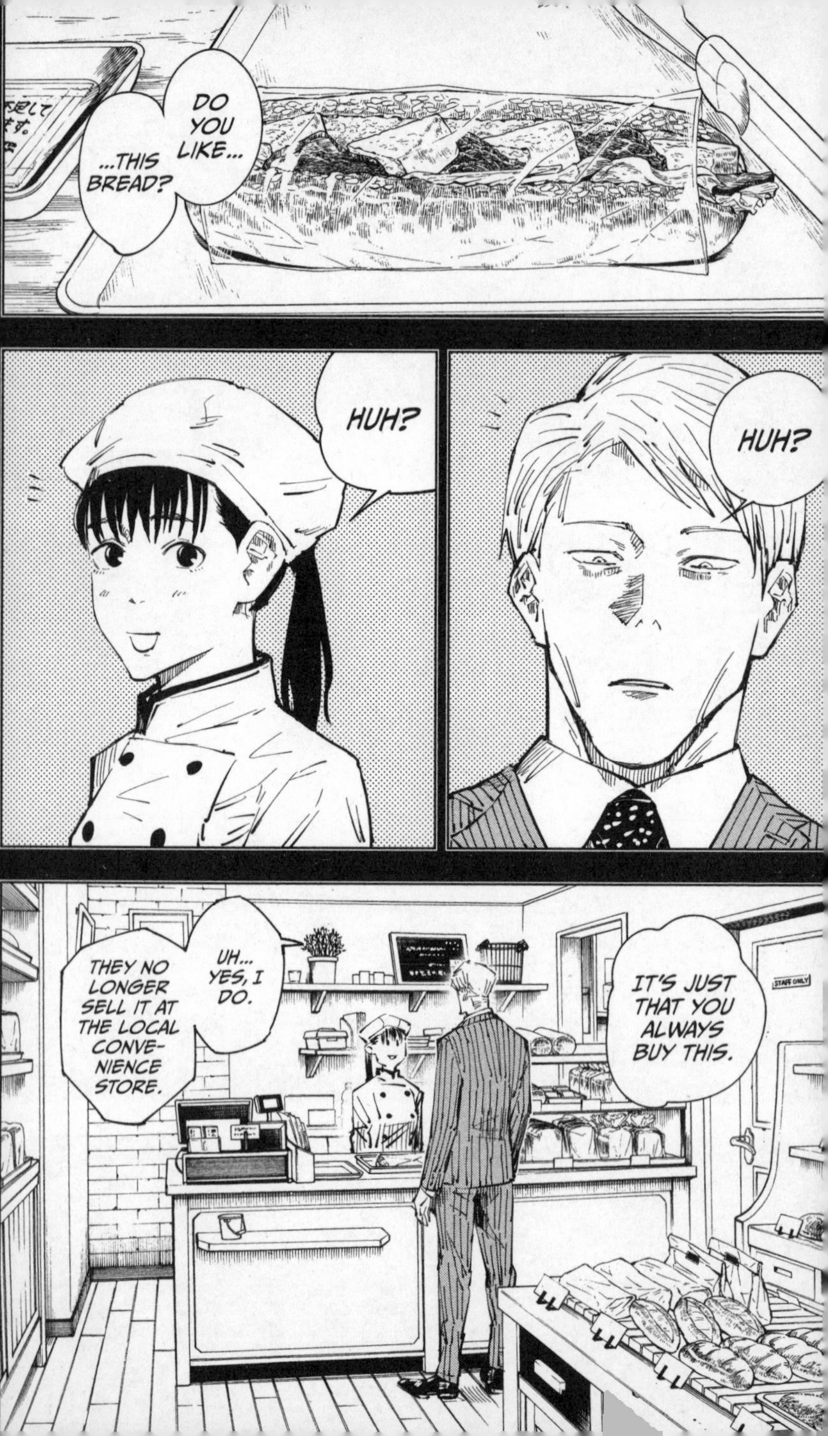
DO YOU LIKE...
...THIS BREAD?
HUH?
HUH?
IT'S JUST THAT YOU ALWAYS BUY THIS.
STAFF ONLY
UH... YES, I DO.
THEY NO LONGER SELL IT AT THE LOCAL CONVE-NIENCE STORE.

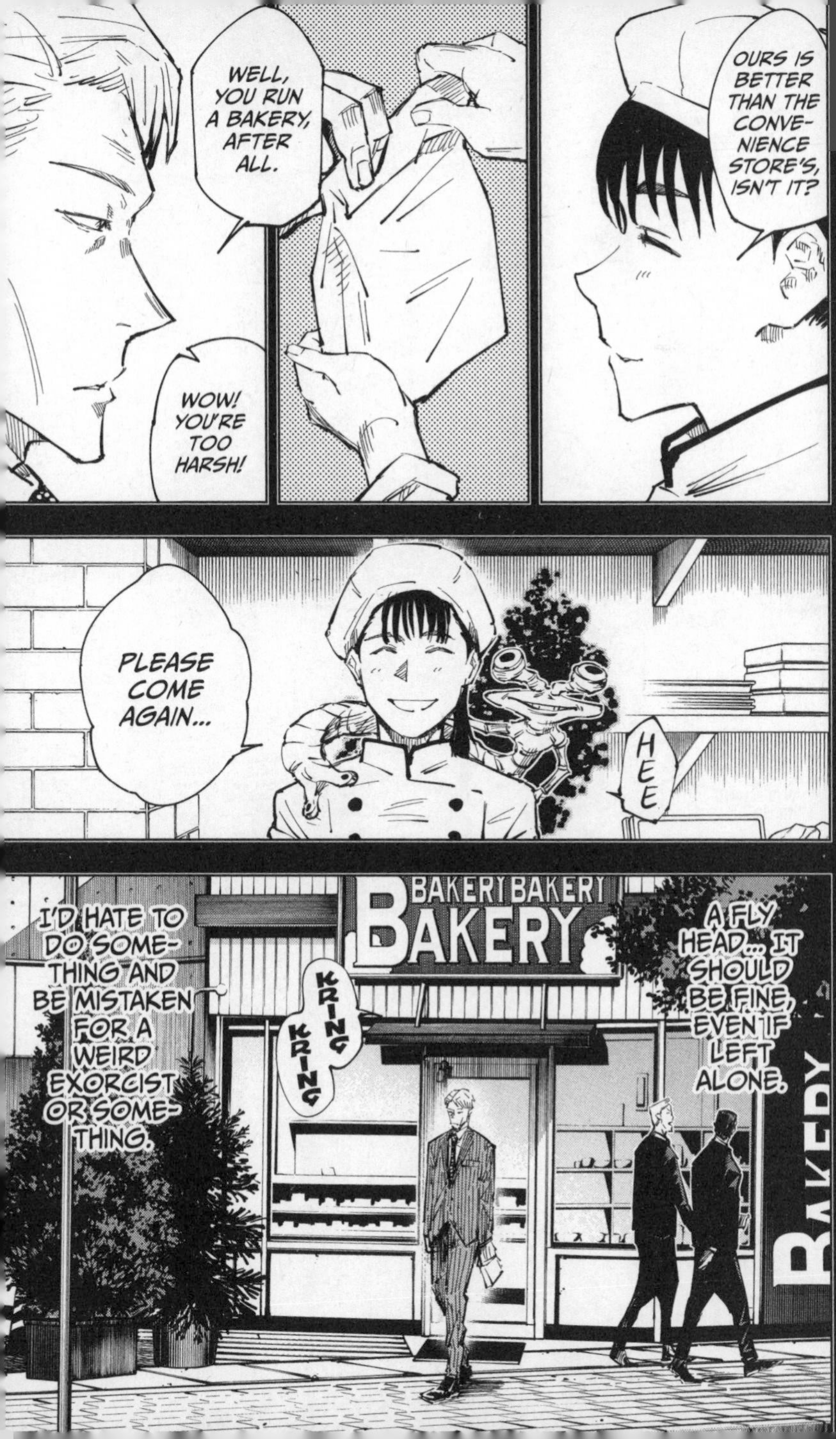
OURS IS BETTER THAN THE CONVENIENCE STORE'S, ISN'T IT?
WELL, YOU RUN A BAKERY, AFTER ALL.
WOW! YOU'RE TOO HARSH!
HEE
PLEASE COME AGAIN...
A FLY HEAD... IT SHOULD BE FINE, EVEN IF LEFT ALONE.
BAKERY BAKERY
BAKERY
BAKERY
KRING KRING
I'D HATE TO DO SOMETHING AND BE MISTAKEN FOR A WEIRD EXORCIST OR SOMETHING.

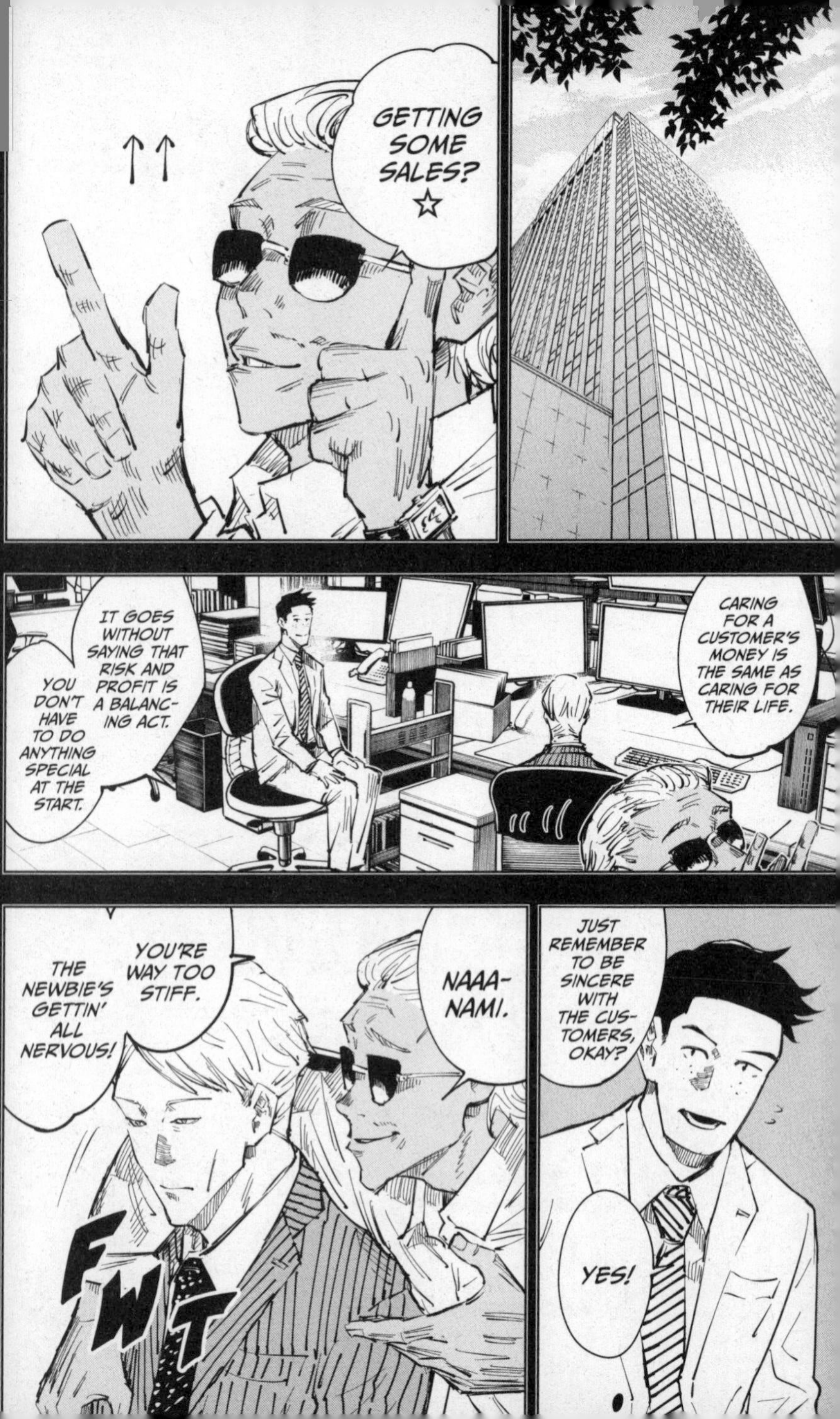
GETTING SOME SALES? ☆
CARING FOR A CUSTOMER'S MONEY IS THE SAME AS CARING FOR THEIR LIFE.
IT GOES WITHOUT SAYING THAT RISK AND PROFIT IS A BALANC-ING ACT.
YOU DON'T HAVE TO DO ANYTHING SPECIAL AT THE START.
JUST REMEMBER TO BE SINCERE WITH THE CUS-TOMERS, OKAY?
YES!
NAAA-NAMI.
YOU'RE WAY TOO STIFF.
THE NEWBIE'S GETTIN' ALL NERVOUS!
FWT

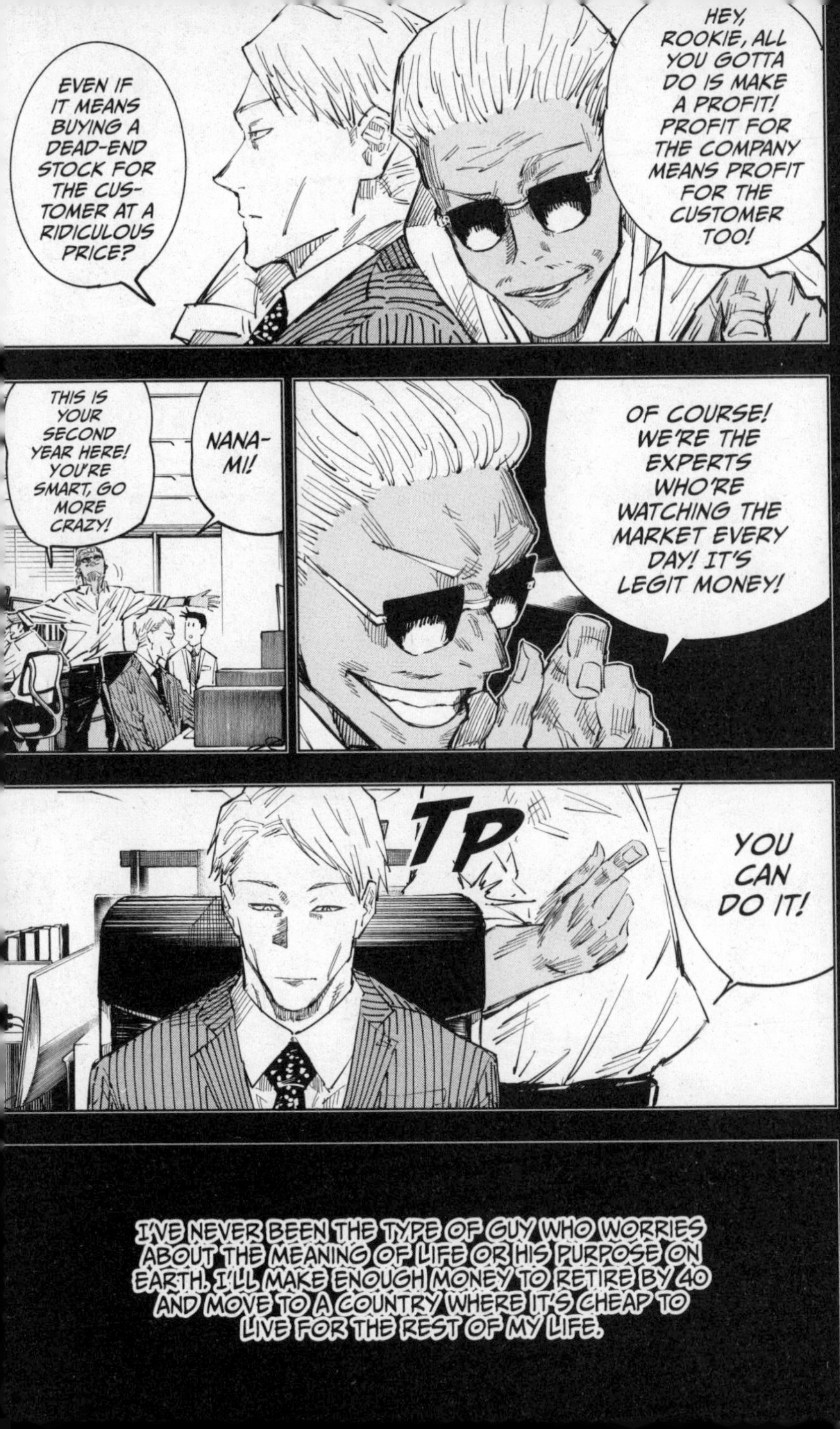
HEY, ROOKIE, ALL YOU GOTTA DO IS MAKE A PROFIT! PROFIT FOR THE COMPANY MEANS PROFIT FOR THE CUSTOMER TOO!
EVEN IF IT MEANS BUYING A DEAD-END STOCK FOR THE CUS-TOMER AT A RIDICULOUS PRICE?
OF COURSE! WE'RE THE EXPERTS WHO'RE WATCHING THE MARKET EVERY DAY! IT'S LEGIT MONEY!
NANA-MI!
THIS IS YOUR SECOND YEAR HERE! YOU'RE SMART, GO MORE CRAZY!
TP
YOU CAN DO IT!
I'VE NEVER BEEN THE TYPE OF GUY WHO WORRIES ABOUT THE MEANING OF LIFE OR HIS PURPOSE ON EARTH. I'LL MAKE ENOUGH MONEY TO RETIRE BY 40 AND MOVE TO A COUNTRY WHERE IT'S CHEAP TO LIVE FOR THE REST OF MY LIFE.

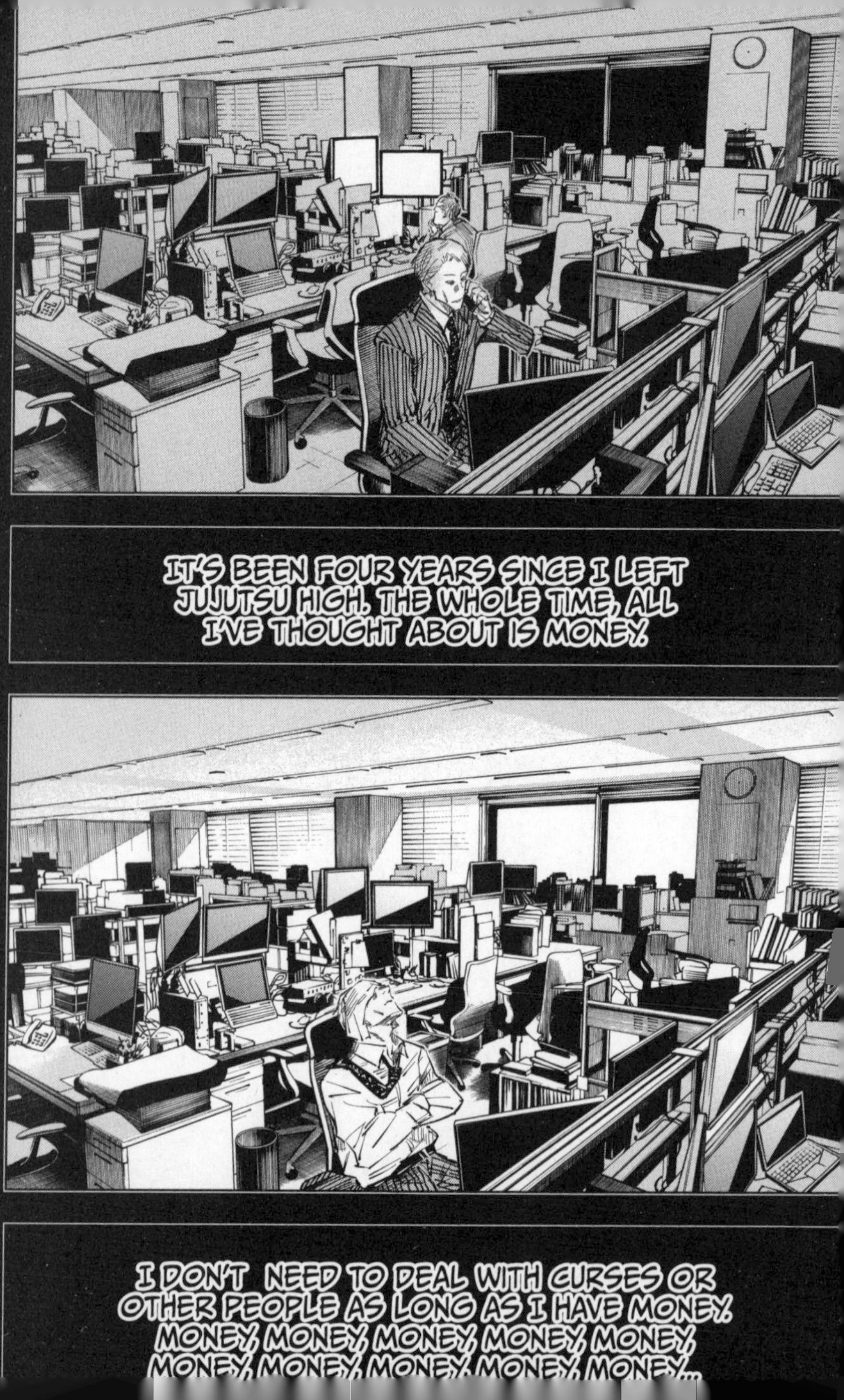
IT'S BEEN FOUR YEARS SINCE I LEFT JUJUTSU HIGH. THE WHOLE TIME, ALL I'VE THOUGHT ABOUT IS MONEY.
I DON'T NEED TO DEAL WITH CURSES OR OTHER PEOPLE AS LONG AS I HAVE MONEY. MONEY, MONEY, MONEY, MONEY, MONEY, MONEY, MONEY, MONEY, MONEY, MONEY...

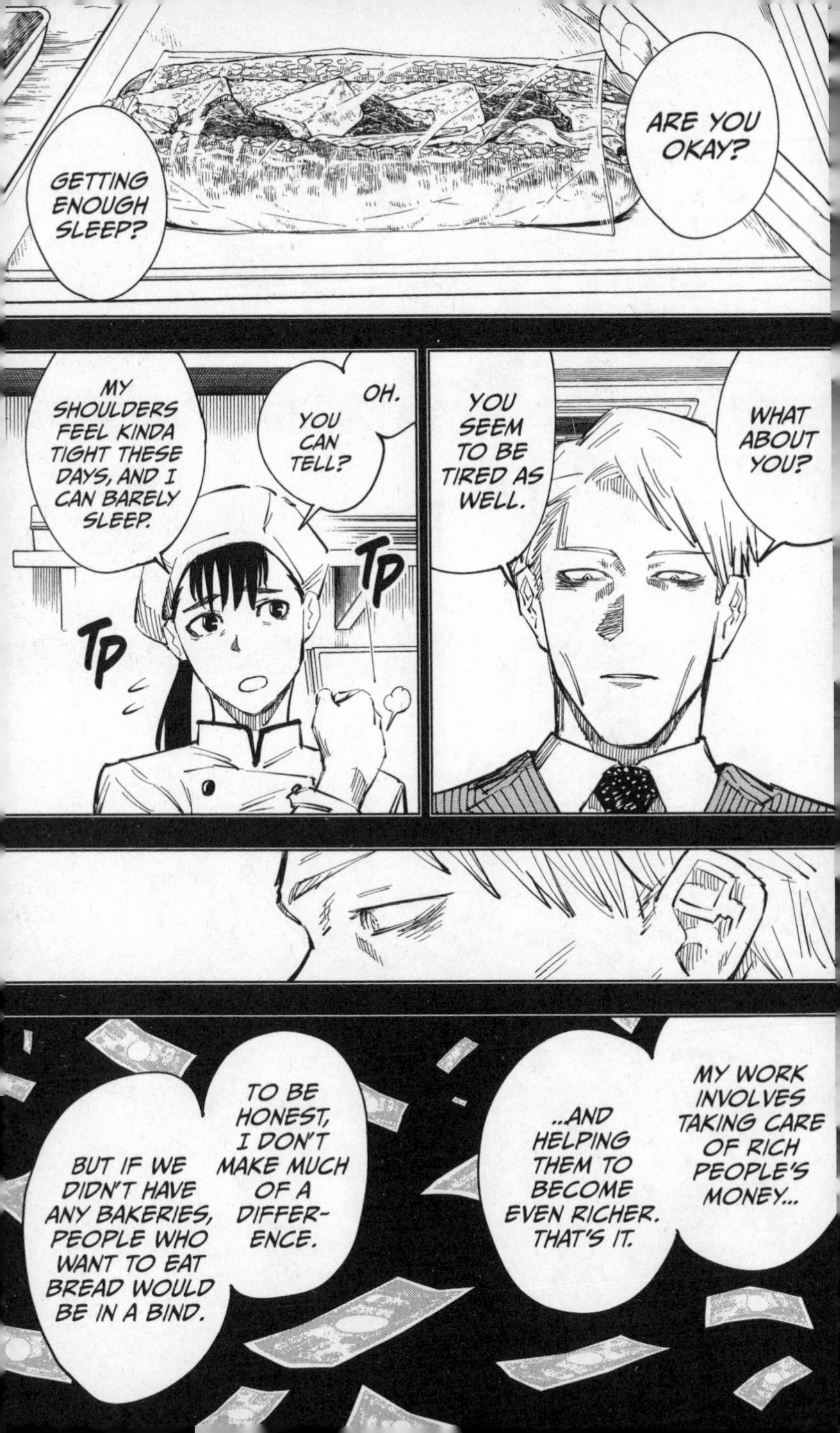
ARE YOU OKAY?
GETTING ENOUGH SLEEP?
WHAT ABOUT YOU?
YOU SEEM TO BE TIRED AS WELL.
OH.
YOU CAN TELL?
TP
MY SHOULDERS FEEL KINDA TIGHT THESE DAYS, AND I CAN BARELY SLEEP.
TP
MY WORK INVOLVES TAKING CARE OF RICH PEOPLE'S MONEY...
...AND HELPING THEM TO BECOME EVEN RICHER. THAT'S IT.
TO BE HONEST, I DON'T MAKE MUCH OF A DIFFER-ENCE.
BUT IF WE DIDN'T HAVE ANY BAKERIES, PEOPLE WHO WANT TO EAT BREAD WOULD BE IN A BIND.

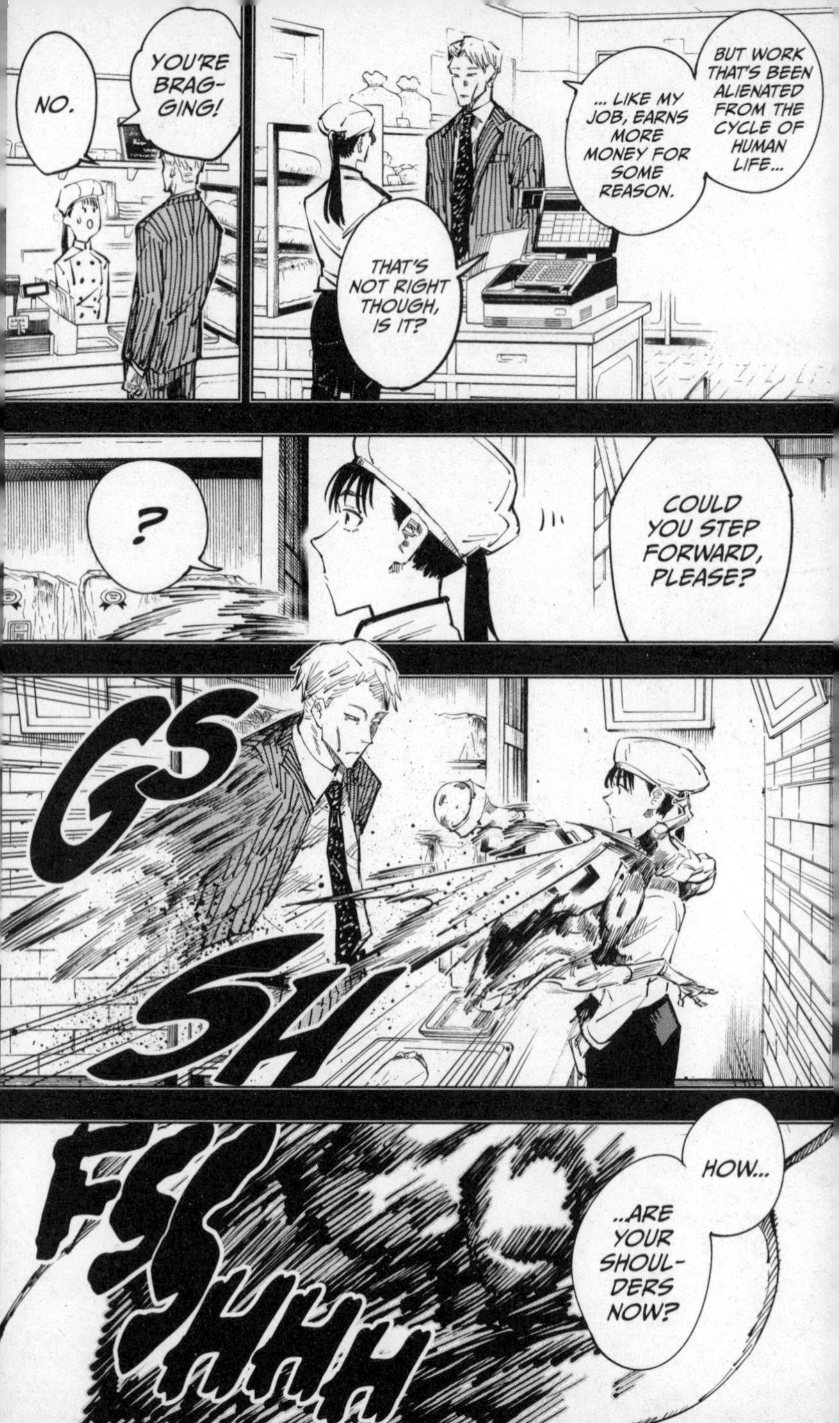
BUT WORK THAT'S BEEN ALIENATED FROM THE CYCLE OF HUMAN LIFE...
... LIKE MY JOB, EARNS MORE MONEY FOR SOME REASON.
THAT'S NOT RIGHT THOUGH, IS IT?
YOU'RE BRAG-GING!
NO.
COULD YOU STEP FORWARD, PLEASE?
?
GSSH
HOW...
...ARE YOUR SHOUL-DERS NOW?
FSSHHH

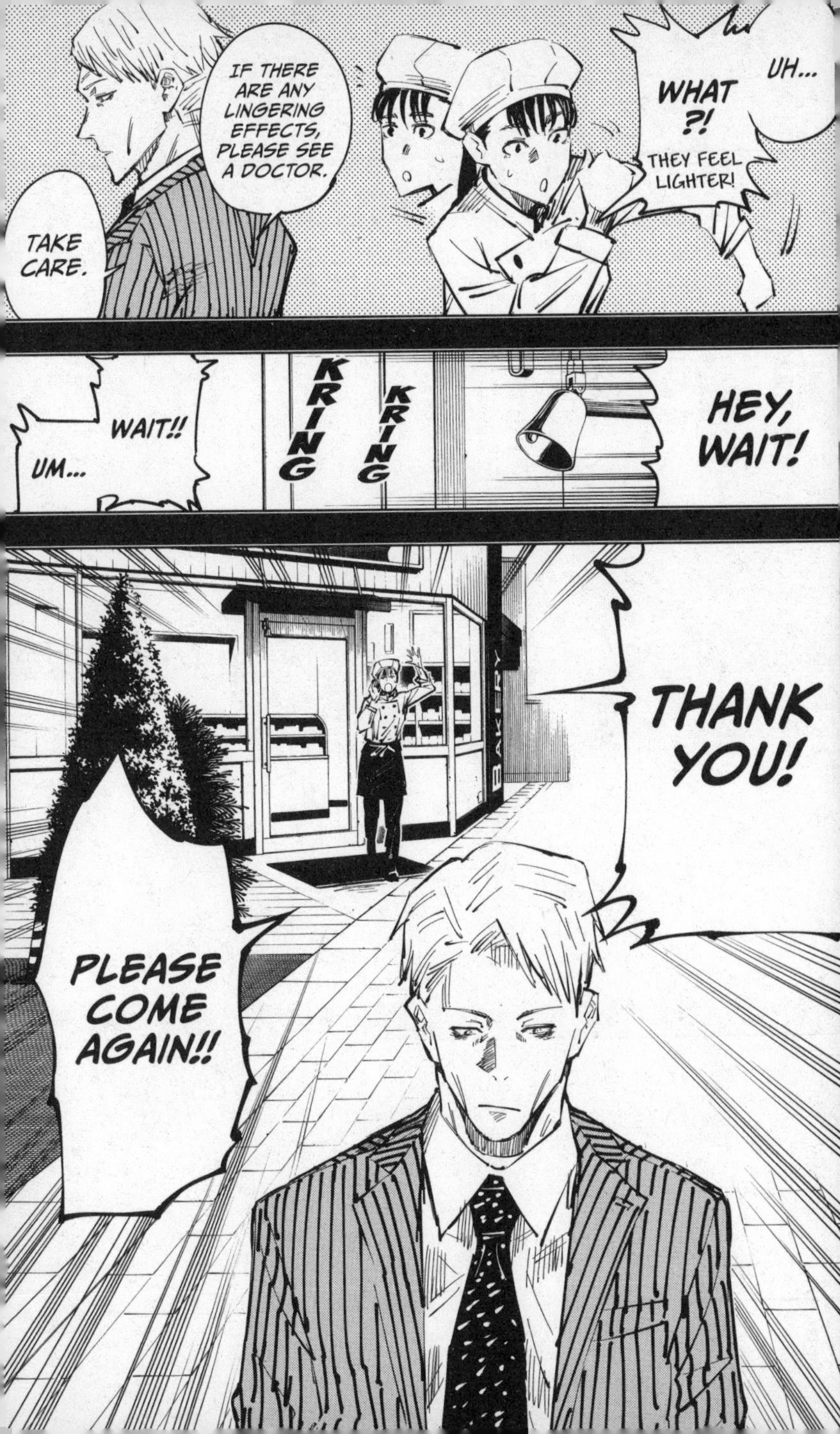
UH...
WHAT?! THEY FEEL LIGHTER!
IF THERE ARE ANY LINGERING EFFECTS, PLEASE SEE A DOCTOR.
TAKE CARE.
HEY, WAIT!
KRING KRING
WAIT!! UM...
THANK YOU!
BAKERY
PLEASE COME AGAIN!!

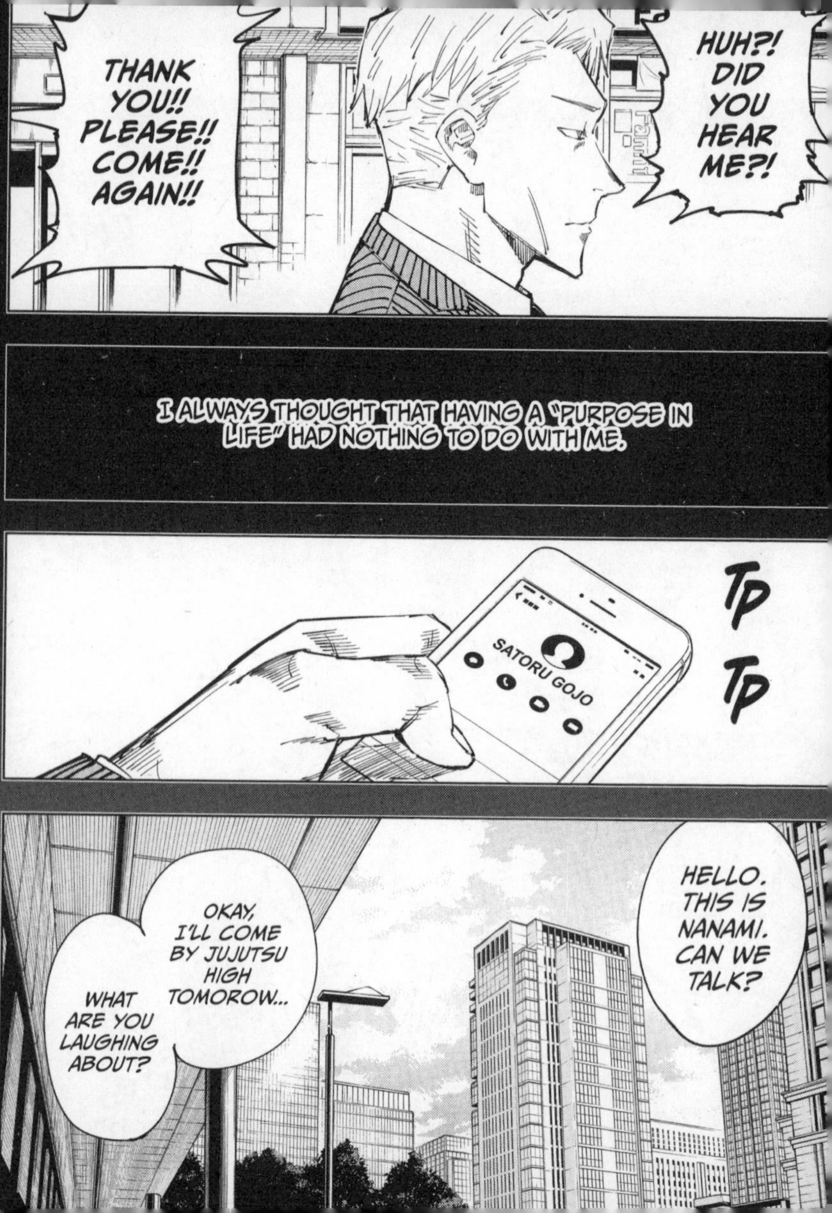
HUH?! DID YOU HEAR ME?!
THANK YOU!! PLEASE!! COME!! AGAIN!!
I ALWAYS THOUGHT THAT HAVING A "PURPOSE IN LIFE" HAD NOTHING TO DO WITH ME.
TP
TP
SATORU GOJO
HELLO. THIS IS NANAMI. CAN WE TALK?
OKAY, I'LL COME BY JUJUTSU HIGH TOMOROW...
WHAT ARE YOU LAUGHING ABOUT?

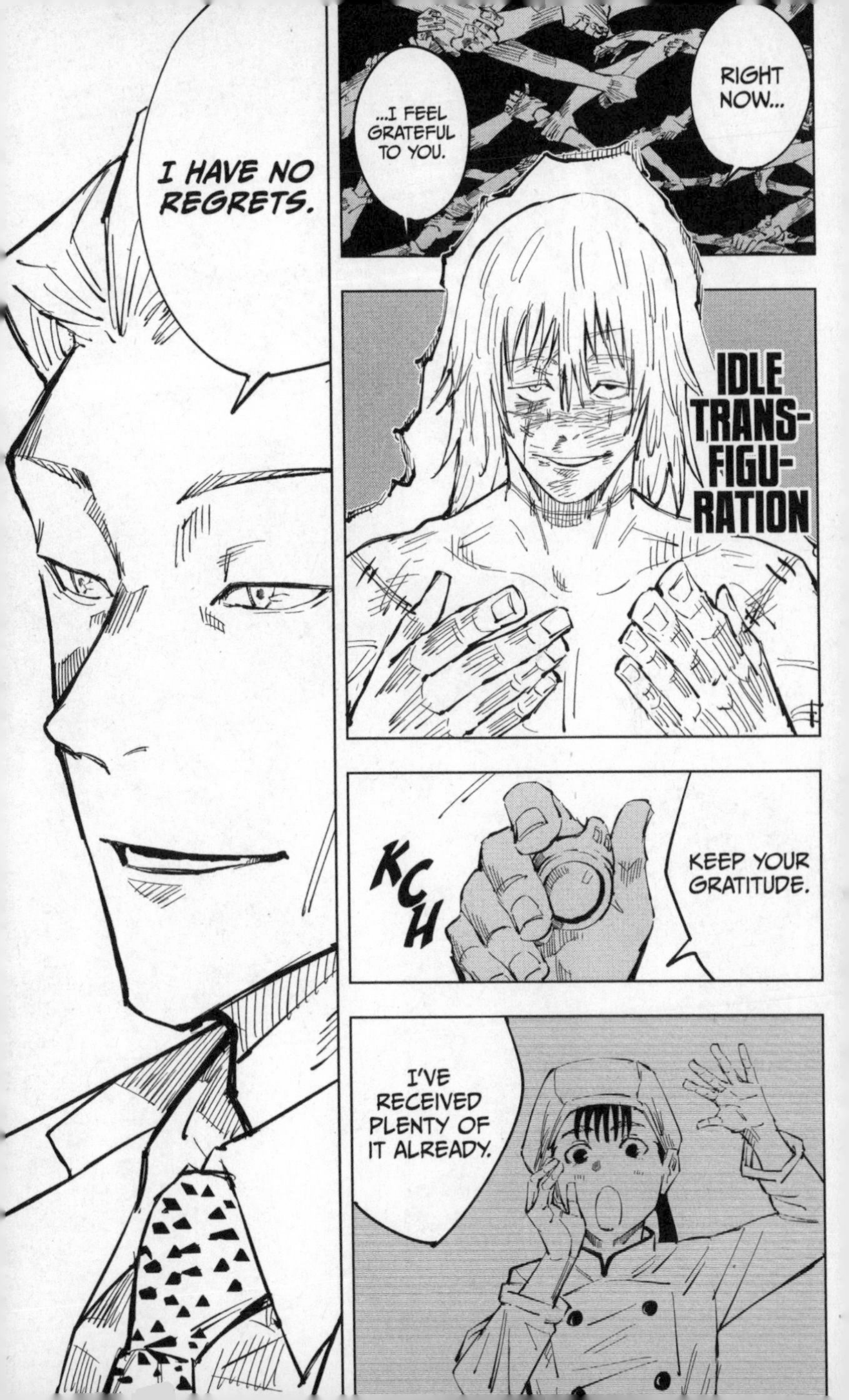
RIGHT NOW...
...I FEEL GRATEFUL TO YOU.
IDLE TRANS-FIGU-RATION
KEEP YOUR GRATITUDE.
KCH
I'VE RECEIVED PLENTY OF IT ALREADY.
I HAVE NO REGRETS.

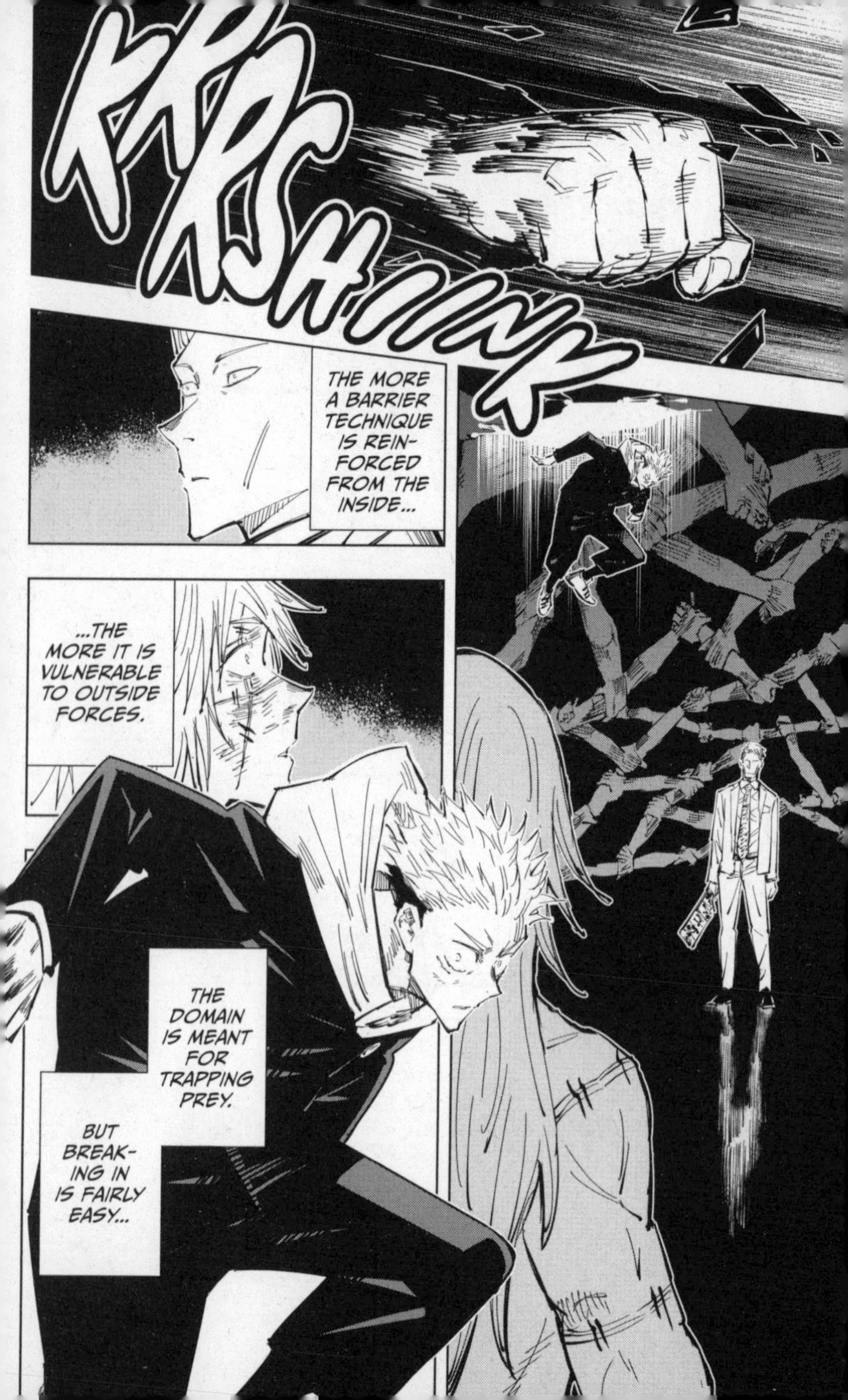
KRSHUNK
THE MORE A BARRIER TECHNIQUE IS REIN-FORCED FROM THE INSIDE...
...THE MORE IT IS VULNERABLE TO OUTSIDE FORCES.
THE DOMAIN IS MEANT FOR TRAPPING PREY.
BUT BREAK-ING IN IS FAIRLY EASY...

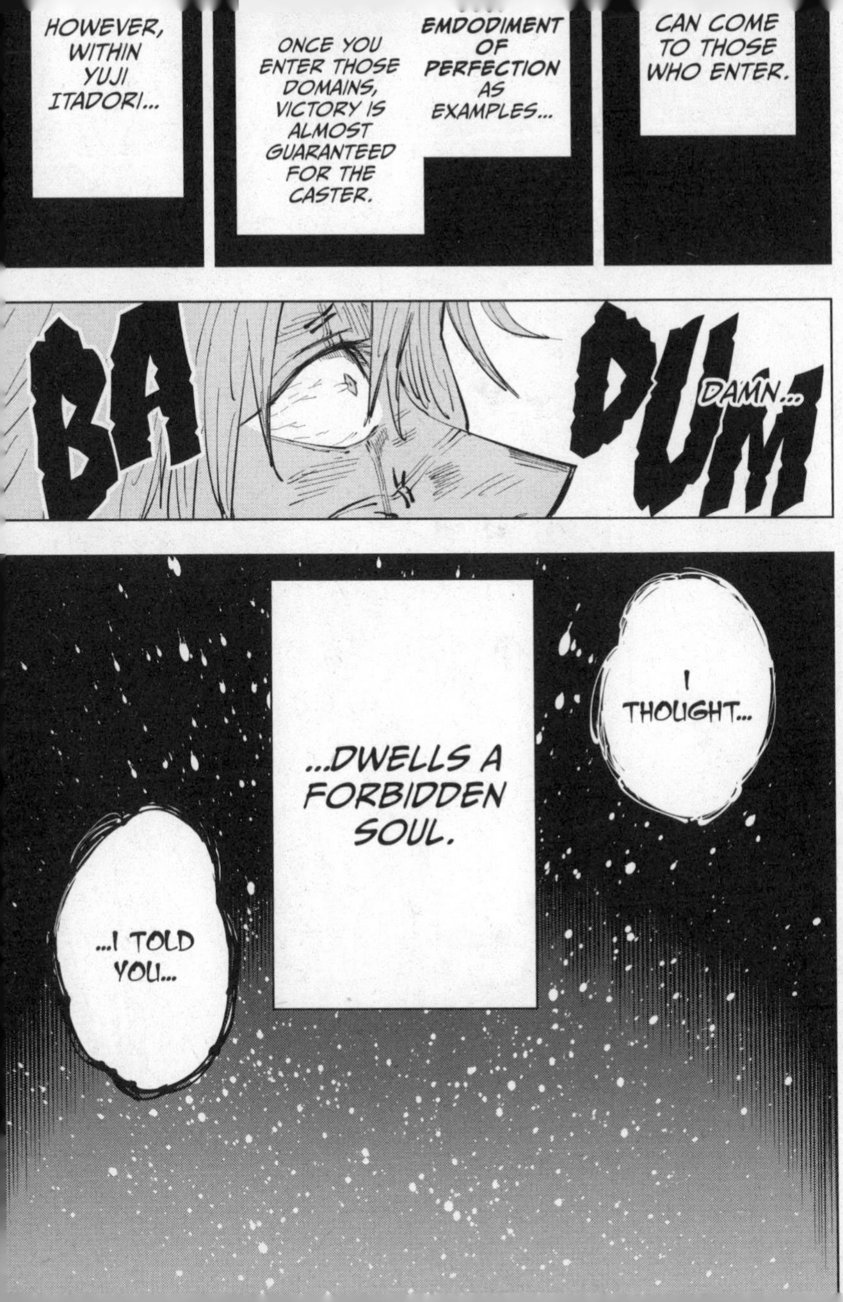
CAN COME TO THOSE WHO ENTER.
EMDODIMENT OF PERFECTION AS EXAMPLES...
ONCE YOU ENTER THOSE DOMAINS, VICTORY IS ALMOST GUARANTEED FOR THE CASTER.
HOWEVER, WITHIN YUJI ITADORI...
BA
DUM
DAMN...
I THOUGHT...
...DWELLS A FORBIDDEN SOUL.
...I TOLD YOU...

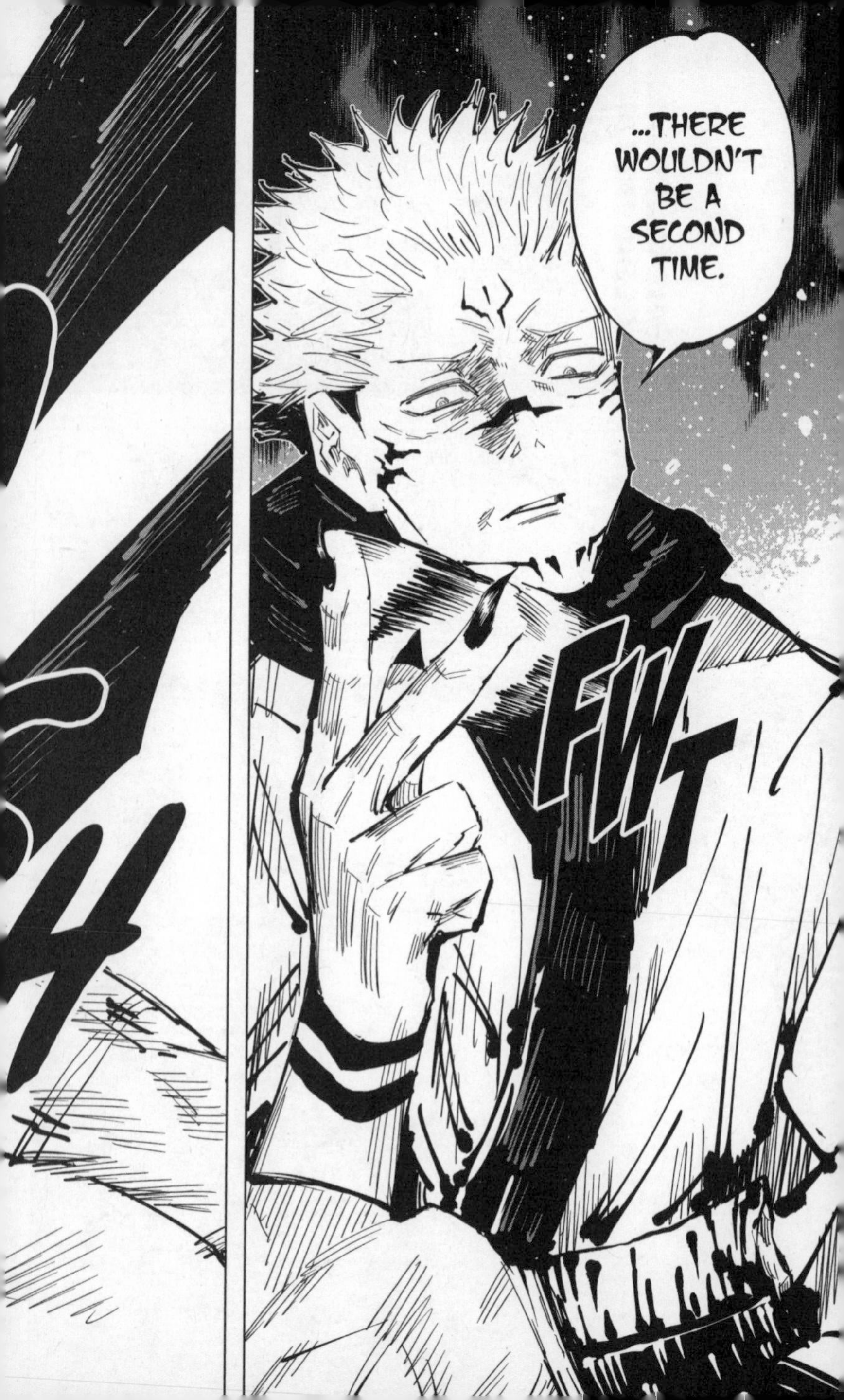
...THERE WOULDN'T BE A SECOND TIME.

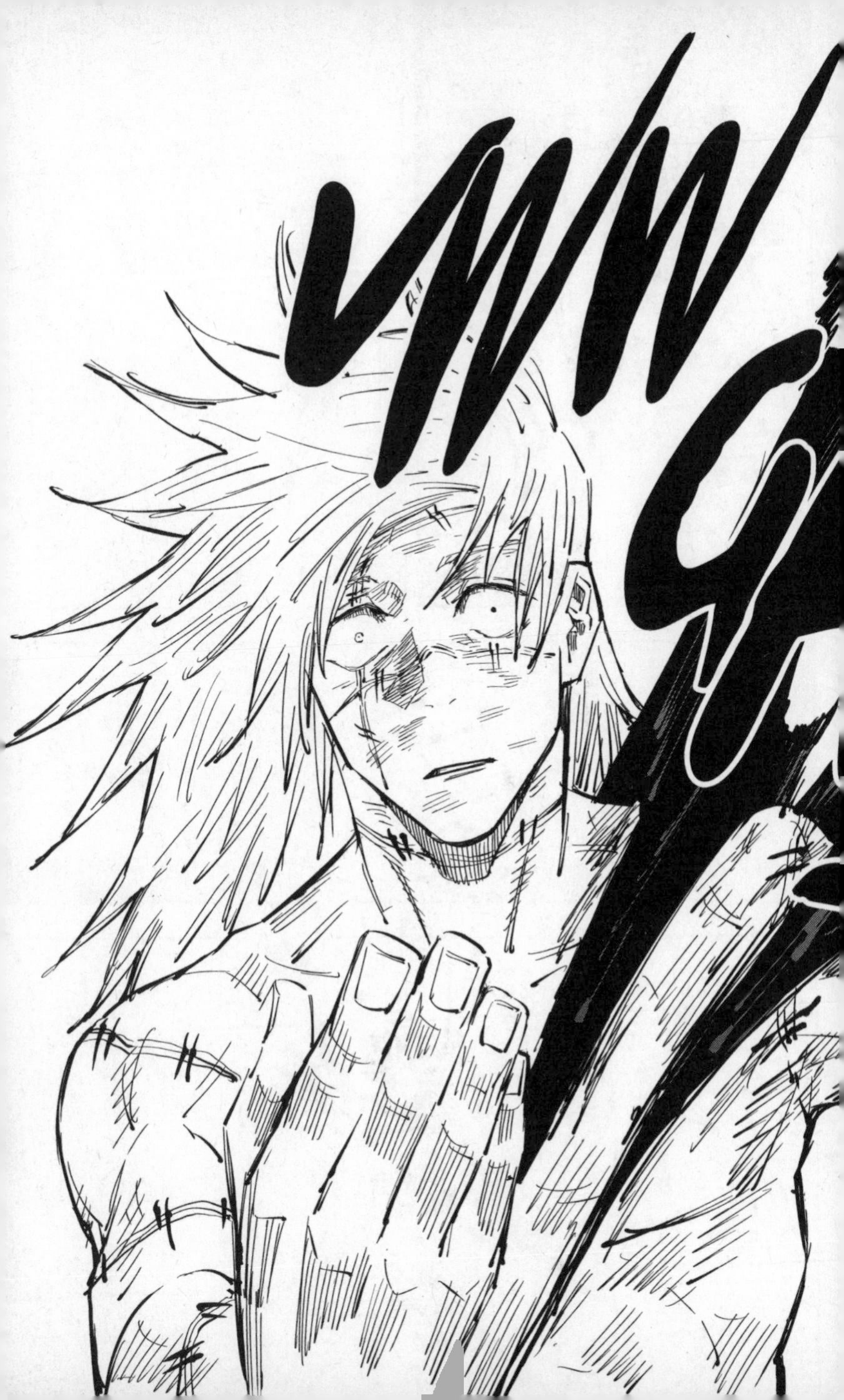

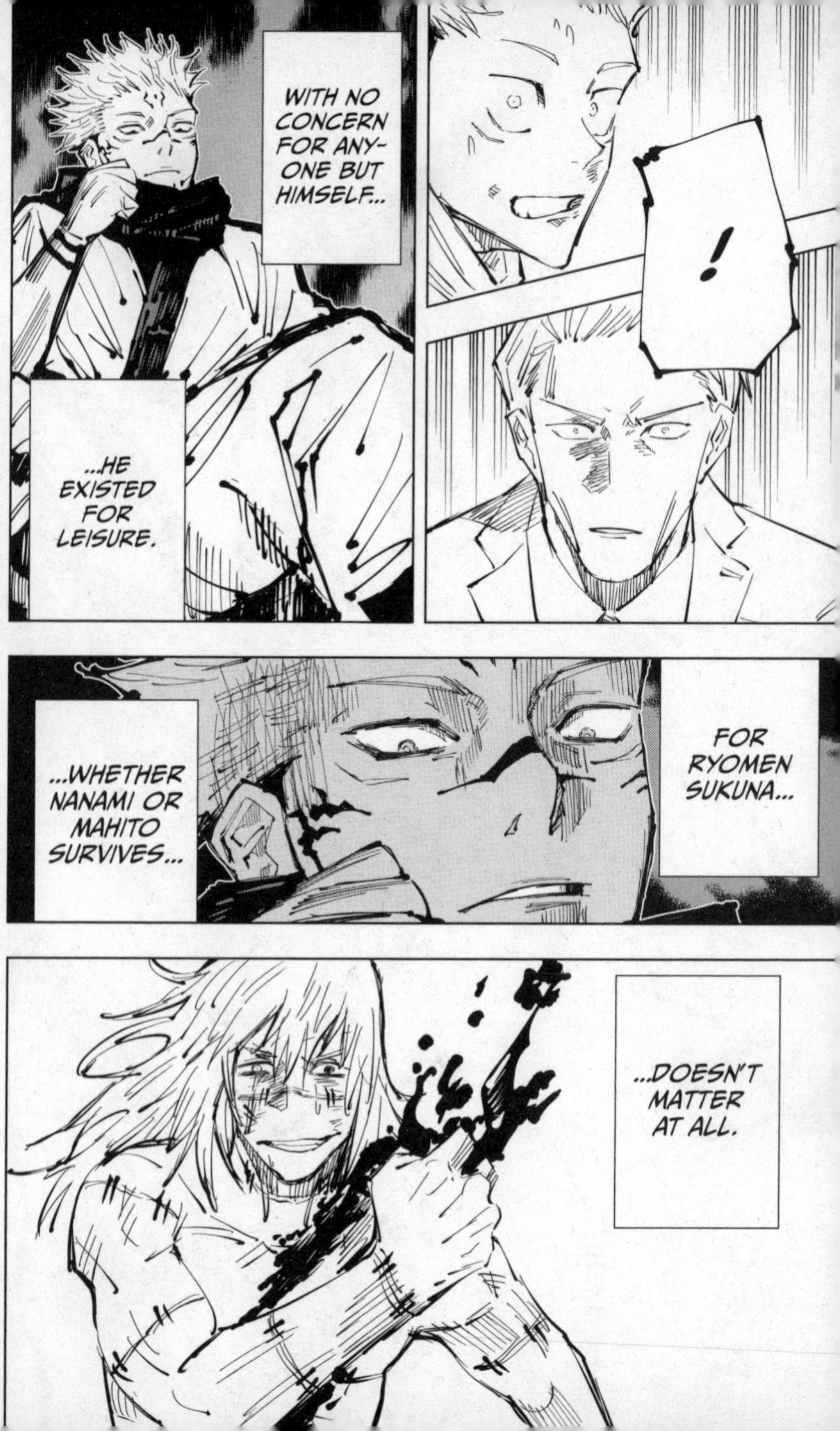
!
WITH NO CONCERN FOR ANY-ONE BUT HIMSELF...
...HE EXISTED FOR LEISURE.
FOR RYOMEN SUKUNA...
...WHETHER NANAMI OR MAHITO SURVIVES...
...DOESN'T MATTER AT ALL.

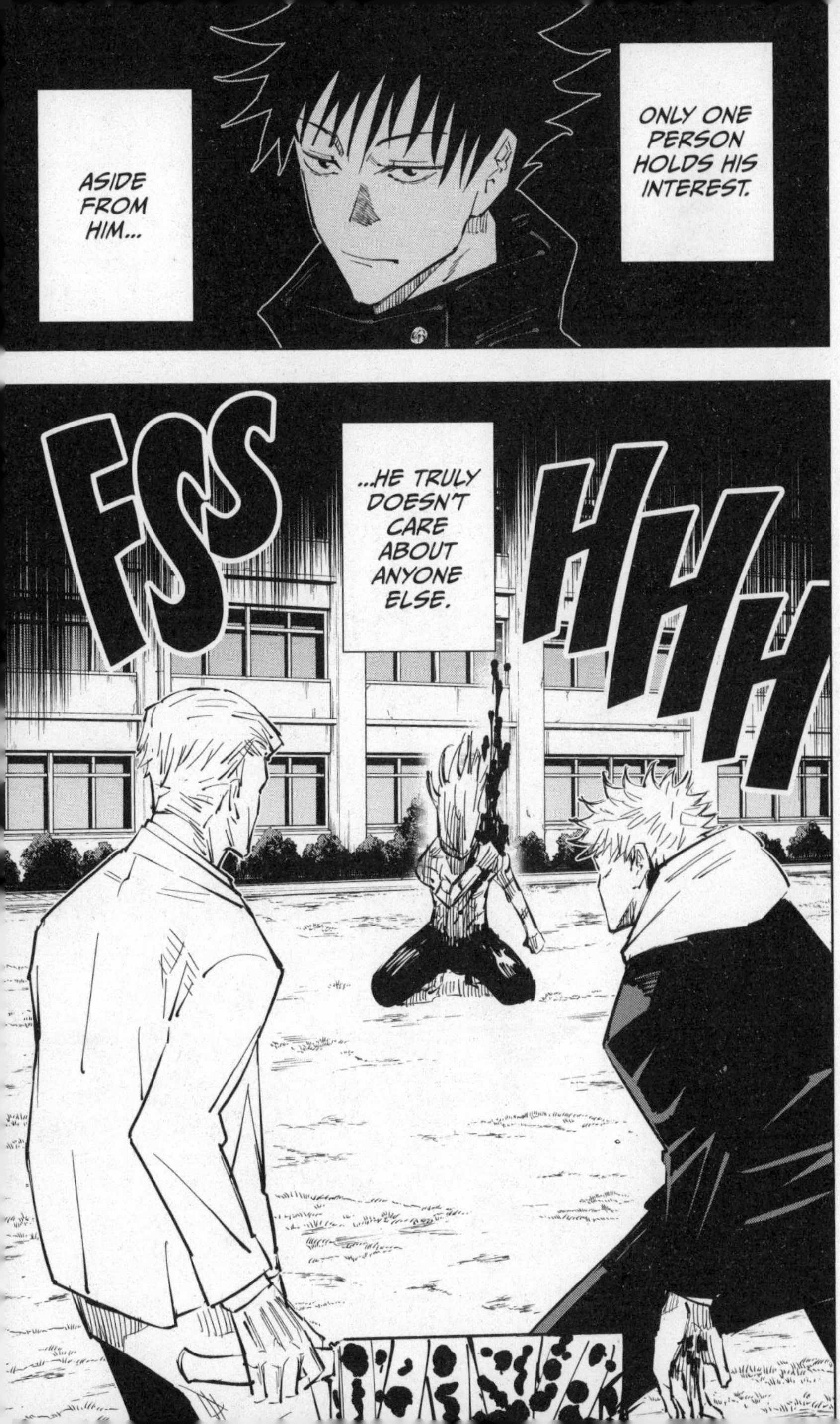
ONLY ONE PERSON HOLDS HIS INTEREST.
ASIDE FROM HIM...
...HE TRULY DOESN'T CARE ABOUT ANYONE ELSE.
FSSHHH

MAHITO'S FIGHT EXPLANATION, PART 2

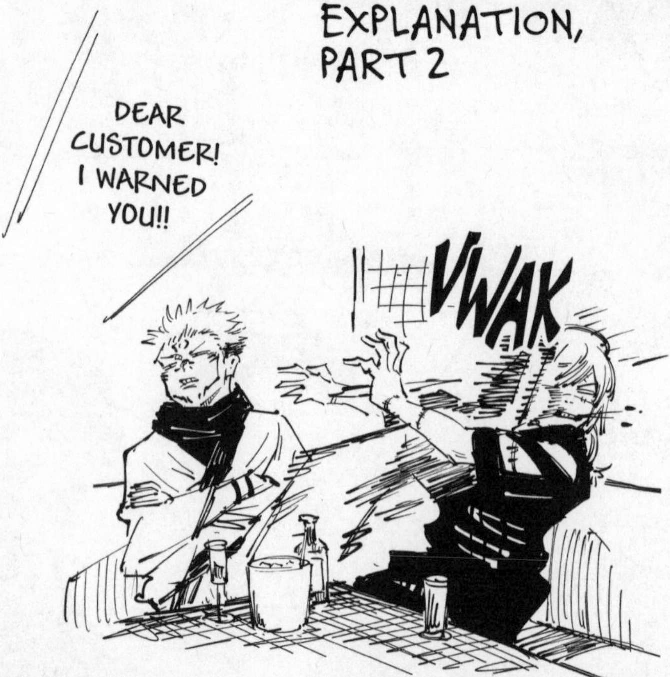
DEAR CUSTOMER! I WARNED YOU!!
VWAK

CHAPTER 31: TOMORROW

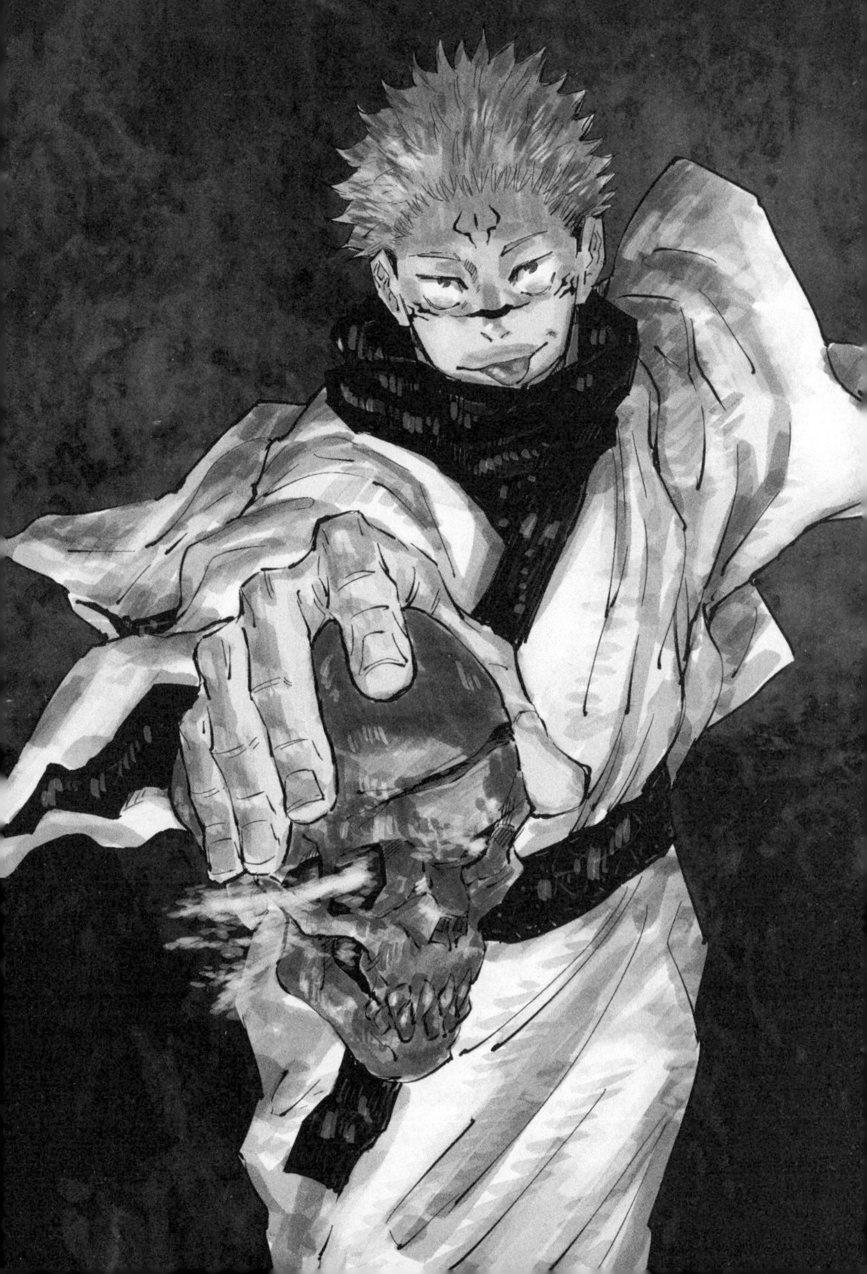

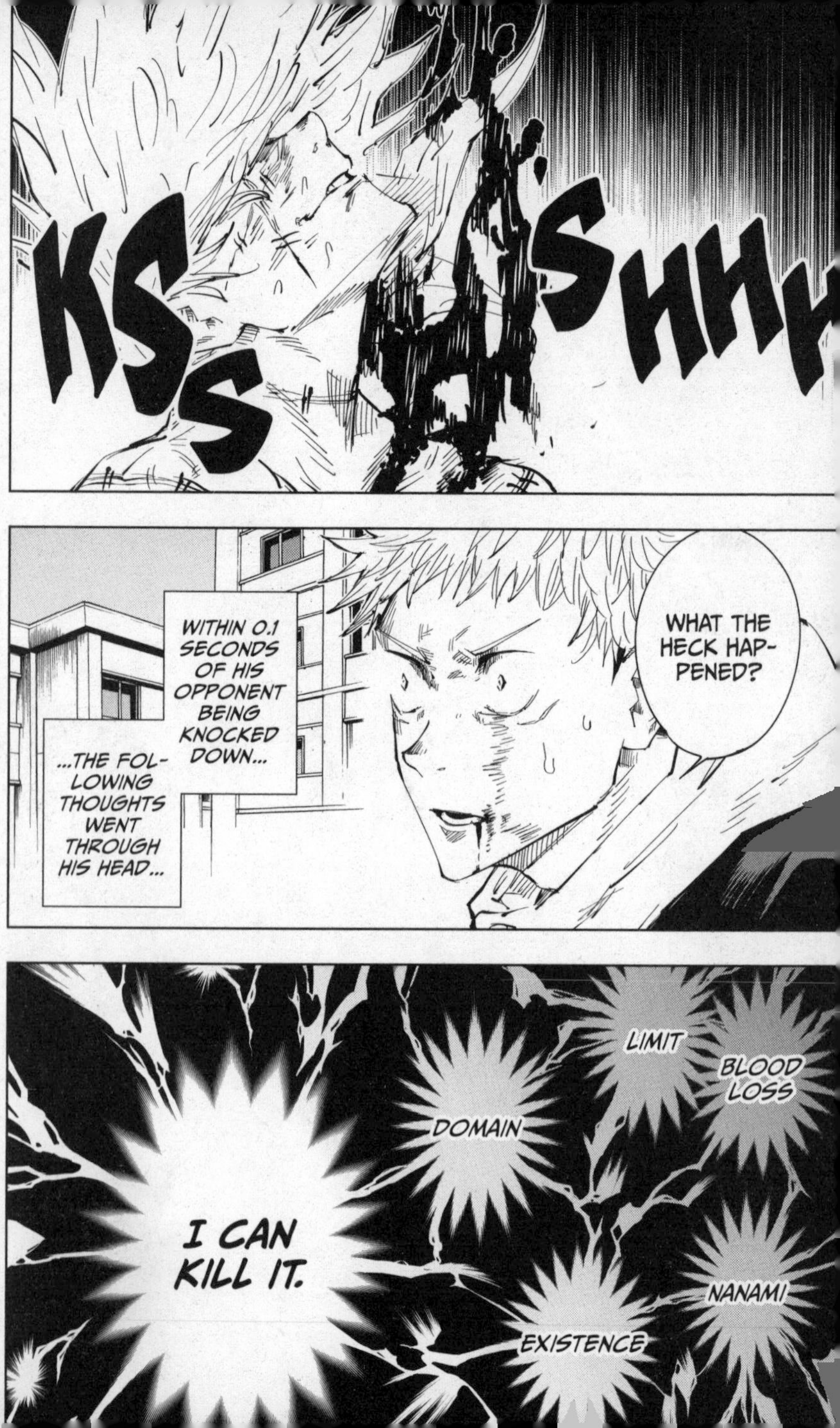
KSSSHHH
WHAT THE HECK HAPPENED?
WITHIN 0.1 SECONDS OF HIS OPPONENT BEING KNOCKED DOWN...
...THE FOLLOWING THOUGHTS WENT THROUGH HIS HEAD...
BLOOD LOSS
LIMIT
DOMAIN
NANAMI
EXISTENCE
I CAN KILL IT.

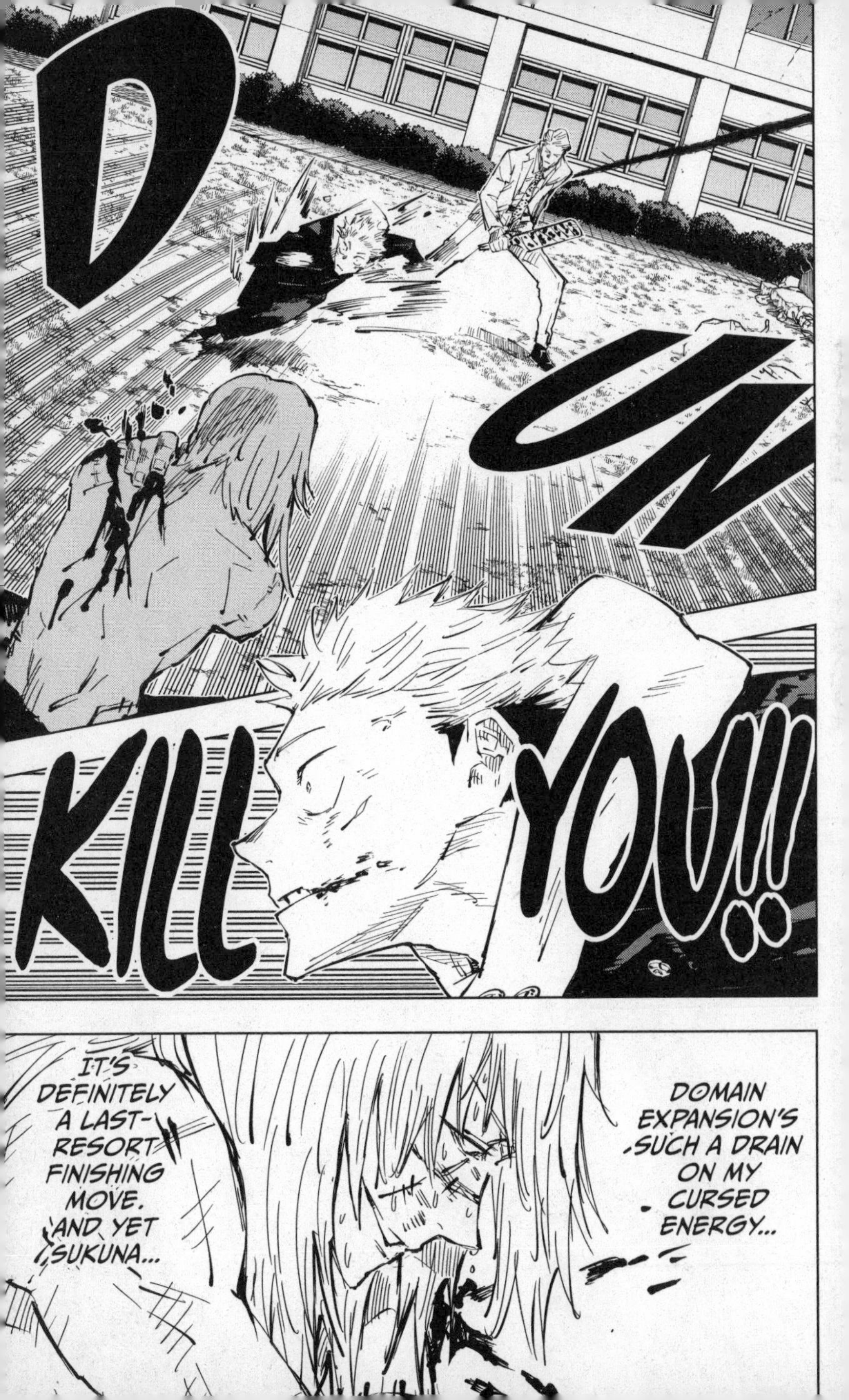
D
N
KILL YOU!!
DOMAIN EXPANSION'S SUCH A DRAIN ON MY CURSED ENERGY...
IT'S DEFINITELY A LAST-RESORT FINISHING MOVE. AND YET SUKUNA...

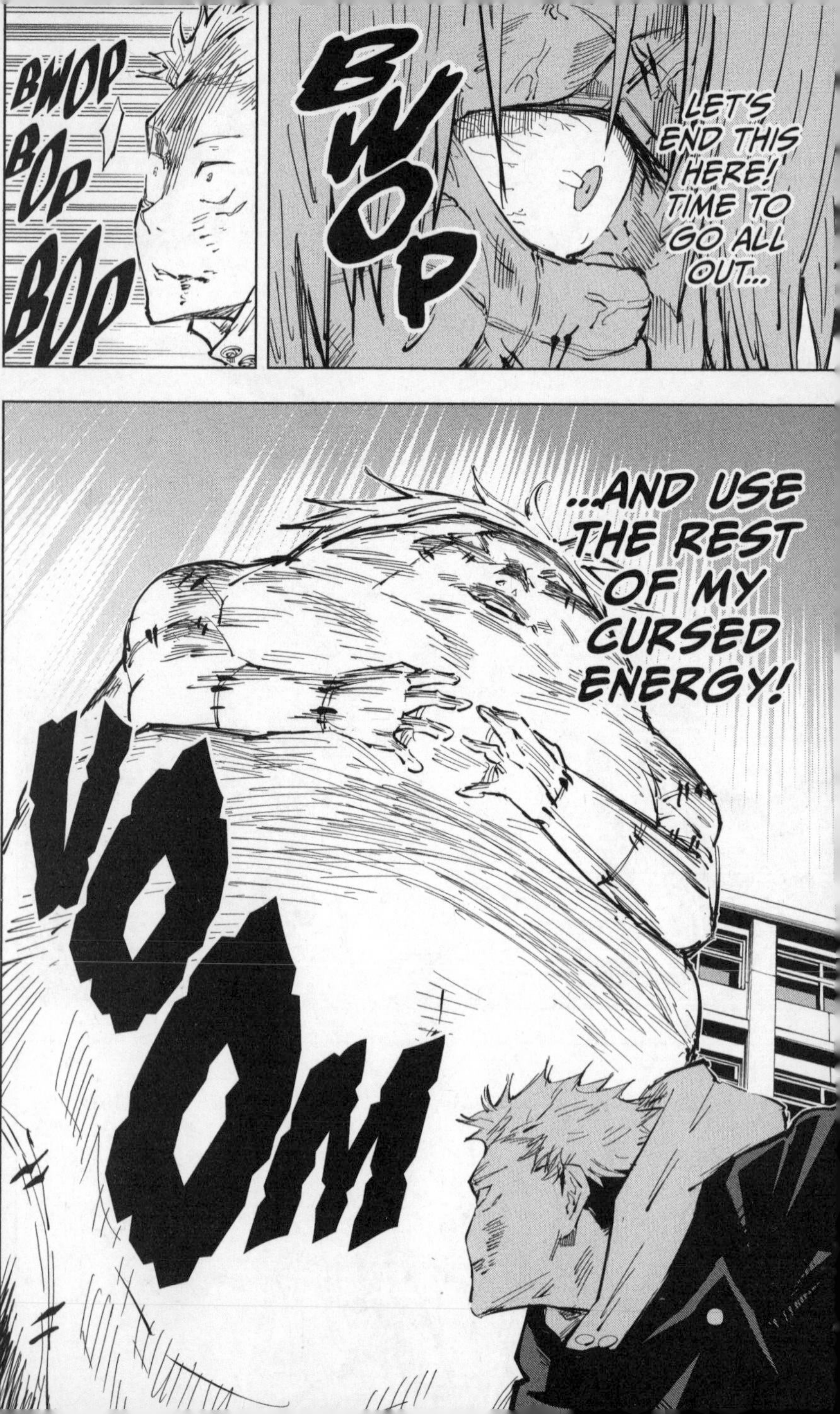
BWOP
LET'S END THIS HERE! TIME TO GO ALL OUT...
BWOP BOP BOP
...AND USE THE REST OF MY CURSED ENERGY!
VOOM

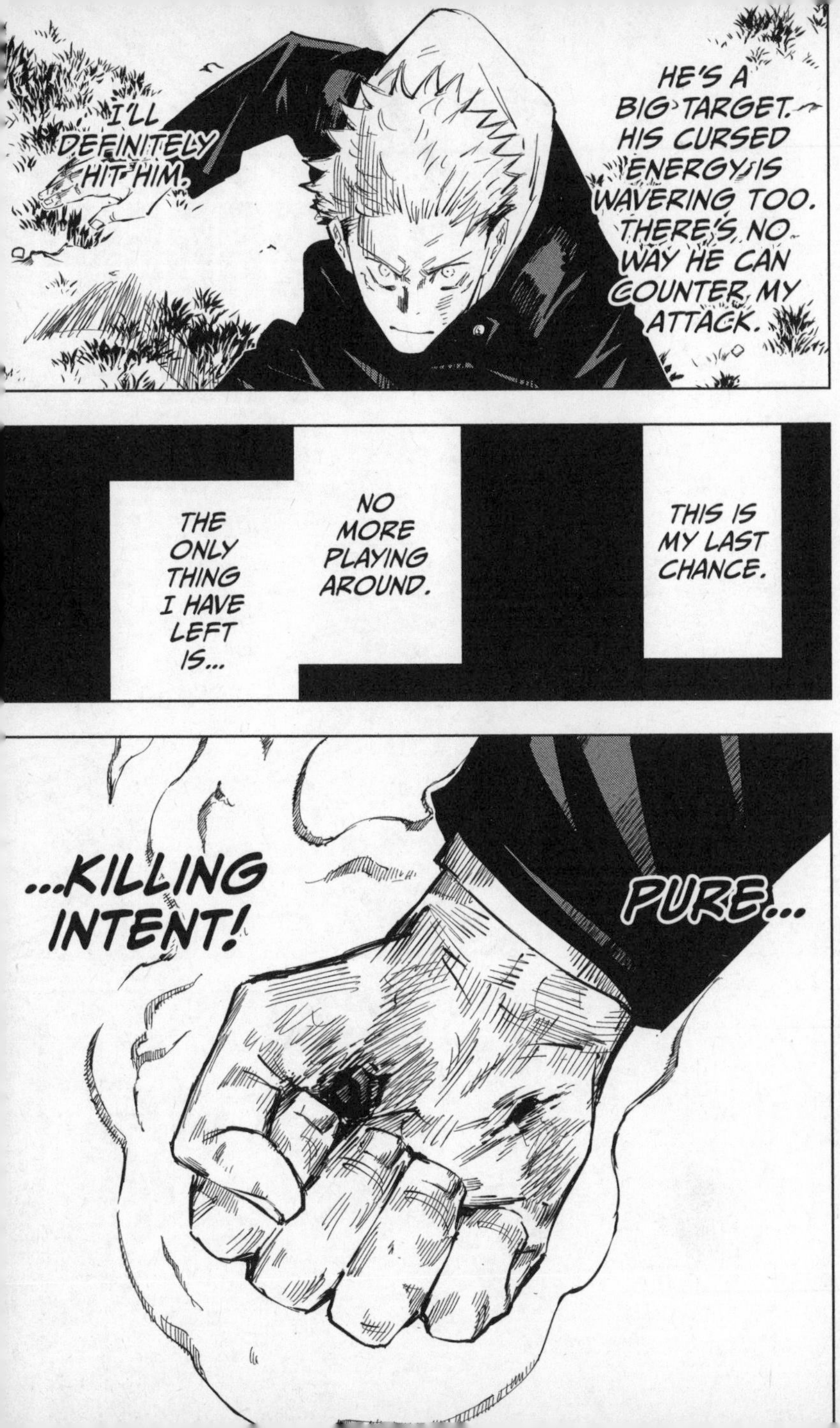
HE'S A BIG TARGET. HIS CURSED ENERGY IS WAVERING TOO. THERE'S NO WAY HE CAN COUNTER MY ATTACK.
I'LL DEFINITELY HIT HIM.
THIS IS MY LAST CHANCE.
NO MORE PLAYING AROUND.
THE ONLY THING I HAVE LEFT IS...
PURE...
...KILLING INTENT!

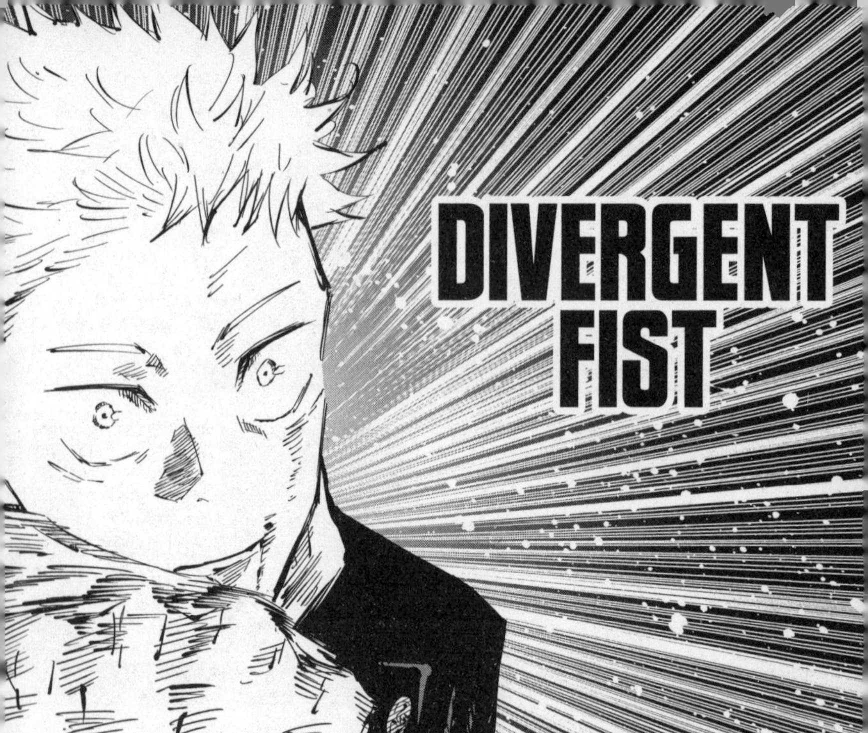
DIVERGENT FIST
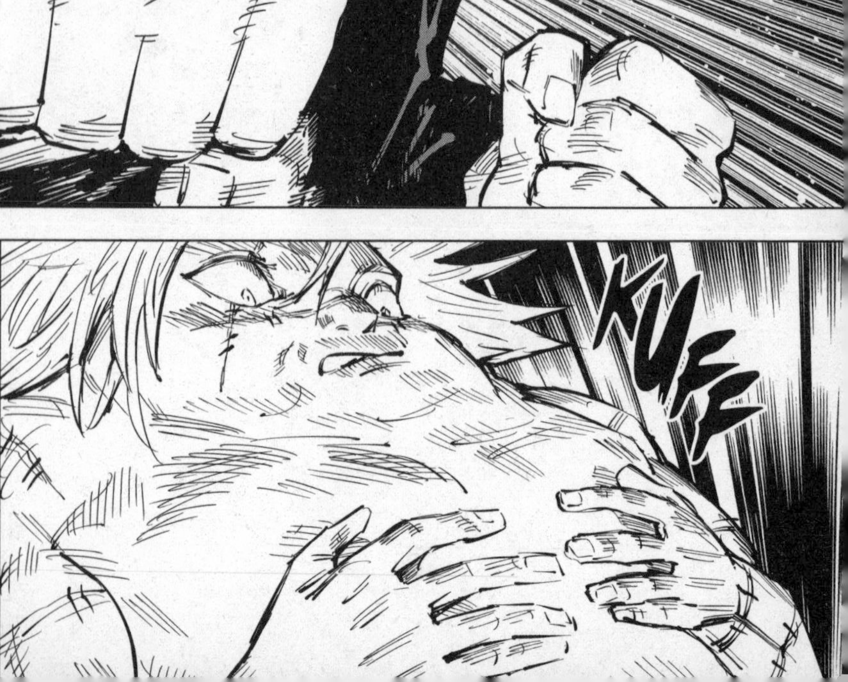
KUFF

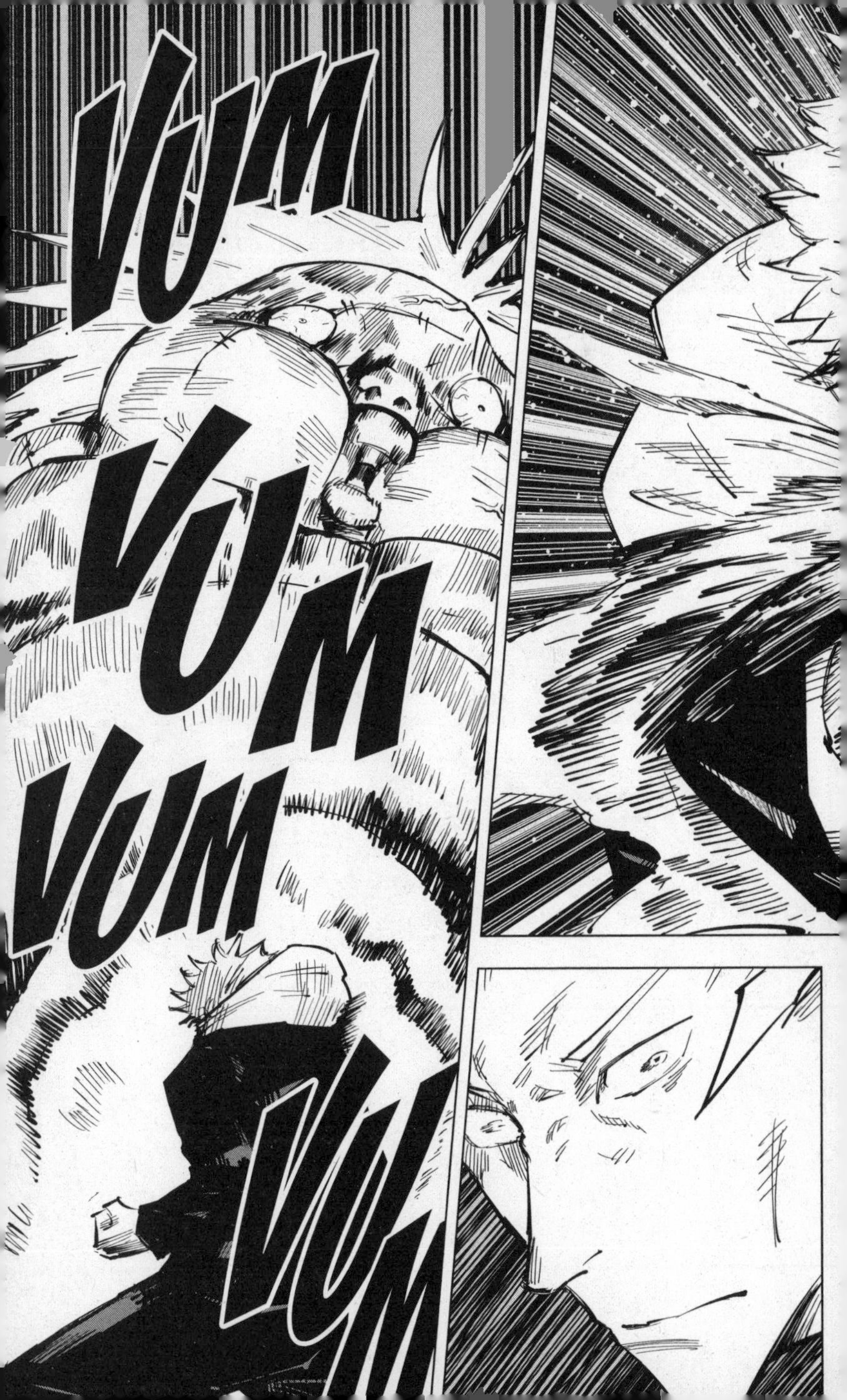
VUM
VUM
VUM
VUM

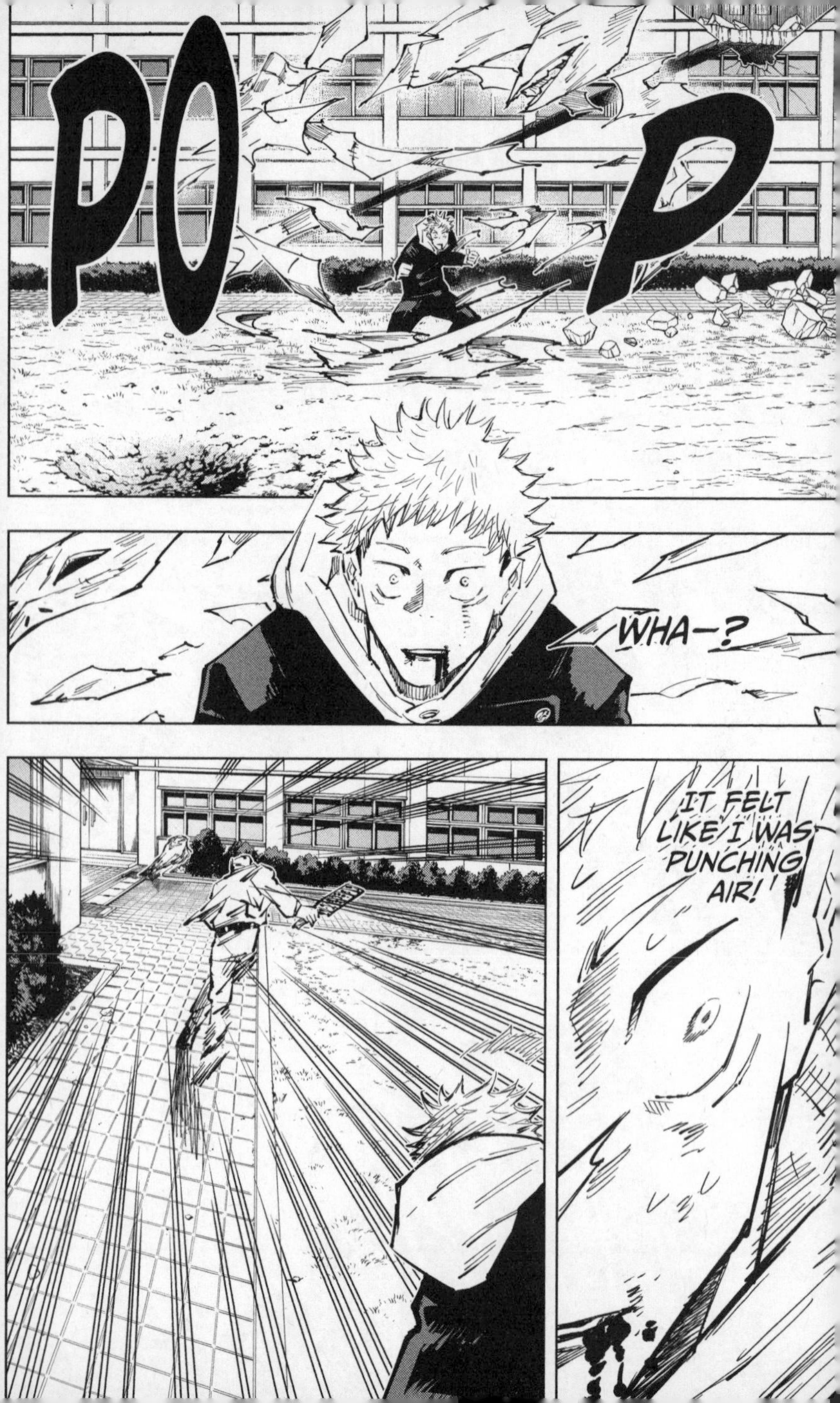
POP
WHA-?
IT FELT LIKE I WAS PUNCHING AIR!

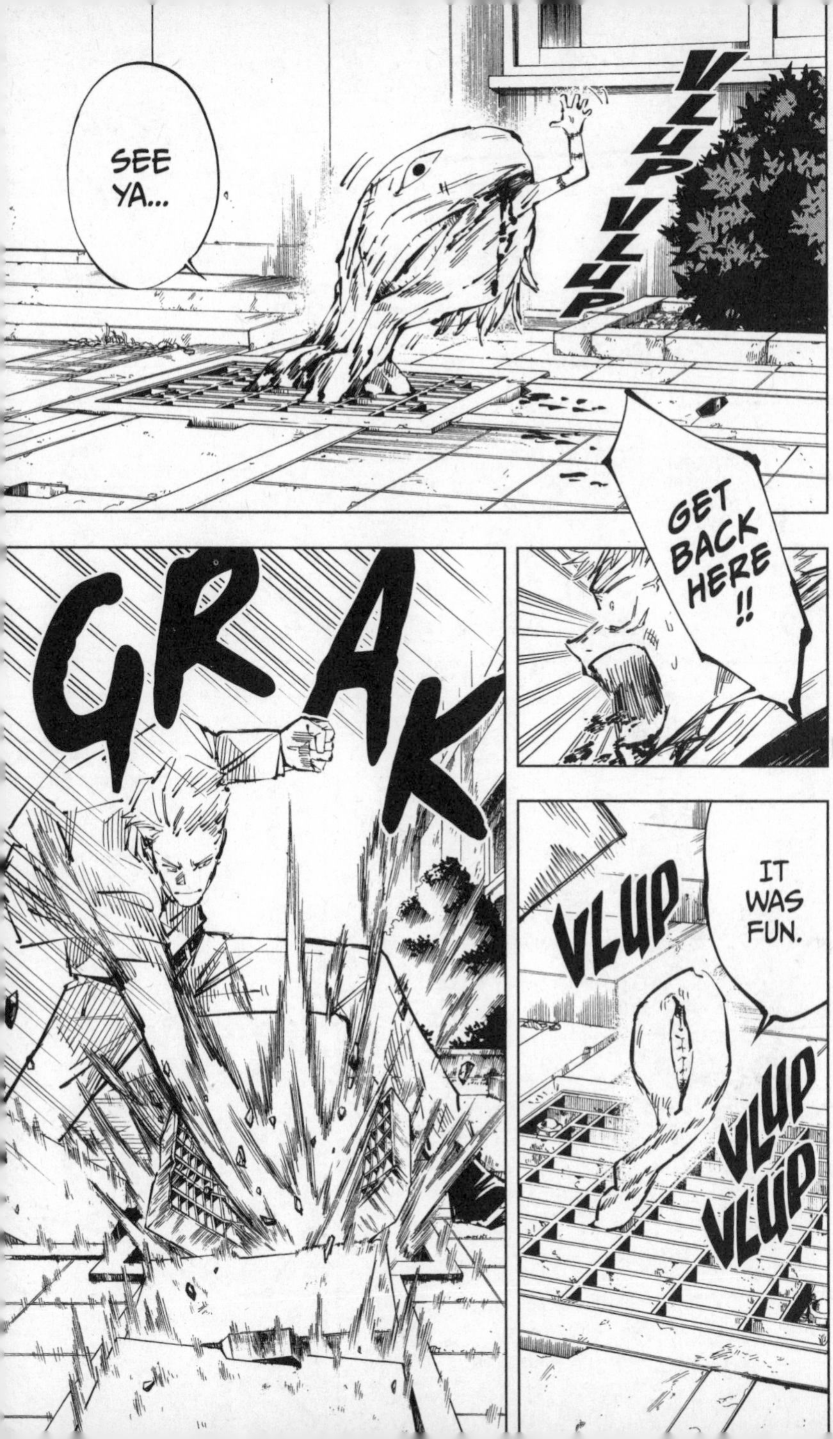
VLUP VLUP
SEE YA...
GET BACK HERE!!
IT WAS FUN.
VLUP
VLUP VLUP
GRAK

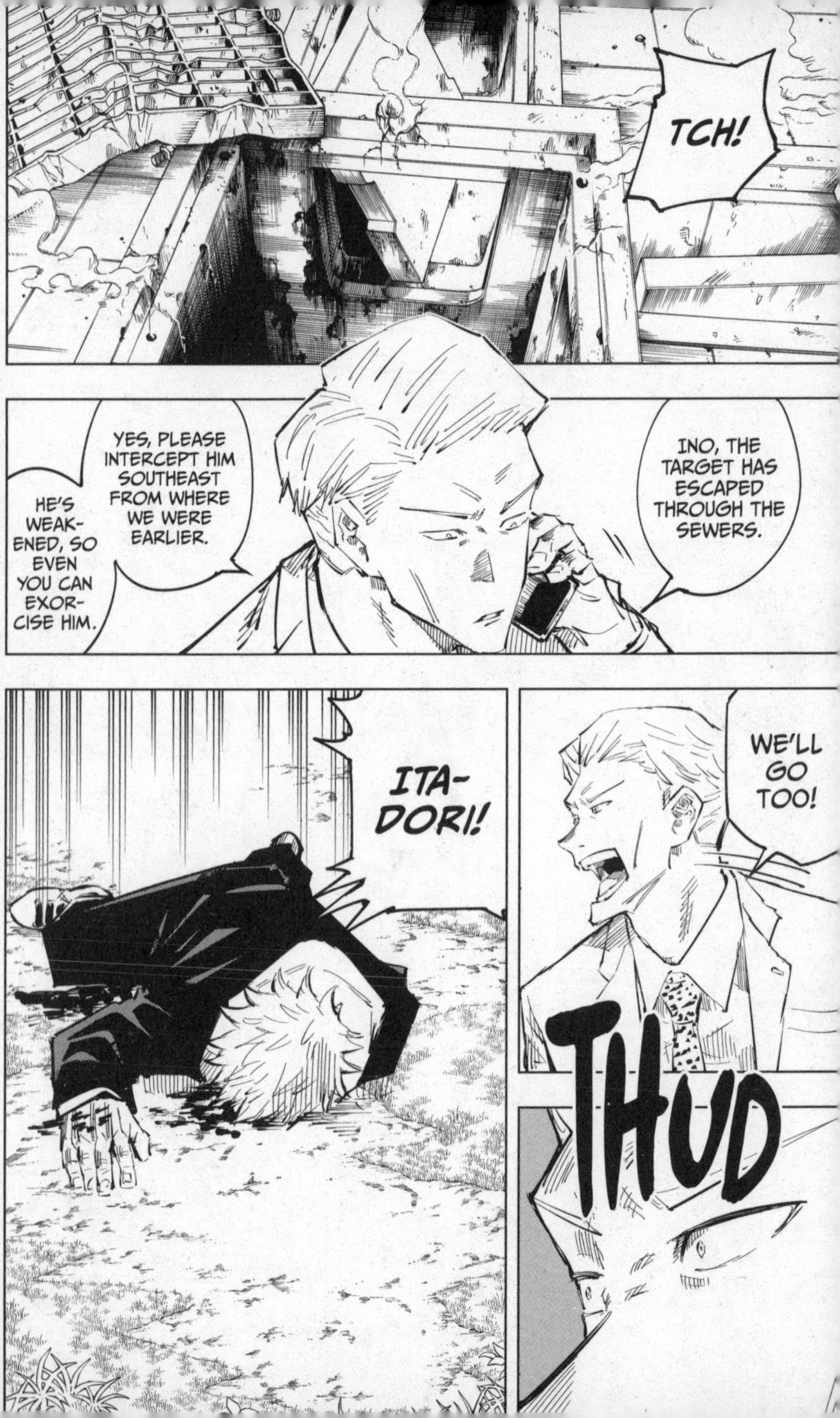
TCH!
INO, THE TARGET HAS ESCAPED THROUGH THE SEWERS.
YES, PLEASE INTERCEPT HIM SOUTHEAST FROM WHERE WE WERE EARLIER.
HE'S WEAK-ENED, SO EVEN YOU CAN EXOR-CISE HIM.
WE'LL GO TOO!
THUD
ITA-DORI!

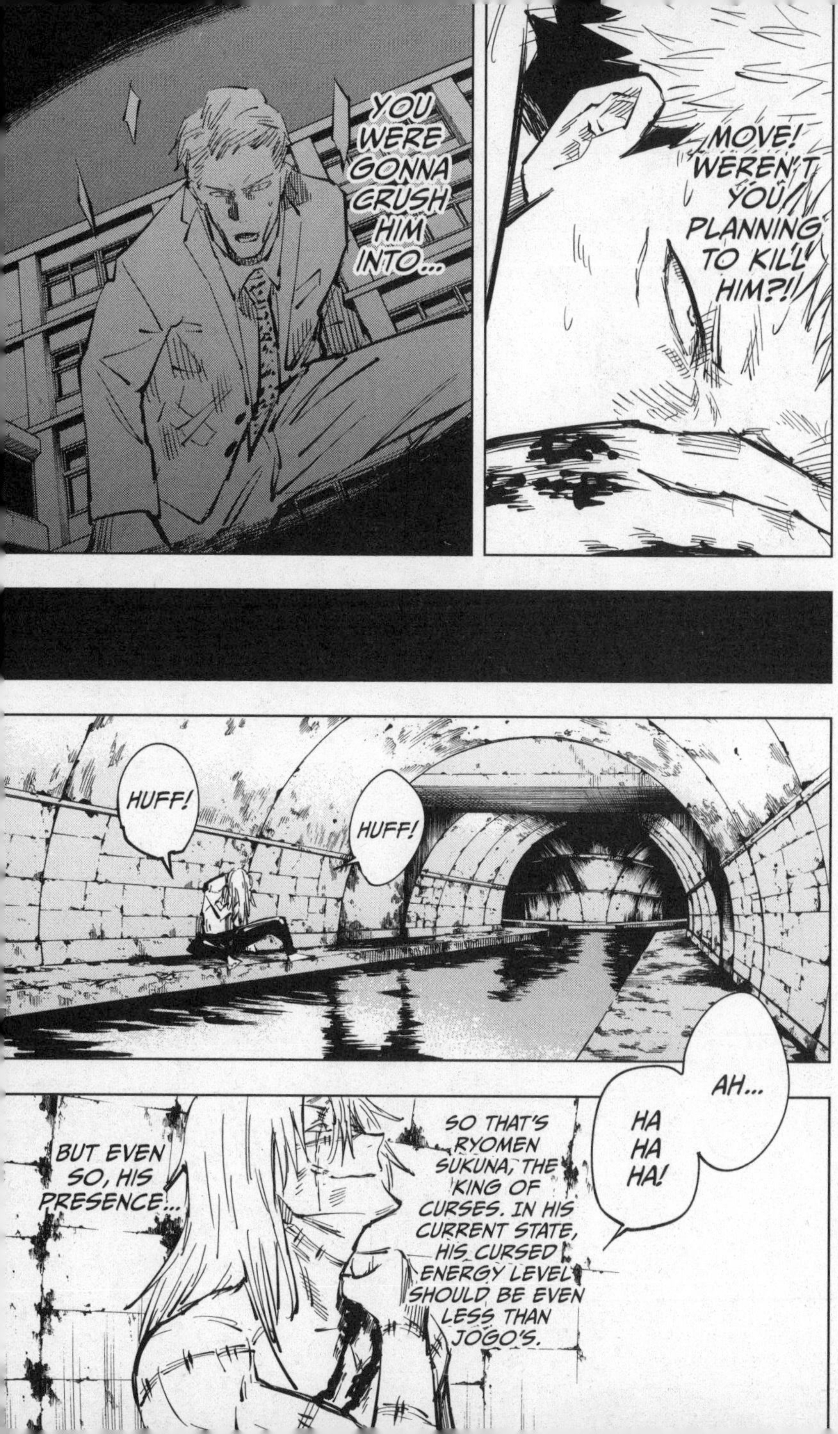
MOVE! WEREN'T YOU PLANNING TO KILL HIM?!
YOU WERE GONNA CRUSH HIM INTO...
HUFF!
HUFF!
AH... HA HA HA!
SO THAT'S RYOMEN SUKUNA, THE KING OF CURSES. IN HIS CURRENT STATE, HIS CURSED ENERGY LEVEL SHOULD BE EVEN LESS THAN JOGO'S.
BUT EVEN SO, HIS PRESENCE...

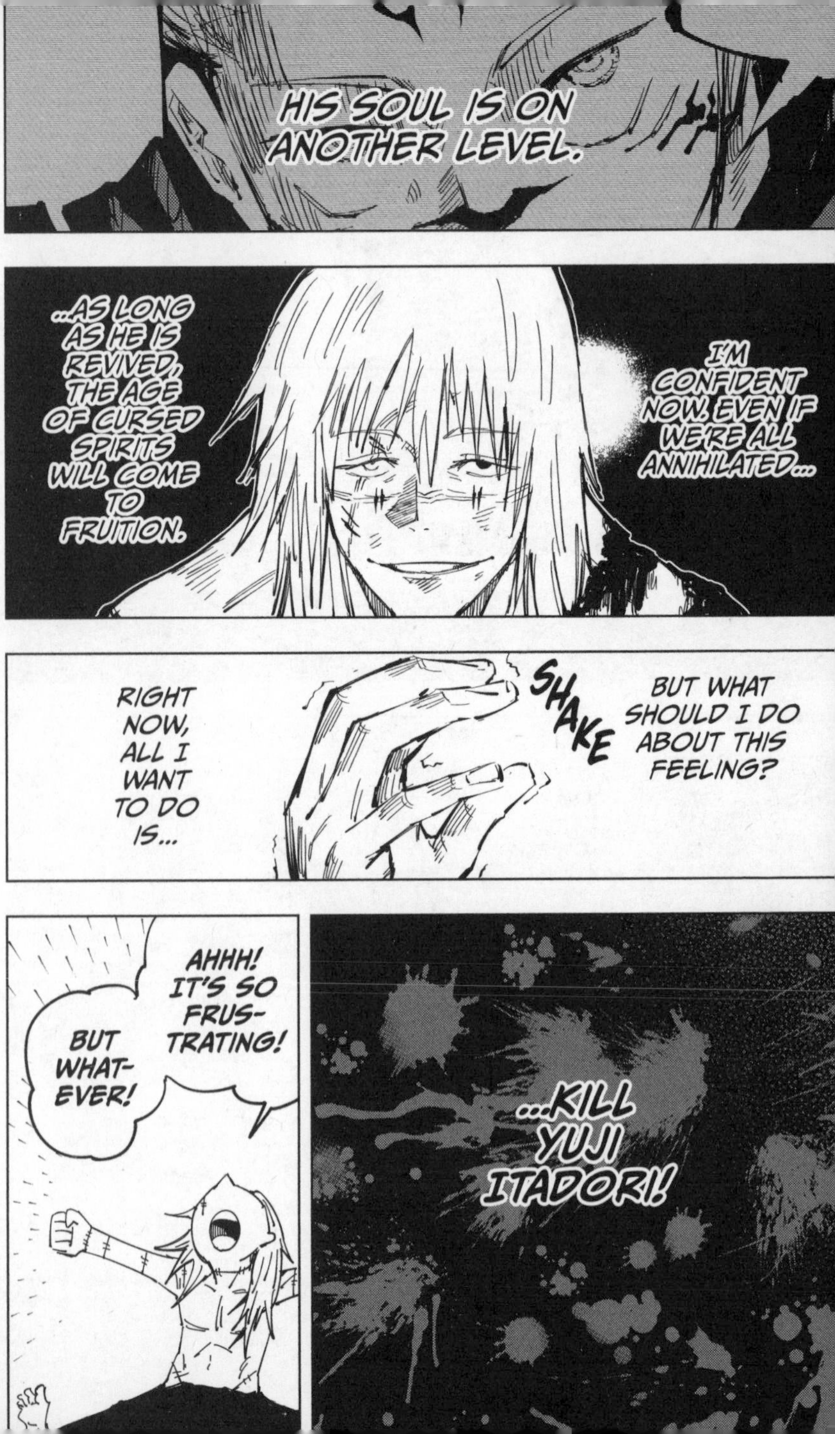
HIS SOUL IS ON ANOTHER LEVEL.
I'M CONFIDENT NOW. EVEN IF WE'RE ALL ANNIHILATED...
...AS LONG AS HE IS REVIVED, THE AGE OF CURSED SPIRITS WILL COME TO FRUITION.
BUT WHAT SHOULD I DO ABOUT THIS FEELING?
SHAKE
RIGHT NOW, ALL I WANT TO DO IS...
...KILL YUJI ITADORI!
AHHH! IT'S SO FRUS-TRATING!
BUT WHAT-EVER!

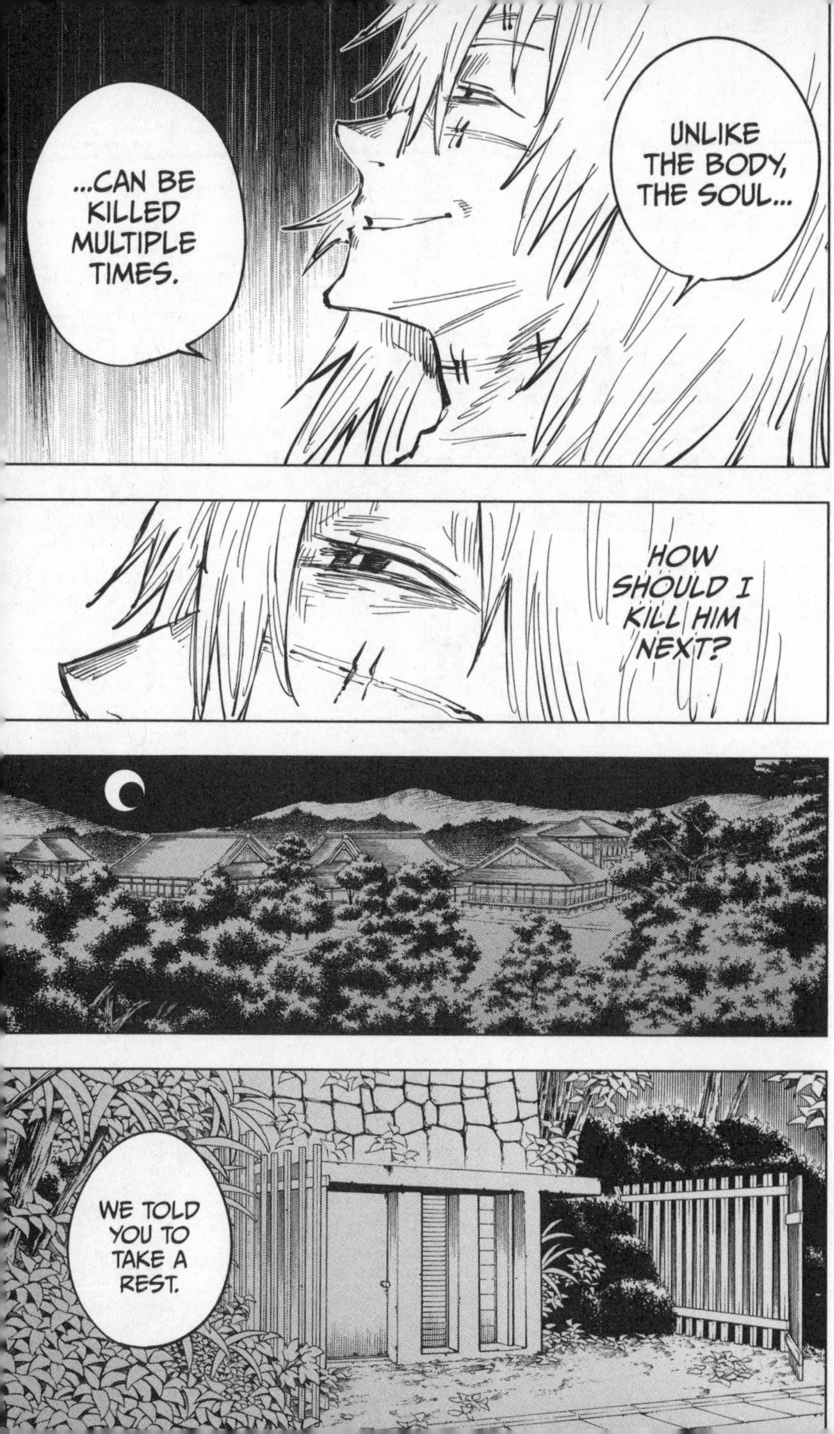
UNLIKE THE BODY, THE SOUL...
...CAN BE KILLED MULTIPLE TIMES.
HOW SHOULD I KILL HIM NEXT?
WE TOLD YOU TO TAKE A REST.

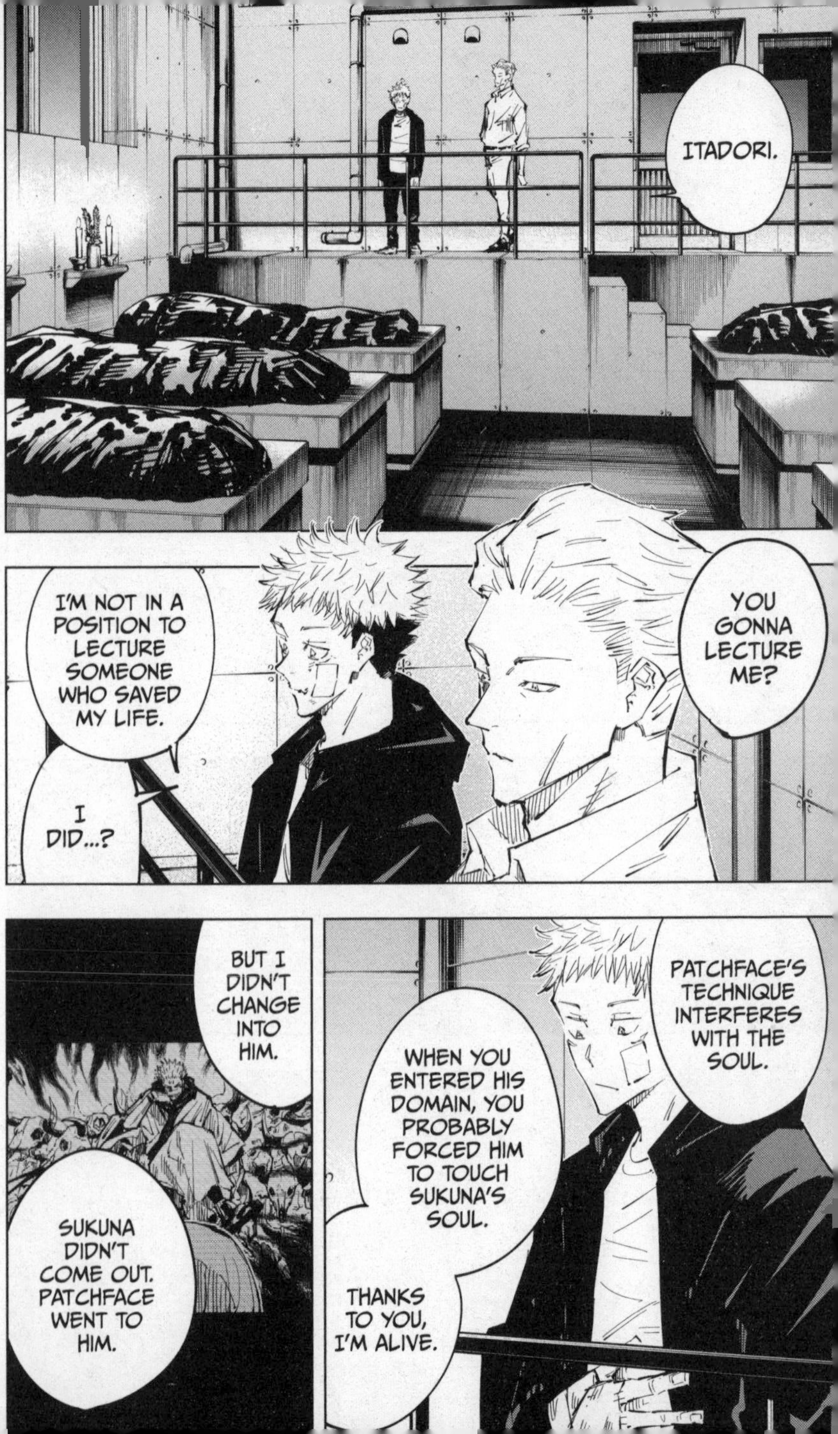
ITADORI.
YOU GONNA LECTURE ME?
I'M NOT IN A POSITION TO LECTURE SOMEONE WHO SAVED MY LIFE.
I DID...?
PATCHFACE'S TECHNIQUE INTERFERES WITH THE SOUL.
WHEN YOU ENTERED HIS DOMAIN, YOU PROBABLY FORCED HIM TO TOUCH SUKUNA'S SOUL.
THANKS TO YOU, I'M ALIVE.
BUT I DIDN'T CHANGE INTO HIM.
SUKUNA DIDN'T COME OUT. PATCHFACE WENT TO HIM.

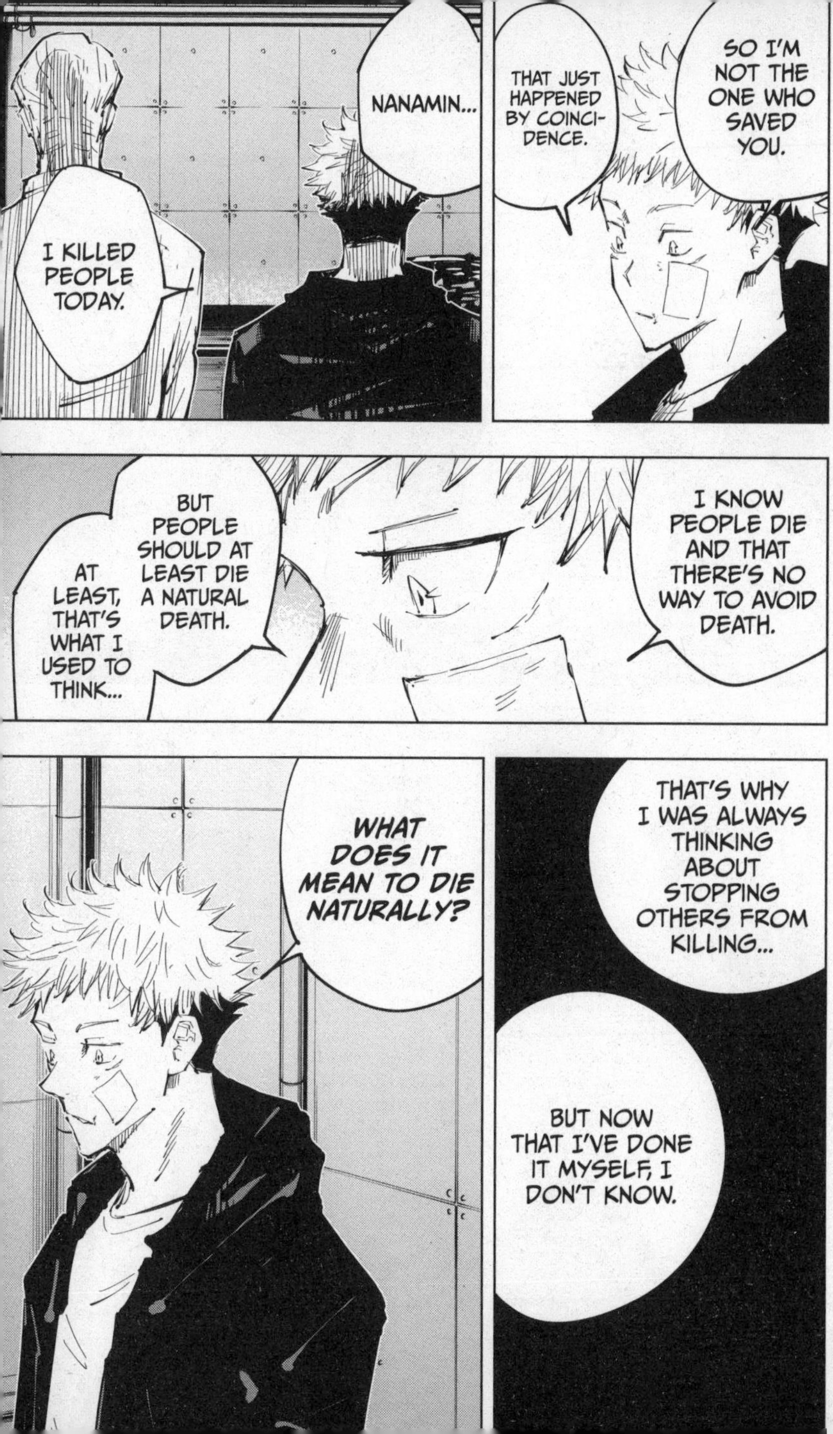
SO I'M NOT THE ONE WHO SAVED YOU.
THAT JUST HAPPENED BY COINCI-DENCE.
NANAMIN...
I KILLED PEOPLE TODAY.
I KNOW PEOPLE DIE AND THAT THERE'S NO WAY TO AVOID DEATH.
BUT PEOPLE SHOULD AT LEAST DIE A NATURAL DEATH.
AT LEAST, THAT'S WHAT I USED TO THINK...
THAT'S WHY I WAS ALWAYS THINKING ABOUT STOPPING OTHERS FROM KILLING...
BUT NOW THAT I'VE DONE IT MYSELF, I DON'T KNOW.
WHAT DOES IT MEAN TO DIE NATURALLY?

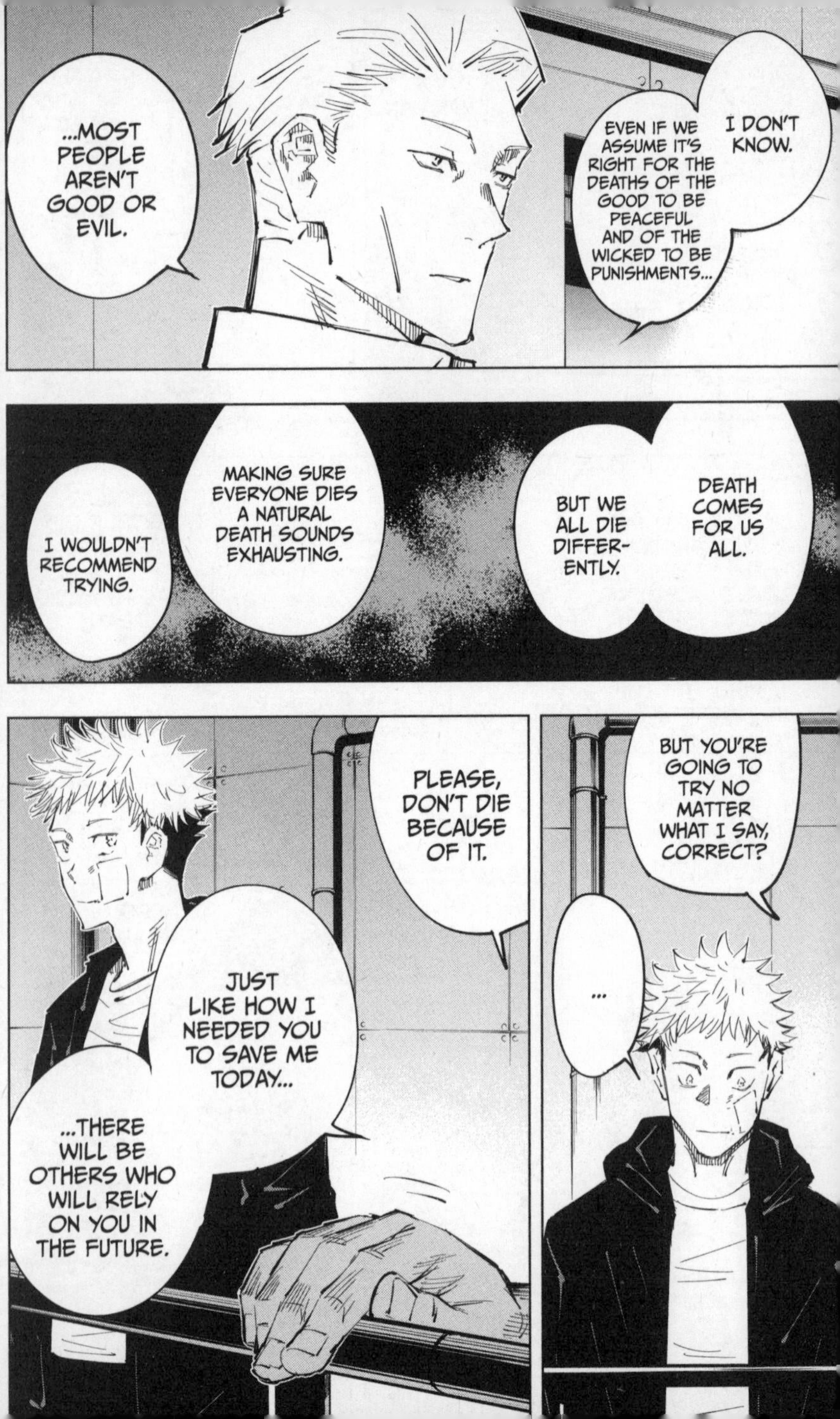
I DON'T KNOW.
EVEN IF WE ASSUME IT'S RIGHT FOR THE DEATHS OF THE GOOD TO BE PEACEFUL AND OF THE WICKED TO BE PUNISHMENTS...
...MOST PEOPLE AREN'T GOOD OR EVIL.
DEATH COMES FOR US ALL.
BUT WE ALL DIE DIFFER-ENTLY.
MAKING SURE EVERYONE DIES A NATURAL DEATH SOUNDS EXHAUSTING.
I WOULDN'T RECOMMEND TRYING.
BUT YOU'RE GOING TO TRY NO MATTER WHAT I SAY, CORRECT?
...
PLEASE, DON'T DIE BECAUSE OF IT.
JUST LIKE HOW I NEEDED YOU TO SAVE ME TODAY...
...THERE WILL BE OTHERS WHO WILL RELY ON YOU IN THE FUTURE.

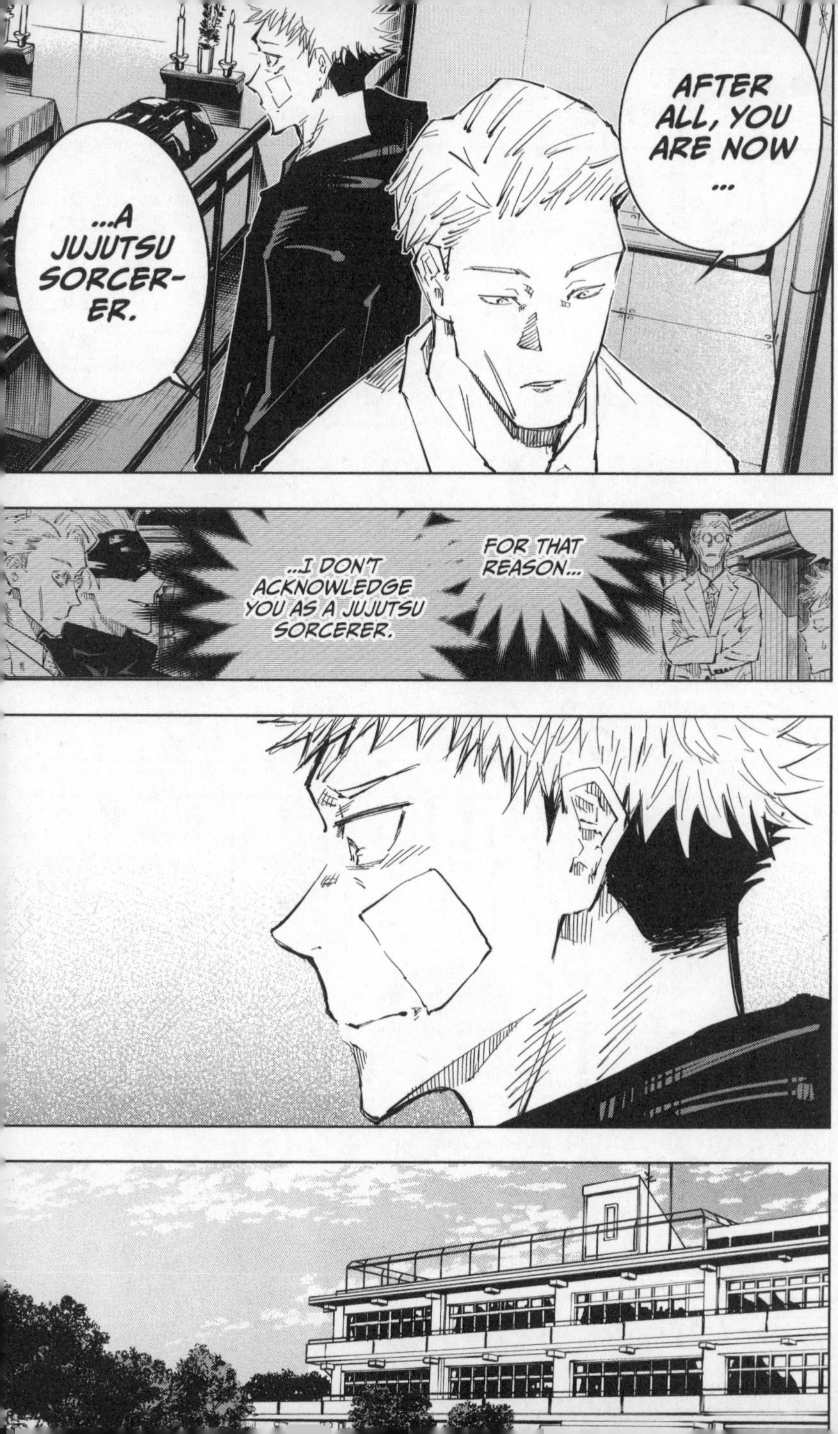
AFTER ALL, YOU ARE NOW ...
...A JUJUTSU SORCERER.
FOR THAT REASON...
...I DON'T ACKNOWLEDGE YOU AS A JUJUTSU SORCERER.

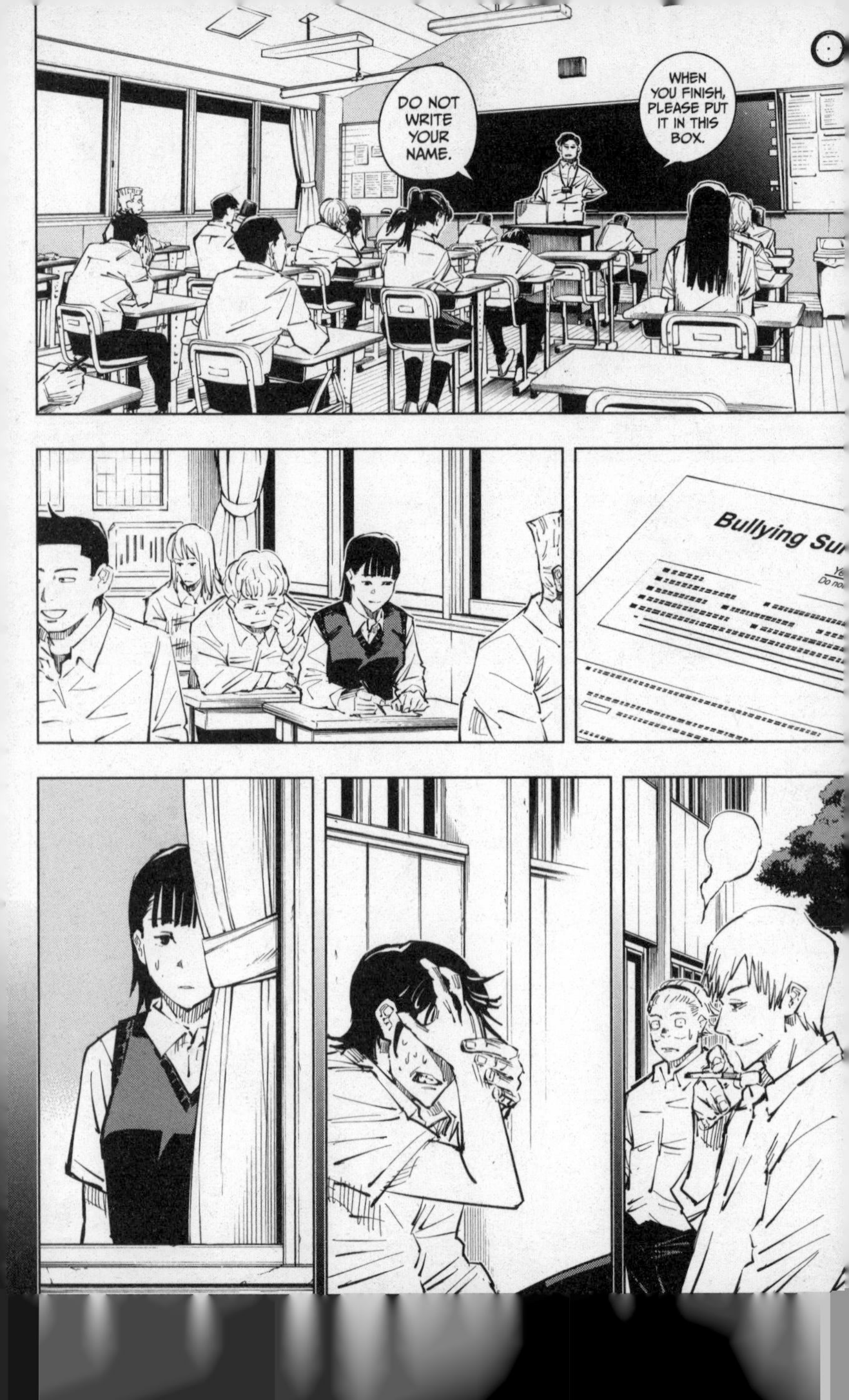
WHEN YOU FINISH, PLEASE PUT IT IN THIS BOX.
DO NOT WRITE YOUR NAME.

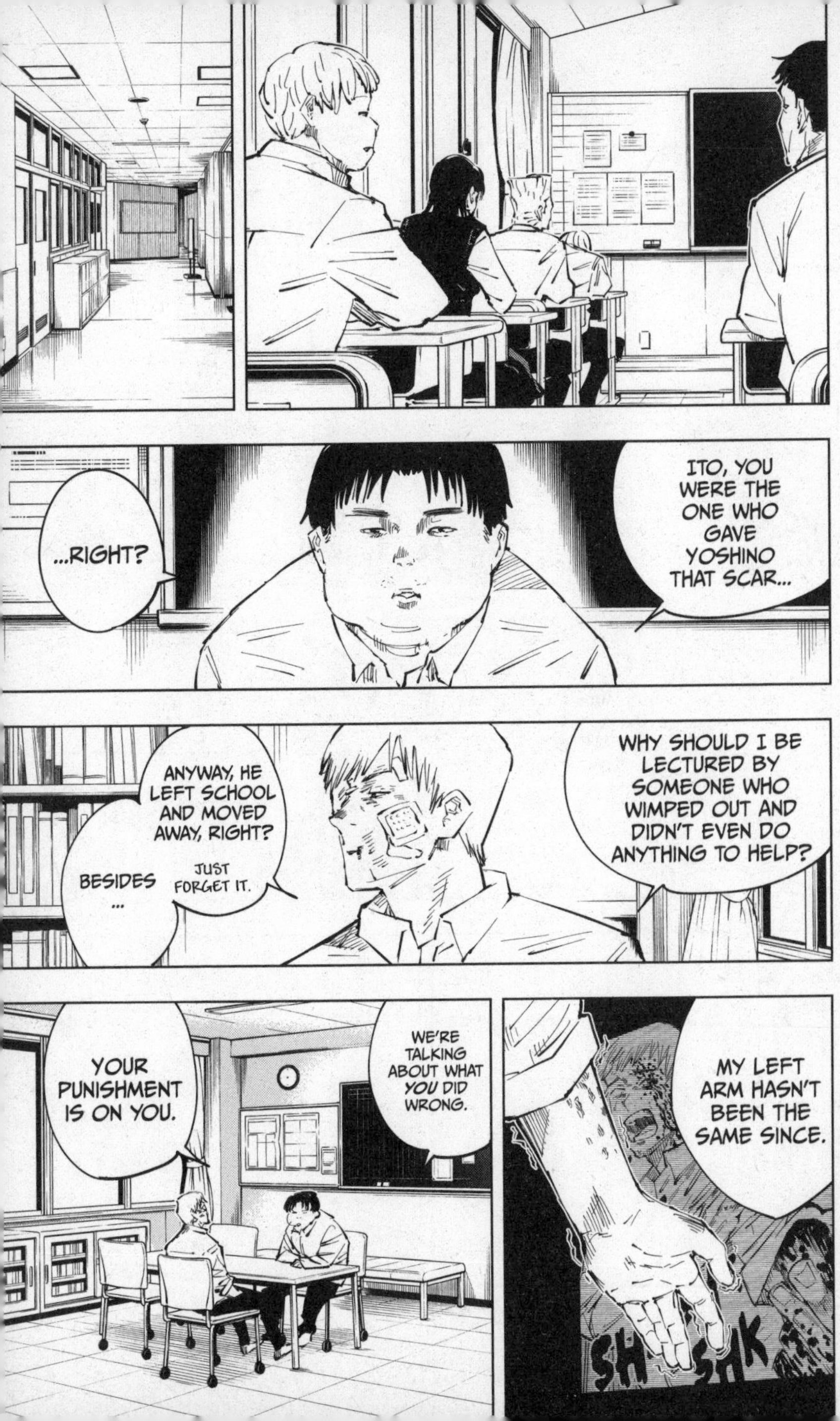

ITO, YOU WERE THE ONE WHO GAVE YOSHINO THAT SCAR...
...RIGHT?
WHY SHOULD I BE LECTURED BY SOMEONE WHO WIMPED OUT AND DIDN'T EVEN DO ANYTHING TO HELP?
ANYWAY, HE LEFT SCHOOL AND MOVED AWAY, RIGHT?
JUST FORGET IT.
BESIDES...
MY LEFT ARM HASN'T BEEN THE SAME SINCE.
SHK SHK
WE'RE TALKING ABOUT WHAT YOU DID WRONG.
YOUR PUNISHMENT IS ON YOU.

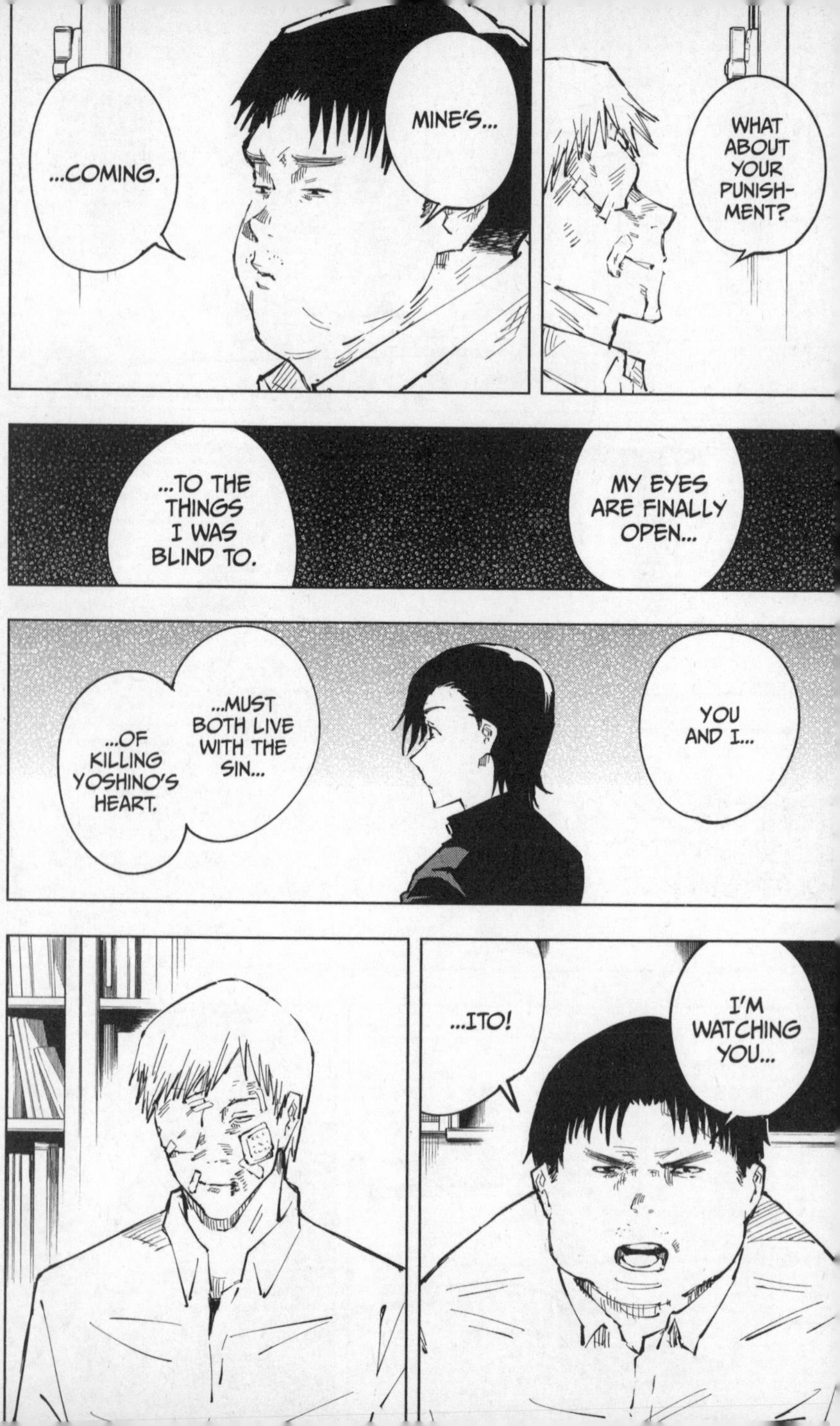
WHAT ABOUT YOUR PUNISHMENT?
MINE'S...
...COMING.
MY EYES ARE FINALLY OPEN...
...TO THE THINGS I WAS BLIND TO.
YOU AND I...
...MUST BOTH LIVE WITH THE SIN...
...OF KILLING YOSHINO'S HEART.
I'M WATCHING YOU...
...ITO!

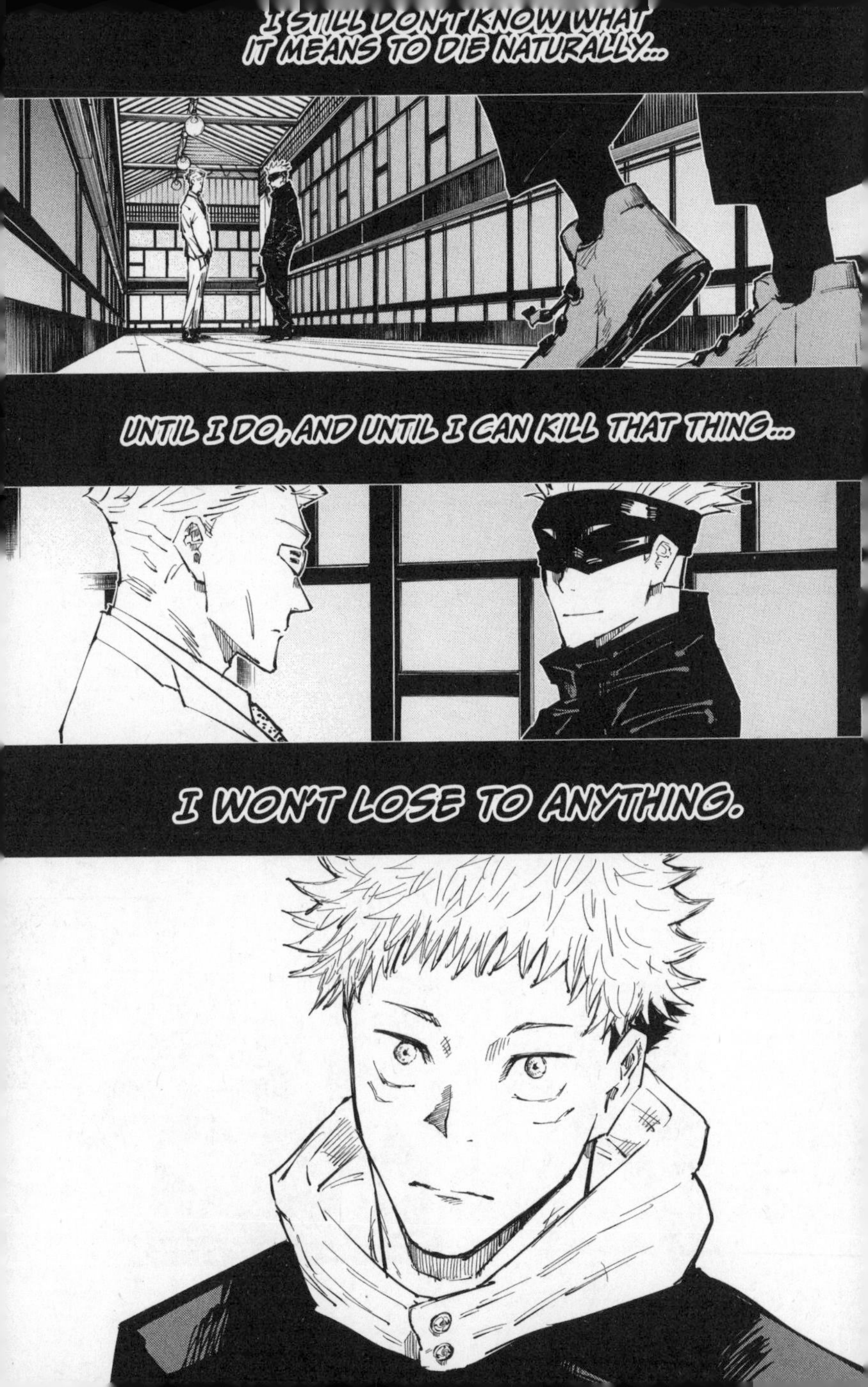
I STILL DON'T KNOW WHAT IT MEANS TO DIE NATURALLY...
UNTIL I DO, AND UNTIL I CAN KILL THAT THING...
I WON'T LOSE TO ANYTHING.

MAHITO'S FIGHT EXPLANATION, PART 3

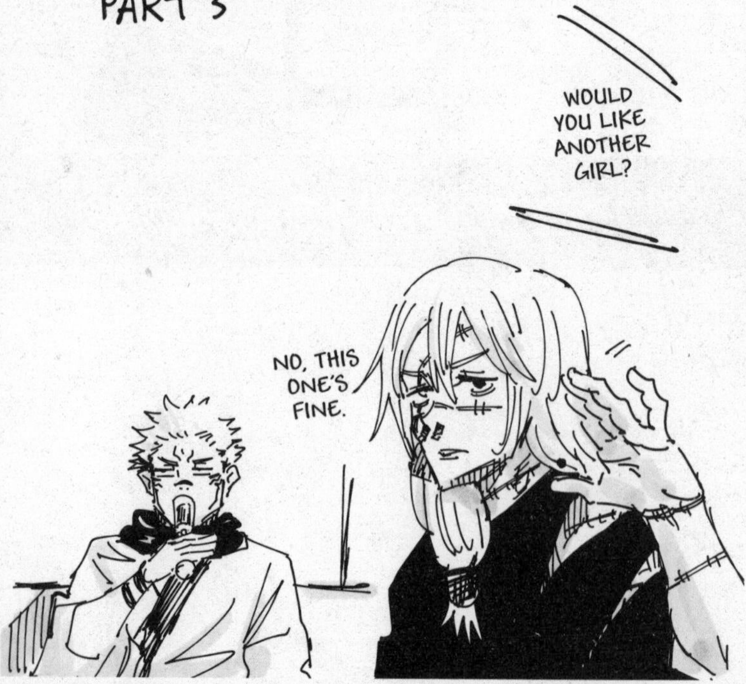
WOULD YOU LIKE ANOTHER GIRL?
NO, THIS ONE'S FINE.

CHAPTER 32: INTROSPECTION

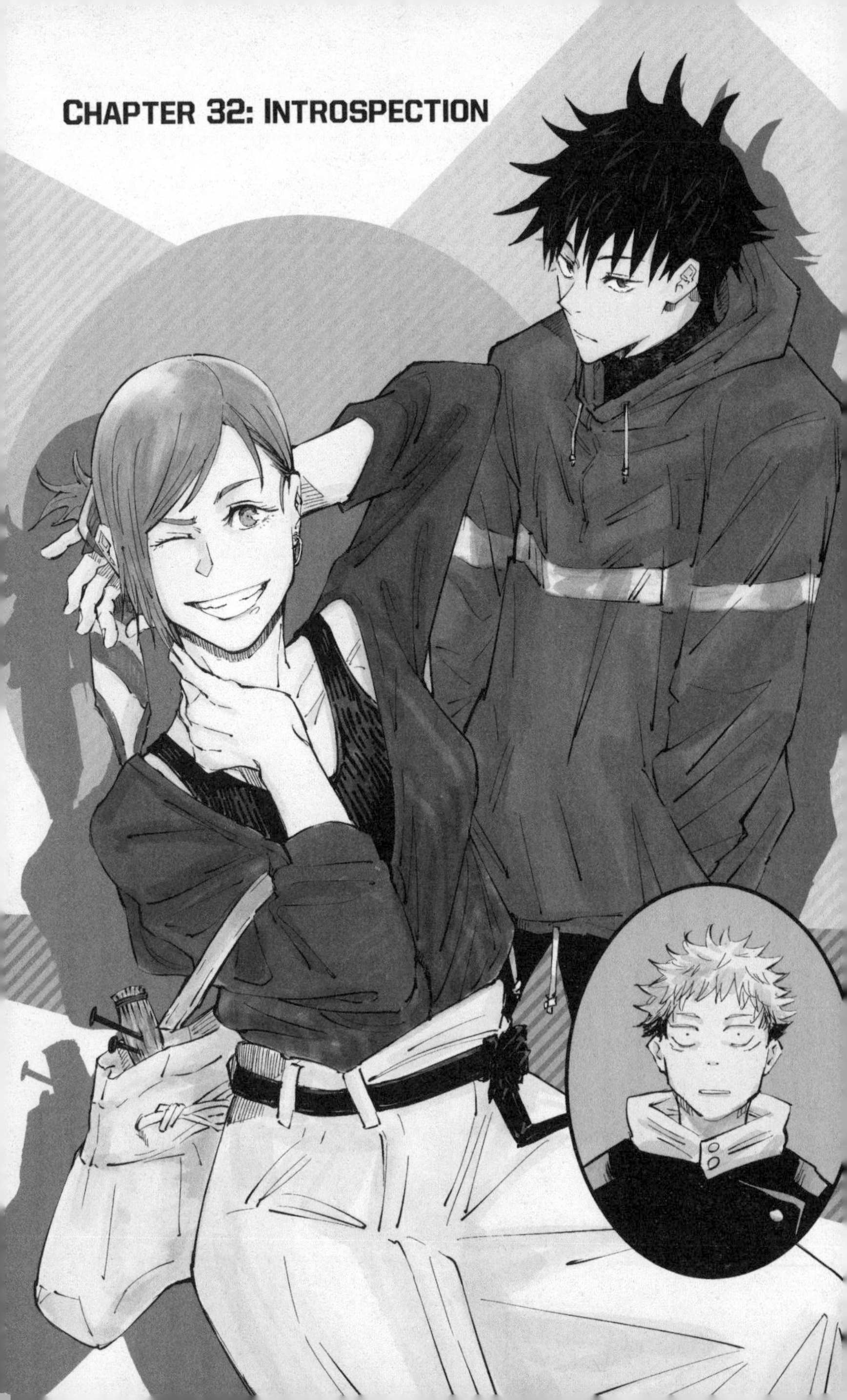

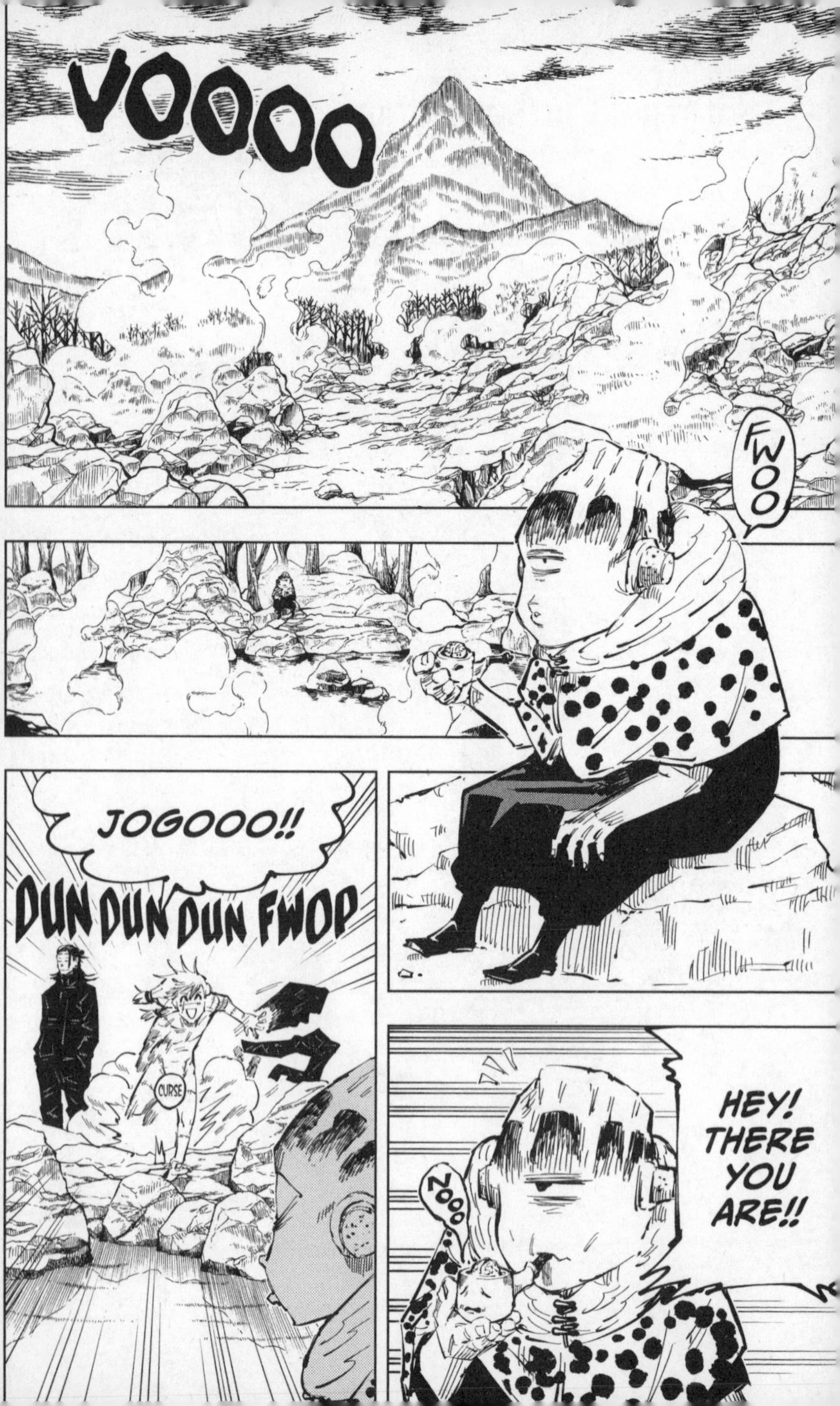
VOOOO
FWOO
HEY! THERE YOU ARE!!
NOOO
JOGOOO!!
DUN DUN DUN FWOP
CURSE

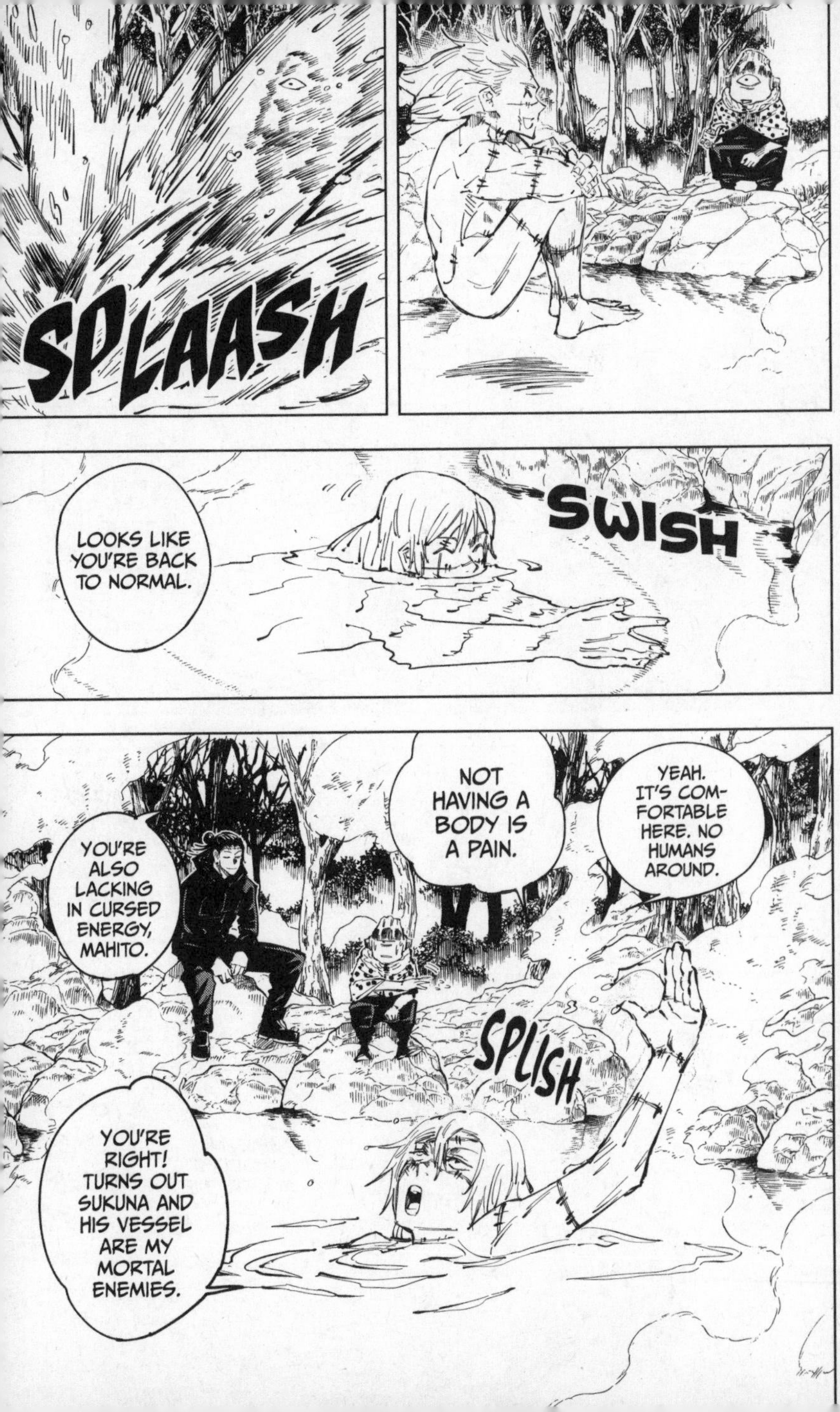
SPLAASH
SWISH
LOOKS LIKE YOU'RE BACK TO NORMAL.
YEAH. IT'S COMFORTABLE HERE. NO HUMANS AROUND.
NOT HAVING A BODY IS A PAIN.
YOU'RE ALSO LACKING IN CURSED ENERGY, MAHITO.
SPLISH
YOU'RE RIGHT! TURNS OUT SUKUNA AND HIS VESSEL ARE MY MORTAL ENEMIES.

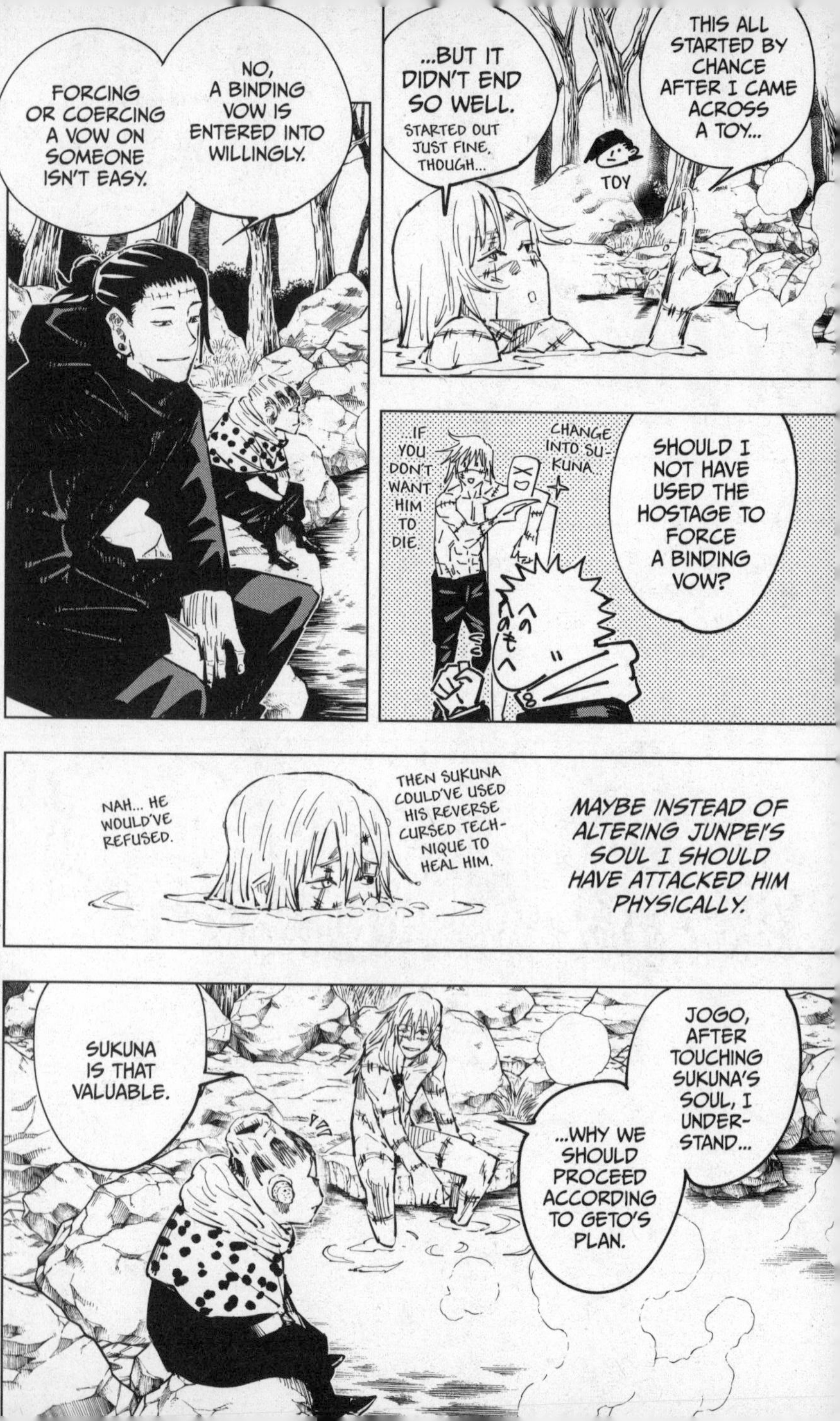
THIS ALL STARTED BY CHANCE AFTER I CAME ACROSS A TOY...
TOY
...BUT IT DIDN'T END SO WELL.
STARTED OUT JUST FINE, THOUGH...
SHOULD I NOT HAVE USED THE HOSTAGE TO FORCE A BINDING VOW?
CHANGE INTO SUKUNA.
IF YOU DON'T WANT HIM TO DIE.
NO, A BINDING VOW IS ENTERED INTO WILLINGLY.
FORCING OR COERCING A VOW ON SOMEONE ISN'T EASY.
MAYBE INSTEAD OF ALTERING JUNPEI'S SOUL I SHOULD HAVE ATTACKED HIM PHYSICALLY.
THEN SUKUNA COULD'VE USED HIS REVERSE CURSED TECH-NIQUE TO HEAL HIM.
NAH... HE WOULD'VE REFUSED.
JOGO, AFTER TOUCHING SUKUNA'S SOUL, I UNDER-STAND...
...WHY WE SHOULD PROCEED ACCORDING TO GETO'S PLAN.
SUKUNA IS THAT VALUABLE.

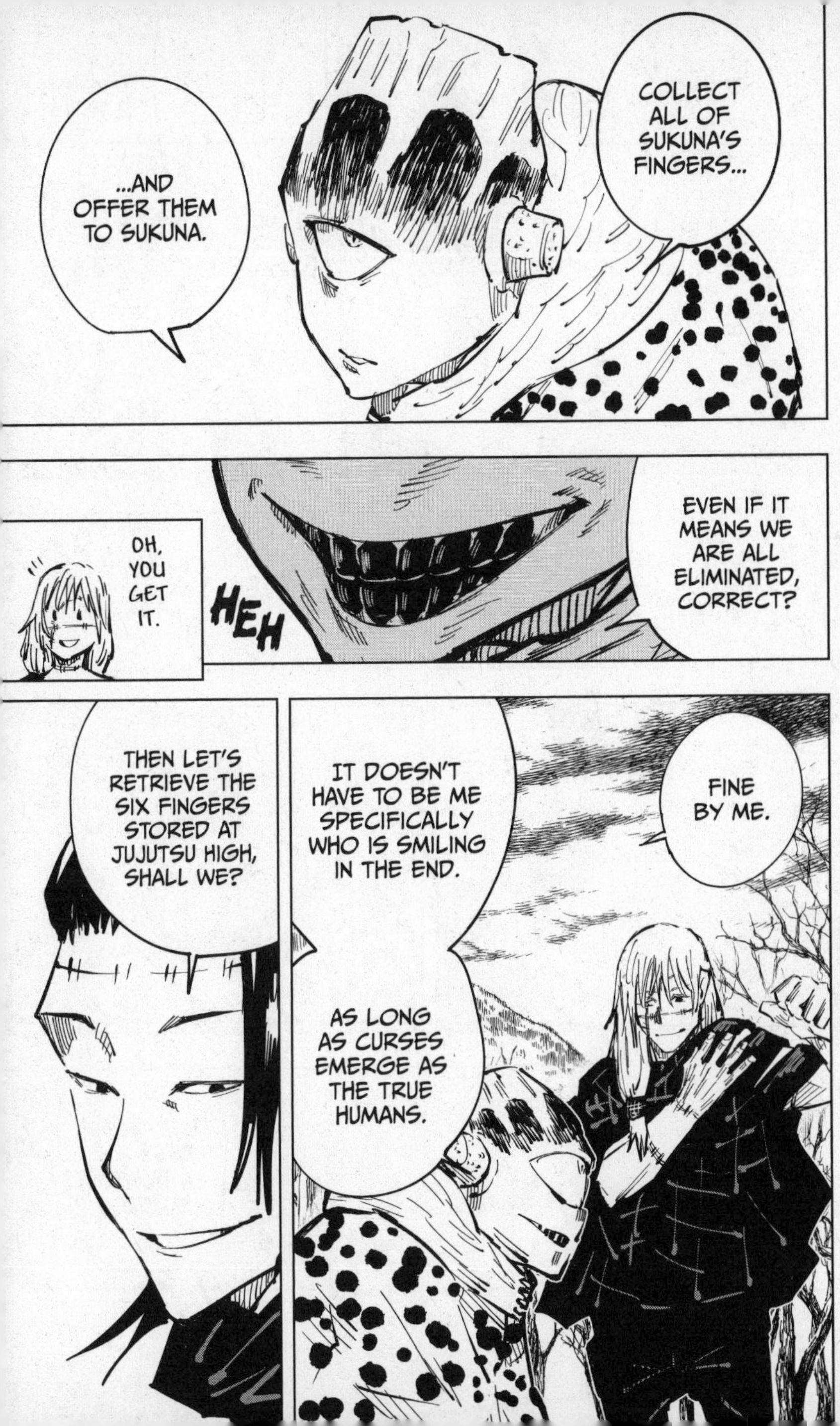
COLLECT ALL OF SUKUNA'S FINGERS...
...AND OFFER THEM TO SUKUNA.
EVEN IF IT MEANS WE ARE ALL ELIMINATED, CORRECT?
HEH
OH, YOU GET IT.
FINE BY ME.
IT DOESN'T HAVE TO BE ME SPECIFICALLY WHO IS SMILING IN THE END.
AS LONG AS CURSES EMERGE AS THE TRUE HUMANS.
THEN LET'S RETRIEVE THE SIX FINGERS STORED AT JUJUTSU HIGH, SHALL WE?

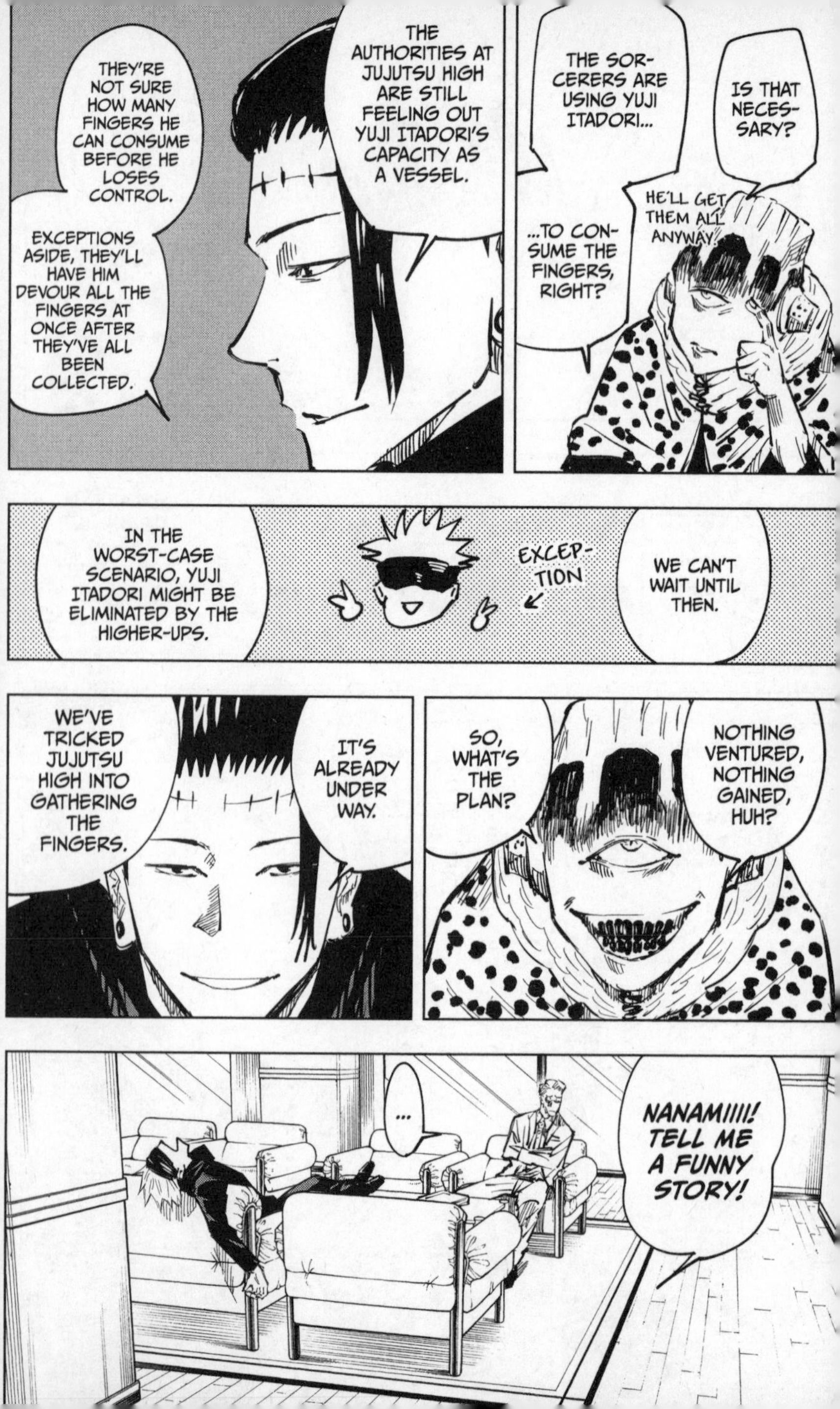
THE SORCERERS ARE USING YUJI ITADORI...
...TO CONSUME THE FINGERS, RIGHT?
IS THAT NECESSARY?
HE'LL GET THEM ALL ANYWAY.
THE AUTHORITIES AT JUJUTSU HIGH ARE STILL FEELING OUT YUJI ITADORI'S CAPACITY AS A VESSEL.
THEY'RE NOT SURE HOW MANY FINGERS HE CAN CONSUME BEFORE HE LOSES CONTROL.
EXCEPTIONS ASIDE, THEY'LL HAVE HIM DEVOUR ALL THE FINGERS AT ONCE AFTER THEY'VE ALL BEEN COLLECTED.
WE CAN'T WAIT UNTIL THEN.
EXCEPTION
IN THE WORST-CASE SCENARIO, YUJI ITADORI MIGHT BE ELIMINATED BY THE HIGHER-UPS.
NOTHING VENTURED, NOTHING GAINED, HUH?
SO, WHAT'S THE PLAN?
IT'S ALREADY UNDER WAY.
WE'VE TRICKED JUJUTSU HIGH INTO GATHERING THE FINGERS.
NANAMIIII! TELL ME A FUNNY STORY!
...

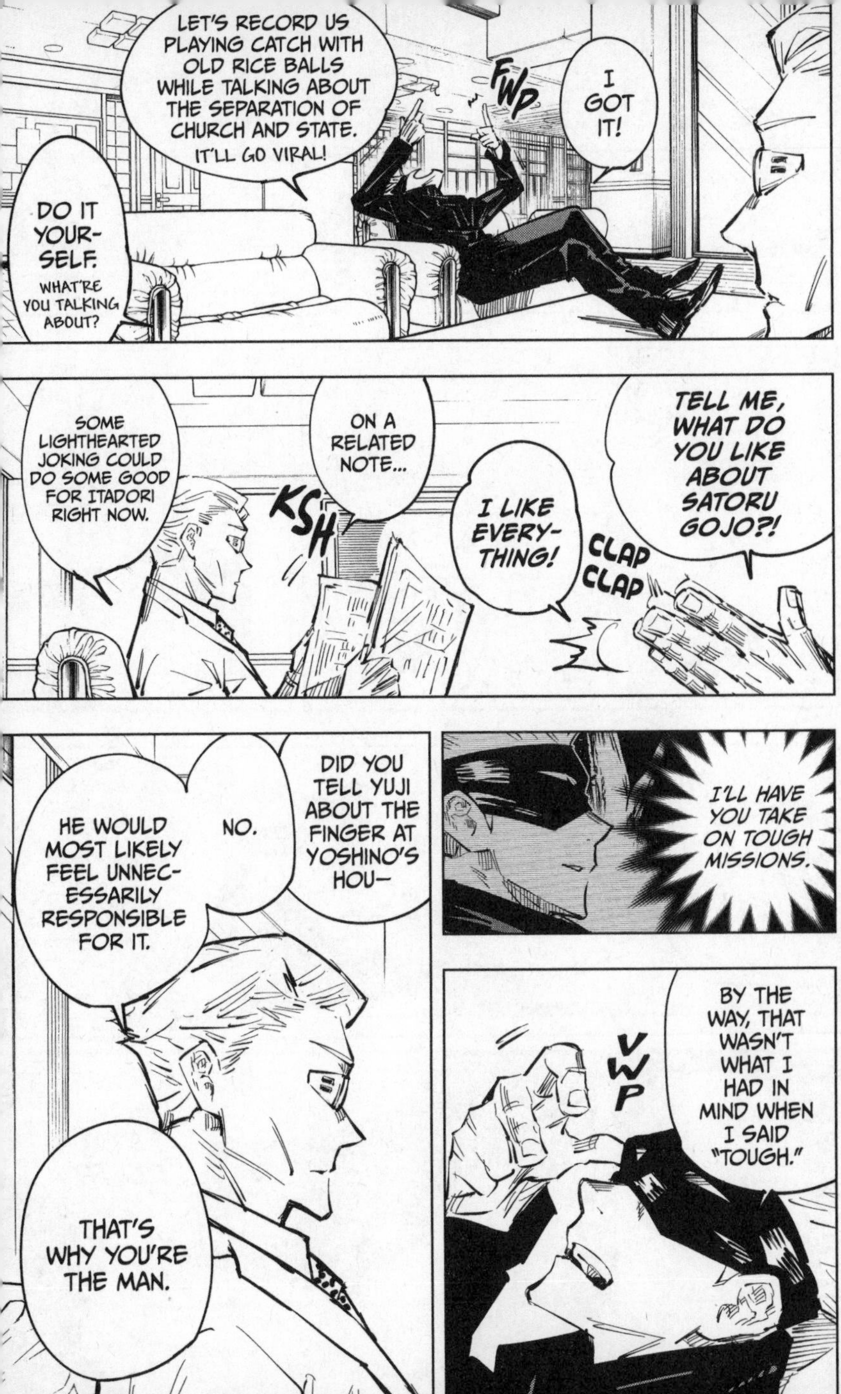
I GOT IT!
FWP
LET'S RECORD US PLAYING CATCH WITH OLD RICE BALLS WHILE TALKING ABOUT THE SEPARATION OF CHURCH AND STATE. IT'LL GO VIRAL!
DO IT YOURSELF. WHAT'RE YOU TALKING ABOUT?
TELL ME, WHAT DO YOU LIKE ABOUT SATORU GOJO?!
CLAP CLAP
I LIKE EVERYTHING!
ON A RELATED NOTE...
KSH
SOME LIGHTHEARTED JOKING COULD DO SOME GOOD FOR ITADORI RIGHT NOW.
I'LL HAVE YOU TAKE ON TOUGH MISSIONS.
BY THE WAY, THAT WASN'T WHAT I HAD IN MIND WHEN I SAID "TOUGH."
VWP
DID YOU TELL YUJI ABOUT THE FINGER AT YOSHINO'S HOU—
NO.
HE WOULD MOST LIKELY FEEL UNNECESSARILY RESPONSIBLE FOR IT.
THAT'S WHY YOU'RE THE MAN.

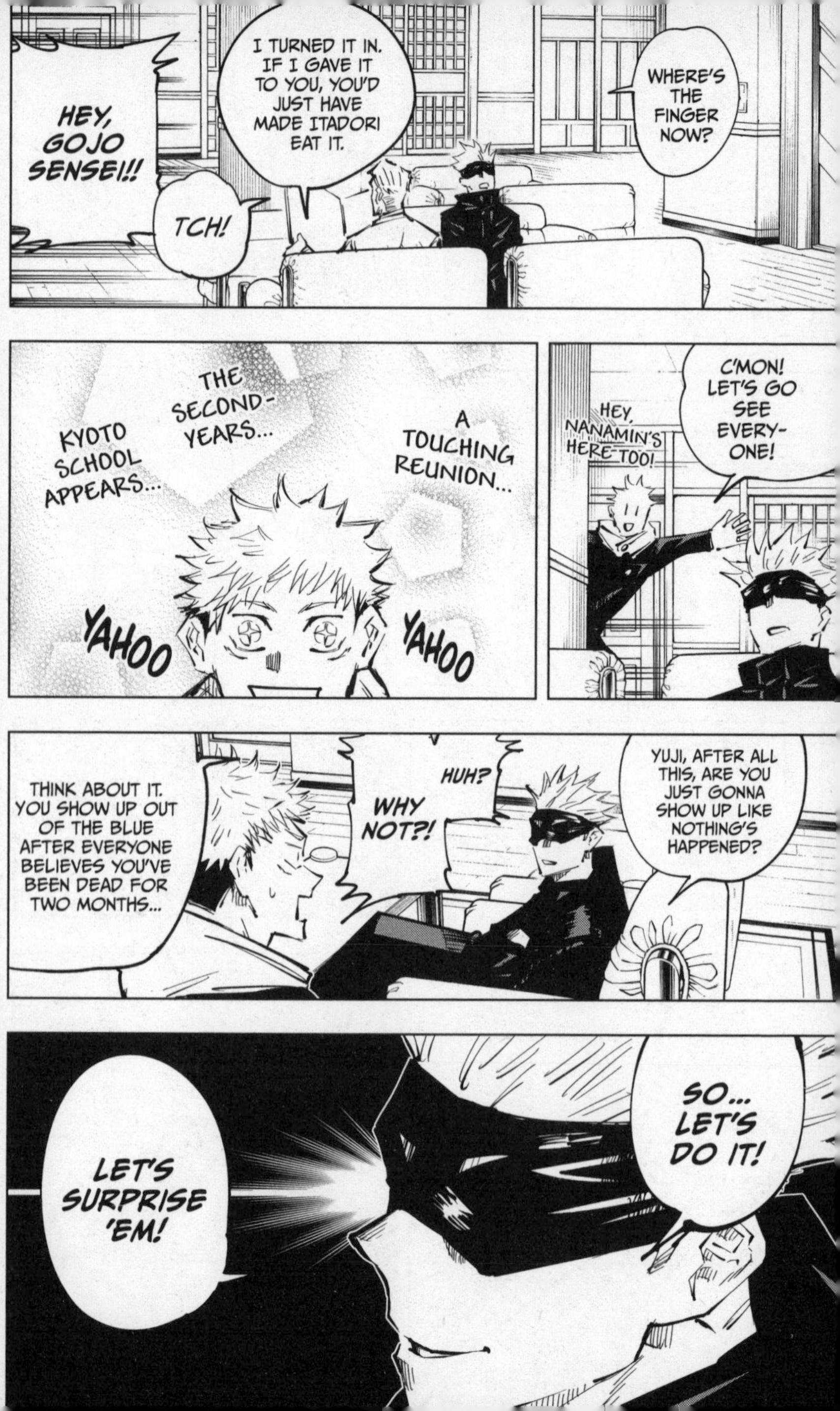

WHERE'S THE FINGER NOW?
I TURNED IT IN. IF I GAVE IT TO YOU, YOU'D JUST HAVE MADE ITADORI EAT IT.
TCH!
HEY, GOJO SENSEI!!
C'MON! LET'S GO SEE EVERY-ONE!
HEY, NANAMIN'S HERE TOO!
A TOUCHING REUNION...
THE SECOND-YEARS...
KYOTO SCHOOL APPEARS...
YAHOO
YAHOO
YUJI, AFTER ALL THIS, ARE YOU JUST GONNA SHOW UP LIKE NOTHING'S HAPPENED?
HUH?
WHY NOT?!
THINK ABOUT IT. YOU SHOW UP OUT OF THE BLUE AFTER EVERYONE BELIEVES YOU'VE BEEN DEAD FOR TWO MONTHS...
SO... LET'S DO IT!
LET'S SURPRISE 'EM!

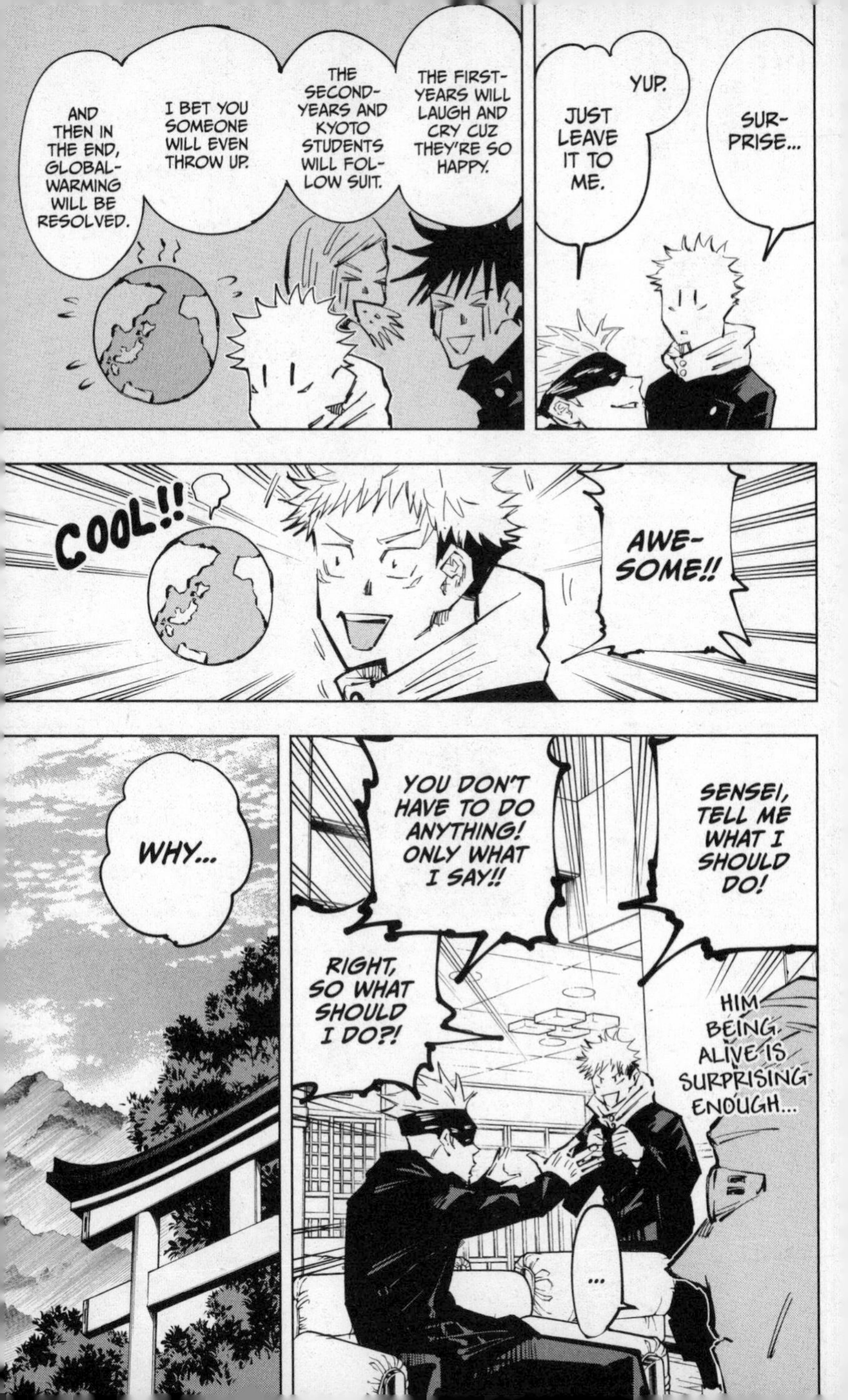
SUR-PRISE...
YUP.
JUST LEAVE IT TO ME.
THE FIRST-YEARS WILL LAUGH AND CRY CUZ THEY'RE SO HAPPY.
THE SECOND-YEARS AND KYOTO STUDENTS WILL FOL-LOW SUIT.
I BET YOU SOMEONE WILL EVEN THROW UP.
AND THEN IN THE END, GLOBAL-WARMING WILL BE RESOLVED.
AWE-SOME!!
COOL!!
SENSEI, TELL ME WHAT I SHOULD DO!
YOU DON'T HAVE TO DO ANYTHING! ONLY WHAT I SAY!!
HIM BEING ALIVE IS SURPRISING ENOUGH...
RIGHT, SO WHAT SHOULD I DO?!
...
WHY...

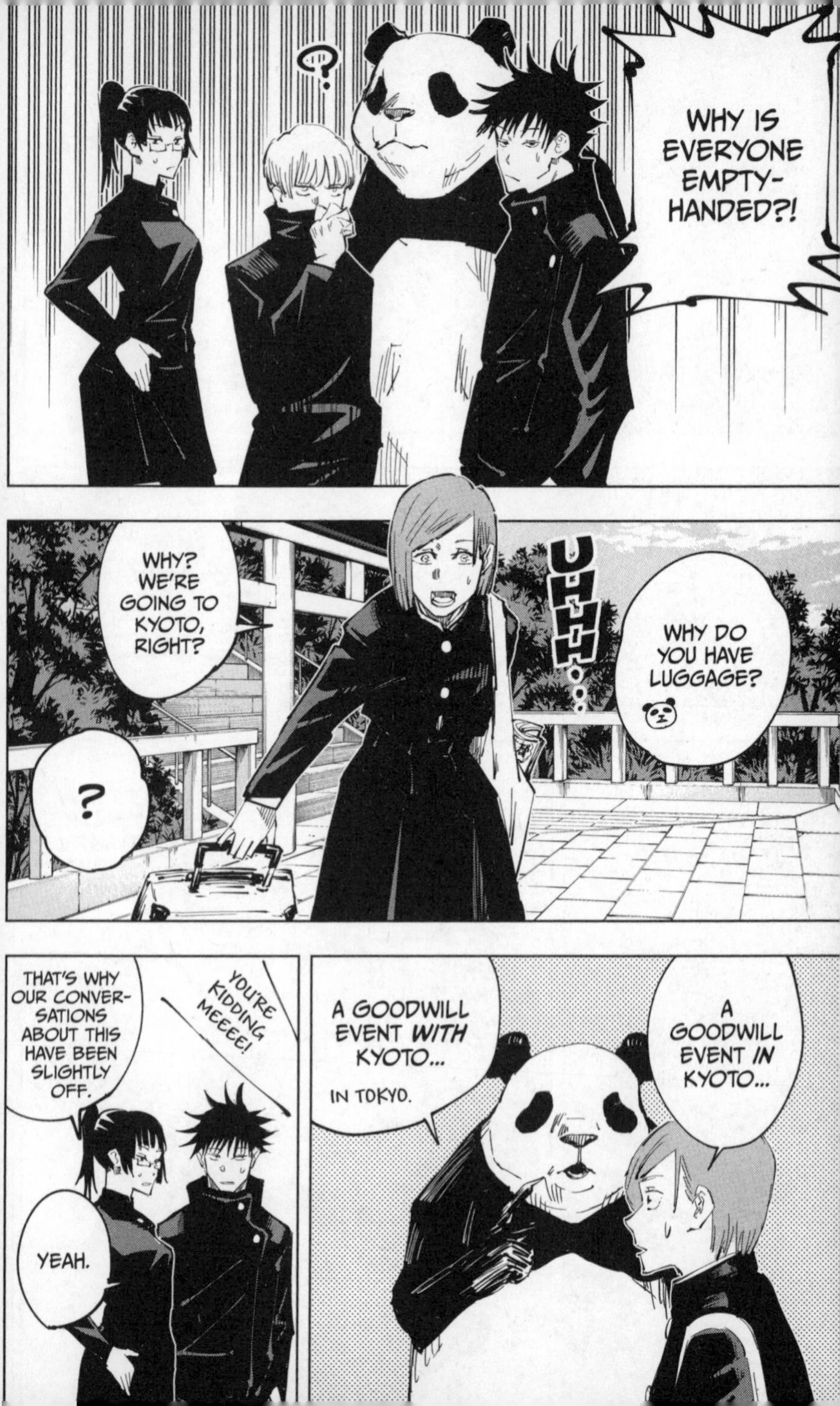
WHY IS EVERYONE EMPTY-HANDED?!
?
WHY DO YOU HAVE LUGGAGE?
UHHH...
WHY? WE'RE GOING TO KYOTO, RIGHT?
?
A GOODWILL EVENT *IN* KYOTO...
A GOODWILL EVENT *WITH* KYOTO...
IN TOKYO.
YOU'RE KIDDING MEEEE!
THAT'S WHY OUR CONVER-SATIONS ABOUT THIS HAVE BEEN SLIGHTLY OFF.
YEAH.

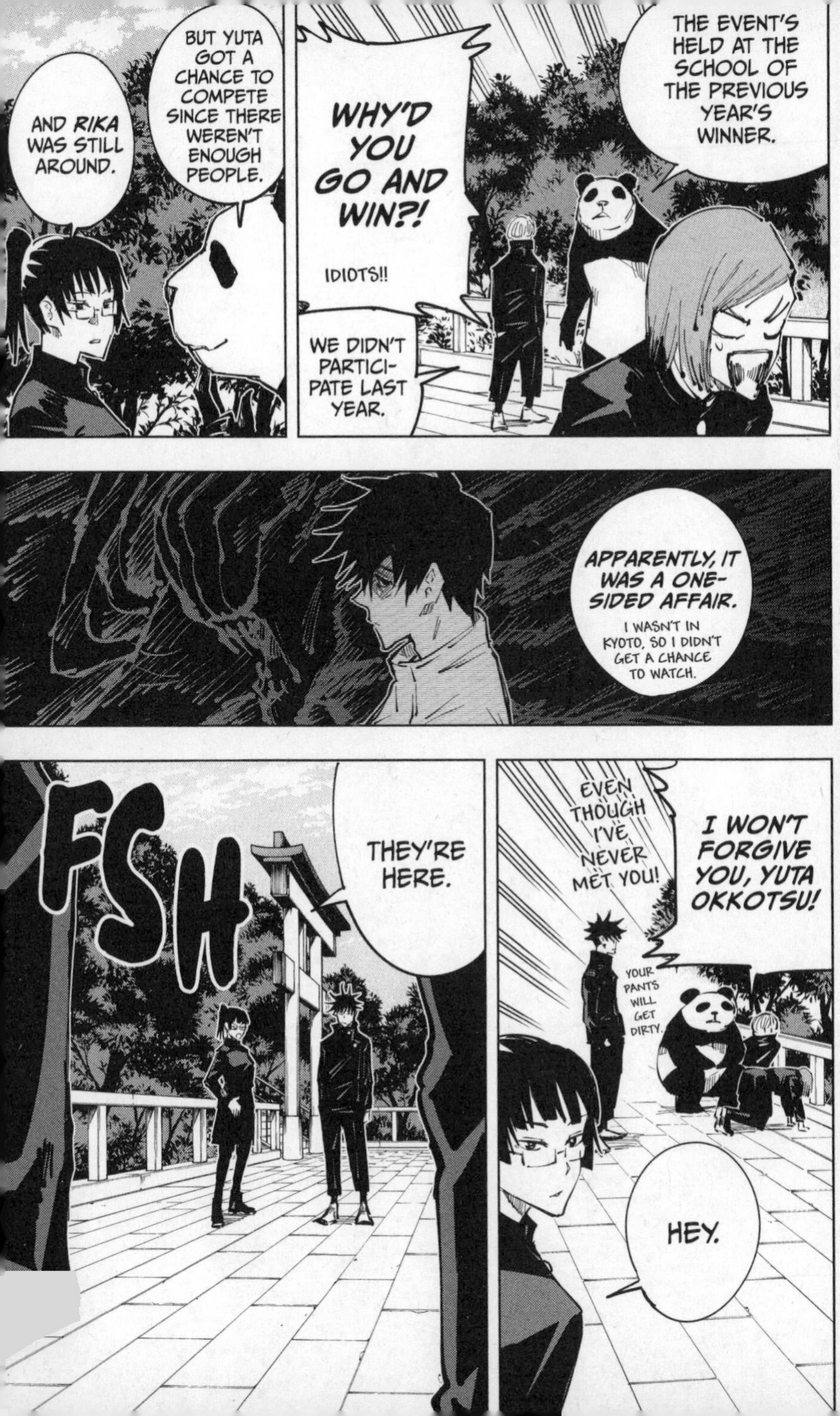
THE EVENT'S HELD AT THE SCHOOL OF THE PREVIOUS YEAR'S WINNER.
WHY'D YOU GO AND WIN?!
IDIOTS!!
WE DIDN'T PARTICIPATE LAST YEAR.
BUT YUTA GOT A CHANCE TO COMPETE SINCE THERE WEREN'T ENOUGH PEOPLE.
AND RIKA WAS STILL AROUND.
APPARENTLY, IT WAS A ONE-SIDED AFFAIR.
I WASN'T IN KYOTO, SO I DIDN'T GET A CHANCE TO WATCH.
I WON'T FORGIVE YOU, YUTA OKKOTSU!
EVEN THOUGH I'VE NEVER MET YOU!
YOUR PANTS WILL GET DIRTY.
HEY.
THEY'RE HERE.
FSH

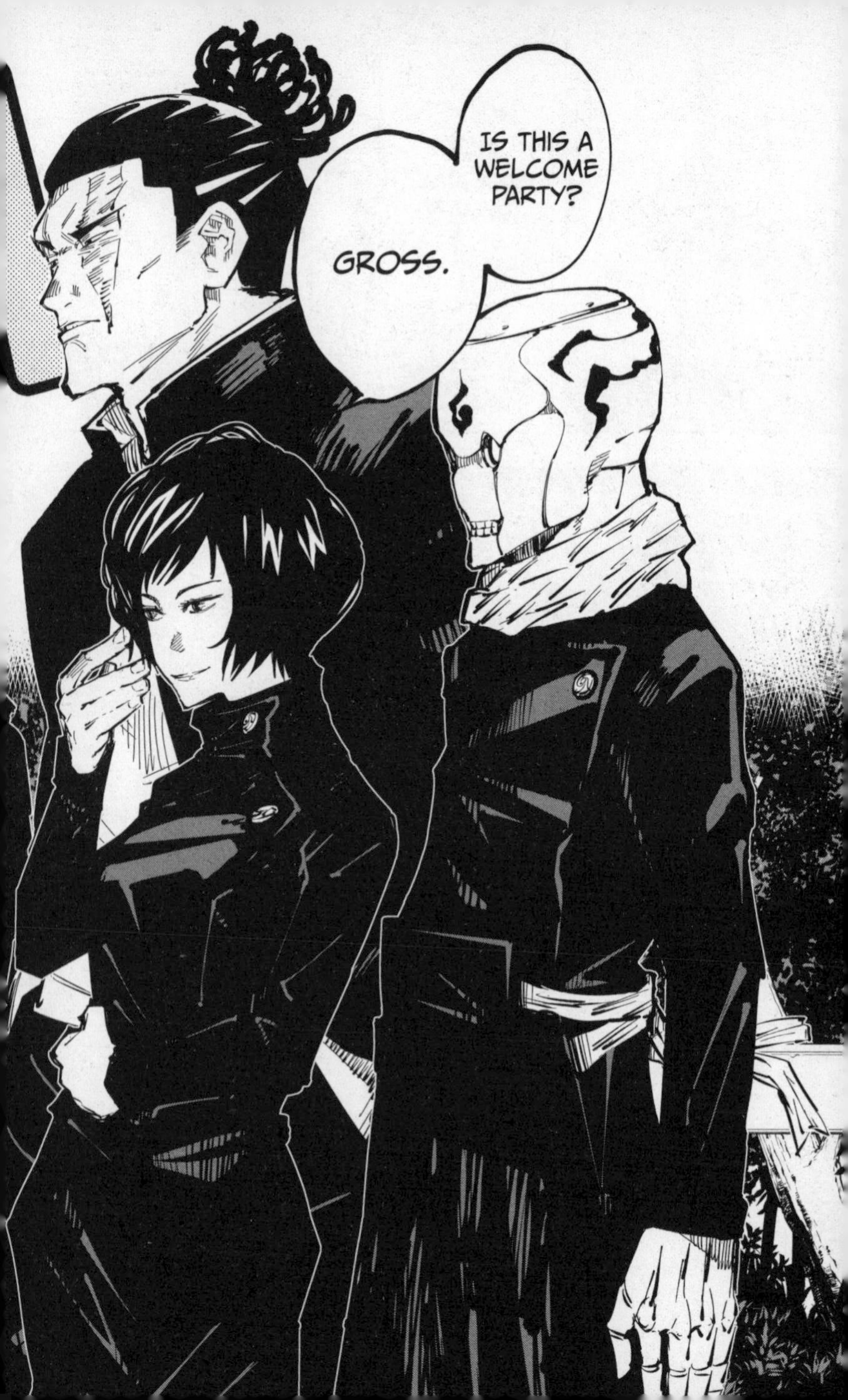
IS THIS A WELCOME PARTY?
GROSS.

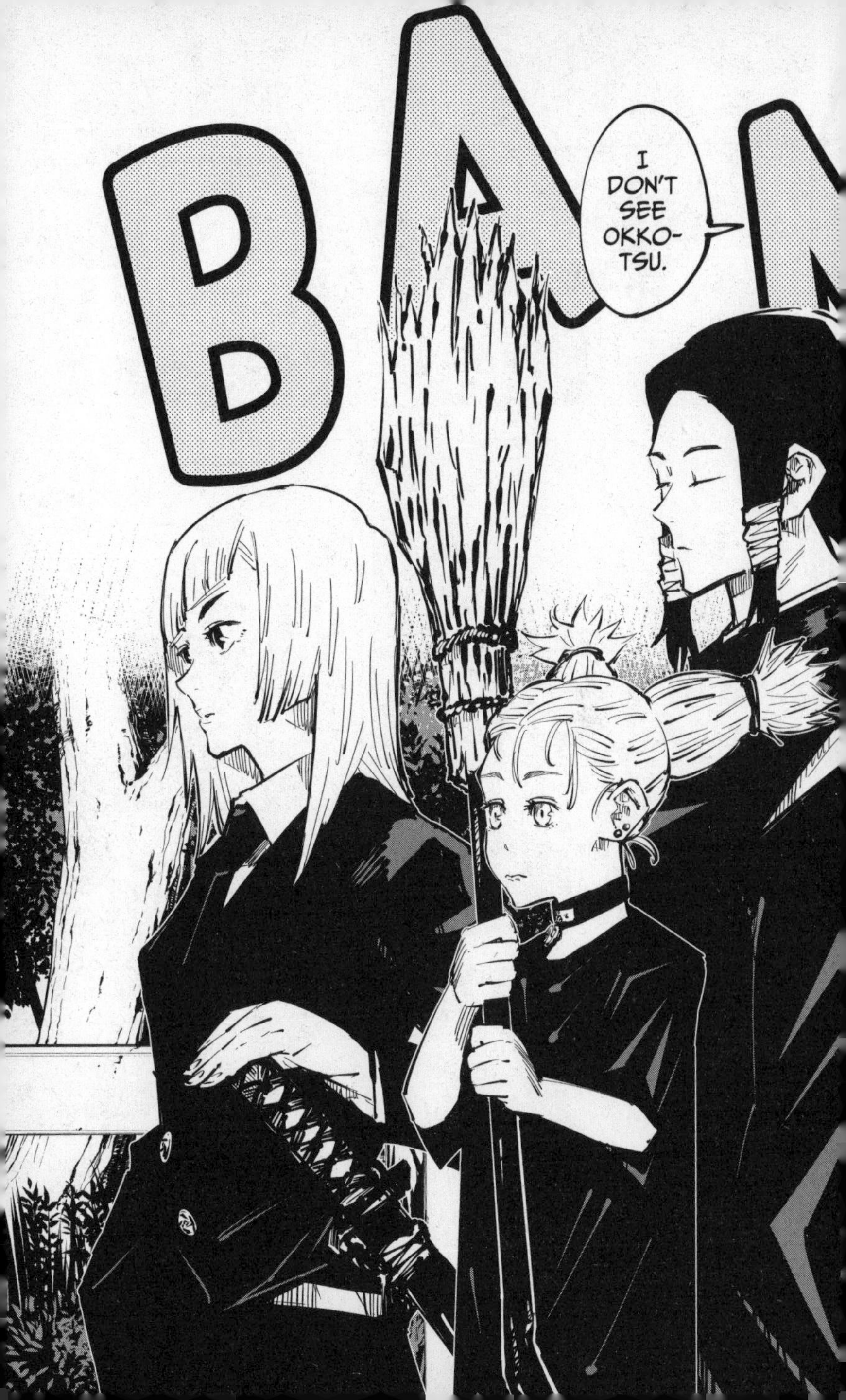
BAM
I DON'T SEE OKKO-TSU.

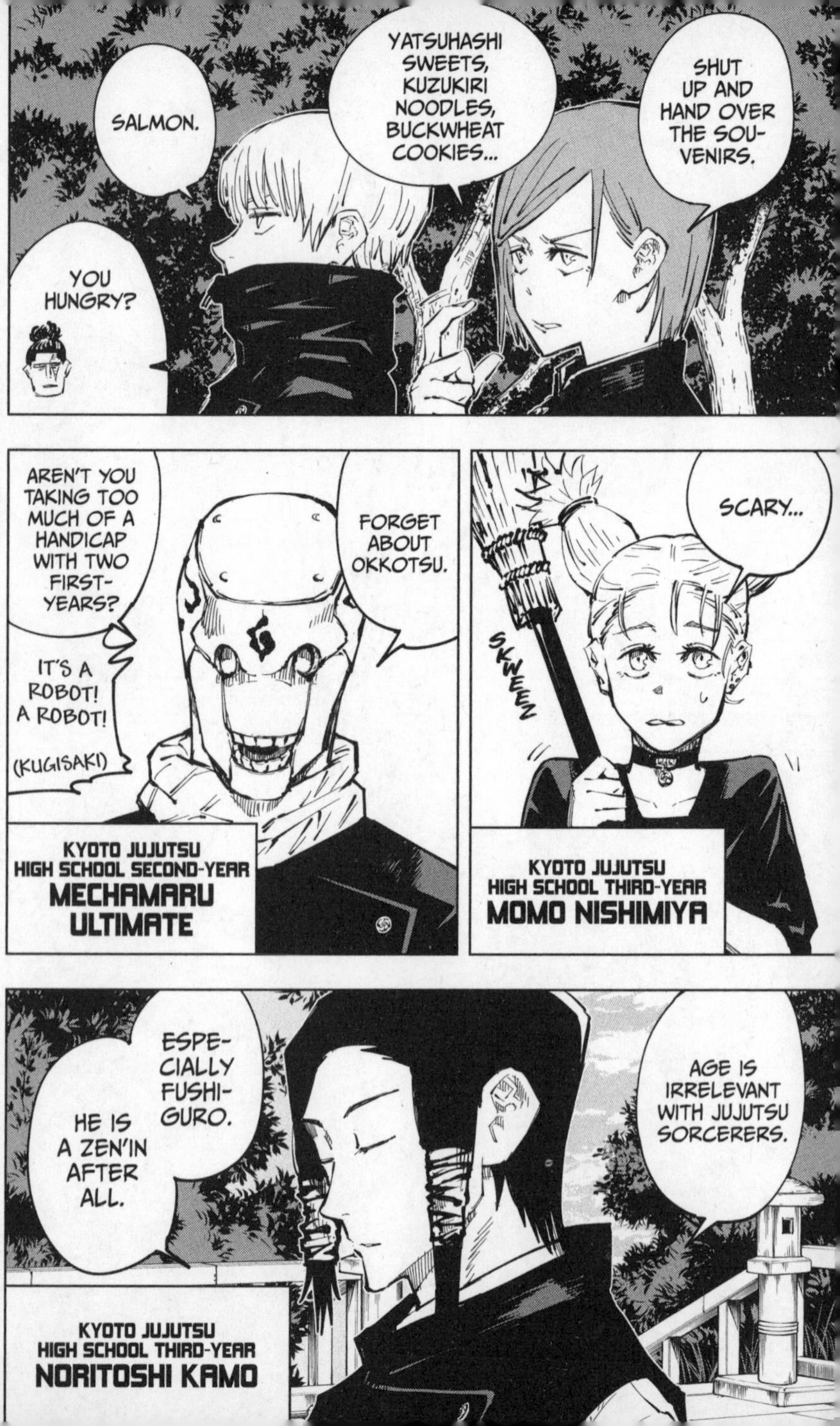
SHUT UP AND HAND OVER THE SOUVENIRS.
YATSUHASHI SWEETS, KUZUKIRI NOODLES, BUCKWHEAT COOKIES...
SALMON.
YOU HUNGRY?
SCARY...
SKWEEZ
KYOTO JUJUTSU HIGH SCHOOL THIRD-YEAR
MOMO NISHIMIYA
FORGET ABOUT OKKOTSU.
AREN'T YOU TAKING TOO MUCH OF A HANDICAP WITH TWO FIRST-YEARS?
IT'S A ROBOT! A ROBOT!
(KUGISAKI)
KYOTO JUJUTSU HIGH SCHOOL SECOND-YEAR
MECHAMARU ULTIMATE
AGE IS IRRELEVANT WITH JUJUTSU SORCERERS.
ESPECIALLY FUSHIGURO.
HE IS A ZEN'IN AFTER ALL.
KYOTO JUJUTSU HIGH SCHOOL THIRD-YEAR
NORITOSHI KAMO

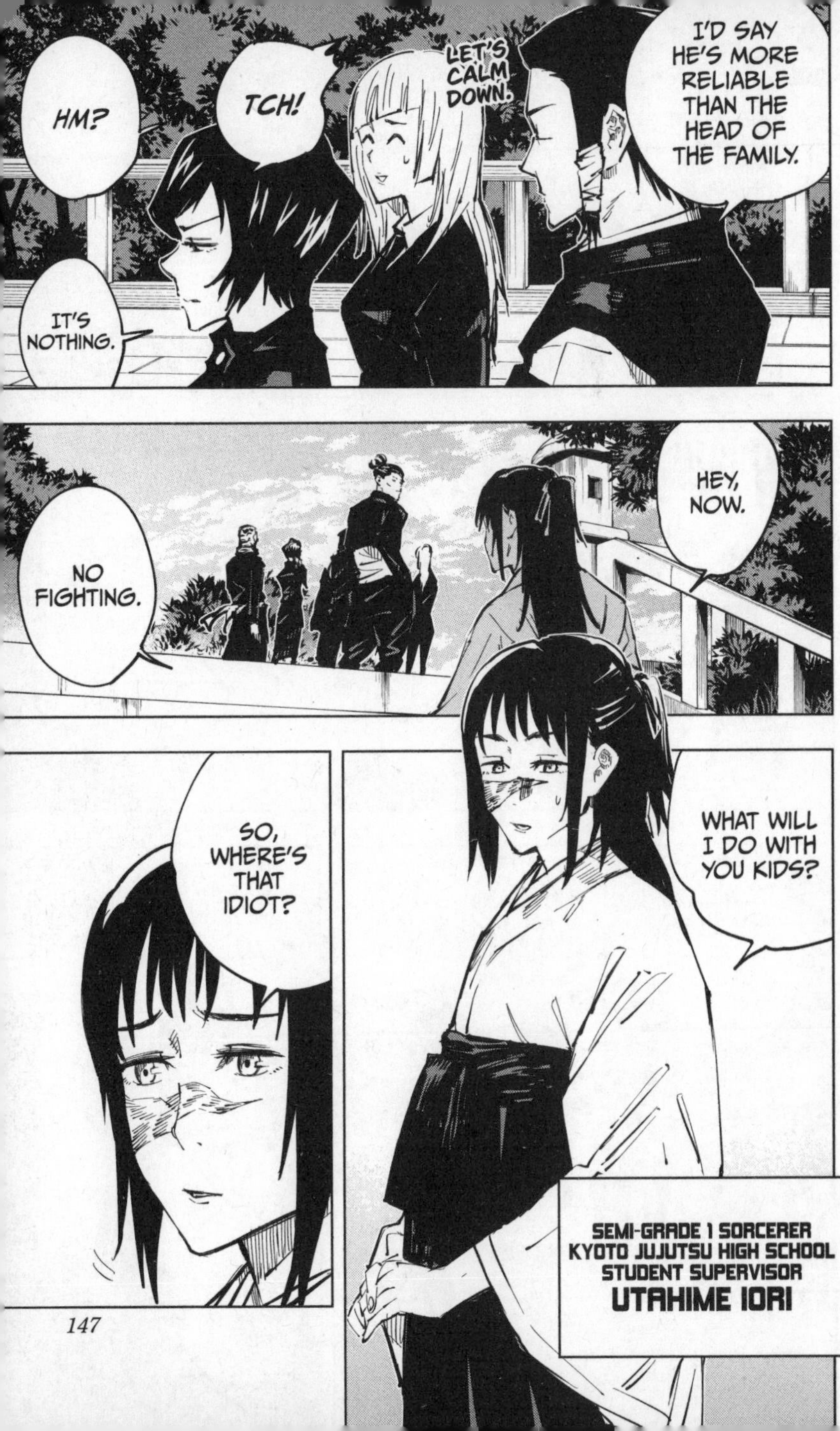
I'D SAY HE'S MORE RELIABLE THAN THE HEAD OF THE FAMILY.
LET'S CALM DOWN.
TCH!
HM?
IT'S NOTHING.
HEY, NOW.
NO FIGHTING.
WHAT WILL I DO WITH YOU KIDS?
SEMI-GRADE 1 SORCERER
KYOTO JUJUTSU HIGH SCHOOL
STUDENT SUPERVISOR
UTAHIME IORI
SO, WHERE'S THAT IDIOT?

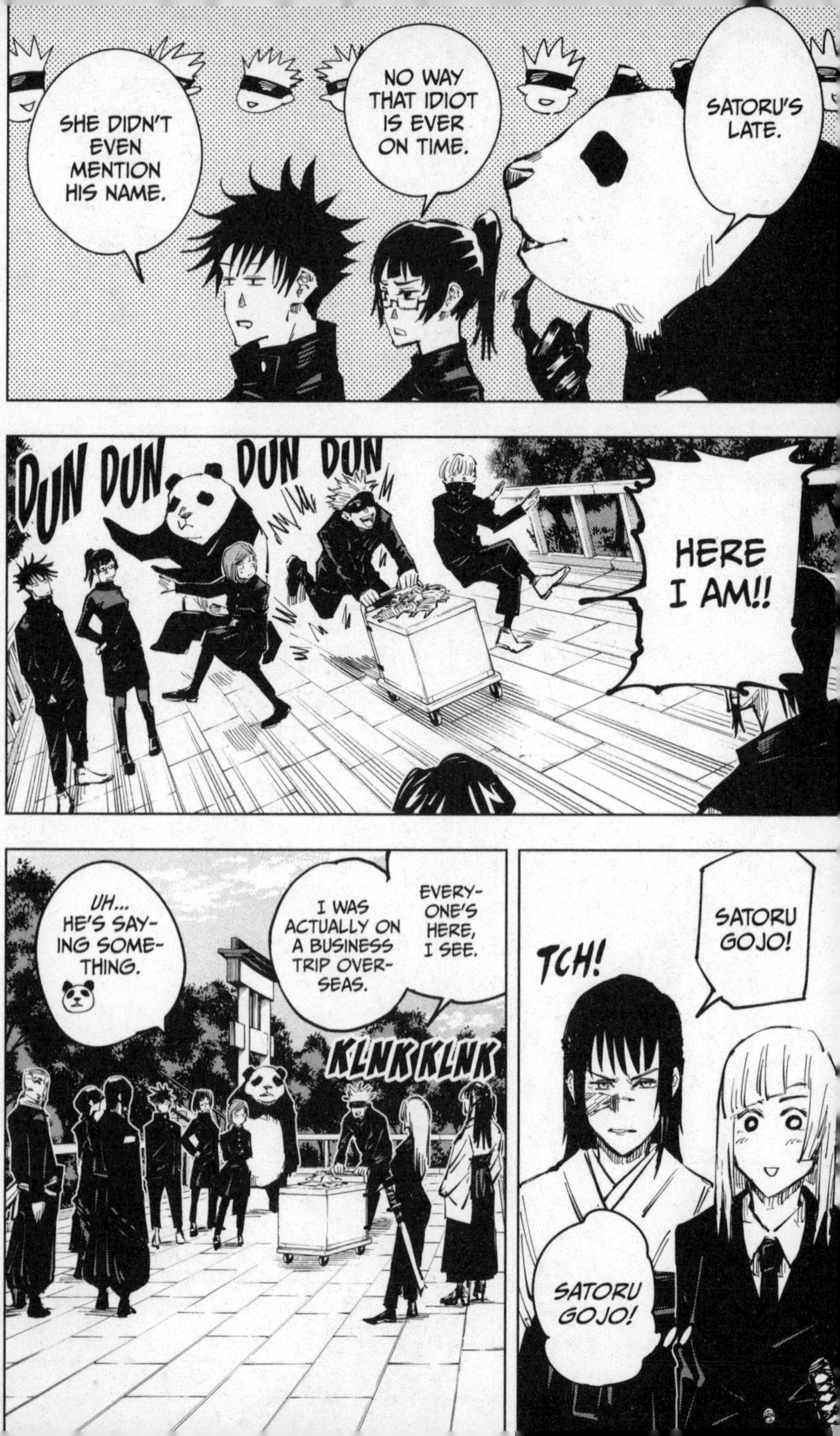
SATORU'S LATE.
NO WAY THAT IDIOT IS EVER ON TIME.
SHE DIDN'T EVEN MENTION HIS NAME.
HERE I AM!!
DUN DUN DUN DUN
SATORU GOJO!
TCH!
SATORU GOJO!
EVERY-ONE'S HERE, I SEE.
I WAS ACTUALLY ON A BUSINESS TRIP OVER-SEAS.
KLNK KLNK
UH... HE'S SAY-ING SOME-THING.

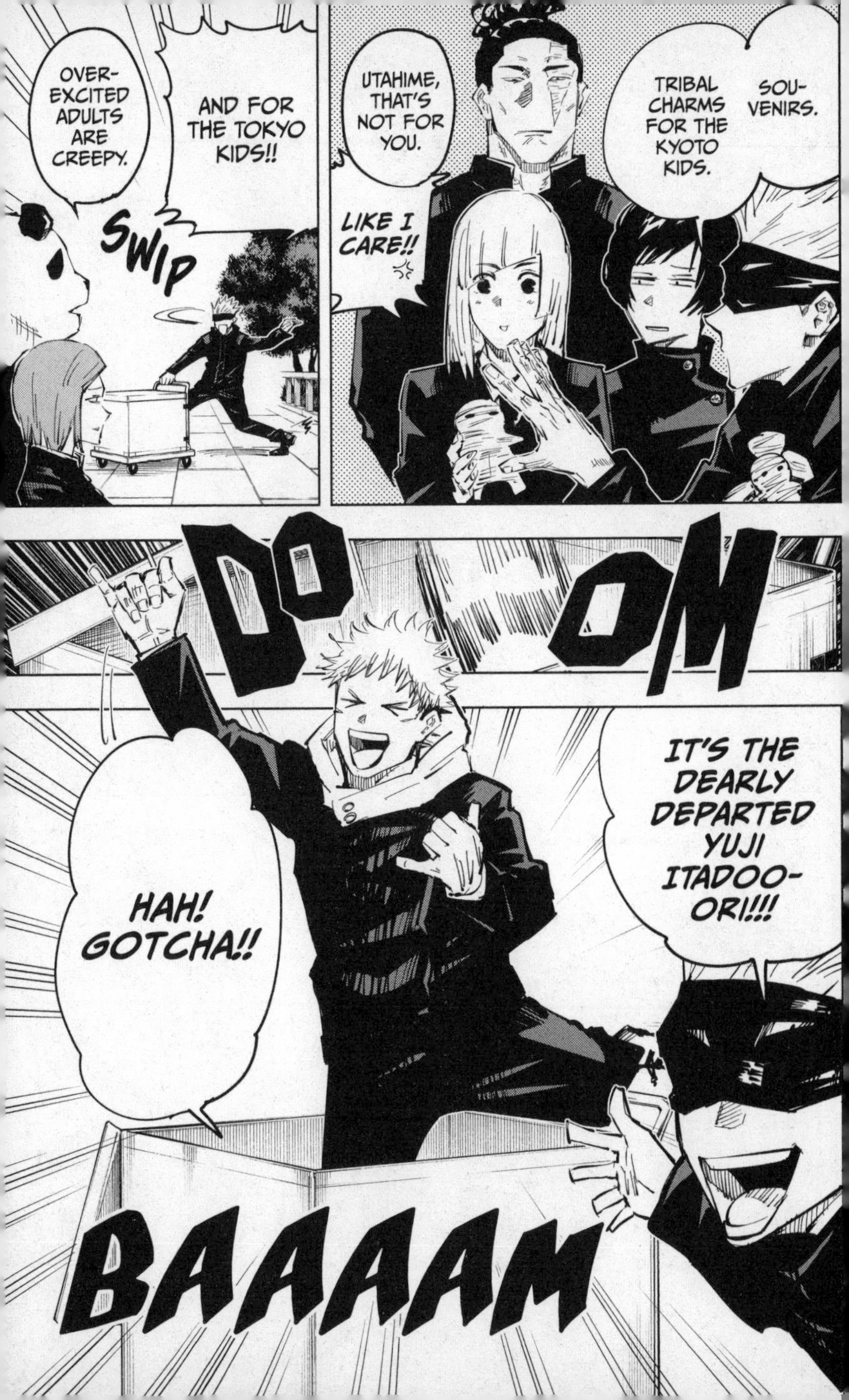
SOU-VENIRS.
TRIBAL CHARMS FOR THE KYOTO KIDS.
UTAHIME, THAT'S NOT FOR YOU.
LIKE I CARE!!
AND FOR THE TOKYO KIDS!!
SWIP
OVER-EXCITED ADULTS ARE CREEPY.
DOOM
IT'S THE DEARLY DEPARTED YUJI ITADOO-ORI!!!
HAH! GOTCHA!!
BAAAAM

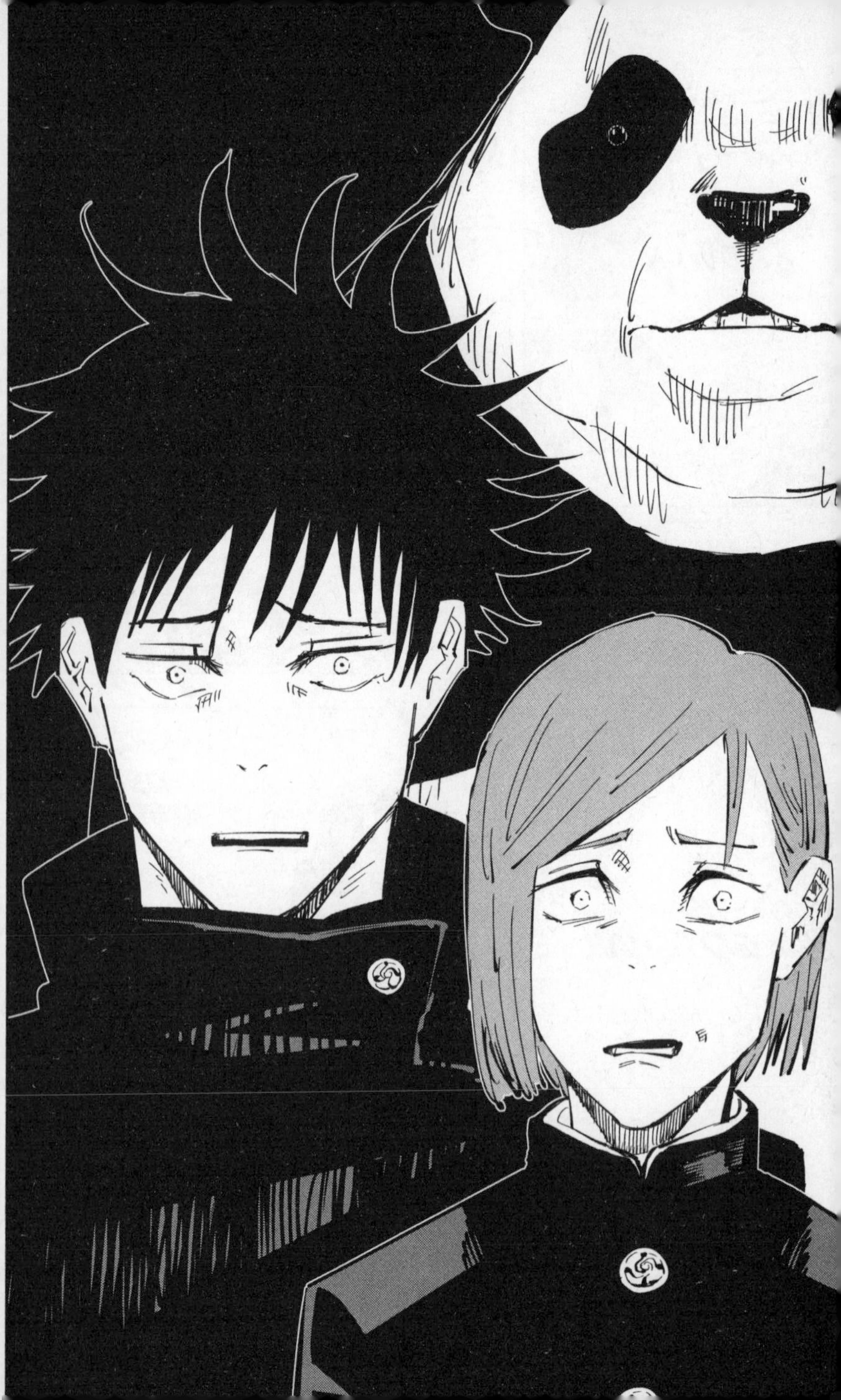

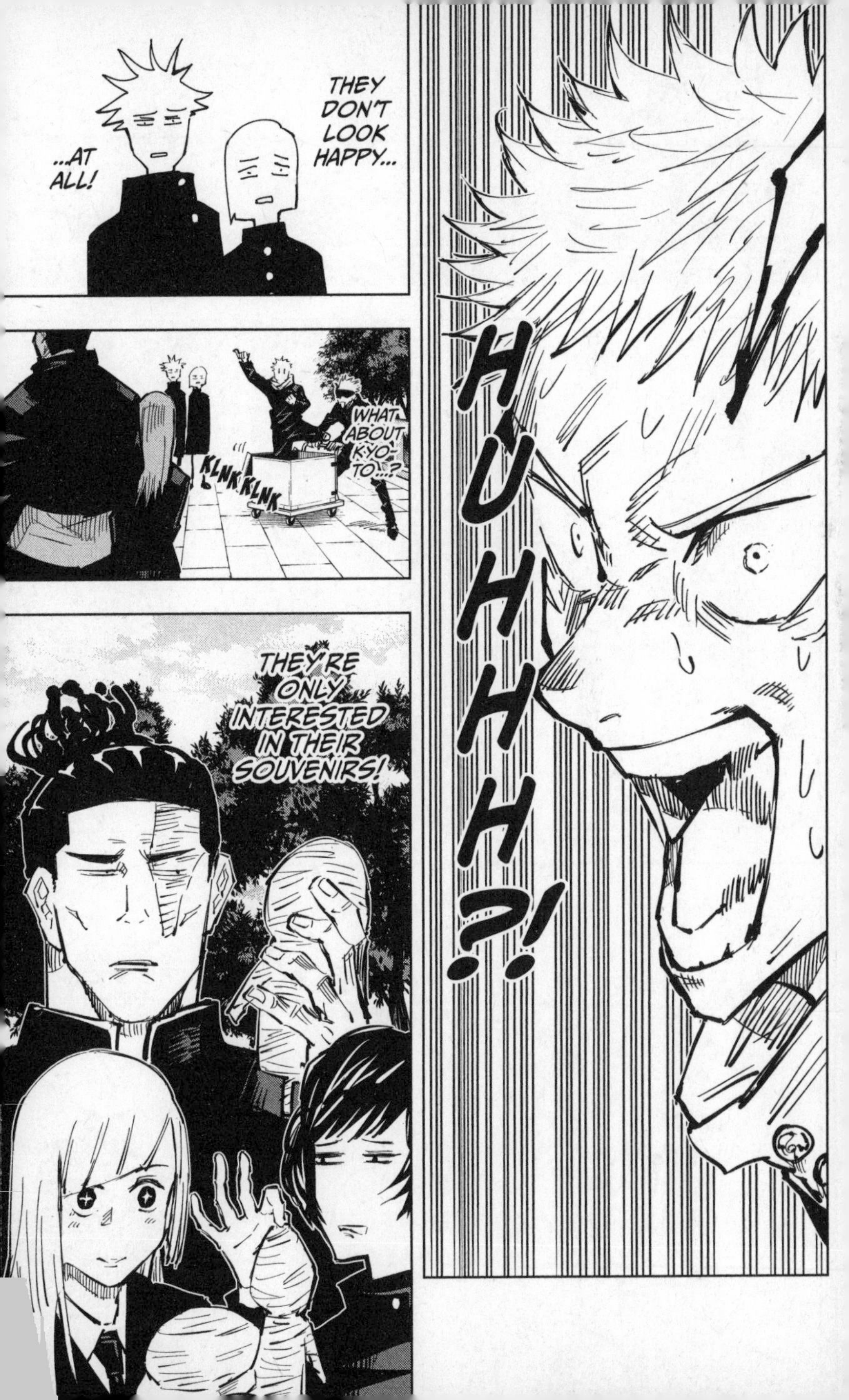
HUHHHH?!
THEY DON'T LOOK HAPPY...
...AT ALL!
WHAT ABOUT KYO-TO...?
KLNK KLNK
THEY'RE ONLY INTERESTED IN THEIR SOUVENIRS!

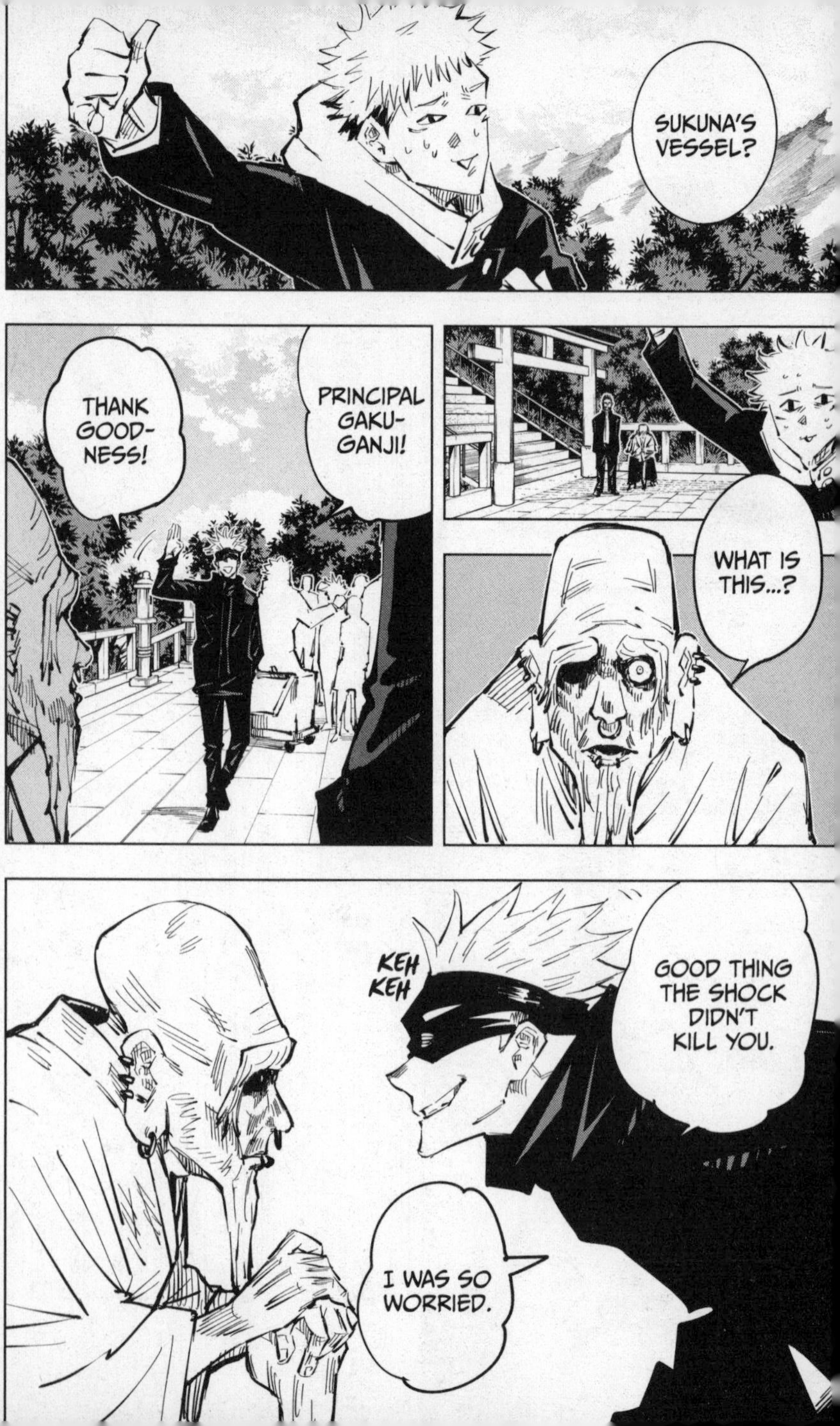
SUKUNA'S VESSEL?
WHAT IS THIS...?
PRINCIPAL GAKU-GANJI!
THANK GOOD-NESS!
GOOD THING THE SHOCK DIDN'T KILL YOU.
KEH KEH
I WAS SO WORRIED.

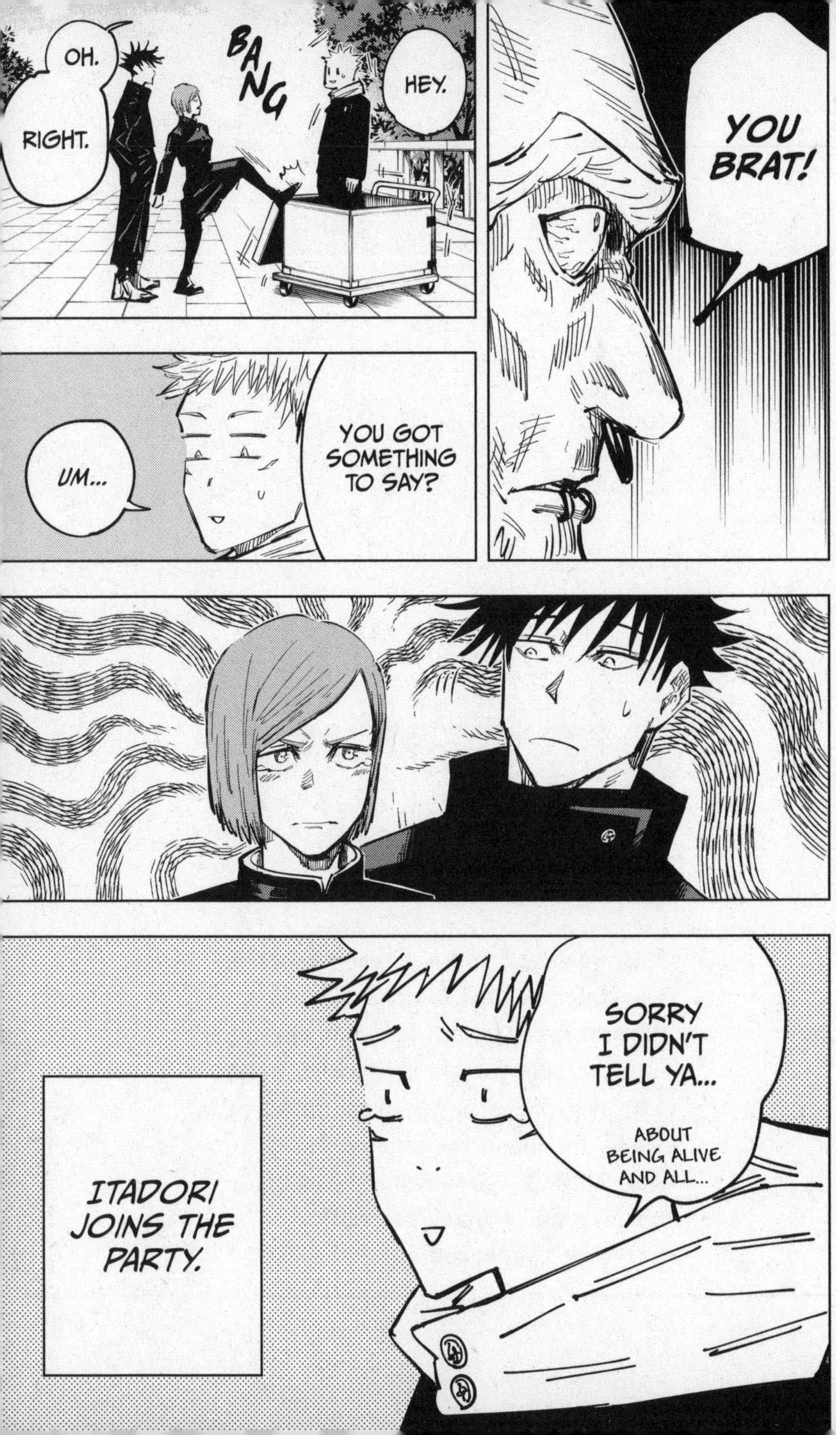
YOU BRAT!
HEY.
BANG
OH. RIGHT.
YOU GOT SOMETHING TO SAY?
UM...
SORRY I DIDN'T TELL YA...
ABOUT BEING ALIVE AND ALL...
ITADORI JOINS THE PARTY.

Have you ever told a perverted joke or
something related to gender that's a
hit with the guys but falls flat with the
girls, making the atmosphere all tense?
No? It happens to me all the time...
That's the mood I was going for with
chapter 32. I guess it doesn't matter
whether you're a guy or a girl.
Everyone's different.

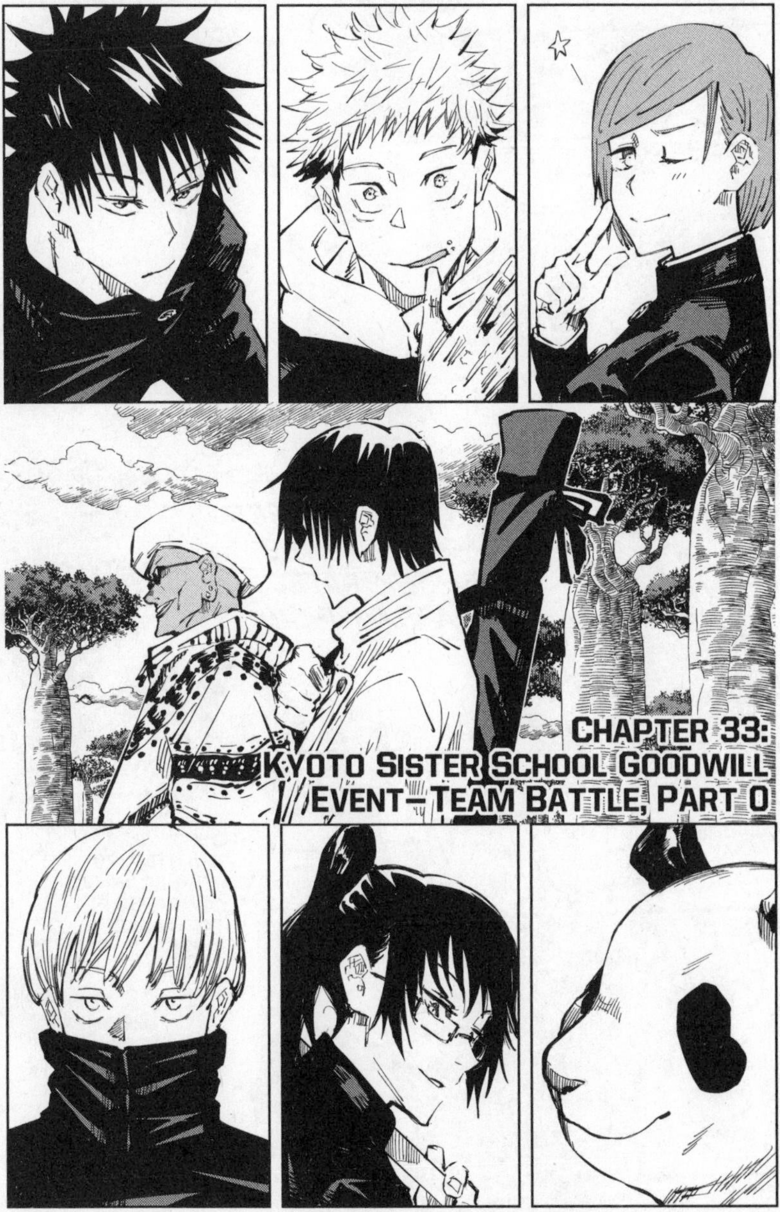
CHAPTER 33:
KYOTO SISTER SCHOOL GOODWILL EVENT– TEAM BATTLE, PART 0

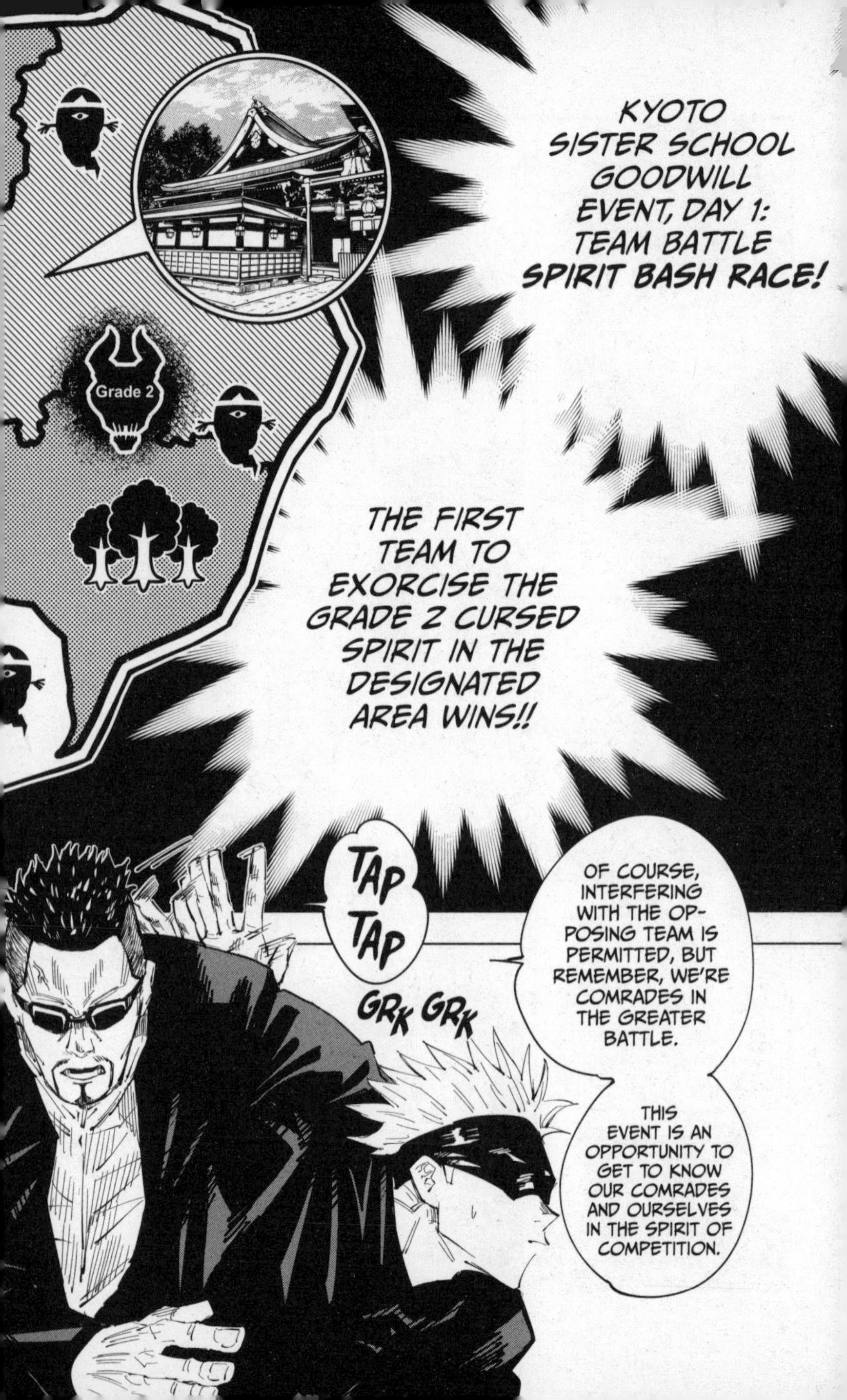
KYOTO SISTER SCHOOL GOODWILL EVENT, DAY 1: TEAM BATTLE SPIRIT BASH RACE!
Grade 2
THE FIRST TEAM TO EXORCISE THE GRADE 2 CURSED SPIRIT IN THE DESIGNATED AREA WINS!!
OF COURSE, INTERFERING WITH THE OP-POSING TEAM IS PERMITTED, BUT REMEMBER, WE'RE COMRADES IN THE GREATER BATTLE.
TAP TAP
GRK GRK
THIS EVENT IS AN OPPORTUNITY TO GET TO KNOW OUR COMRADES AND OURSELVES IN THE SPIRIT OF COMPETITION.

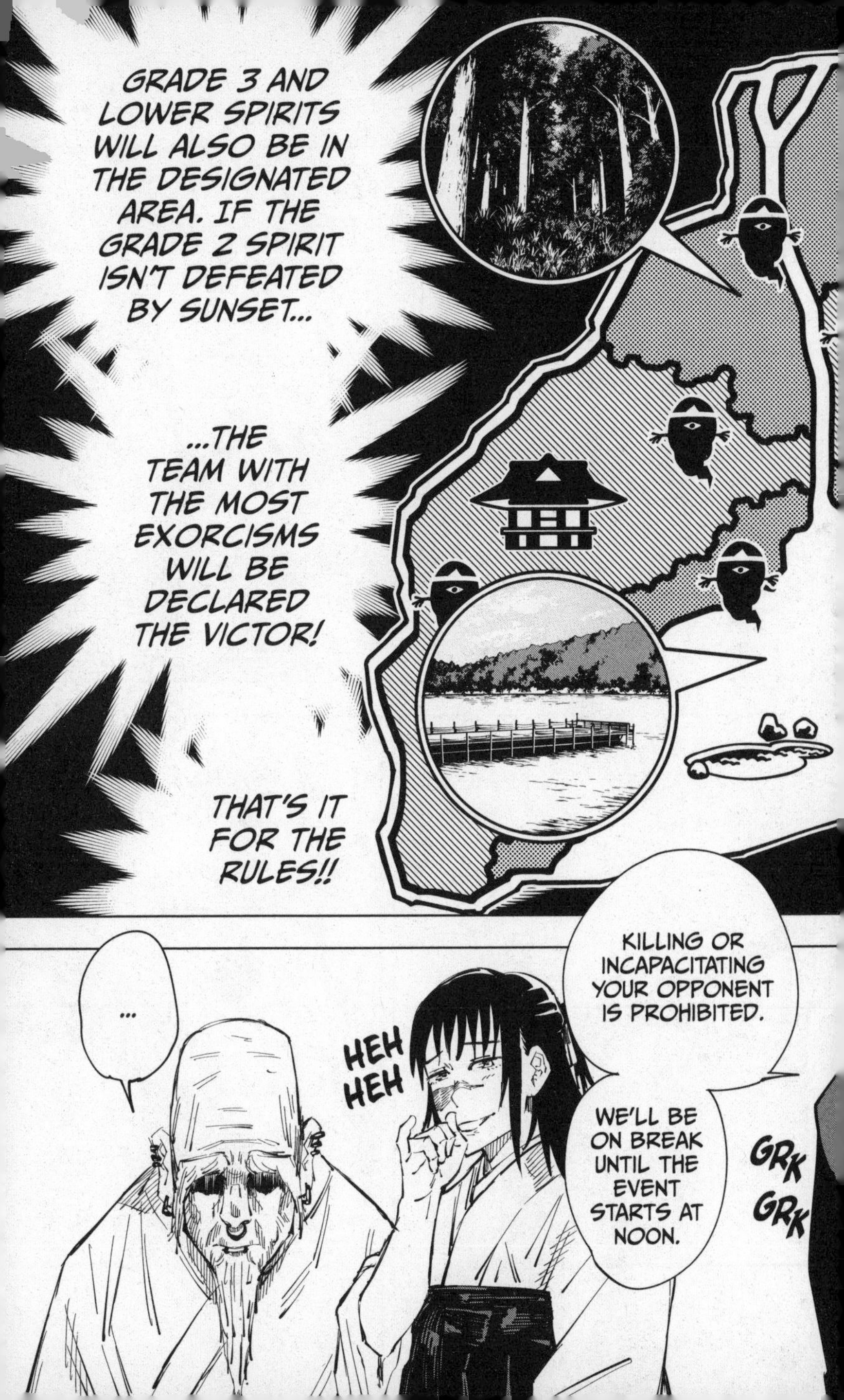
GRADE 3 AND LOWER SPIRITS WILL ALSO BE IN THE DESIGNATED AREA. IF THE GRADE 2 SPIRIT ISN'T DEFEATED BY SUNSET...
...THE TEAM WITH THE MOST EXORCISMS WILL BE DECLARED THE VICTOR!
THAT'S IT FOR THE RULES!!
KILLING OR INCAPACITATING YOUR OPPONENT IS PROHIBITED.
WE'LL BE ON BREAK UNTIL THE EVENT STARTS AT NOON.
GRK GRK
HEH HEH
...

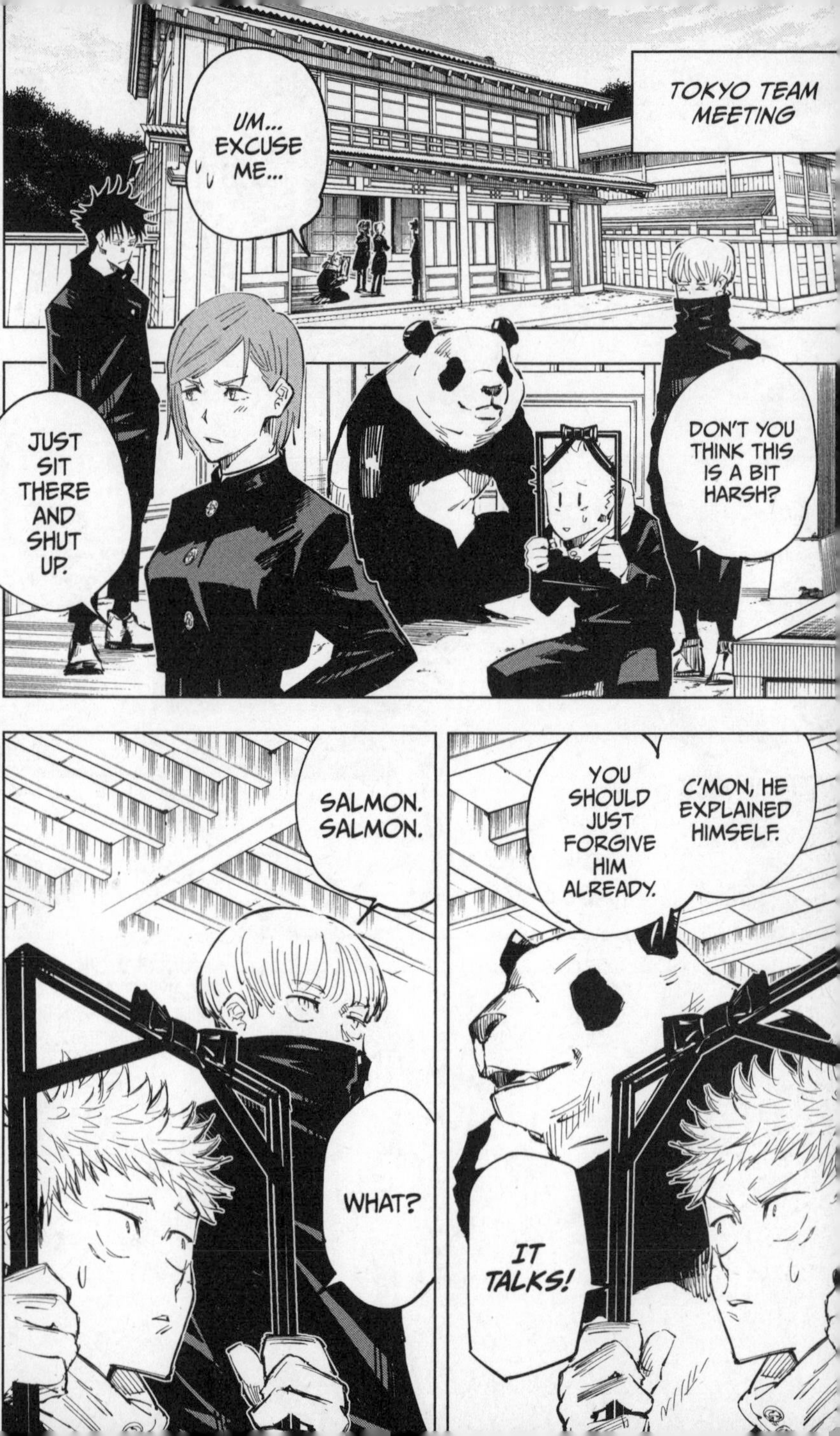
TOKYO TEAM MEETING
UM... EXCUSE ME...
DON'T YOU THINK THIS IS A BIT HARSH?
JUST SIT THERE AND SHUT UP.
C'MON, HE EXPLAINED HIMSELF.
YOU SHOULD JUST FORGIVE HIM ALREADY.
IT TALKS!
SALMON. SALMON.
WHAT?

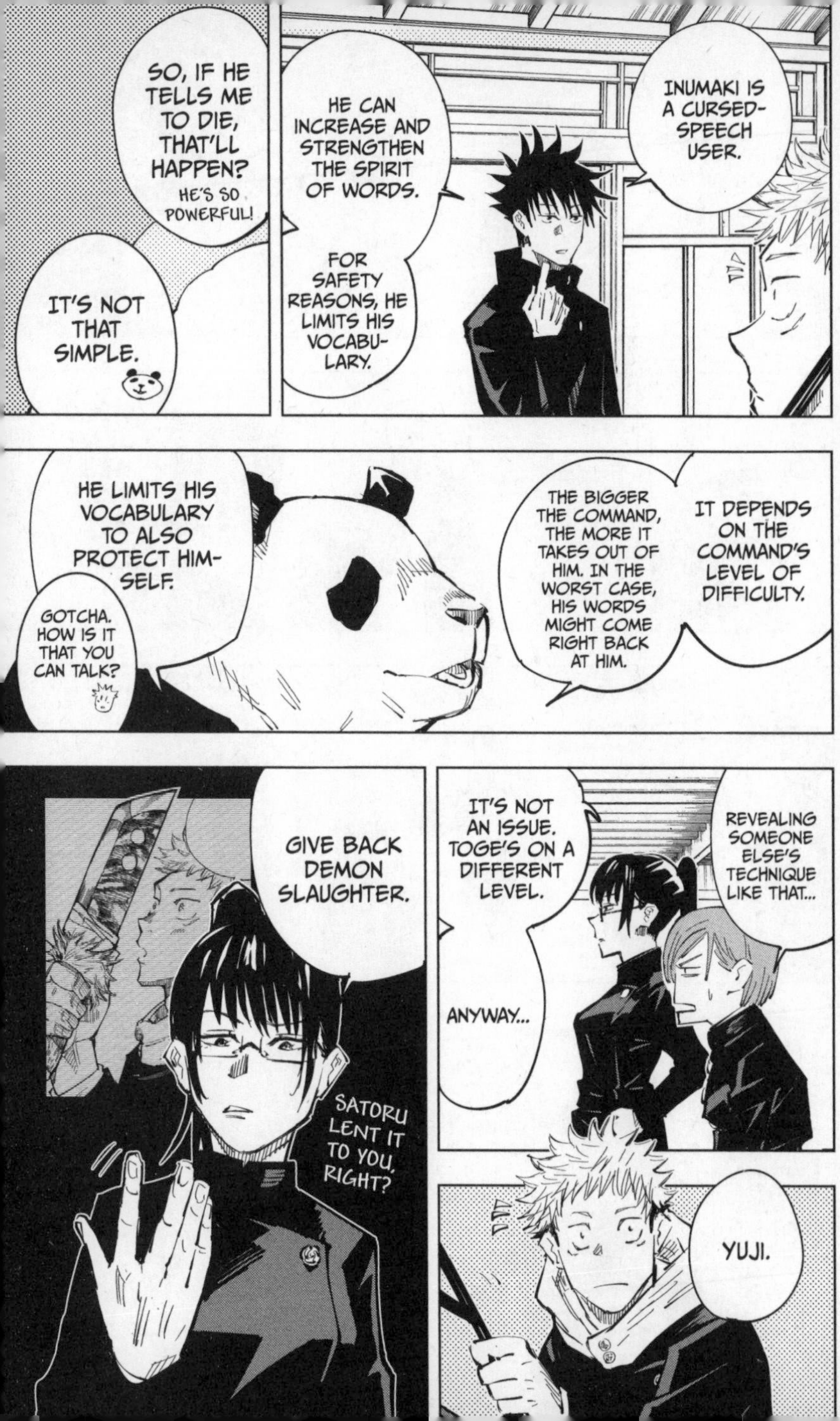
INUMAKI IS A CURSED-SPEECH USER.
HE CAN INCREASE AND STRENGTHEN THE SPIRIT OF WORDS.
FOR SAFETY REASONS, HE LIMITS HIS VOCABU-LARY.
SO, IF HE TELLS ME TO DIE, THAT'LL HAPPEN?
HE'S SO POWERFUL!
IT'S NOT THAT SIMPLE.
IT DEPENDS ON THE COMMAND'S LEVEL OF DIFFICULTY.
THE BIGGER THE COMMAND, THE MORE IT TAKES OUT OF HIM. IN THE WORST CASE, HIS WORDS MIGHT COME RIGHT BACK AT HIM.
HE LIMITS HIS VOCABULARY TO ALSO PROTECT HIM-SELF.
GOTCHA. HOW IS IT THAT YOU CAN TALK?
REVEALING SOMEONE ELSE'S TECHNIQUE LIKE THAT...
IT'S NOT AN ISSUE. TOGE'S ON A DIFFERENT LEVEL.
ANYWAY...
YUJI.
GIVE BACK DEMON SLAUGHTER.
SATORU LENT IT TO YOU, RIGHT?

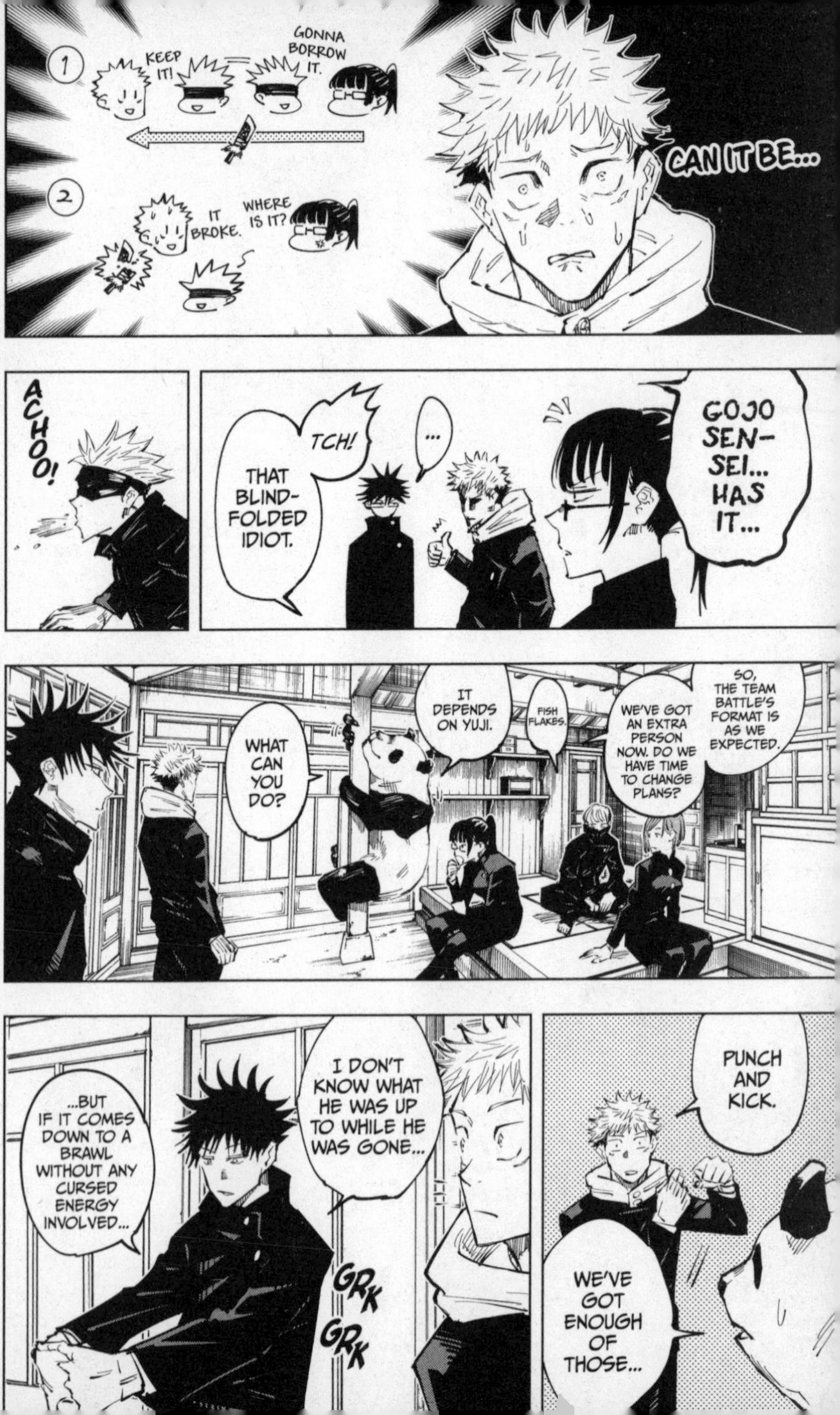
CAN IT BE...
1
GONNA BORROW IT.
KEEP IT!
2
WHERE IS IT?
IT BROKE.
GOJO SENSEI... HAS IT...
...
TCH!
THAT BLINDFOLDED IDIOT.
ACHOO!
SO, THE TEAM BATTLE'S FORMAT IS AS WE EXPECTED.
WE'VE GOT AN EXTRA PERSON NOW. DO WE HAVE TIME TO CHANGE PLANS?
FISH FLAKES.
IT DEPENDS ON YUJI.
WHAT CAN YOU DO?
PUNCH AND KICK.
WE'VE GOT ENOUGH OF THOSE...
I DON'T KNOW WHAT HE WAS UP TO WHILE HE WAS GONE...
...BUT IF IT COMES DOWN TO A BRAWL WITHOUT ANY CURSED ENERGY INVOLVED...
GRK
GRK

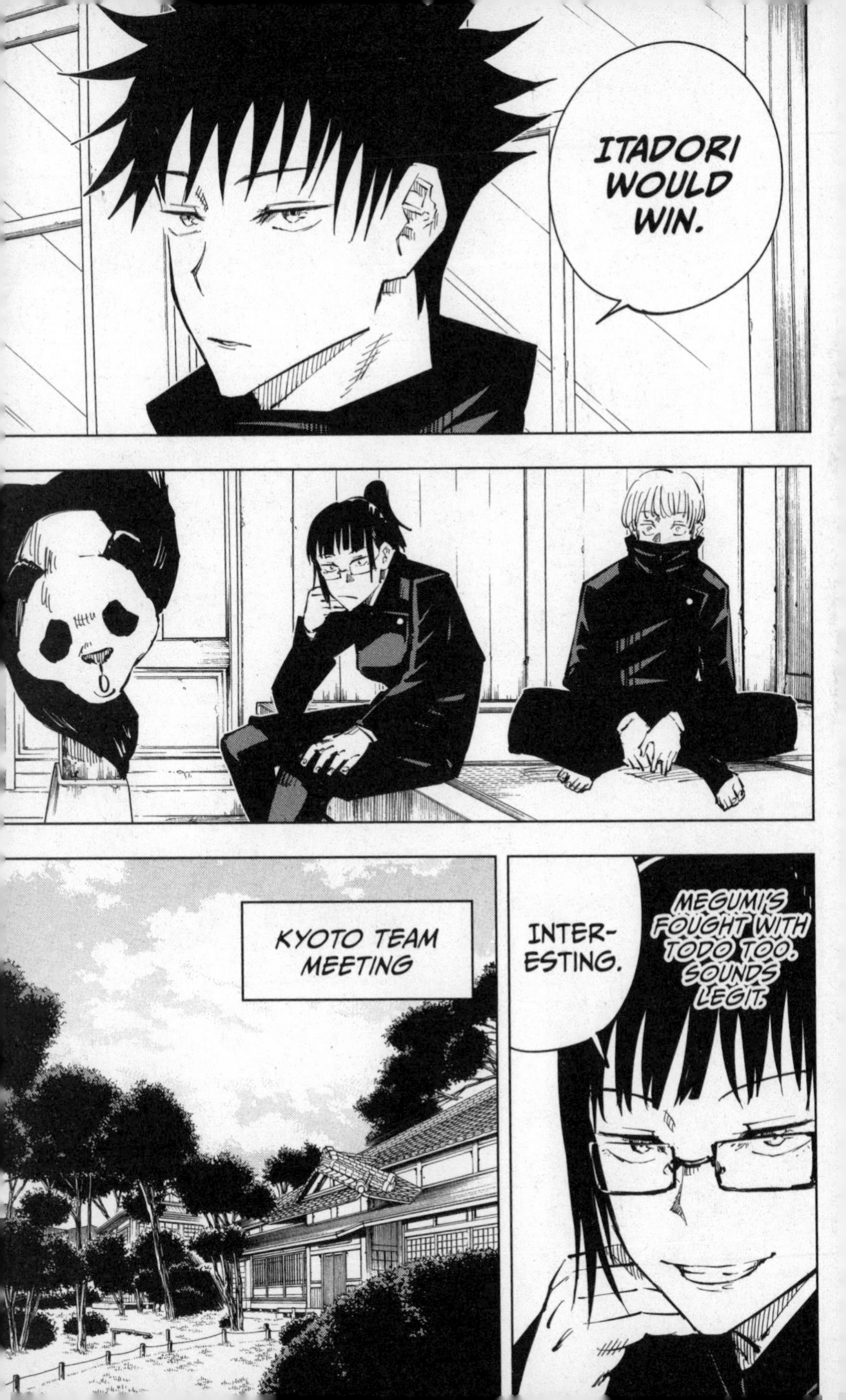
ITADORI WOULD WIN.
MEGUMI'S FOUGHT WITH TODO TOO. SOUNDS LEGIT.
INTER-ESTING.
KYOTO TEAM MEETING

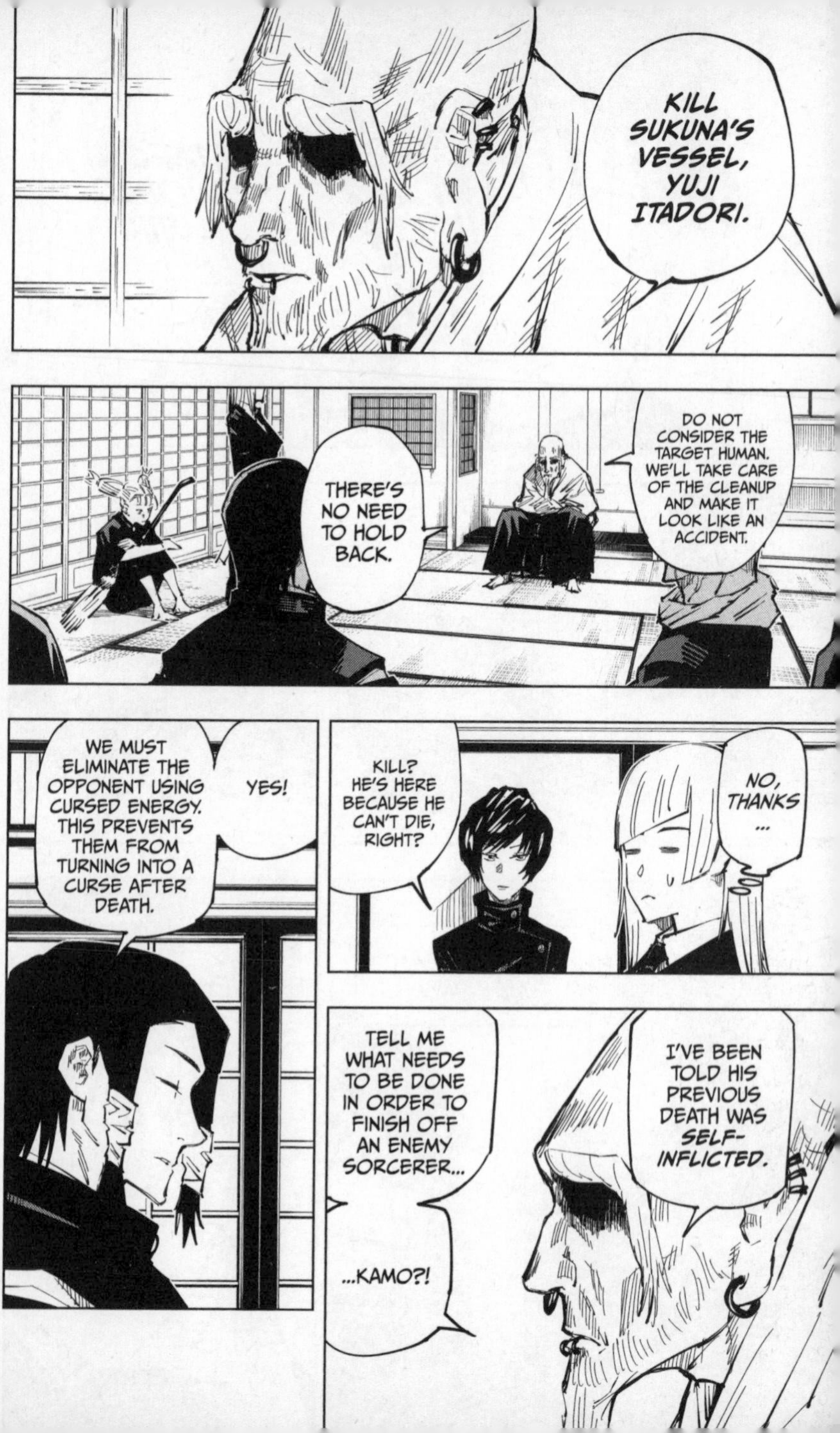
KILL SUKUNA'S VESSEL, YUJI ITADORI.
DO NOT CONSIDER THE TARGET HUMAN. WE'LL TAKE CARE OF THE CLEANUP AND MAKE IT LOOK LIKE AN ACCIDENT.
THERE'S NO NEED TO HOLD BACK.
NO, THANKS ...
KILL? HE'S HERE BECAUSE HE CAN'T DIE, RIGHT?
I'VE BEEN TOLD HIS PREVIOUS DEATH WAS SELF-INFLICTED.
TELL ME WHAT NEEDS TO BE DONE IN ORDER TO FINISH OFF AN ENEMY SORCERER...
...KAMO?!
YES!
WE MUST ELIMINATE THE OPPONENT USING CURSED ENERGY. THIS PREVENTS THEM FROM TURNING INTO A CURSE AFTER DEATH.

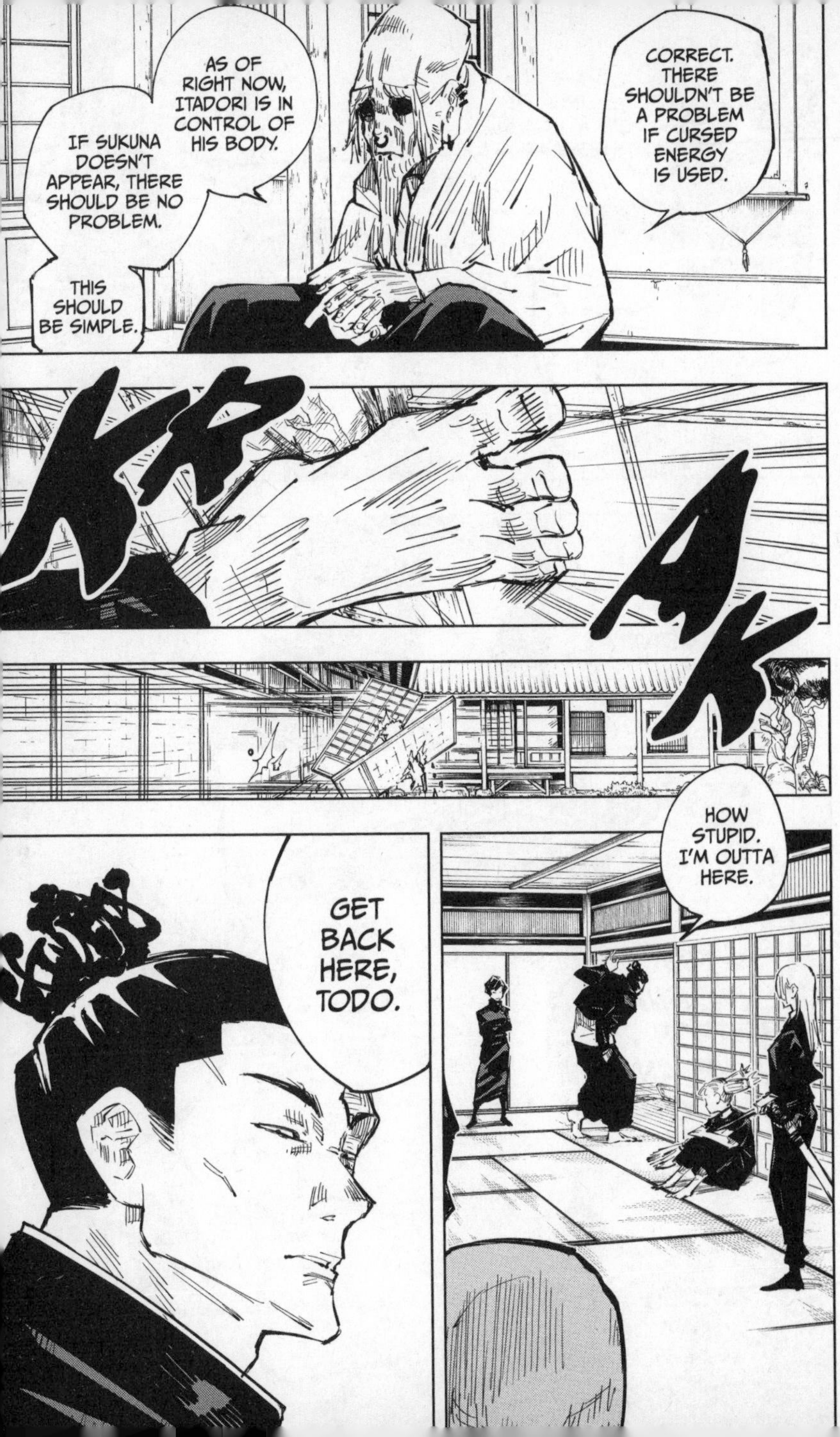
CORRECT. THERE SHOULDN'T BE A PROBLEM IF CURSED ENERGY IS USED.
AS OF RIGHT NOW, ITADORI IS IN CONTROL OF HIS BODY.
IF SUKUNA DOESN'T APPEAR, THERE SHOULD BE NO PROBLEM.
THIS SHOULD BE SIMPLE.
KRAK
HOW STUPID. I'M OUTTA HERE.
GET BACK HERE, TODO.

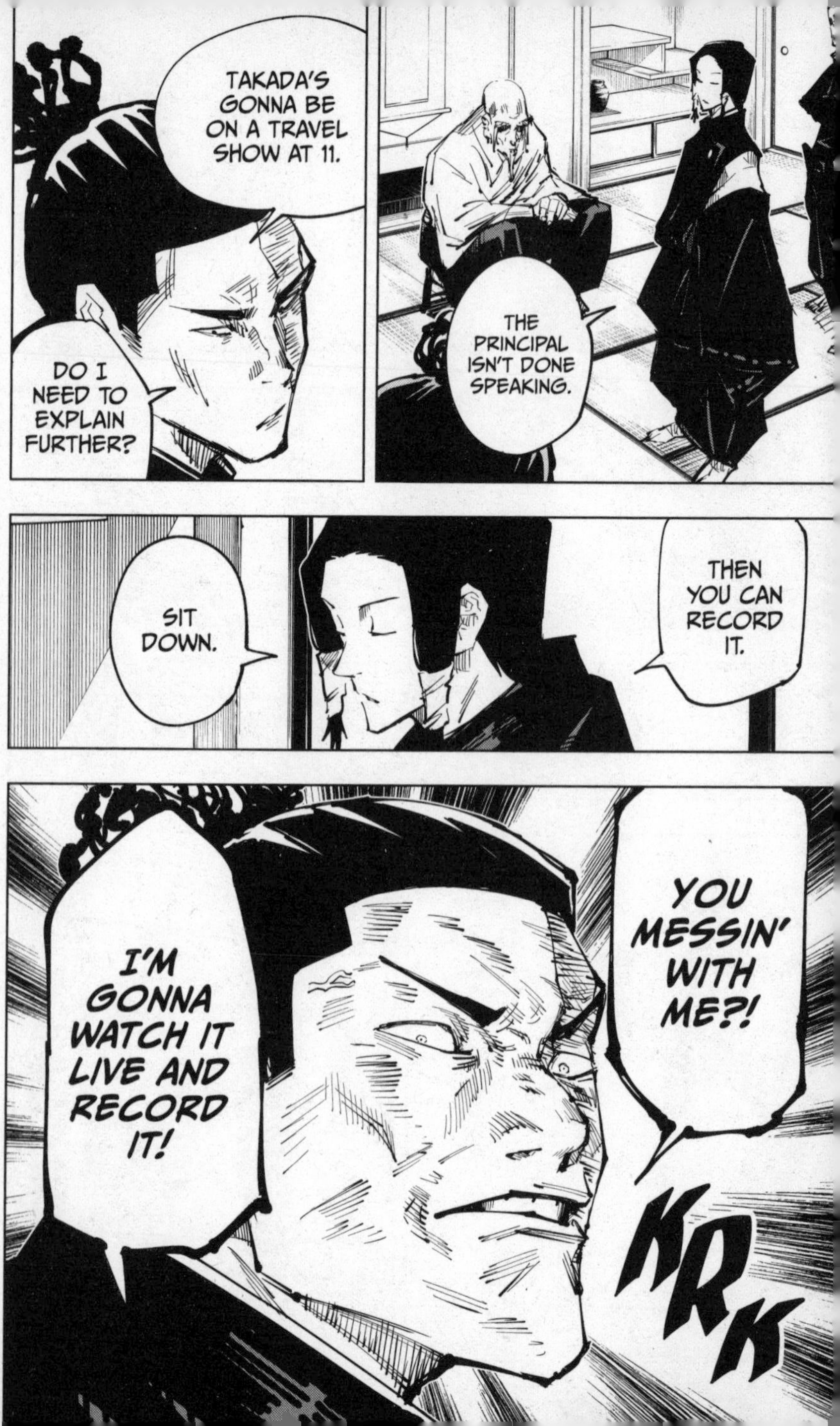
THE PRINCIPAL ISN'T DONE SPEAKING.
TAKADA'S GONNA BE ON A TRAVEL SHOW AT 11.
DO I NEED TO EXPLAIN FURTHER?
THEN YOU CAN RECORD IT.
SIT DOWN.
YOU MESSIN' WITH ME?!
I'M GONNA WATCH IT LIVE AND RECORD IT!
KRK

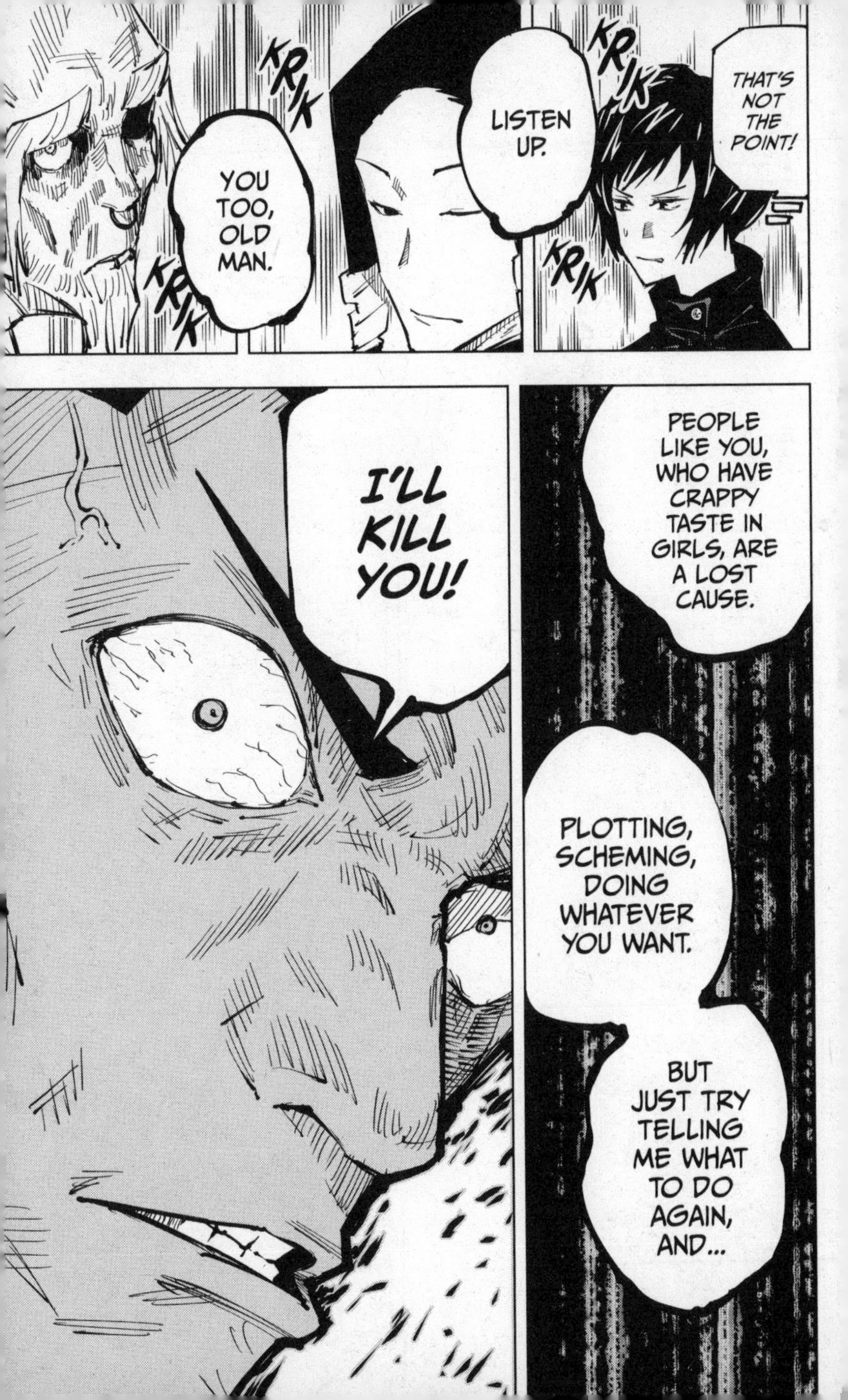
THAT'S NOT THE POINT!
KRIK
KRIK
LISTEN UP.
KRIK
KRIK
YOU TOO, OLD MAN.
PEOPLE LIKE YOU, WHO HAVE CRAPPY TASTE IN GIRLS, ARE A LOST CAUSE.
PLOTTING, SCHEMING, DOING WHATEVER YOU WANT.
BUT JUST TRY TELLING ME WHAT TO DO AGAIN, AND...
I'LL KILL YOU!

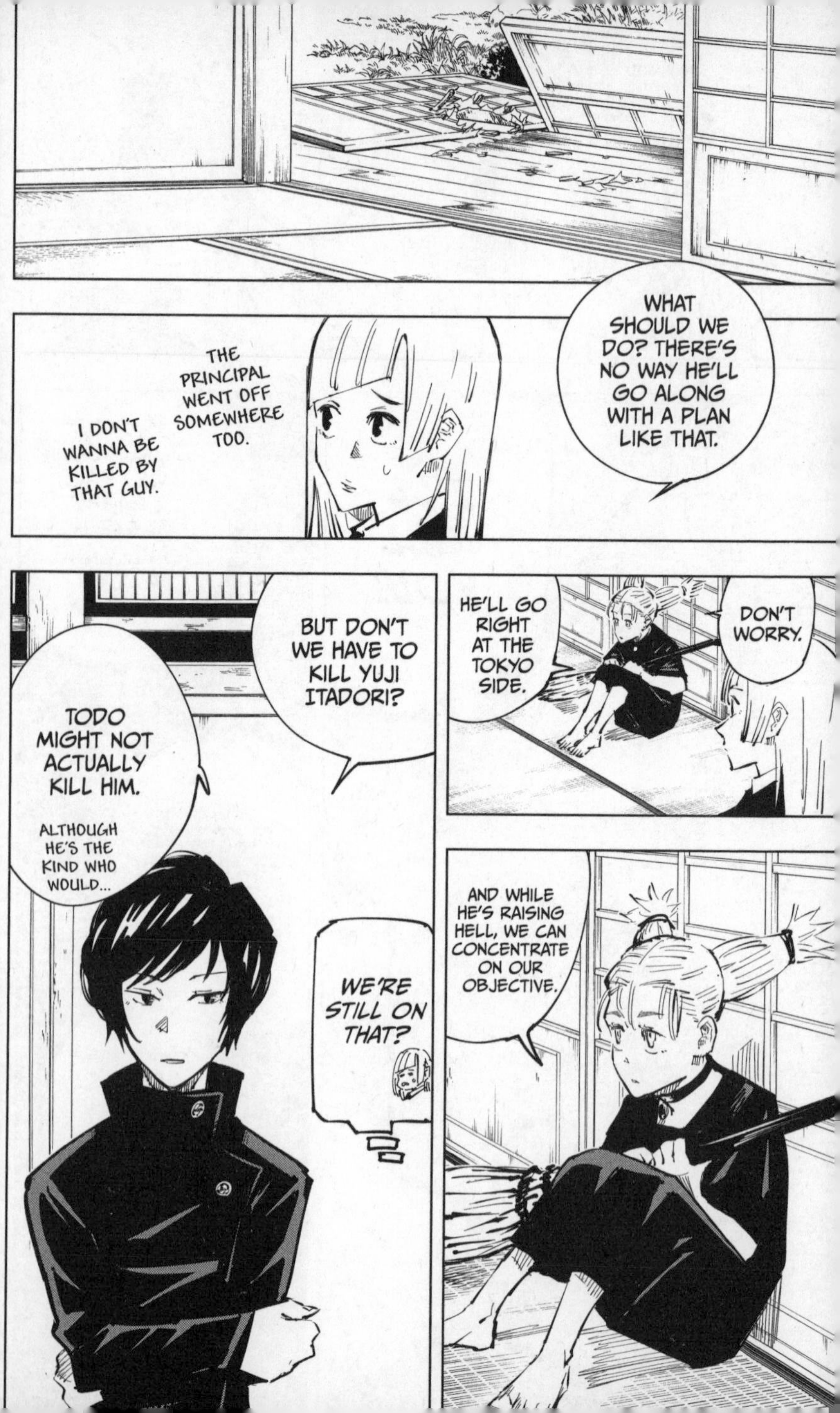
WHAT SHOULD WE DO? THERE'S NO WAY HE'LL GO ALONG WITH A PLAN LIKE THAT.
THE PRINCIPAL WENT OFF SOMEWHERE TOO.
I DON'T WANNA BE KILLED BY THAT GUY.
DON'T WORRY.
HE'LL GO RIGHT AT THE TOKYO SIDE.
AND WHILE HE'S RAISING HELL, WE CAN CONCENTRATE ON OUR OBJECTIVE.
BUT DON'T WE HAVE TO KILL YUJI ITADORI?
TODO MIGHT NOT ACTUALLY KILL HIM.
ALTHOUGH HE'S THE KIND WHO WOULD...
WE'RE STILL ON THAT?

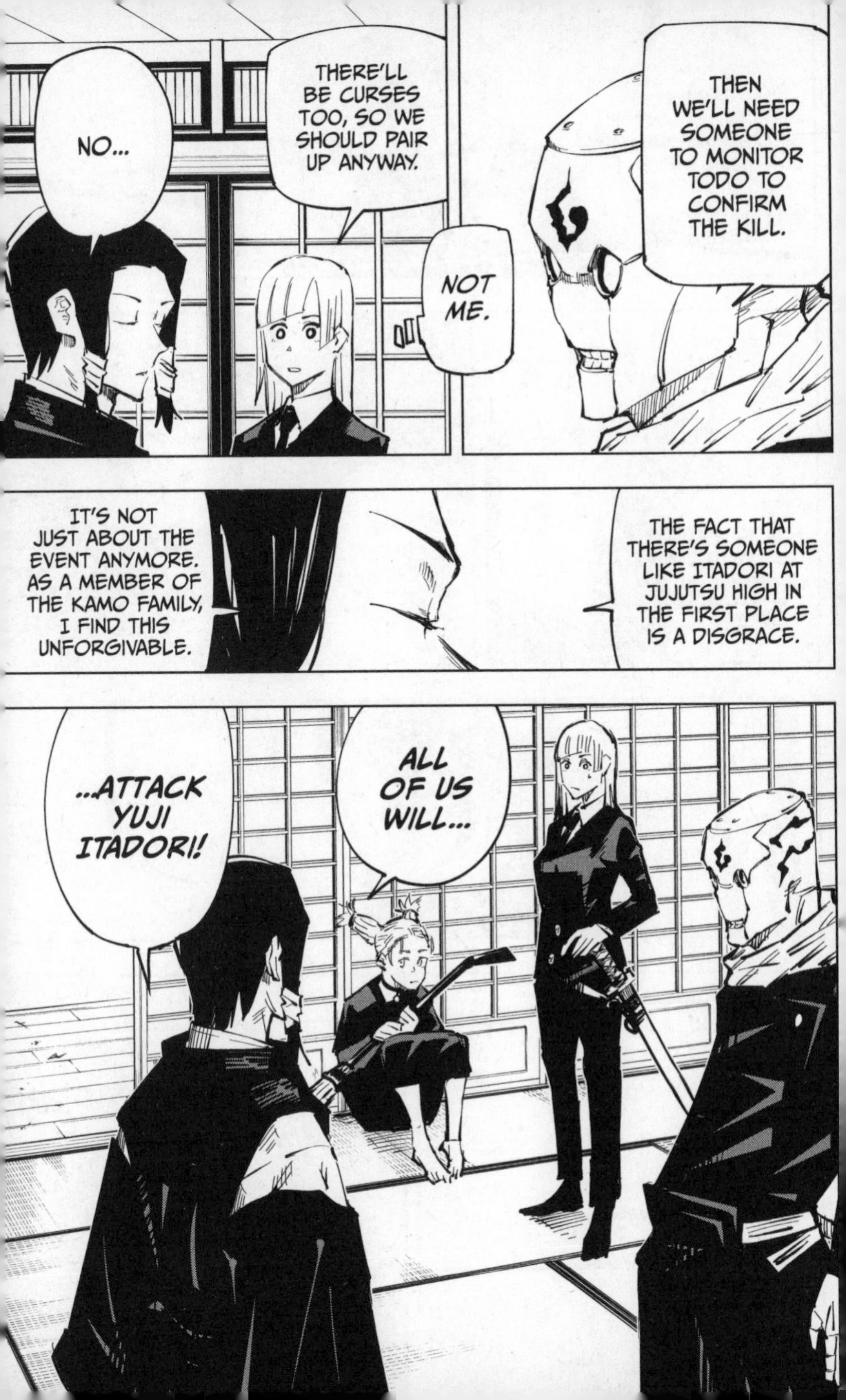
THEN WE'LL NEED SOMEONE TO MONITOR TODO TO CONFIRM THE KILL.
NOT ME.
THERE'LL BE CURSES TOO, SO WE SHOULD PAIR UP ANYWAY.
NO...
THE FACT THAT THERE'S SOMEONE LIKE ITADORI AT JUJUTSU HIGH IN THE FIRST PLACE IS A DISGRACE.
IT'S NOT JUST ABOUT THE EVENT ANYMORE. AS A MEMBER OF THE KAMO FAMILY, I FIND THIS UNFORGIVABLE.
ALL OF US WILL...
...ATTACK YUJI ITADORI!

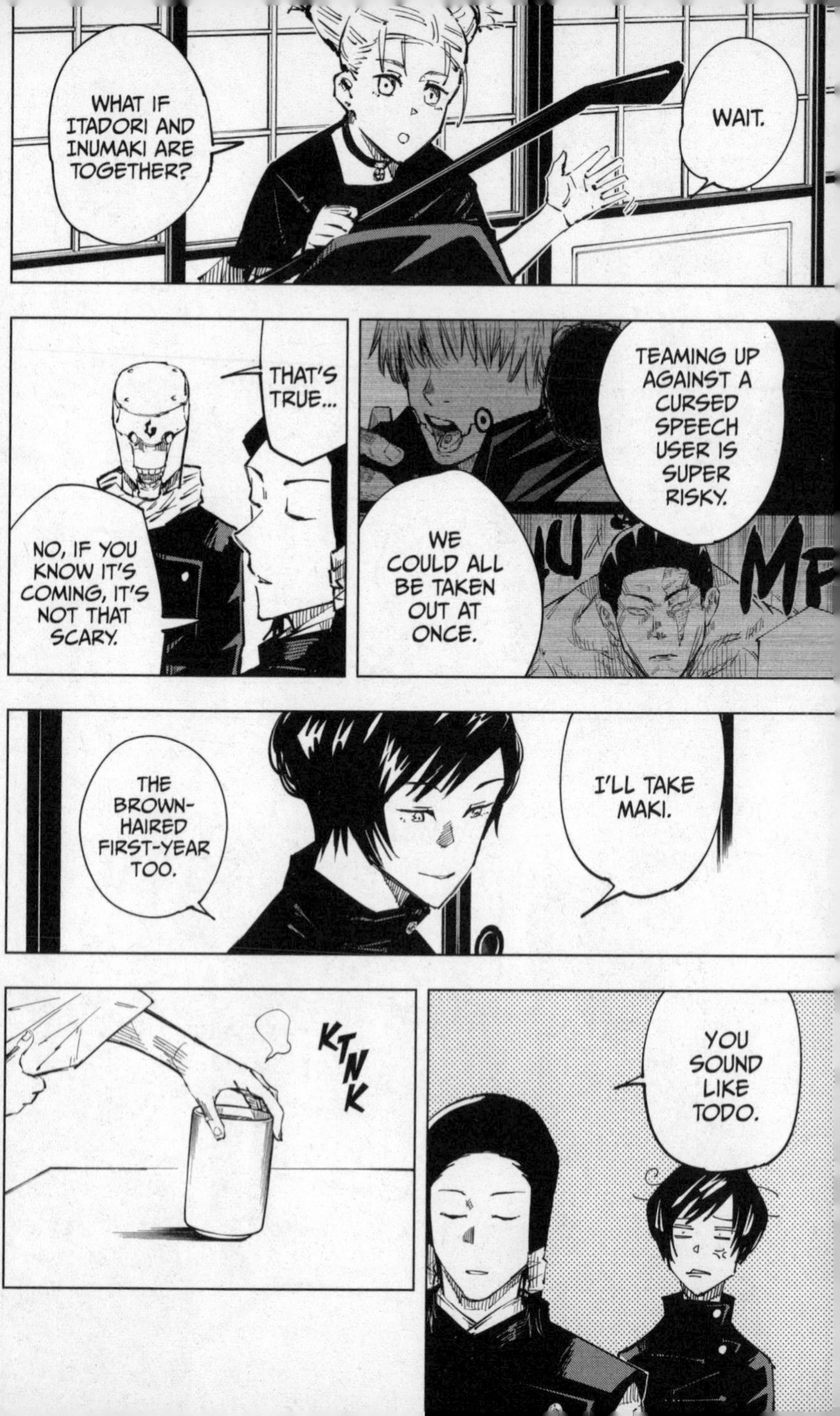
WAIT.
WHAT IF ITADORI AND INUMAKI ARE TOGETHER?
TEAMING UP AGAINST A CURSED SPEECH USER IS SUPER RISKY.
WE COULD ALL BE TAKEN OUT AT ONCE.
THAT'S TRUE...
NO, IF YOU KNOW IT'S COMING, IT'S NOT THAT SCARY.
I'LL TAKE MAKI.
THE BROWN-HAIRED FIRST-YEAR TOO.
YOU SOUND LIKE TODO.
KTNK

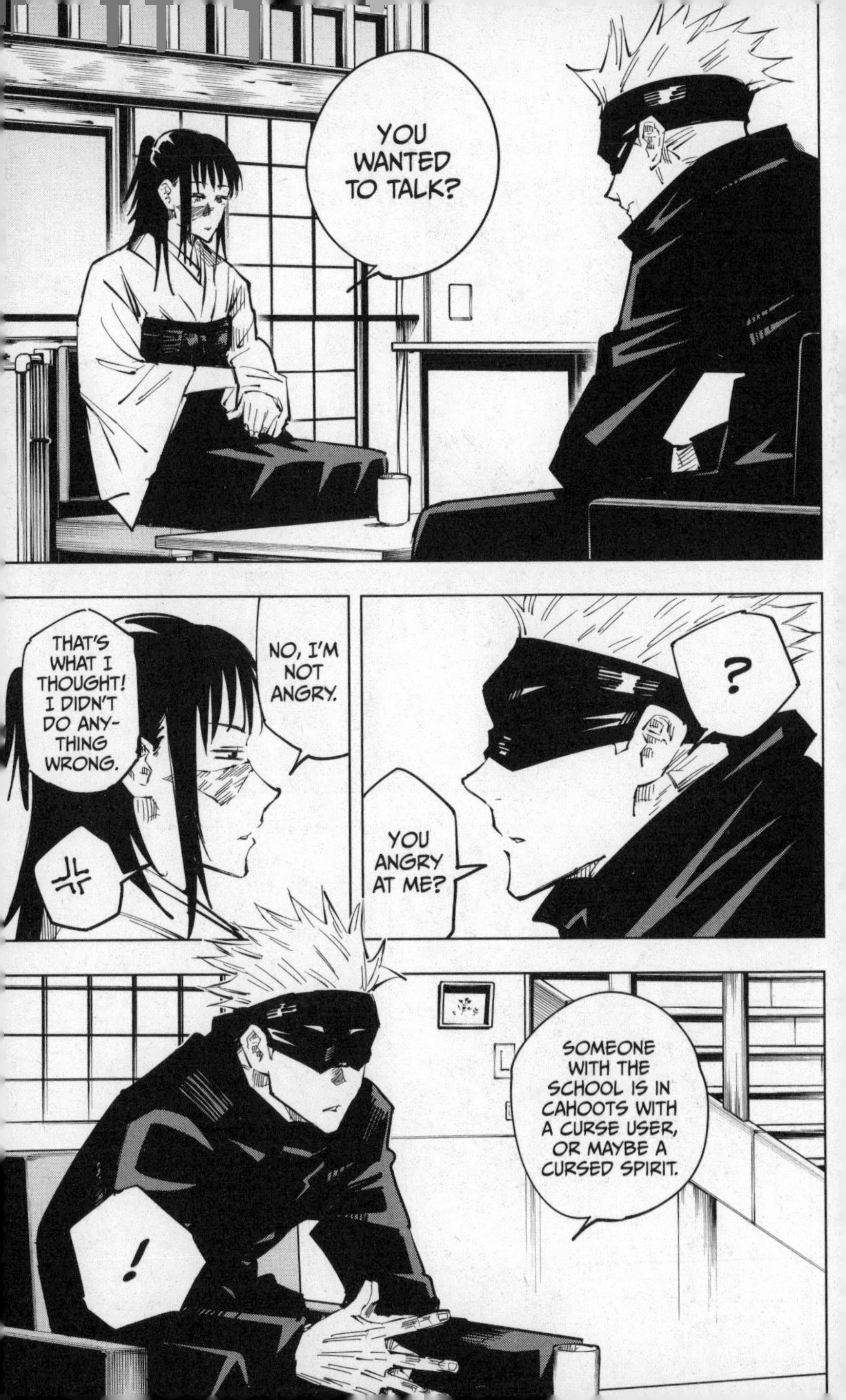
YOU WANTED TO TALK?
?
YOU ANGRY AT ME?
NO, I'M NOT ANGRY.
THAT'S WHAT I THOUGHT! I DIDN'T DO ANY-THING WRONG.
SOMEONE WITH THE SCHOOL IS IN CAHOOTS WITH A CURSE USER, OR MAYBE A CURSED SPIRIT.
!

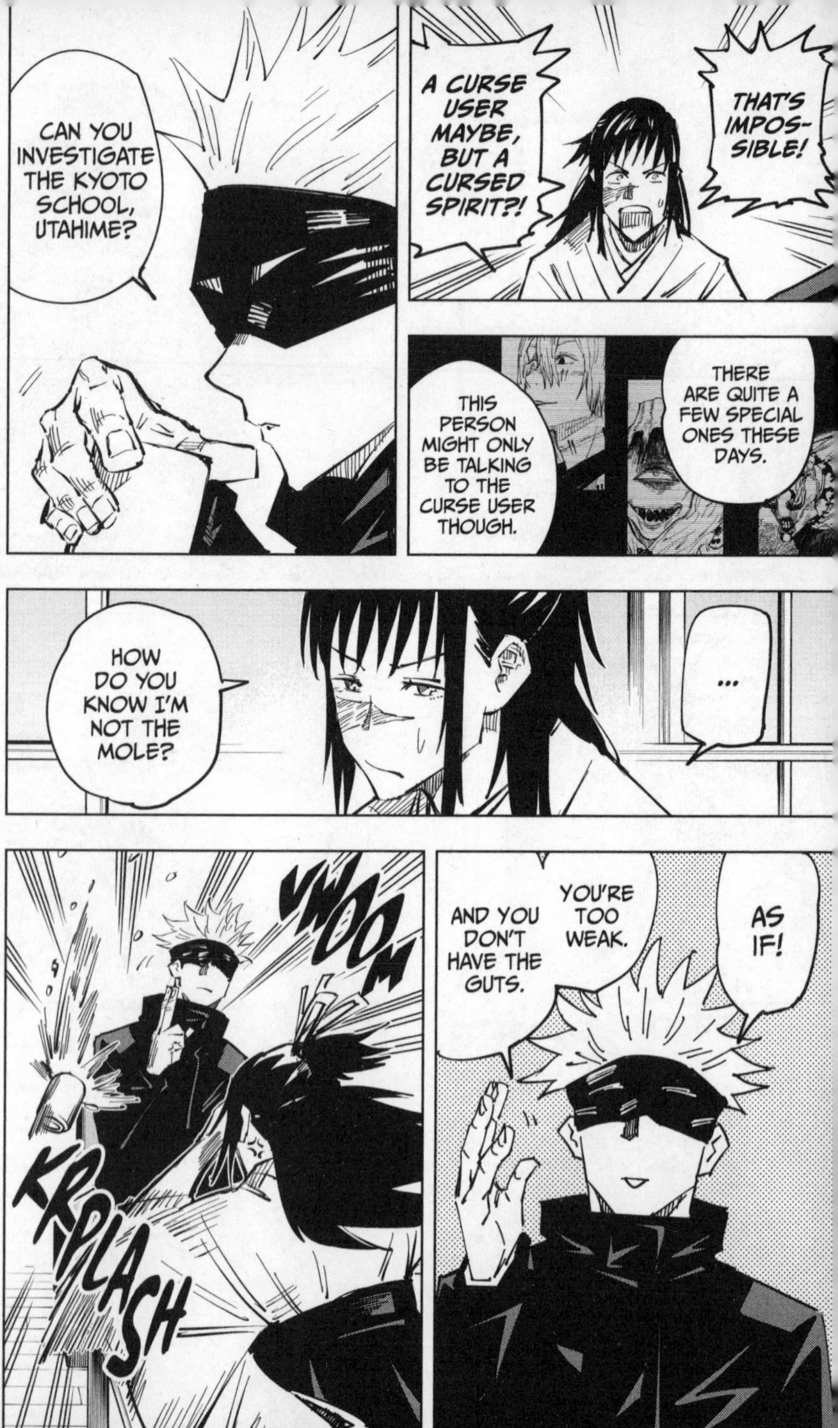
THAT'S IMPOSSIBLE!
A CURSE USER MAYBE, BUT A CURSED SPIRIT?!
THERE ARE QUITE A FEW SPECIAL ONES THESE DAYS.
THIS PERSON MIGHT ONLY BE TALKING TO THE CURSE USER THOUGH.
CAN YOU INVESTIGATE THE KYOTO SCHOOL, UTAHIME?
...
HOW DO YOU KNOW I'M NOT THE MOLE?
AS IF!
YOU'RE TOO WEAK.
AND YOU DON'T HAVE THE GUTS.
VWOOM
KRPLASH

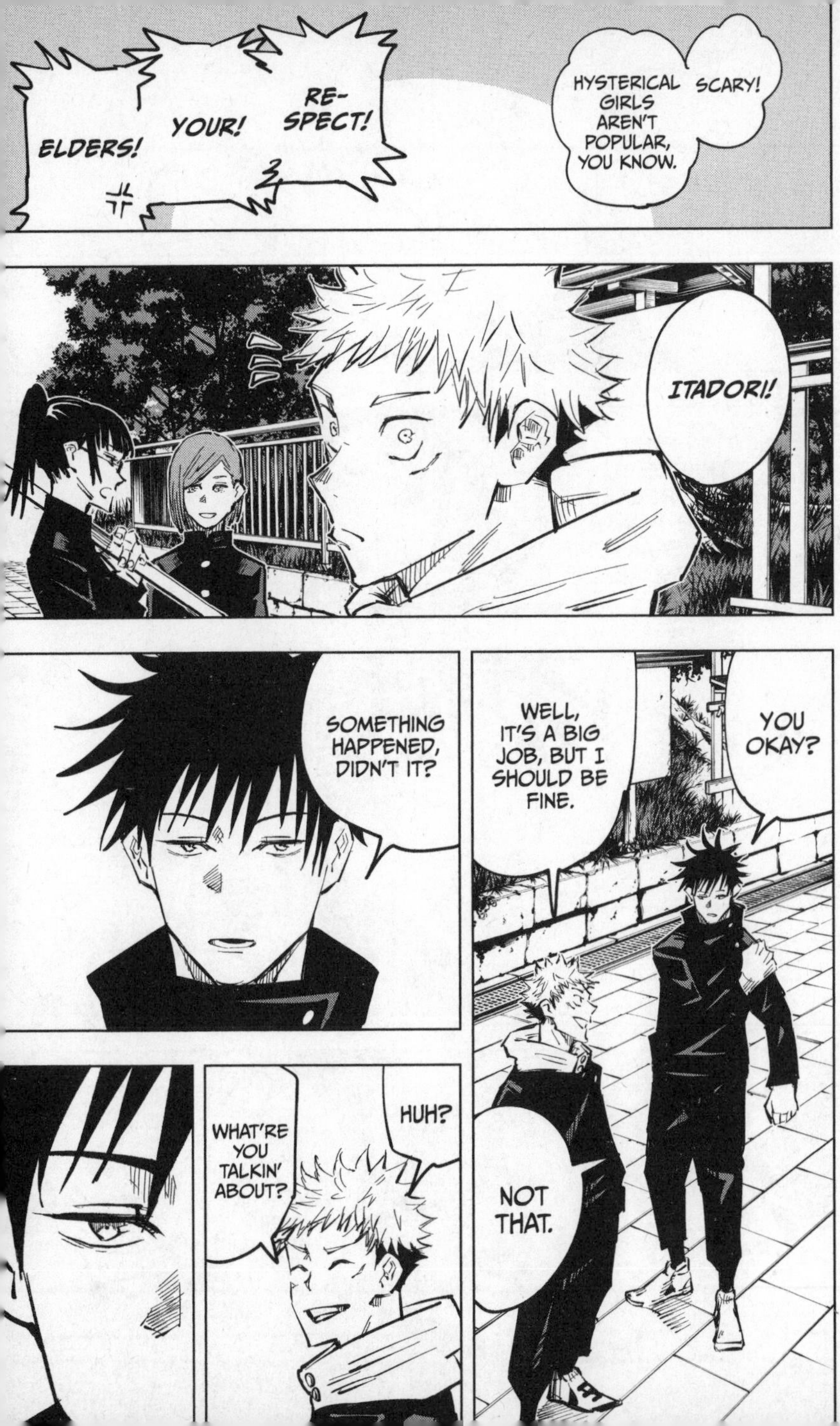

SCARY!
HYSTERICAL GIRLS AREN'T POPULAR, YOU KNOW.
RE-SPECT!
YOUR!
ELDERS!
ITADORI!
YOU OKAY?
WELL, IT'S A BIG JOB, BUT I SHOULD BE FINE.
NOT THAT.
SOMETHING HAPPENED, DIDN'T IT?
HUH?
WHAT'RE YOU TALKIN' ABOUT?

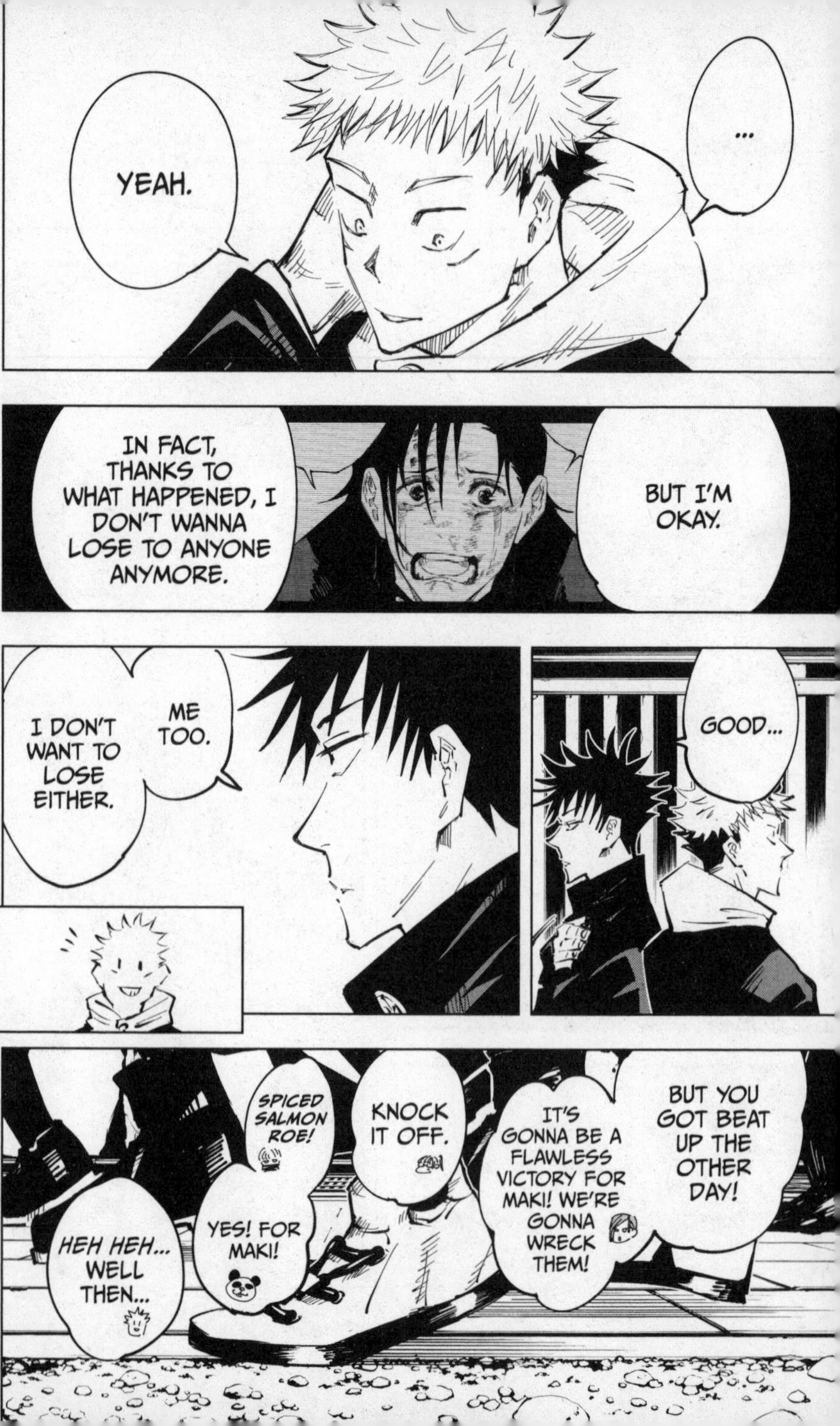
...
YEAH.
BUT I'M OKAY.
IN FACT, THANKS TO WHAT HAPPENED, I DON'T WANNA LOSE TO ANYONE ANYMORE.
GOOD...
ME TOO.
I DON'T WANT TO LOSE EITHER.
BUT YOU GOT BEAT UP THE OTHER DAY!
IT'S GONNA BE A FLAWLESS VICTORY FOR MAKI! WE'RE GONNA WRECK THEM!
KNOCK IT OFF.
SPICED SALMON ROE!
YES! FOR MAKI!
HEH HEH... WELL THEN...

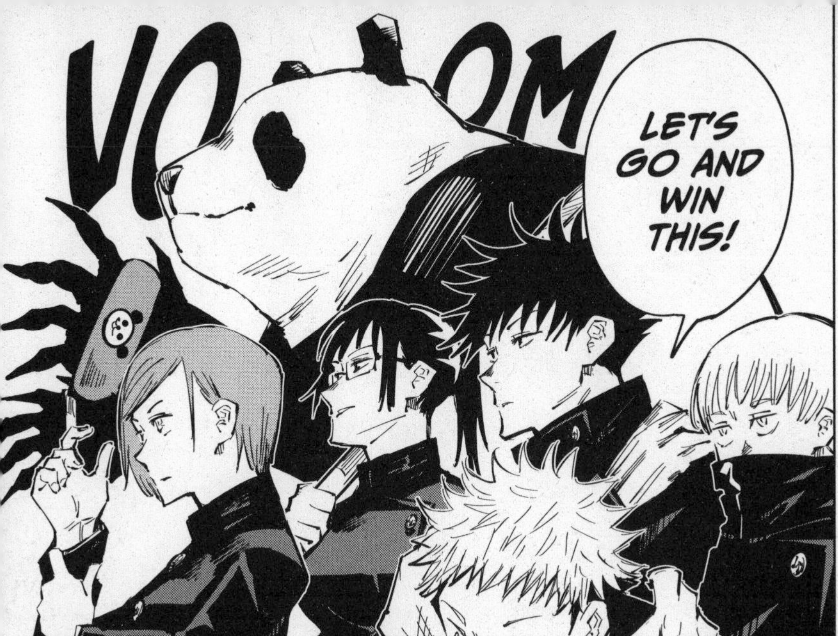
LET'S GO AND WIN THIS!
VO OM

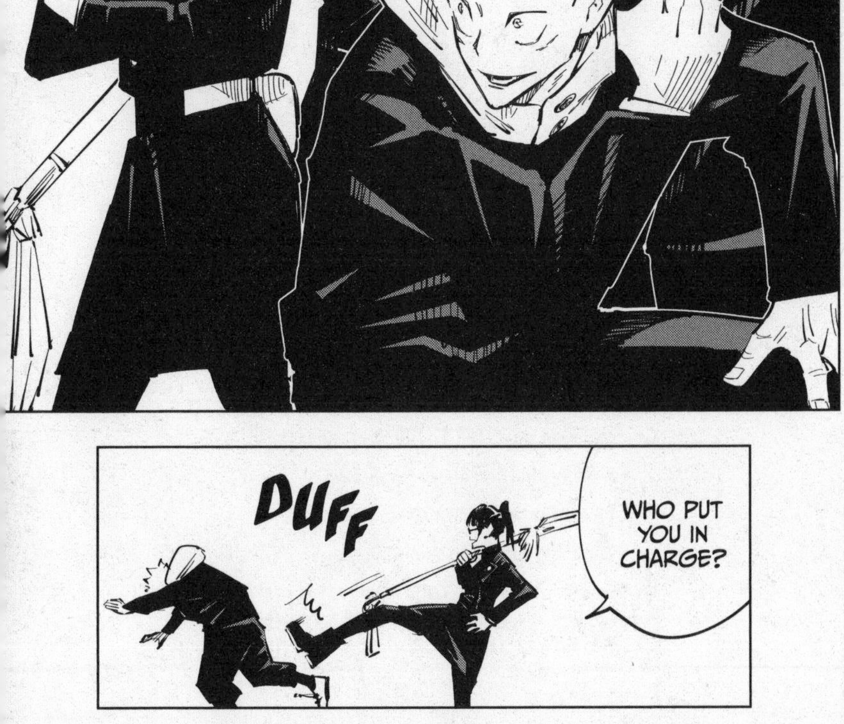
WHO PUT YOU IN CHARGE?
DUFF

I've been getting a lot of letters asking about this scene.

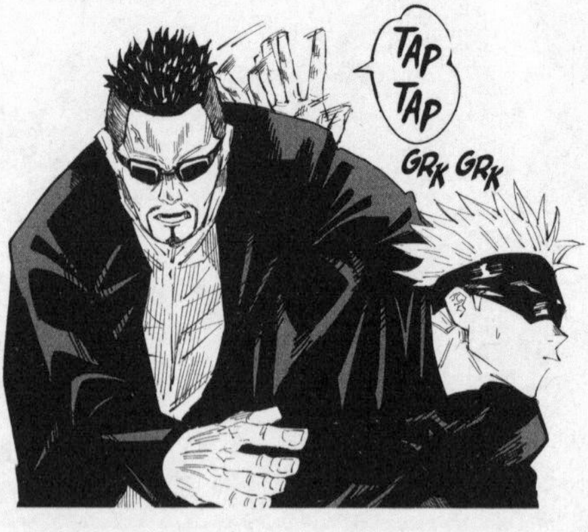
TAP TAP
GRK GRK

Gojo is being punished for three reason:

- the fact that Itadori was still alive
- for messing with Principal Gakuganji
- for being just plain annoying

By using his technique, Gojo could easily protect himself, but he's "reading the room," so to speak. Besides, the students are watching.

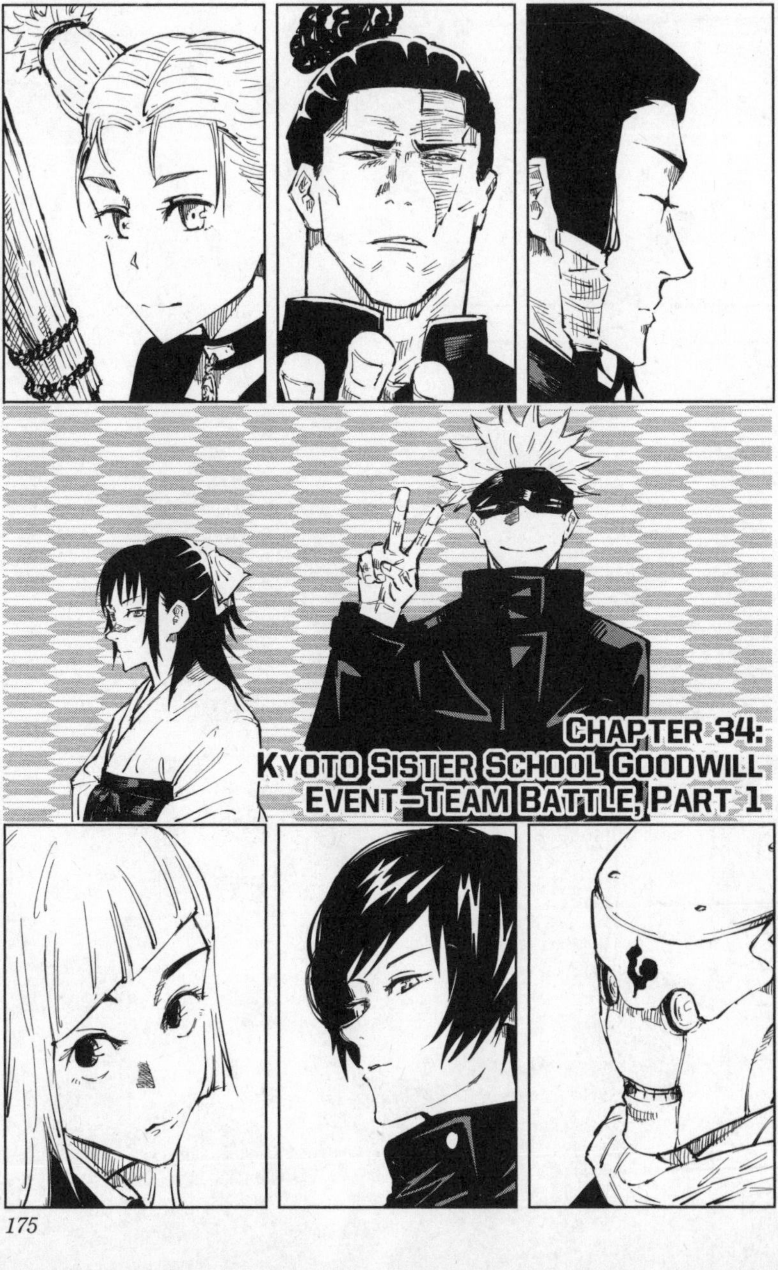
CHAPTER 34:
KYOTO SISTER SCHOOL GOODWILL EVENT–TEAM BATTLE, PART 1

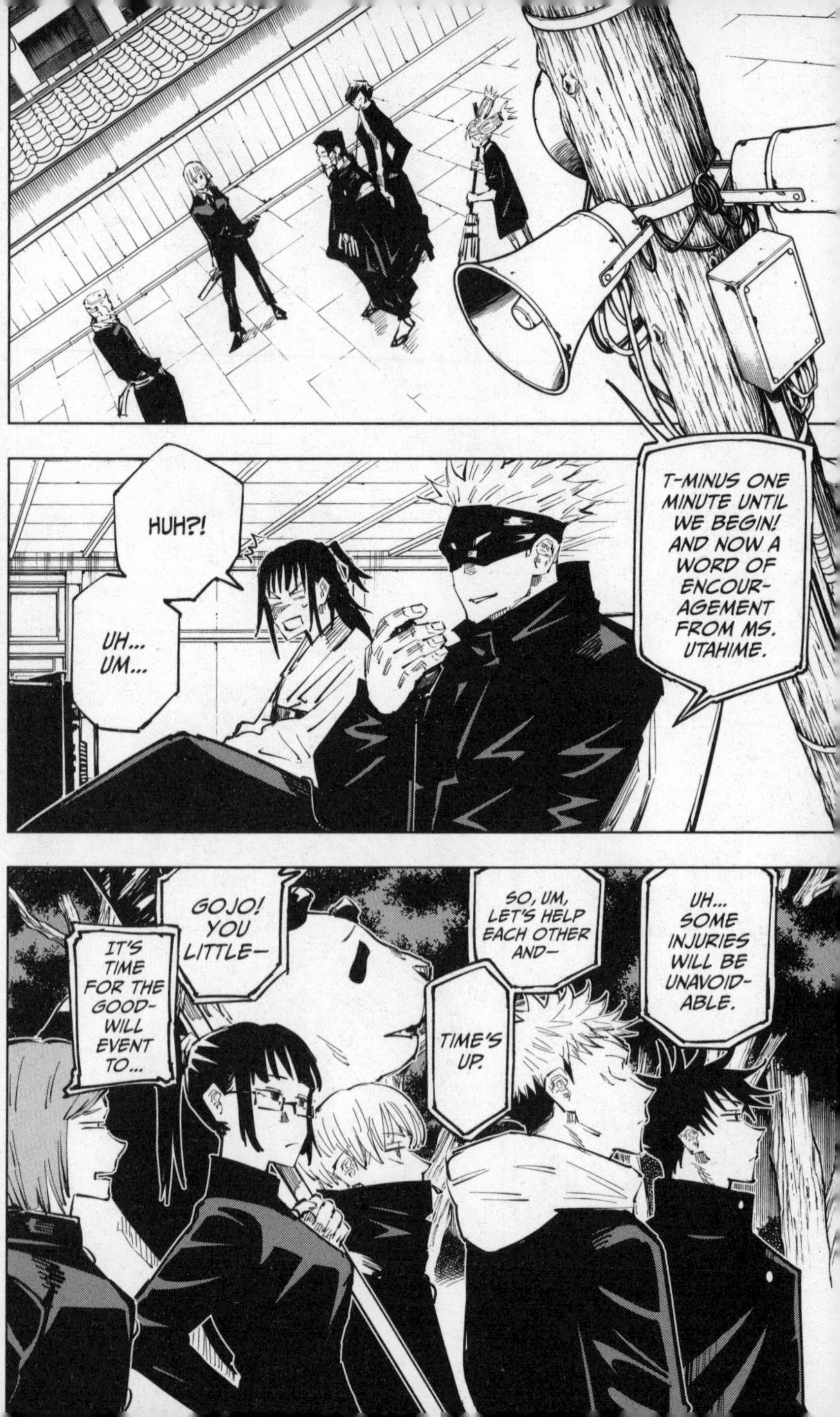
T-MINUS ONE MINUTE UNTIL WE BEGIN! AND NOW A WORD OF ENCOURAGEMENT FROM MS. UTAHIME.
HUH?!
UH... UM...
UH... SOME INJURIES WILL BE UNAVOIDABLE.
SO, UM, LET'S HELP EACH OTHER AND—
TIME'S UP.
GOJO! YOU LITTLE—
IT'S TIME FOR THE GOOD-WILL EVENT TO...

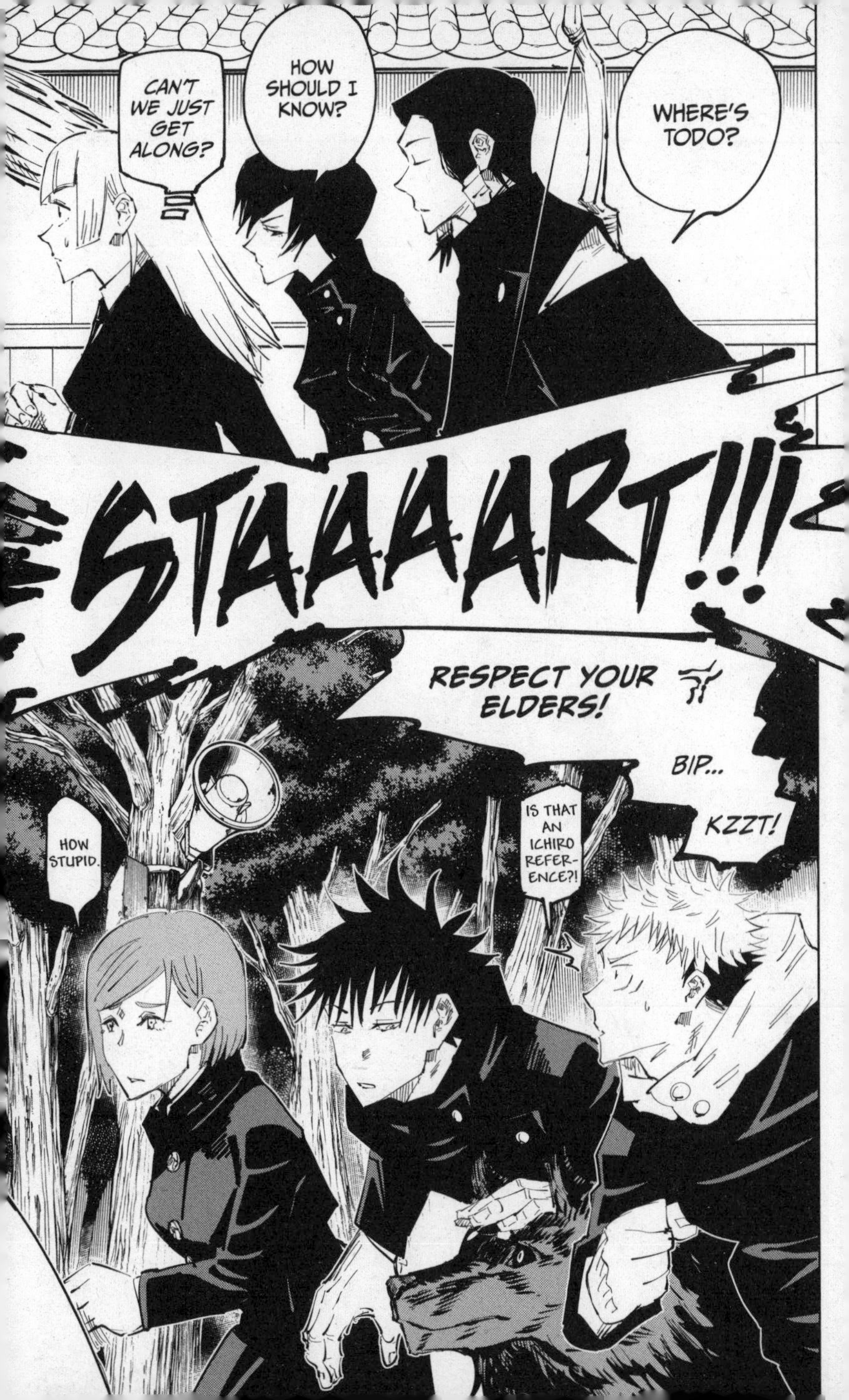
WHERE'S TODO?
HOW SHOULD I KNOW?
CAN'T WE JUST GET ALONG?
STAAAART!!!
RESPECT YOUR ELDERS!
BIP...
KZZT!
IS THAT AN ICHIRO REFERENCE?!
HOW STUPID.

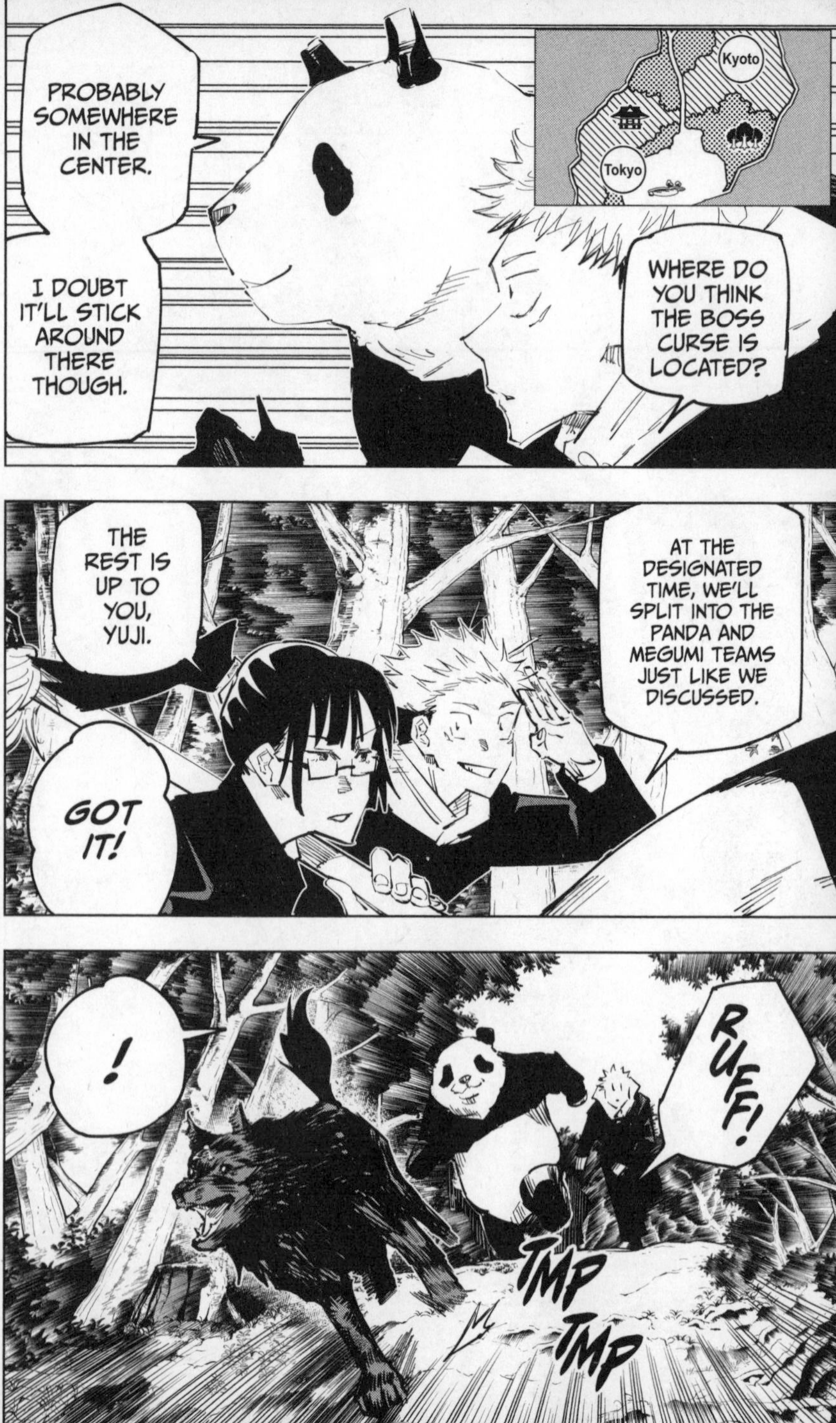
Kyoto
Tokyo
WHERE DO YOU THINK THE BOSS CURSE IS LOCATED?
PROBABLY SOMEWHERE IN THE CENTER.
I DOUBT IT'LL STICK AROUND THERE THOUGH.
AT THE DESIGNATED TIME, WE'LL SPLIT INTO THE PANDA AND MEGUMI TEAMS JUST LIKE WE DISCUSSED.
THE REST IS UP TO YOU, YUJI.
GOT IT!
RUFF!
!
TMP
TMP

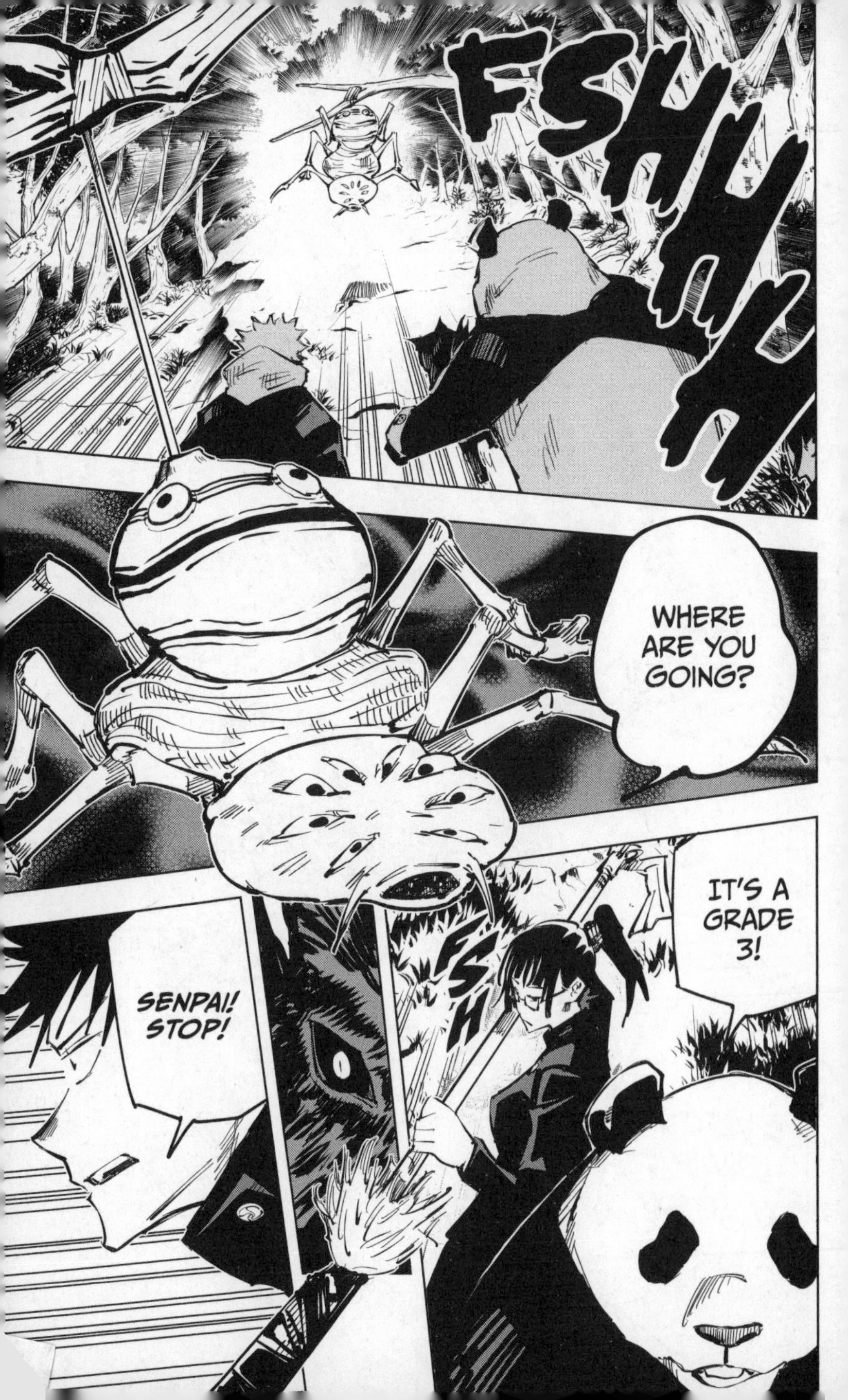
FSHHH
WHERE ARE YOU GOING?
IT'S A GRADE 3!
FSHH
SENPAI! STOP!

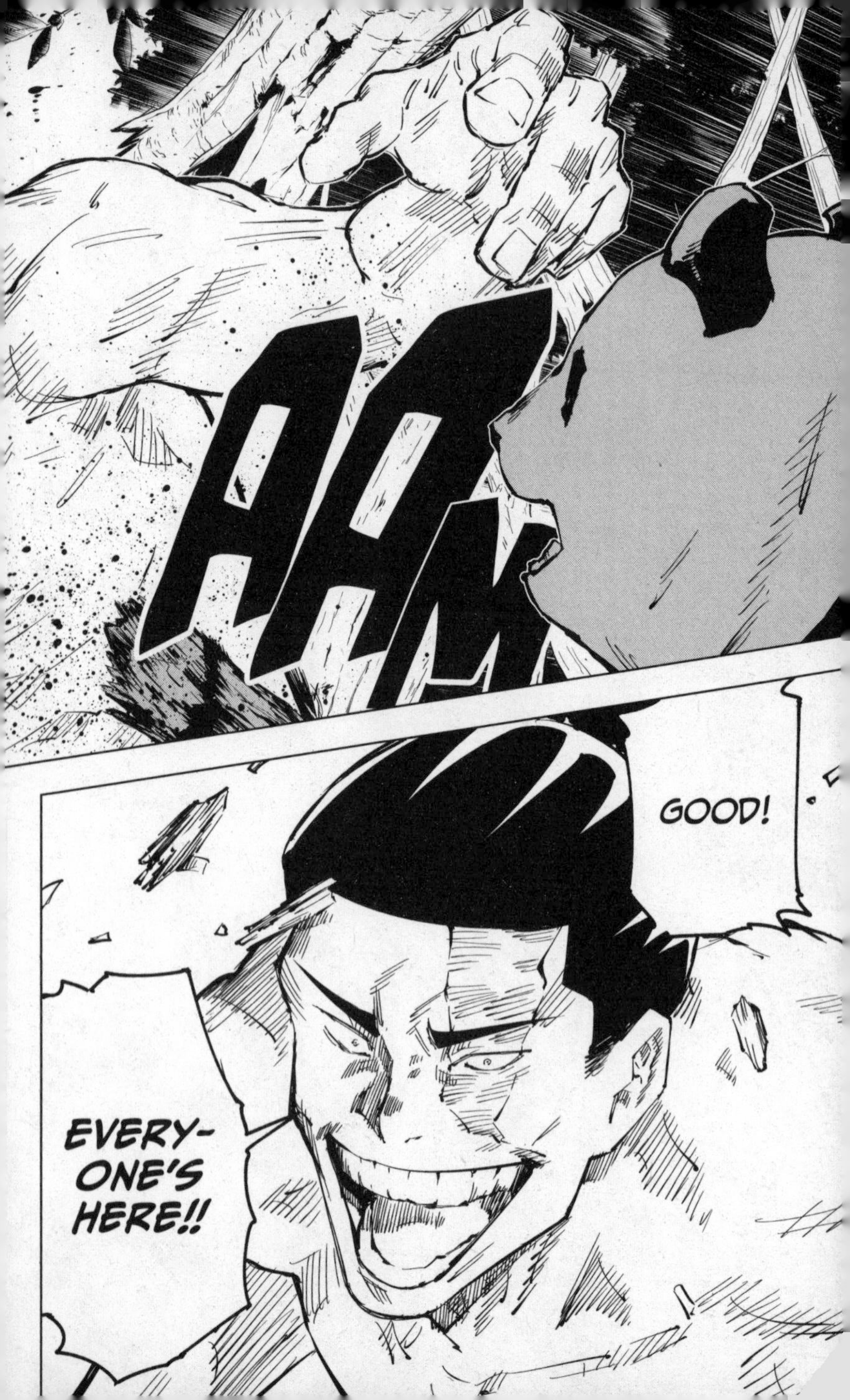
GOOD!
EVERY-ONE'S HERE!!

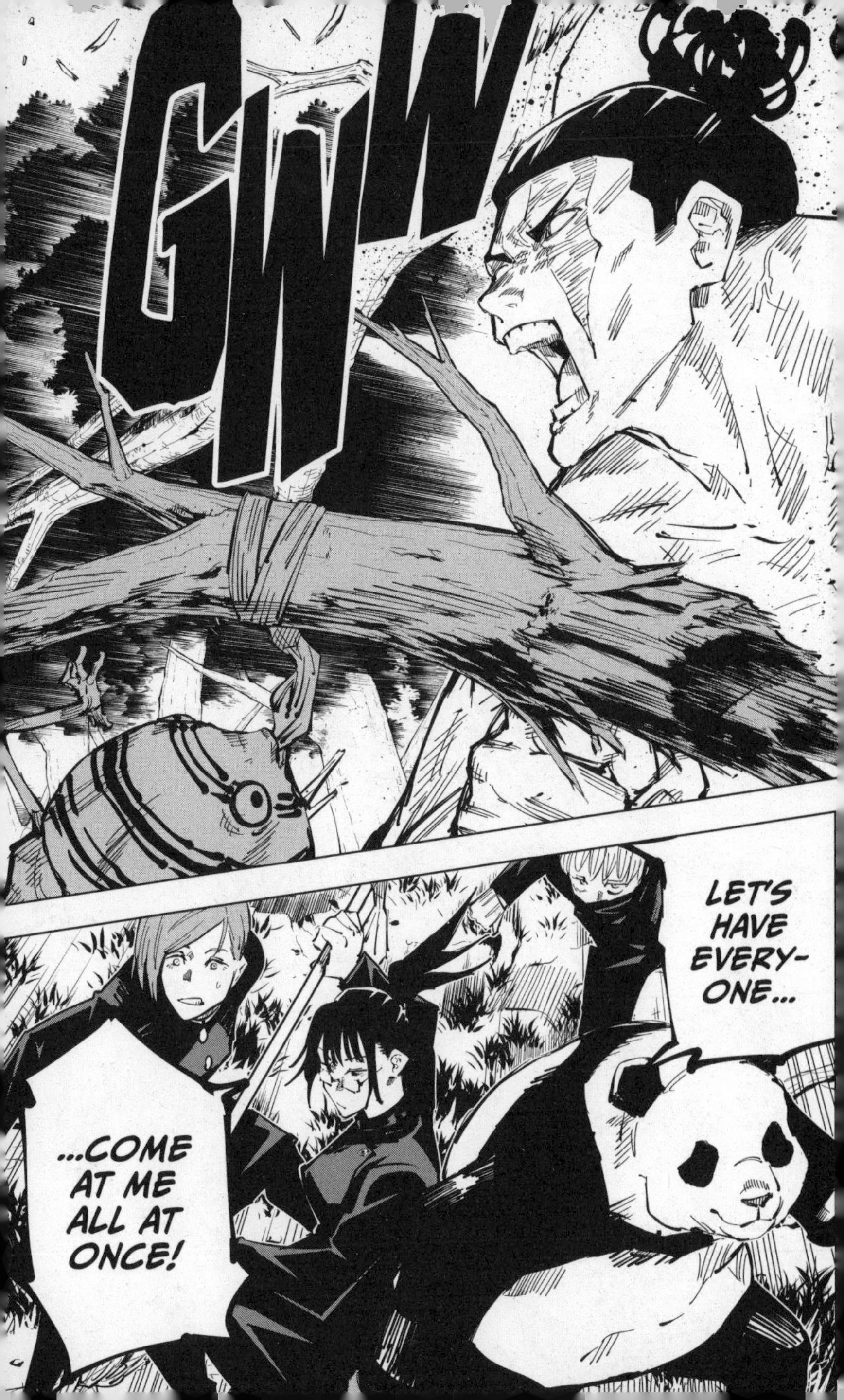
GWW
LET'S HAVE EVERY-ONE...
...COME AT ME ALL AT ONCE!

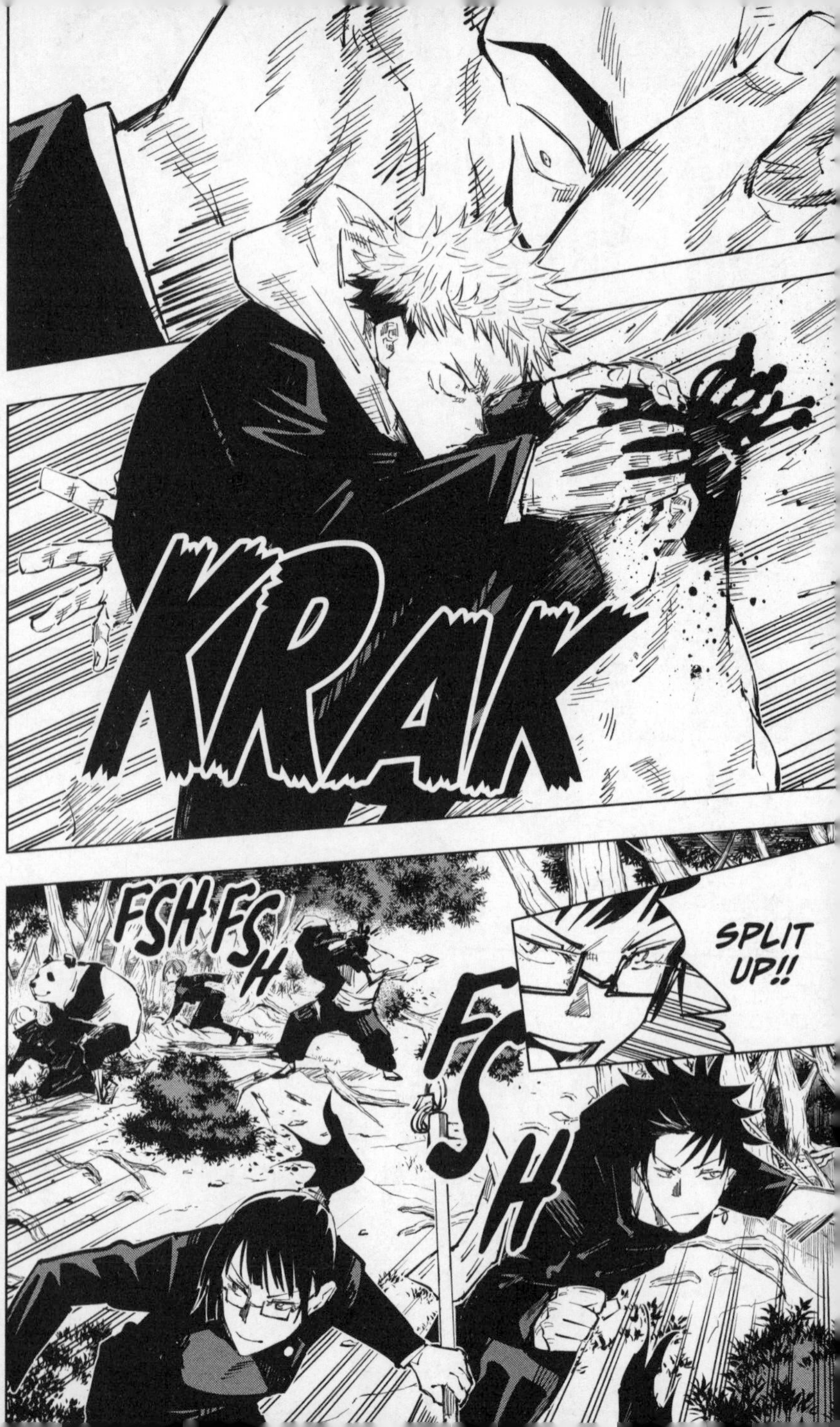
KRAK
SPLIT UP!!
FSH
FSH FSH

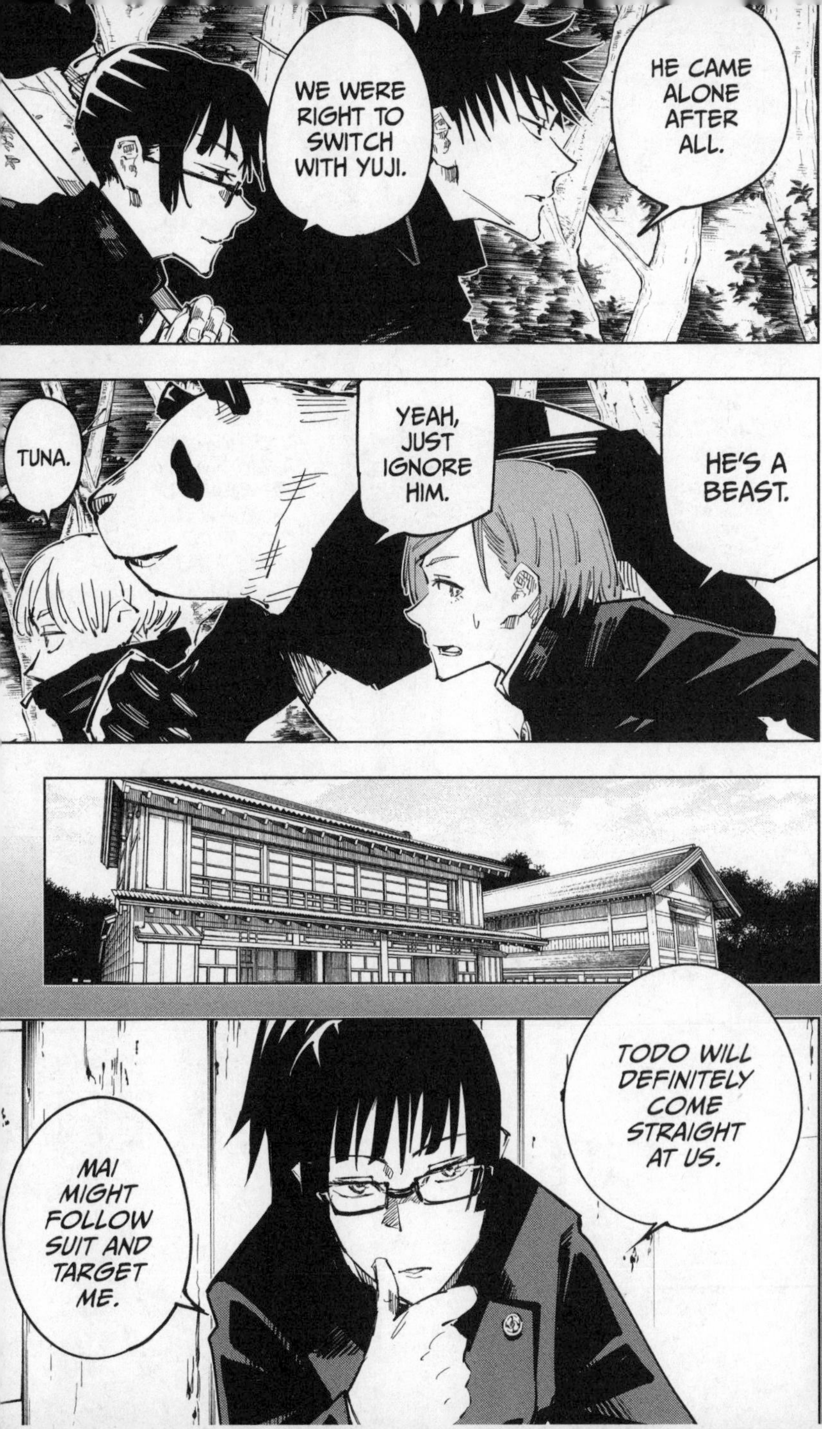
HE CAME ALONE AFTER ALL.
WE WERE RIGHT TO SWITCH WITH YUJI.
HE'S A BEAST.
YEAH, JUST IGNORE HIM.
TUNA.
TODO WILL DEFINITELY COME STRAIGHT AT US.
MAI MIGHT FOLLOW SUIT AND TARGET ME.

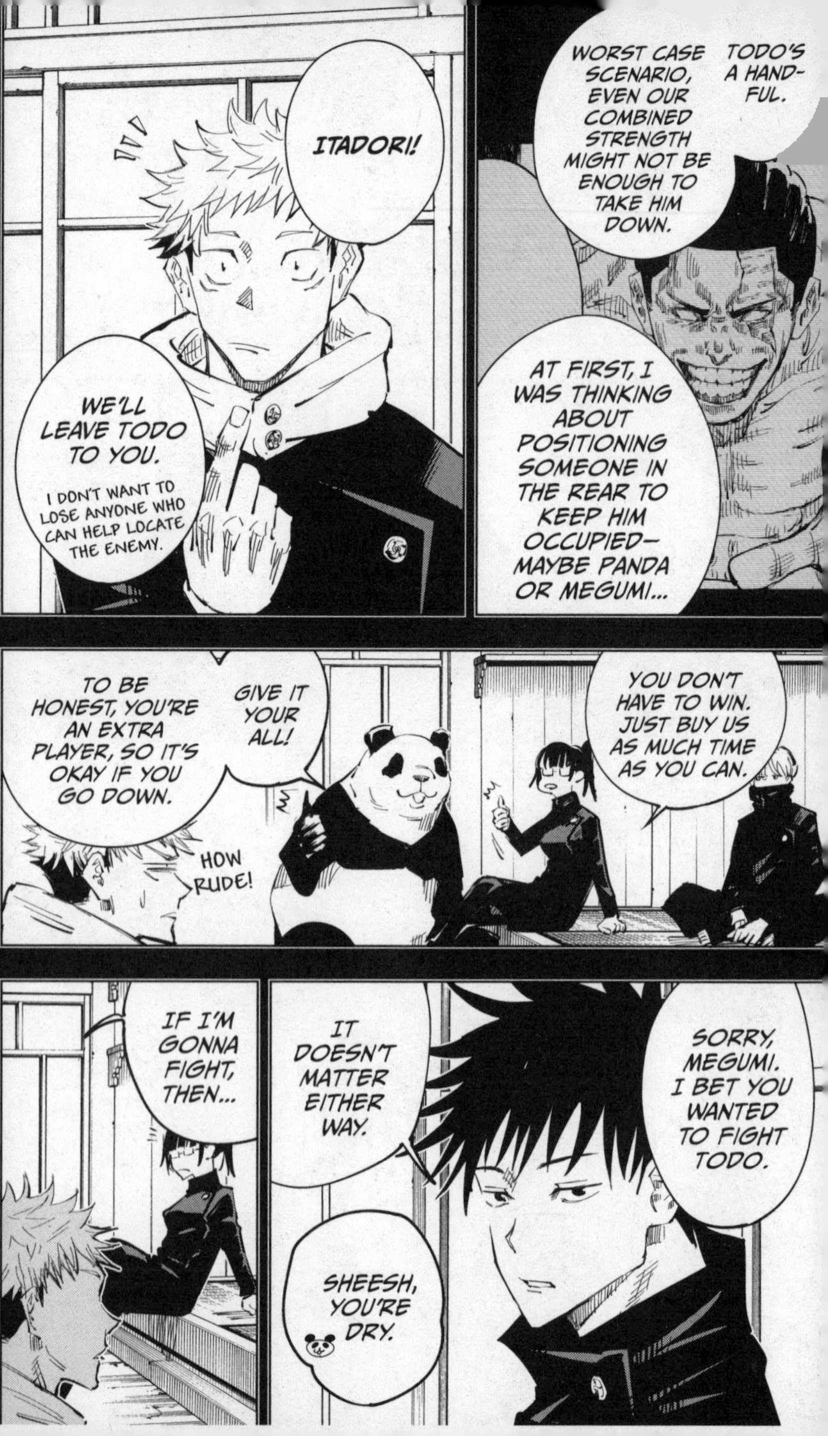
TODO'S A HANDFUL.
WORST CASE SCENARIO, EVEN OUR COMBINED STRENGTH MIGHT NOT BE ENOUGH TO TAKE HIM DOWN.
AT FIRST, I WAS THINKING ABOUT POSITIONING SOMEONE IN THE REAR TO KEEP HIM OCCUPIED— MAYBE PANDA OR MEGUMI...
ITADORI!
WE'LL LEAVE TODO TO YOU.
I DON'T WANT TO LOSE ANYONE WHO CAN HELP LOCATE THE ENEMY.
YOU DON'T HAVE TO WIN. JUST BUY US AS MUCH TIME AS YOU CAN.
GIVE IT YOUR ALL!
TO BE HONEST, YOU'RE AN EXTRA PLAYER, SO IT'S OKAY IF YOU GO DOWN.
HOW RUDE!
SORRY, MEGUMI. I BET YOU WANTED TO FIGHT TODO.
IT DOESN'T MATTER EITHER WAY.
SHEESH, YOU'RE DRY.
IF I'M GONNA FIGHT, THEN...

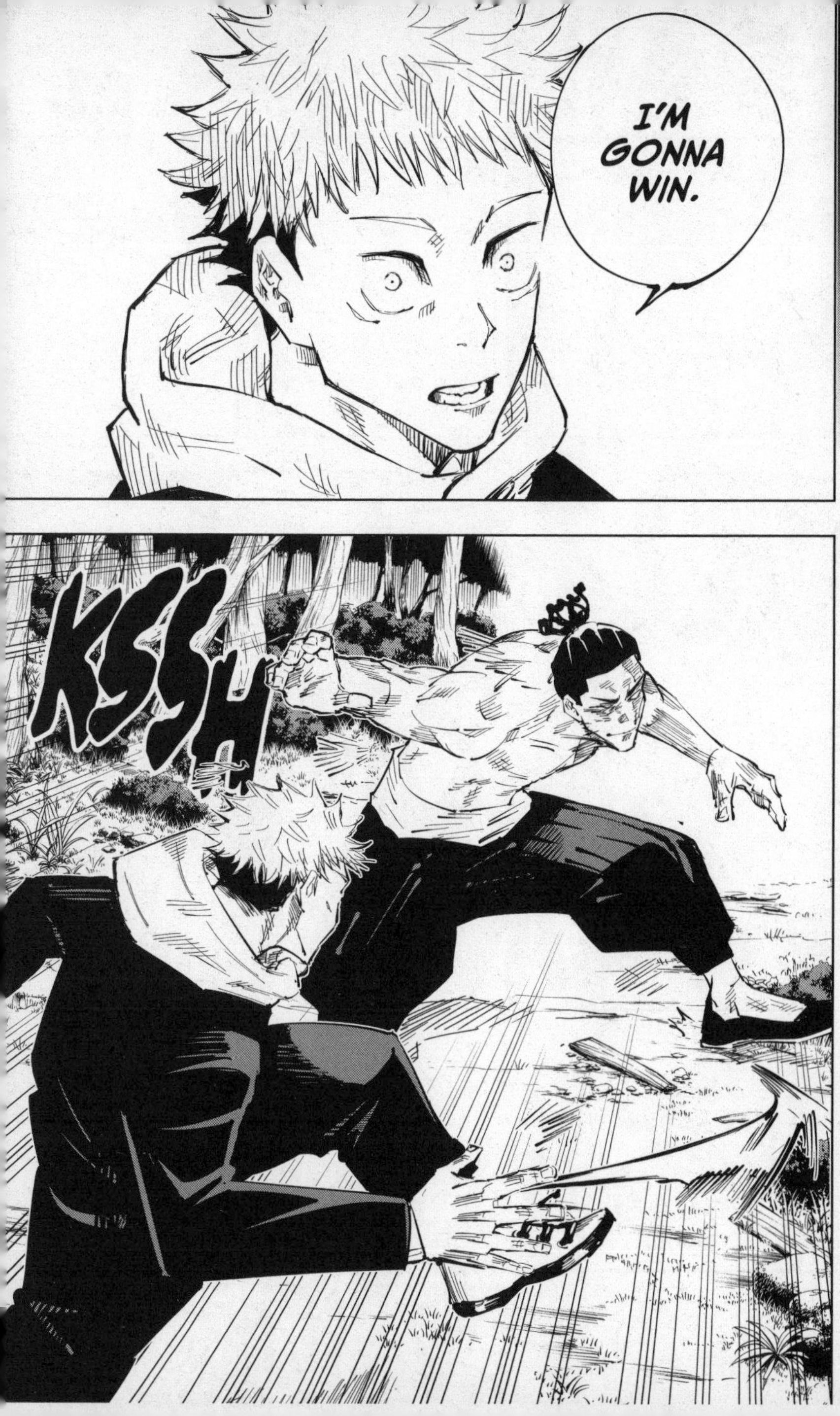
I'M GONNA WIN.
KSSH

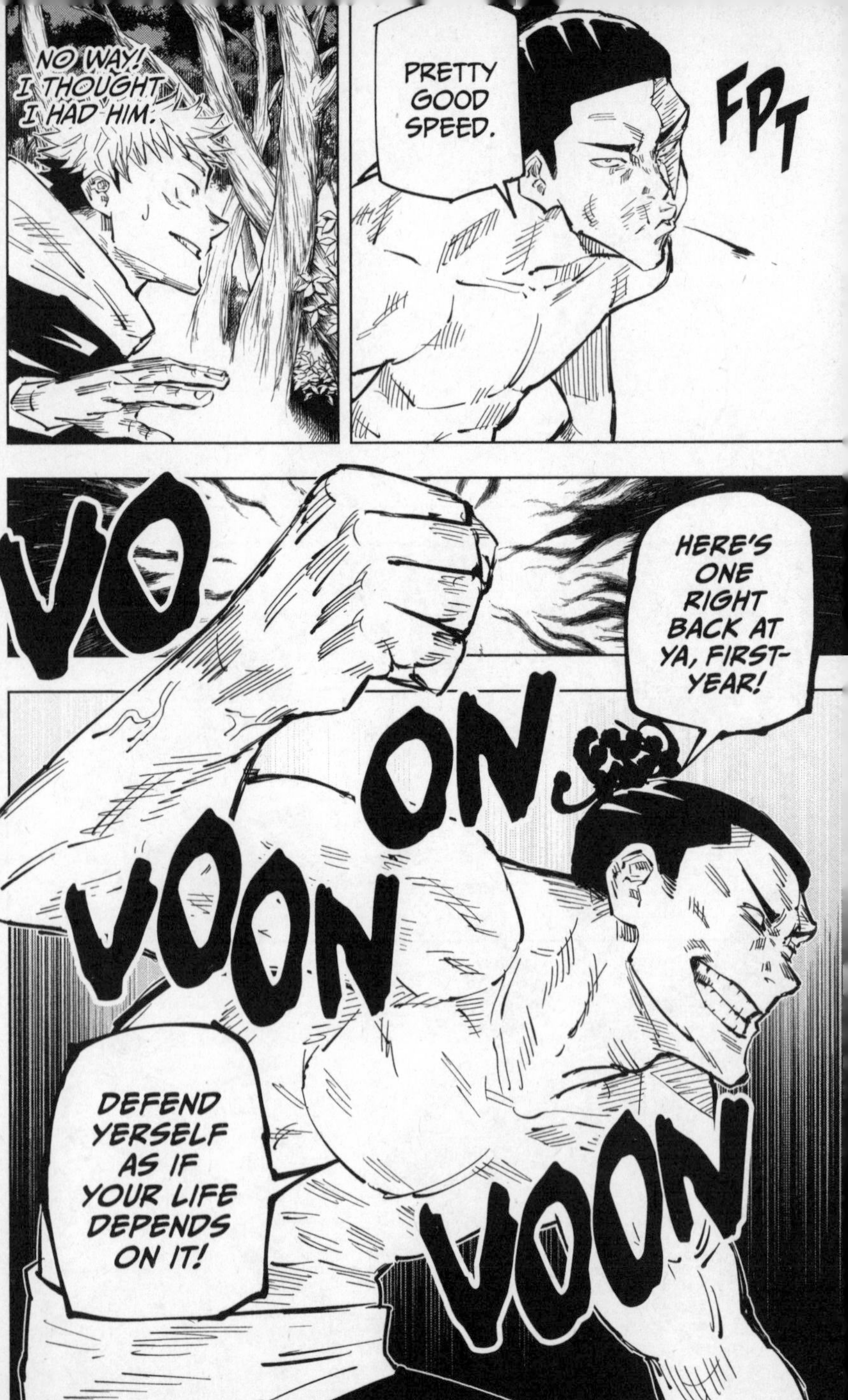
PRETTY GOOD SPEED.
FPT
NO WAY! I THOUGHT I HAD HIM.
HERE'S ONE RIGHT BACK AT YA, FIRST-YEAR!
VO
ON
VOON
VOON
DEFEND YERSELF AS IF YOUR LIFE DEPENDS ON IT!

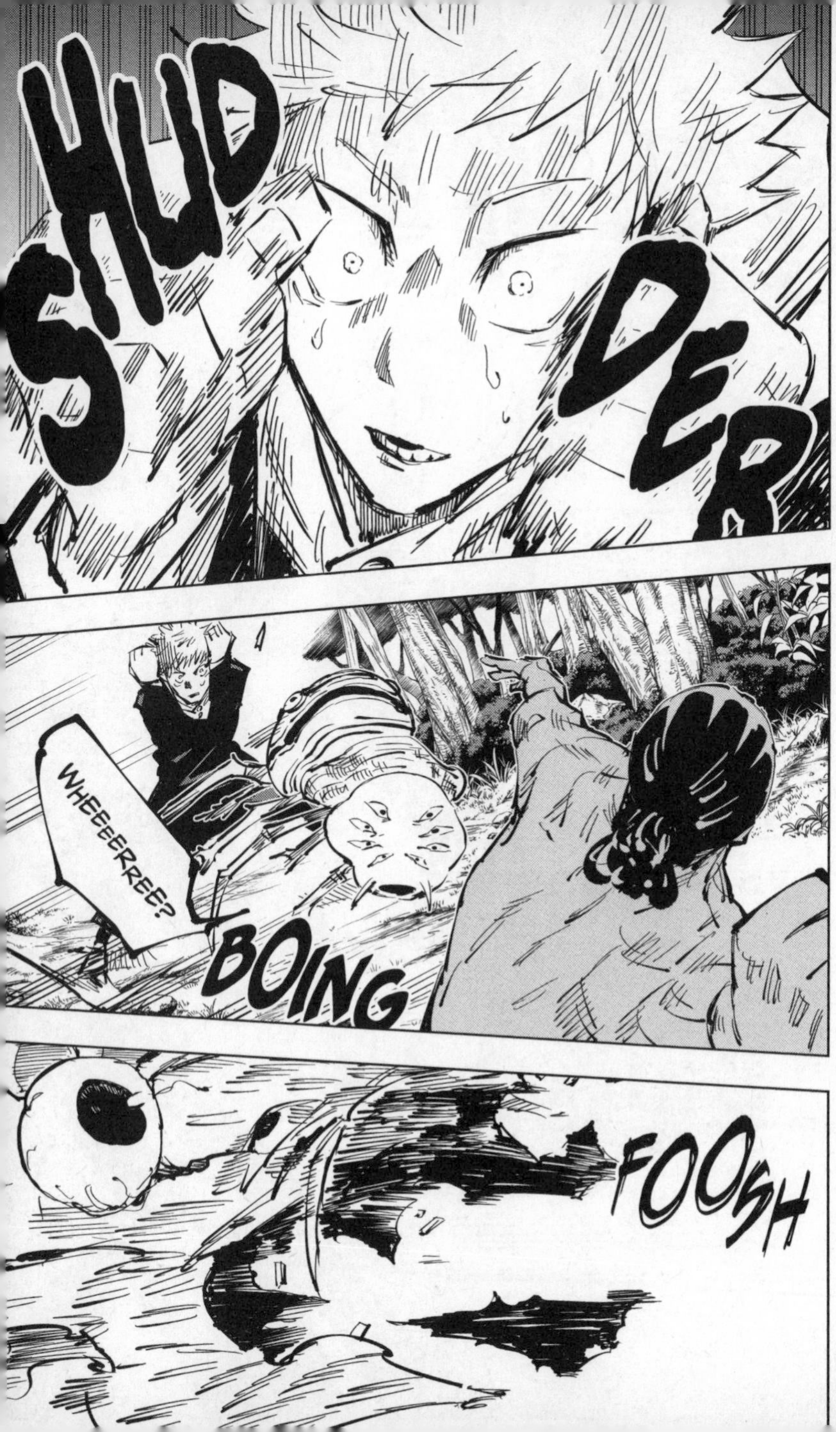
SHUD
DER
BOING
WHEEEERREE?
FOOSH

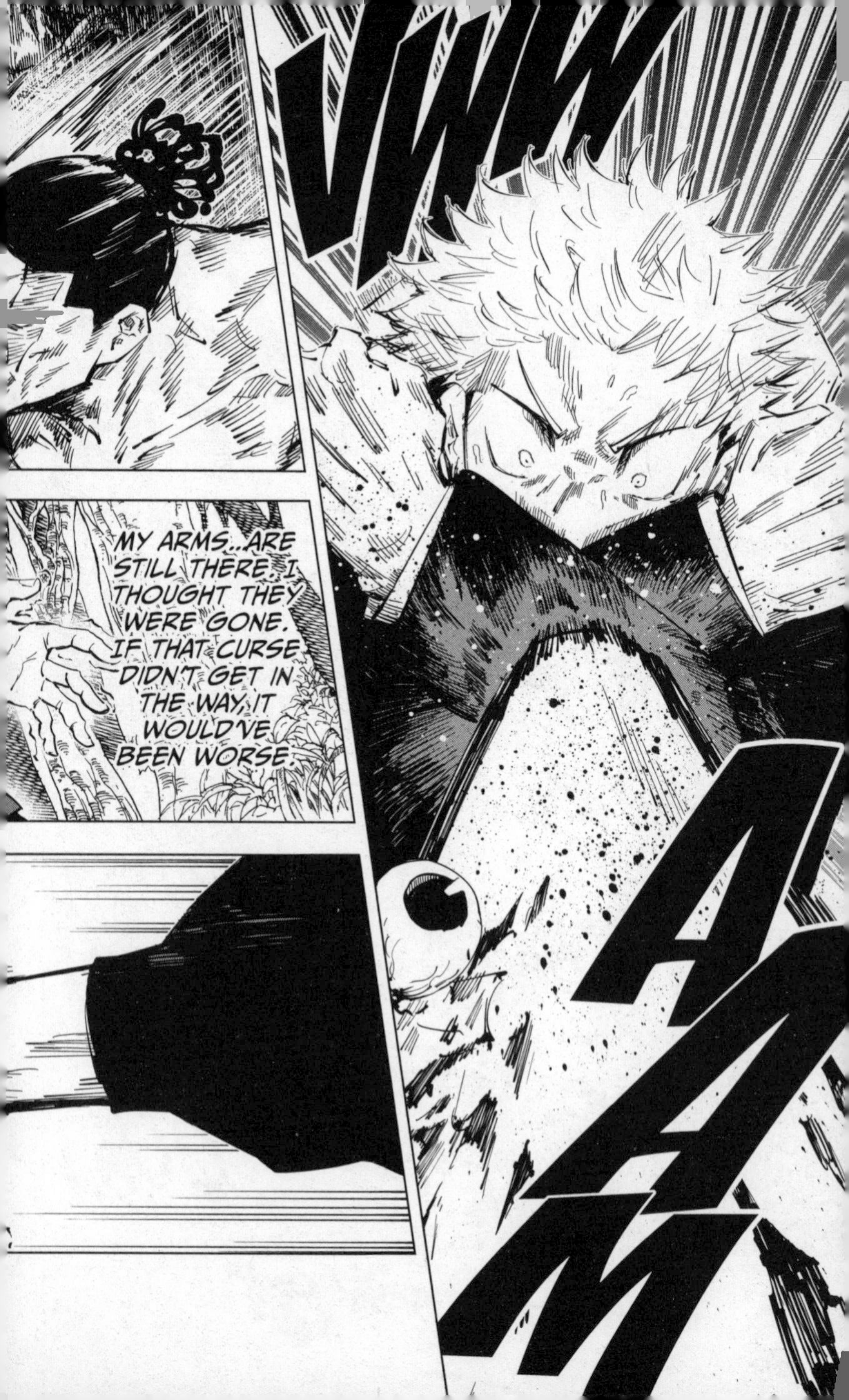
MY ARMS...ARE STILL THERE. I THOUGHT THEY WERE GONE. IF THAT CURSE DIDN'T GET IN THE WAY, IT WOULD'VE BEEN WORSE.

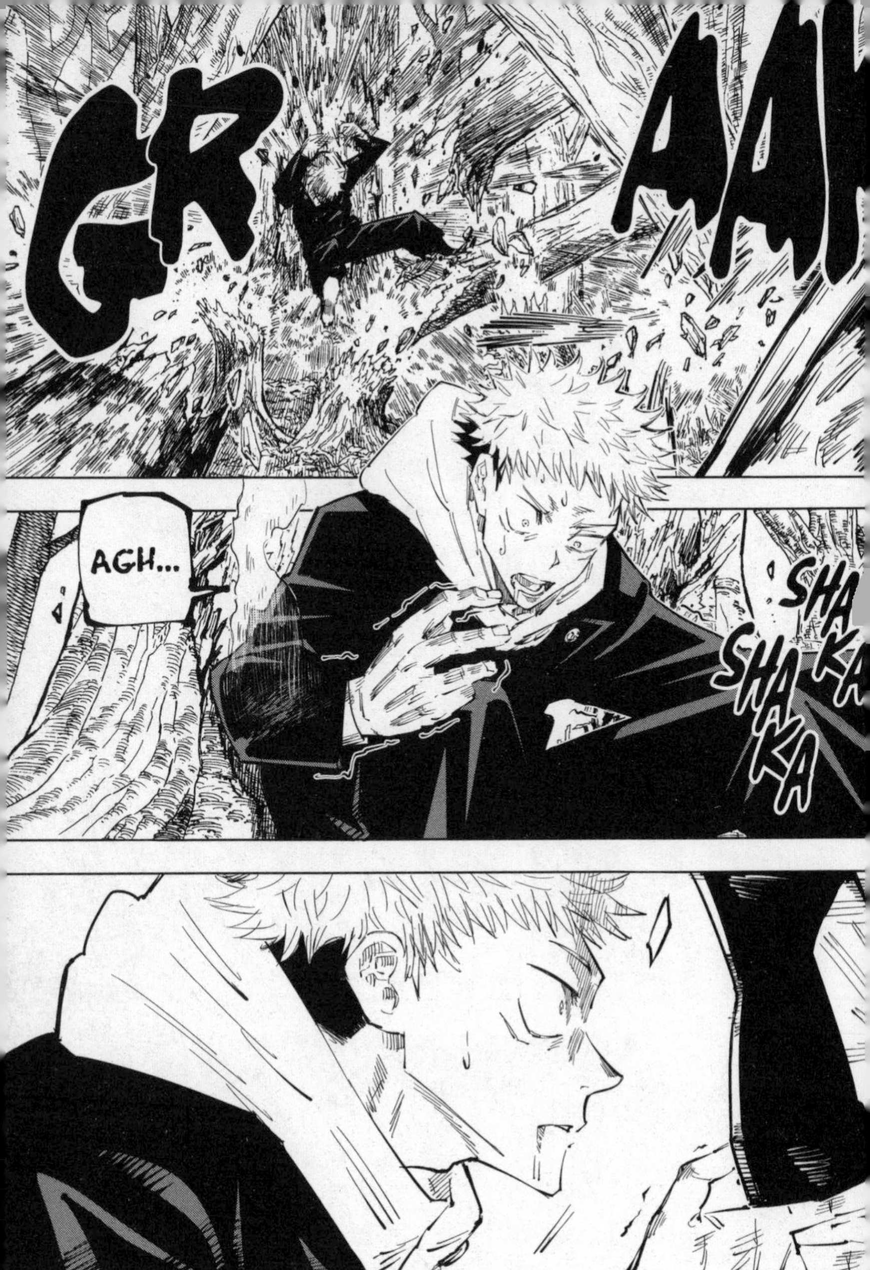
AAH
GR
SHAKA
SHAKA
AGH...

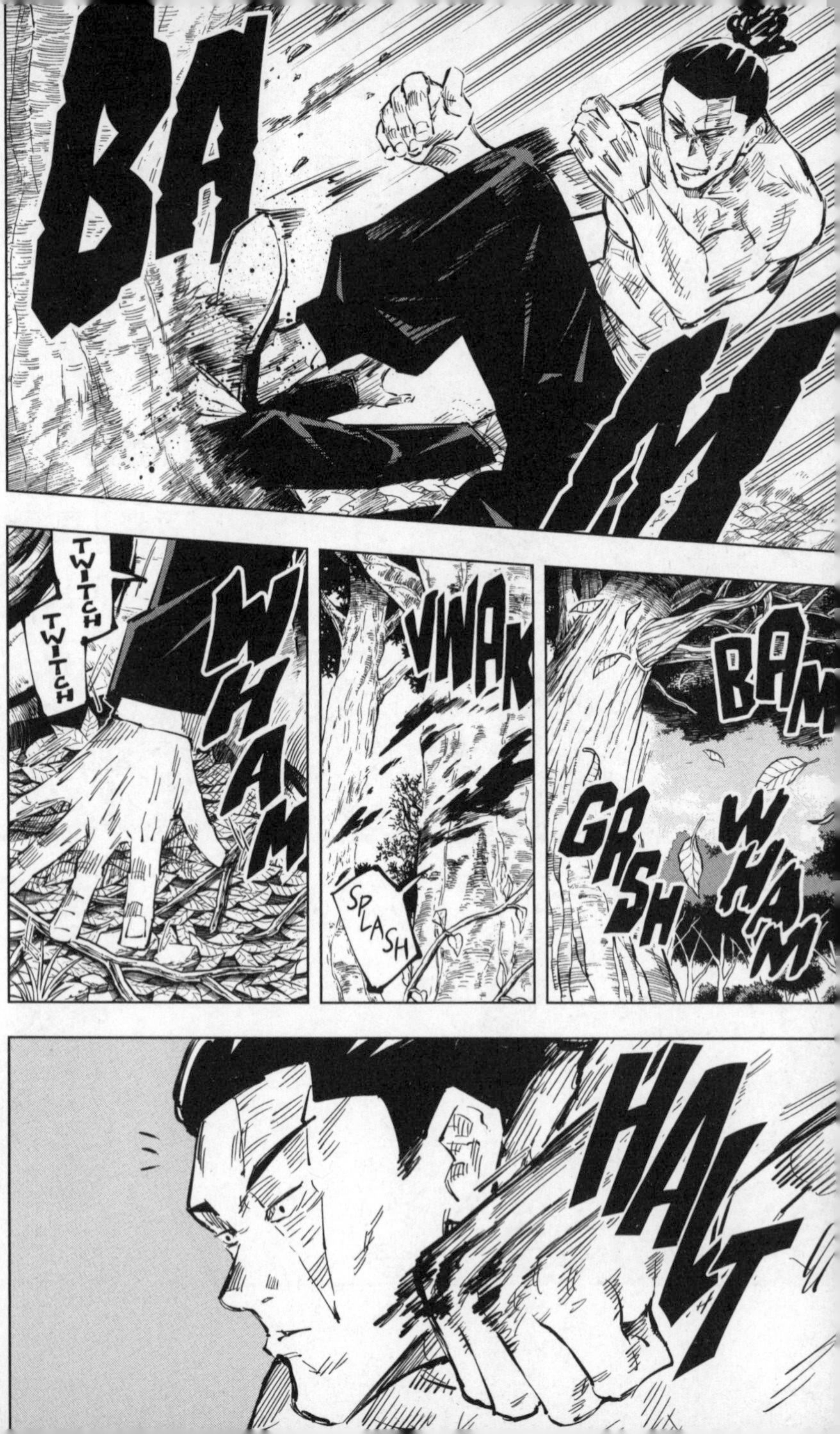
BAM
BAM
WHAM
GRSH
VWAK
SPLASH
TWITCH
TWITCH
WHAM
HALT

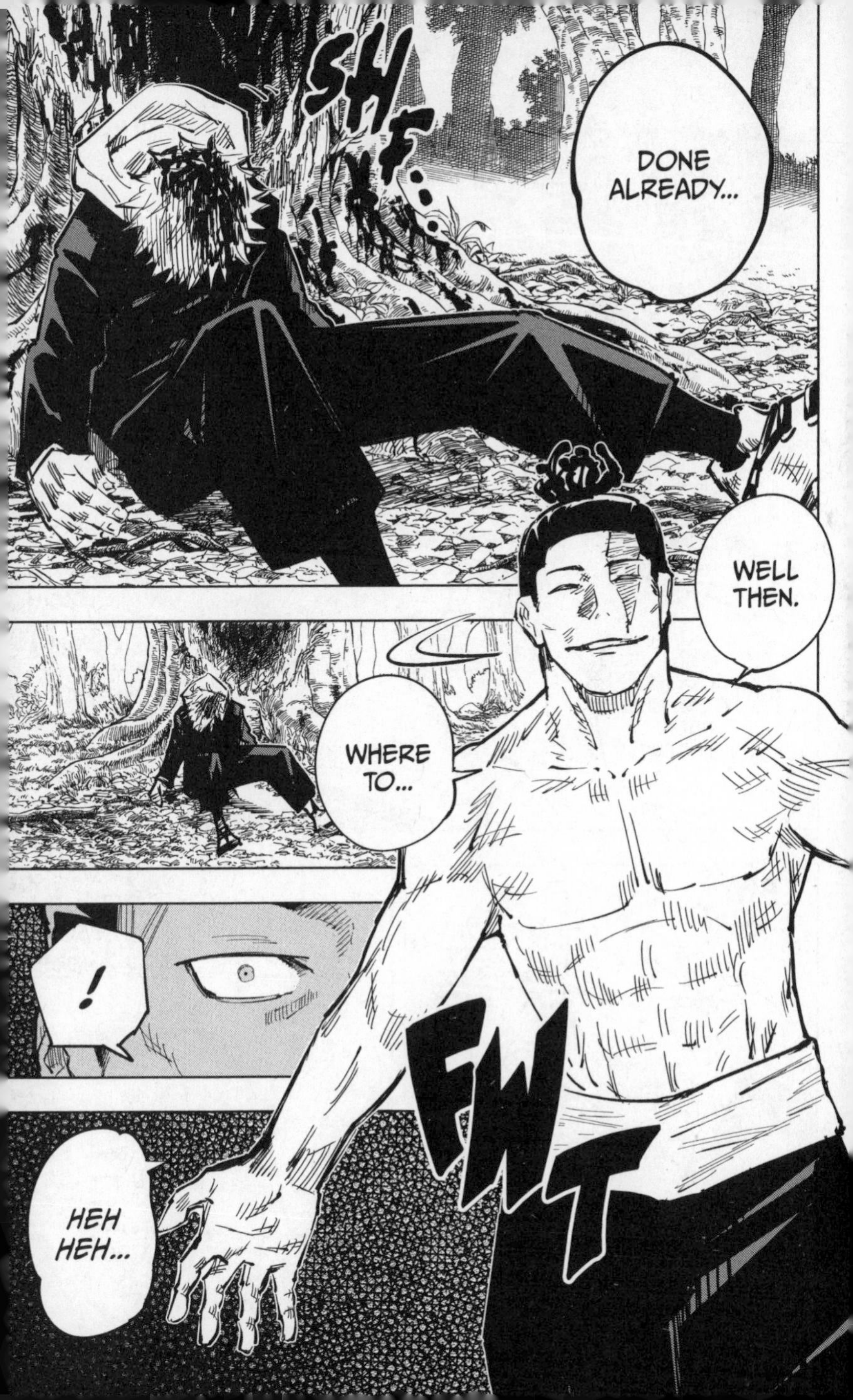
DONE ALREADY...
SHF...
WELL THEN.
WHERE TO...
FWT
!
HEH HEH...

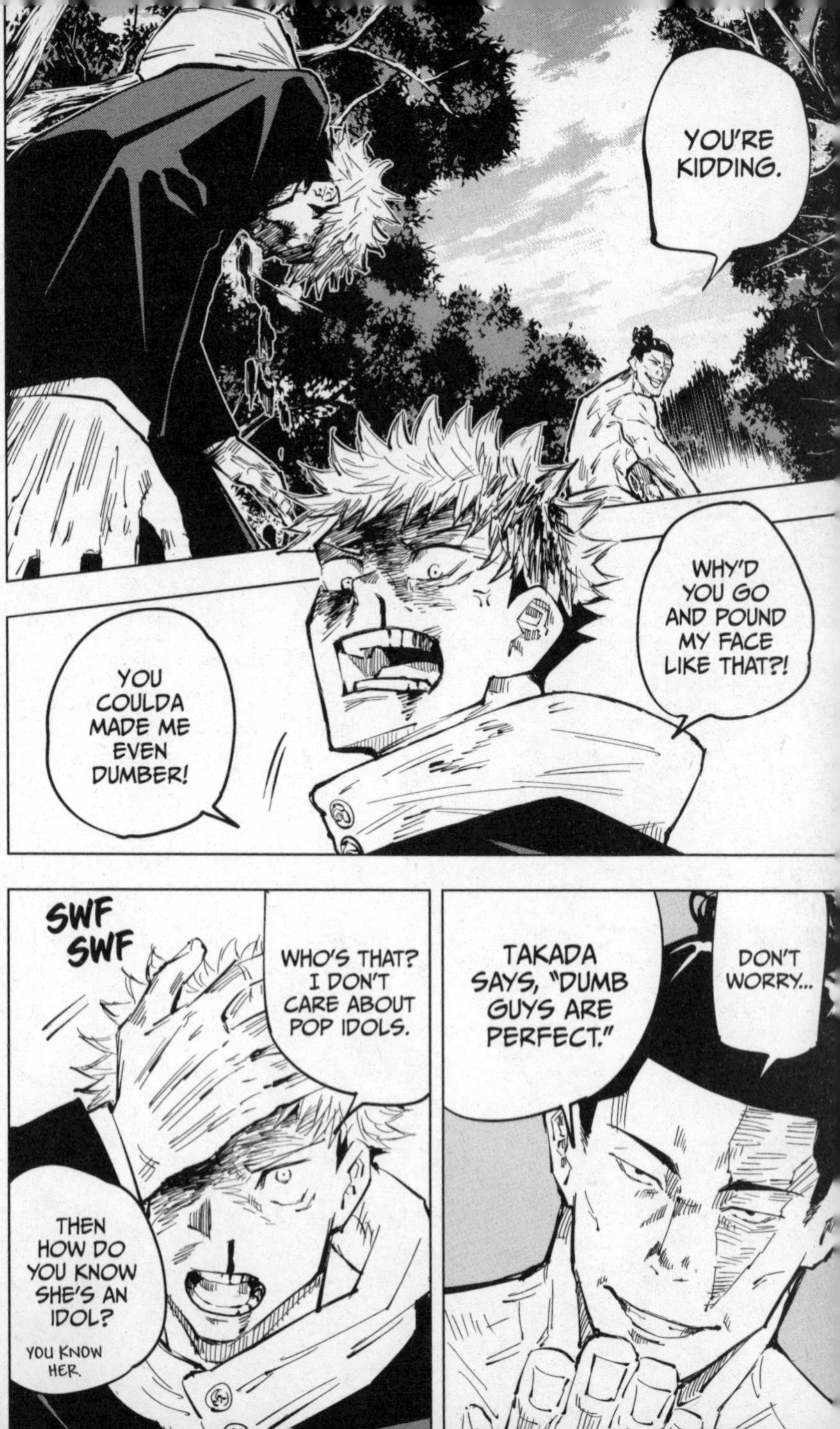
YOU'RE KIDDING.
WHY'D YOU GO AND POUND MY FACE LIKE THAT?!
YOU COULDA MADE ME EVEN DUMBER!
DON'T WORRY...
TAKADA SAYS, "DUMB GUYS ARE PERFECT."
SWF SWF
WHO'S THAT? I DON'T CARE ABOUT POP IDOLS.
THEN HOW DO YOU KNOW SHE'S AN IDOL?
YOU KNOW HER.

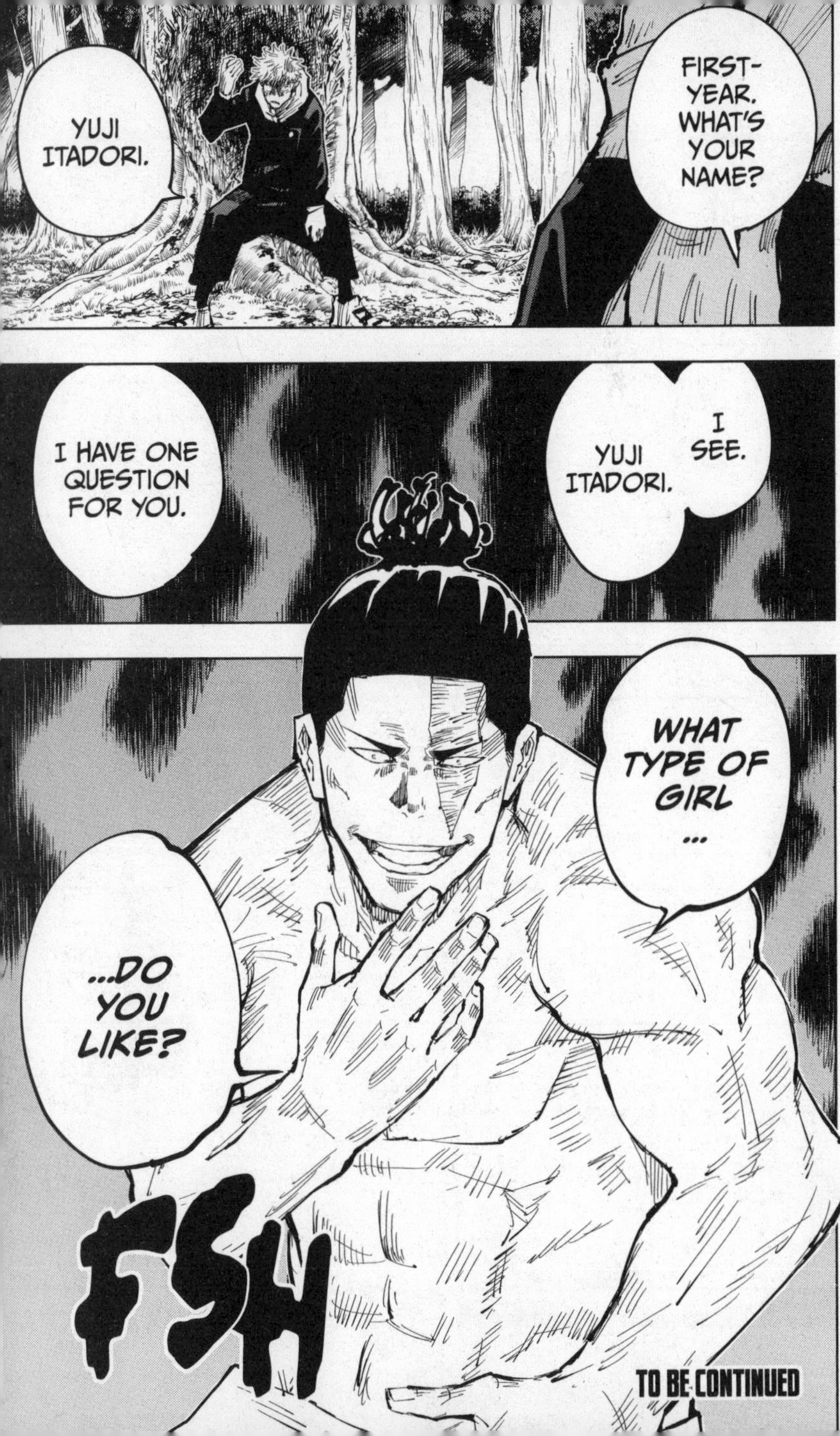
FIRST-YEAR. WHAT'S YOUR NAME?
YUJI ITADORI.
I SEE.
YUJI ITADORI.
I HAVE ONE QUESTION FOR YOU.
WHAT TYPE OF GIRL ...
...DO YOU LIKE?
FSH
TO BE CONTINUED

EXTRA MANGA

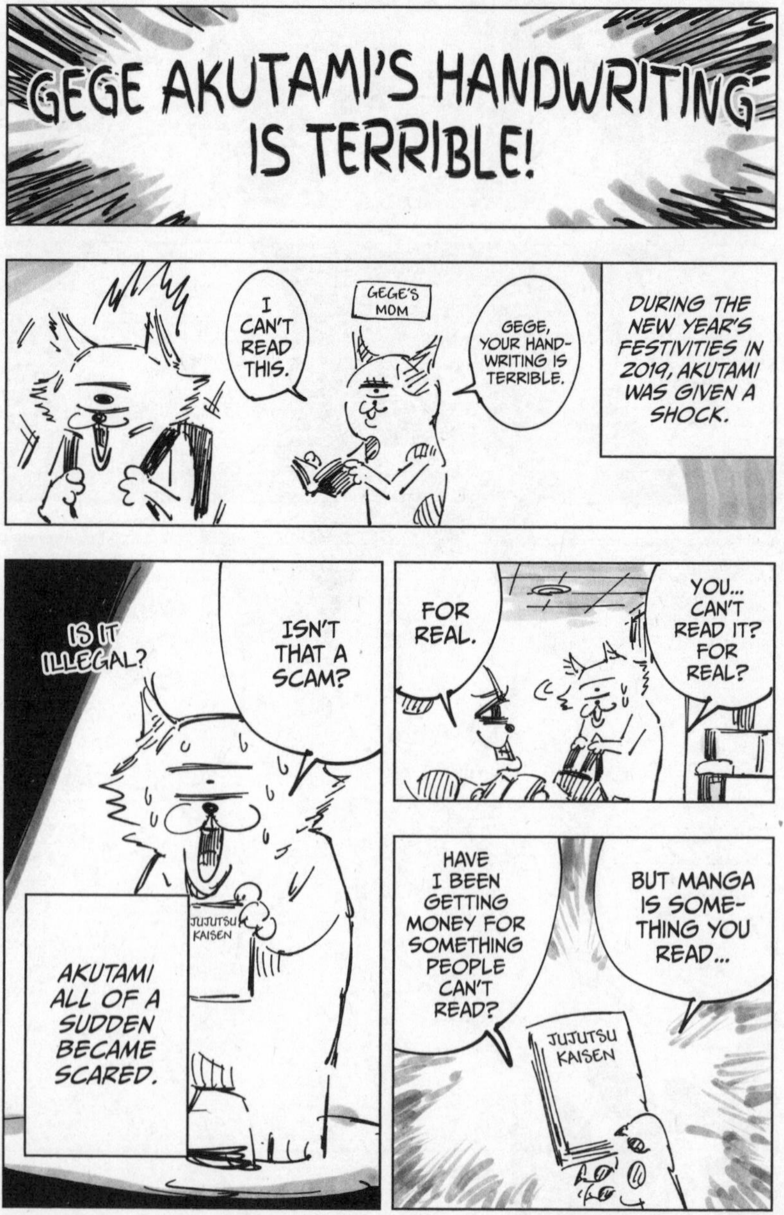
GEGE AKUTAMI'S HANDWRITING IS TERRIBLE!
DURING THE NEW YEAR'S FESTIVITIES IN 2019, AKUTAMI WAS GIVEN A SHOCK.
GEGE, YOUR HAND-WRITING IS TERRIBLE.
GEGE'S MOM
I CAN'T READ THIS.
YOU... CAN'T READ IT? FOR REAL?
FOR REAL.
BUT MANGA IS SOME-THING YOU READ...
HAVE I BEEN GETTING MONEY FOR SOMETHING PEOPLE CAN'T READ?
JUJUTSU KAISEN
ISN'T THAT A SCAM?
IS IT ILLEGAL?
JUJUTSU KAISEN
AKUTAMI ALL OF A SUDDEN BECAME SCARED.

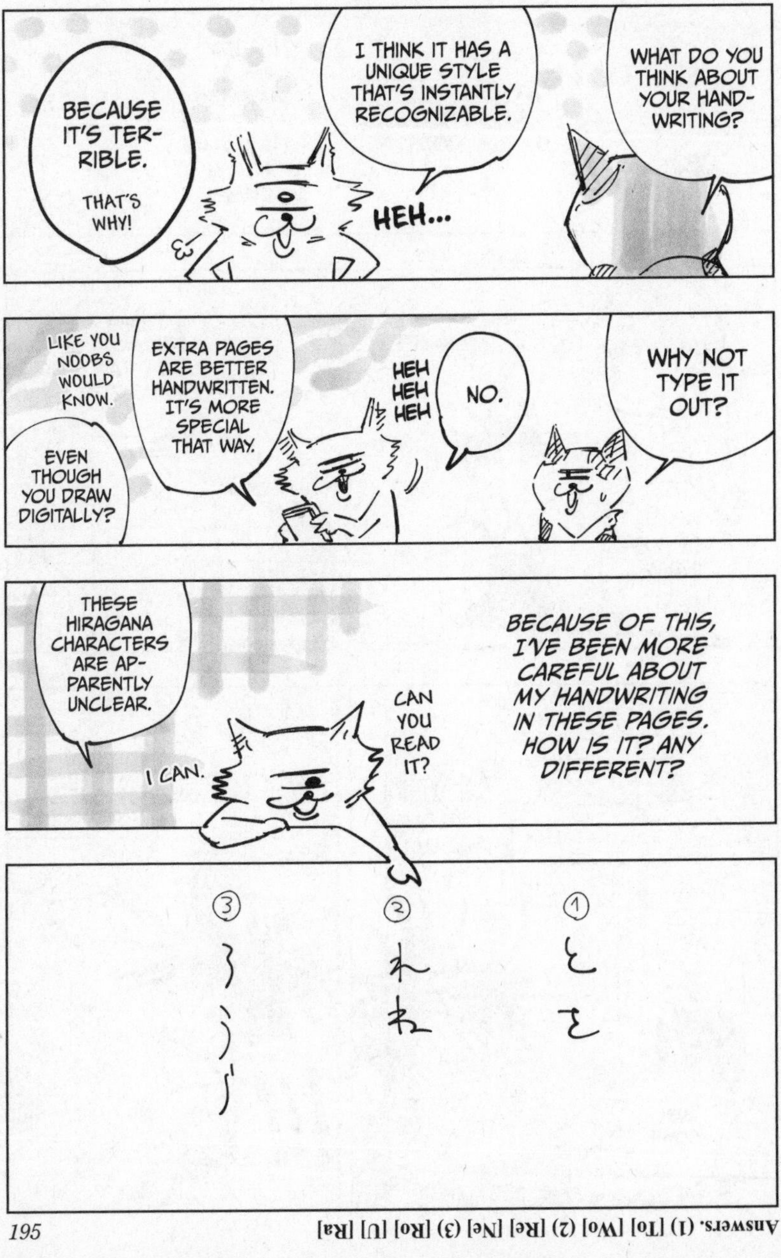
WHAT DO YOU THINK ABOUT YOUR HAND-WRITING?
I THINK IT HAS A UNIQUE STYLE THAT'S INSTANTLY RECOGNIZABLE.
HEH...
BECAUSE IT'S TER-RIBLE.
THAT'S WHY!
WHY NOT TYPE IT OUT?
NO.
HEH HEH HEH
EXTRA PAGES ARE BETTER HANDWRITTEN. IT'S MORE SPECIAL THAT WAY.
LIKE YOU NOOBS WOULD KNOW.
EVEN THOUGH YOU DRAW DIGITALLY?
BECAUSE OF THIS, I'VE BEEN MORE CAREFUL ABOUT MY HANDWRITING IN THESE PAGES. HOW IS IT? ANY DIFFERENT?
CAN YOU READ IT?
THESE HIRAGANA CHARACTERS ARE AP-PARENTLY UNCLEAR.
I CAN.
①
②
③

Answers. (1) [To] [Wo] (2) [Re] [Ne] (3) [Ro] [U] [Ra]

EXTRA MANGA #2

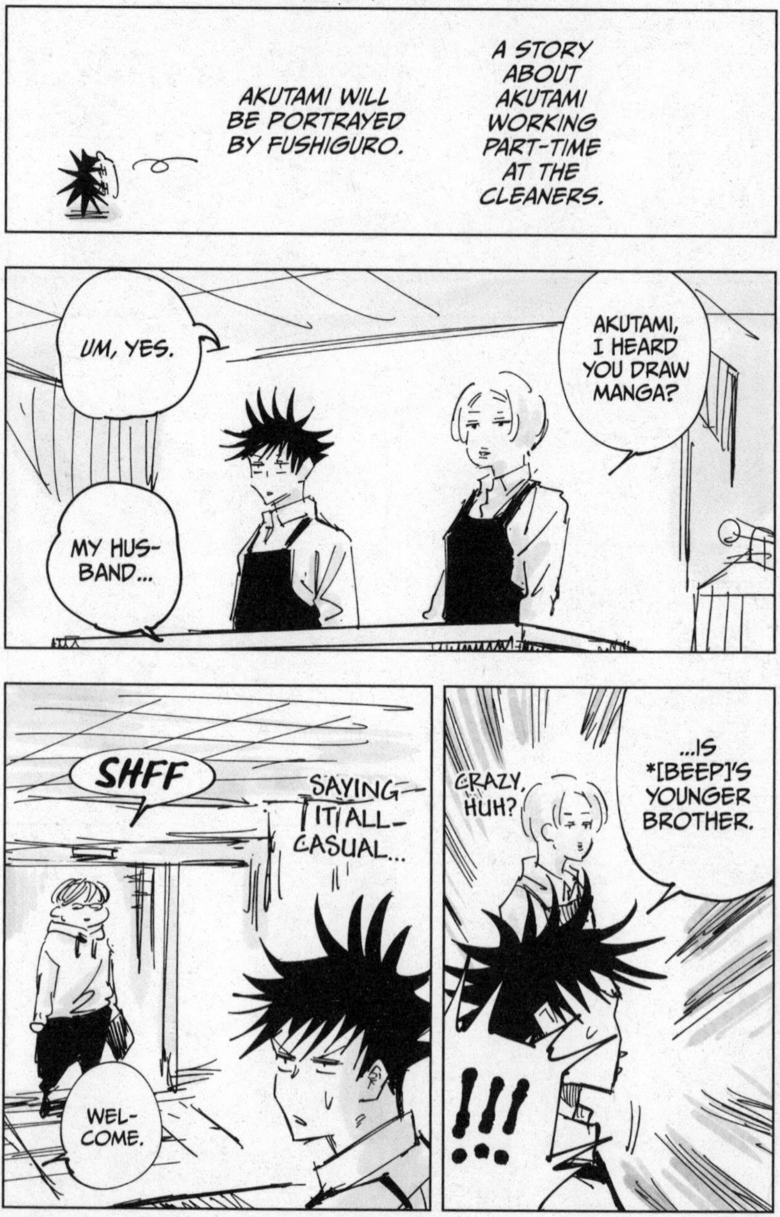

A STORY ABOUT AKUTAMI WORKING PART-TIME AT THE CLEANERS.
AKUTAMI WILL BE PORTRAYED BY FUSHIGURO.
AKUTAMI, I HEARD YOU DRAW MANGA?
UM, YES.
MY HUS-BAND...
...IS *[BEEP]'S YOUNGER BROTHER.
CRAZY, HUH?
!!!
SAYING IT ALL CASUAL...
SHFF
WEL-COME.

*A VERY WELL-KNOWN MANGAKA

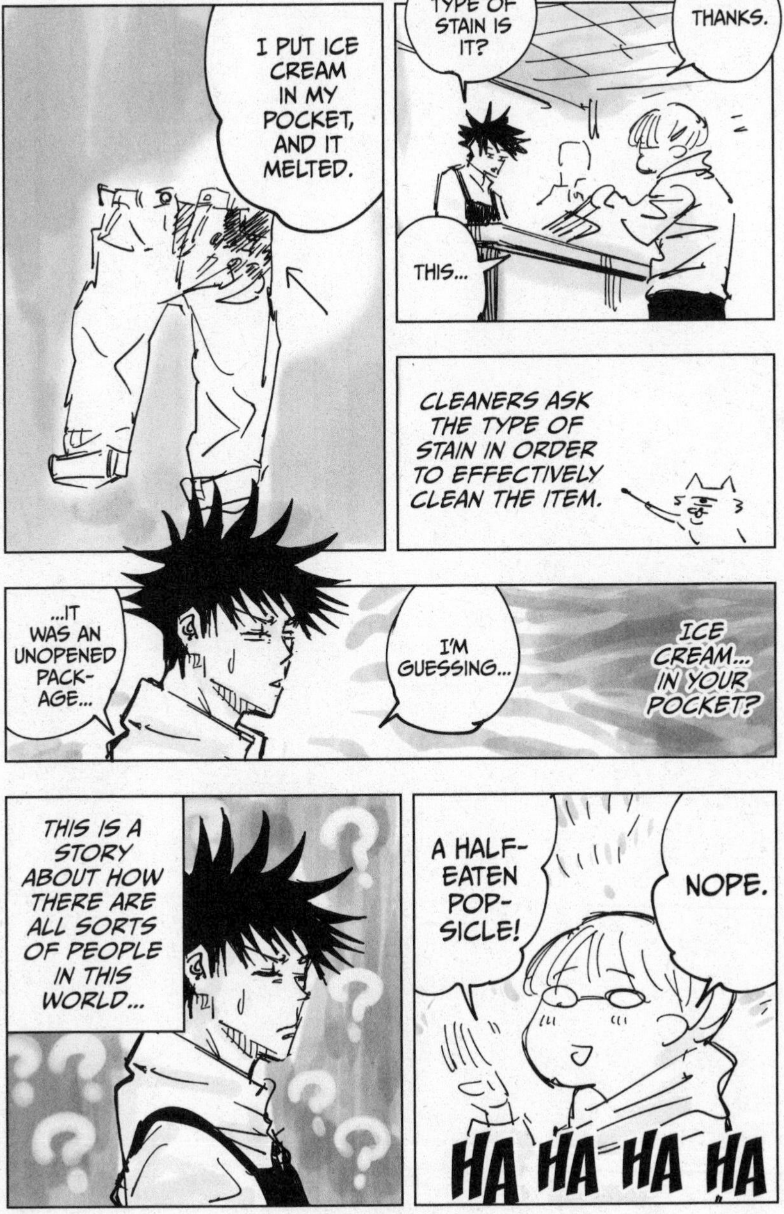
THANKS.
WHAT TYPE OF STAIN IS IT?
THIS...
CLEANERS ASK THE TYPE OF STAIN IN ORDER TO EFFECTIVELY CLEAN THE ITEM.
I PUT ICE CREAM IN MY POCKET, AND IT MELTED.
ICE CREAM... IN YOUR POCKET?
I'M GUESSING...
...IT WAS AN UNOPENED PACKAGE...
NOPE.
A HALF-EATEN POPSICLE!
HA HA HA HA
THIS IS A STORY ABOUT HOW THERE ARE ALL SORTS OF PEOPLE IN THIS WORLD...

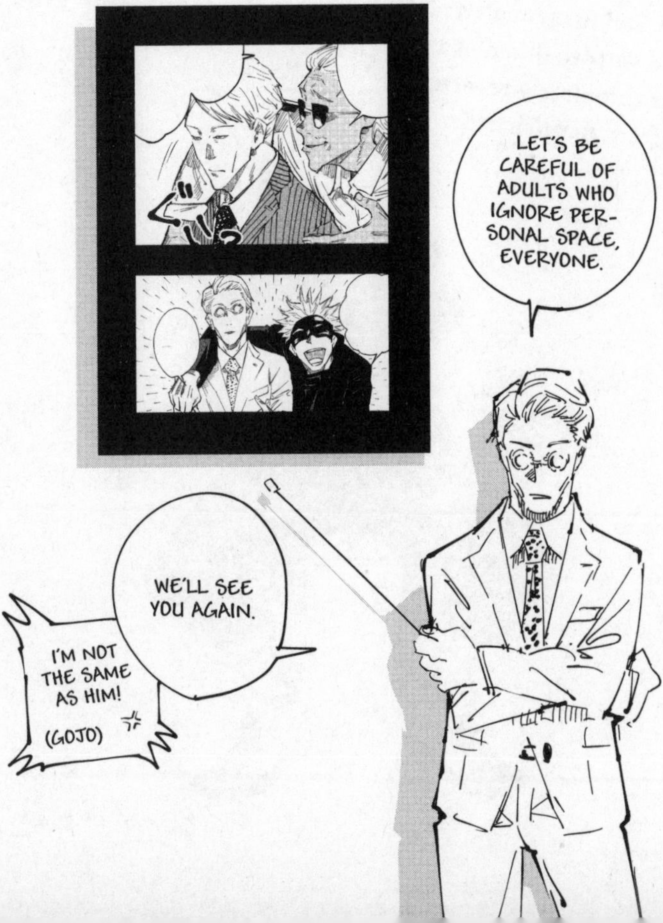
LET'S BE CAREFUL OF ADULTS WHO IGNORE PER-SONAL SPACE, EVERYONE.
WE'LL SEE YOU AGAIN.
I'M NOT THE SAME AS HIM!
(GOJO)

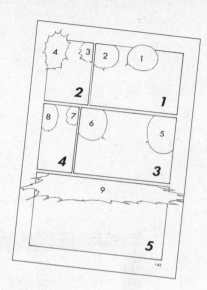

JUJUTSU KAISEN

reads from right to left, starting in the upper-right corner. Japanese is read from right to left, meaning that action, sound effects and word-balloon order are completely reversed from English order.